Specification and Analytical Evaluation of Heterogeneous Dynamic Quorum-Based Data Replication Schemes

W0079801

Christian Storm

Specification and Analytical Evaluation of Heterogeneous Dynamic Quorum-Based Data Replication Schemes

Foreword by Prof. Dr.-Ing. Oliver Theel

 Springer Vieweg

RESEARCH

Christian Storm
Oldenburg, Germany

Dissertation University of Oldenburg, 2011

ISBN 978-3-8348-2380-9 ISBN 978-3-8348-2381-6 (eBook)
DOI 10.1007/978-3-8348-2381-6

The Deutsche Nationalbibliothek lists this publication in the Deutsche Nationalbibliografie; detailed bibliographic data are available in the Internet at http://dnb.d-nb.de.

Springer Vieweg
© Vieweg+Teubner Verlag | Springer Fachmedien Wiesbaden 2012

Cover design: KünkelLopka GmbH, Heidelberg

Printed on acid-free paper

Springer Vieweg is a brand of Springer DE. Springer DE is part of Springer Science+Business Media.
www.springer-vieweg.de

Foreword

Our modern life depends more and more on the correct and continuous functioning of computer systems. This fact bears benefits and risks. Traveling from Hanover to Frankfurt am Main, both in Germany, by train in just a little more than two hours can only be achieved by the cooperation and correct functioning of many computer systems embedded in a high speed train. Parts of them form, for example, a sophisticated brake system or a communication system meant for issuing warnings to the train driver enabling him or her to stop the train in time prior to a potentially deadly collision.

Unfortunately, correct functioning of all these components at all times is impossible: in the absence of perfect components all systems are built out of components that are subject to fail to some extent at some time. Thus, there is always a non-zero probability that a system, such as a high speed train's braking system, fails at a time when its correct functioning is dearly needed. But fortunately, the probability that a system does not work at a particular point in time can be controlled by means of redundancy: as a rule-of-thumb, the more redundancy spent for a system, the higher is its availability and the higher are the costs for building and operating it. Thus, a reasonable trade-off must be found.

In his research work, Christian Storm presents a new universal framework for the specification and implementation of heterogeneous data replication strategies. Data replication is some form of redundant resources, and data replication can be exploited for implementing highly available services, such as information services for the train driver in the high speed train scenario described earlier. Data replication strategies correctly handle the redundant resources, called data replicas. A particular data replication strategy exhibits one particular trade-off between availability and costs. The framework presented allows to model and realize all known, relevant data replication strategies from literature but also goes way beyond. It does so by introducing and exploiting the powerful concept of tree-shaped voting structures. Based on this unifying modeling abstraction, Christian Storm presents a new and efficient analysis technique for heterogeneous, dynamic data replication strategies (that also covers all homogeneous and static cases) based on Petri-Net modeling, reachability and steady-state analyses. It allows to

efficiently analyze and customize data replication strategies helping to identify systems that exhibit the highest availability possible for a certain cost
budget. Since there is no reason to strive for less, researchers and students
should know about the underlying concepts and techniques. This book describes them in a very systematic fashion and is accompanied by carefully
chosen examples and evaluations.

Oliver Theel

Acknowledgments

During the time of my doctorate, too many people to mention them individually have contributed in personal and scientific respects in one or another way. While I owe sincere thankfulness to all, I would like to name a few of them explicitly.

First and foremost, I would like to express my sincerest gratitude and special thanks to my advisor, Prof. Dr.-Ing. Oliver Theel, for his enduring encouragement, support, and his confidence in me. Not only has he given me the freedom to explore and pursue my own ideas but he also provided a pleasant and friendly place to work in. His huge repertoire of anecdotes and stories will be remembered.

Furthermore, I would like to thank my second supervisor Prof. Dr. Wilhelm Hasselbring for refereeing this dissertation.

I am also grateful to the members of the System Software and Distributed Systems Group as well as to the members of the TrustSoft graduate school at the University of Oldenburg. I appreciate the pleasant and productive atmosphere as well as the constructive discussions that developed on various occasions. In particular, I would like to acknowledge Timo Warns, Kinga Kiss-Iakab, Jens Happe, Roland Meyer, Henrik Lipskoch, Heiko Koziolek, and Eike Möhlmann for working together, sharing an office, co-organizing workshops, friendship, and simply having a great time.

Finally, and most importantly, I would like to thank my family for their absolute support and confidence in me throughout my life.

Christian Storm

Abstract

Data replication by employing quorum systems is a well-established concept to improve operation availability on critical data objects in distributed systems that have strong consistency demands. It is therefore an important base concept for constructing dependable distributed systems. Modern distributed systems have become dynamic in nature with processes arriving and deliberately departing at run-time. Traditional data replication schemes are either static, that is, they use a fixed quorum system and cannot adapt to varying numbers of processes in the system, or their dynamics in adapting the quorum system is usually constrained by an upper bound on the number of processes that is predetermined at design-time. These dynamic data replication schemes are homogeneous in the sense that for each set of processes, the quorum system is constructed using the same scheme-inherent quorum system construction strategy. Like there is no single data replication scheme superior for every application scenario, there is also none superior for every set of processes. Motivated by this fact, heterogeneous dynamic data replication schemes are free to use a particular quorum system construction strategy per set of processes.

The first contribution of the thesis is a uniform data replication scheme specification method that combines the potential of heterogeneous dynamic data replication schemes with an unbounded flexibility in the number of processes at run-time. This method provides advanced means to design specifically tailored data replication schemes that can utilize the respective best-option selection of quorum system construction strategies for a specific application scenario.

The choice of a data replication scheme in the design space spawned by static and dynamic, unstructured and structured, and homogeneous and heterogeneous data replication schemes has a strong impact on the performance and dependability of a system and therefore needs a careful evaluation. In light of constantly evolving modern distributed systems, this choice cannot be definitely made at design-time but has to be repeatedly revised and adapted to a changing environment at run-time. For this purpose, evaluation methods based on simulation are inadequate because of their massive time complexity or their approximate nature of results under time constraints. Contrarily, evaluation methods based on analysis are fast and accurate but require a careful crafting of the system model for it to be tractable and to provide meaningful results. To date, the analytical evaluation of dynamic data replication schemes is limited to a subset of the specific subclass of unstructured homogeneous dynamic data replication schemes. The existing approaches are customized to one single data replication scheme and are therefore inapplicable to the evaluation of other schemes.

The second contribution of the thesis is a general and comprehensive approach to the analytical evaluation of data replication schemes that supports unstructured as well as structured homogeneous and moreover heterogeneous dynamic data replication schemes, with static ones being a simple special case. Different data replication schemes are reflected in the system model by merely varying the data replication scheme specification. Furthermore, the system model allows quality measures besides operation availability, such as operation costs, to be evaluated for the write operation as well as for the read operation.

Zusammenfassung

Datenreplikation unter Verwendung von Quoren-Systemen ist ein weit ver-
breitetes Konzept, um die Operationsverfügbarkeit auf kritischen Datenob-
jekten in verteilten Systemen mit hohen Anforderungen an die Datenkonsis-
tenz zu erhöhen. Es ist daher ein wichtiges Basiskonzept zur Konstruktion
zuverlässiger verteilter Systeme. Moderne verteilte Systeme sind natur-
gemäß dynamisch in ihrer Struktur, da Prozesse das System zur Laufzeit
verlassen und neue hinzukommen können. Bisherige Replikationsverfahren
sind allerdings entweder statisch, d.h., sie benutzen ein feststehendes und
nicht an variierende Prozessanzahlen anpassbares Quoren-System, oder ihre
Dynamik in der Anpassung des Quoren-Systems an variierende Prozessanzahlen ist meist durch eine zur Entwicklungszeit festgelegte obere Grenze
beschränkt. Diese dynamischen Replikationsverfahren sind homogen in
dem Sinne, dass zur Konstruktion des Quoren-Systems die gleiche ver-
fahrensspezifische Quoren-Konstruktionsvorschrift für jede Prozessanzahl
benutzt wird. Ebenso wie es kein einzelnes Replikationsverfahren gibt, das
für alle Einsatzszenarien optimal ist, gibt es auch keines, das für alle Prozessanzahlen optimal ist. Daher erlauben heterogen-dynamische Replikationsverfahren die Benutzung verschiedener Quoren-Konstruktionsvorschriften
für verschiedene Prozessanzahlen.

Der erste Beitrag der Dissertation ist eine uniforme Spezifikationsmetho-
de für quoren-basierte Replikationsverfahren, die das Potenzial heterogen-
dynamischer Replikationsverfahren mit einer unbeschränkten Flexibilität
in der Anzahl der Prozesse zur Laufzeit kombiniert. Dadurch bietet diese
Methode die Möglichkeit, spezifisch angepasste Replikationsverfahren für
ein bestimmtes Einsatzszenario unter Verwendung der jeweils besten Kom-
bination von Quoren-Konstruktionsvorschriften zu entwickeln.

Die Auswahl eines Replikationsverfahrens im Entwurfsraum, der durch
statische und dynamische, unstrukturierte und strukturierte sowie durch
homogene und heterogene Replikationsverfahren aufgespannt wird, ist eine
wichtige Entscheidung im Hinblick auf die Performanz und die Zuverläs-
sigkeit eines Systems, weshalb sie sorgfältig evaluiert werden muss. An-
gesichts sich ständig wandelnder moderner verteilter Systeme kann diese
Entscheidung nicht abschließend zur Entwurfszeit getroffen werden, sondern

muss wiederholt zur Laufzeit überprüft und auf ein sich änderndes Einsatzszenario angepasst werden. Evaluationsmethoden, die auf Simulation basieren, sind aufgrund ihrer großen Zeitkomplexität bzw. ihrer approximativen Ergebnisse unter Laufzeitbeschränkung dafür unzureichend. Im Gegensatz dazu sind Evaluationsmethoden, die auf Analyse basieren, schnell und präzise. Allerdings benötigen diese ein sorgfältig erstelltes Systemmodell, das handhabbar ist und sinnvolle Ergebnisse liefert. Bisher ist die analytische Evaluation dynamischer Replikationsverfahren beschränkt auf eine bestimmte Untermenge unstrukturierter homogen-dynamischer Verfahren. Existierende Ansätze sind speziell auf ein Replikationsverfahren ausgerichtet und daher nicht anwendbar auf andere Replikationsverfahren.

Der zweite Beitrag der Dissertation ist ein allgemeiner und umfassender Ansatz zur analytischen Evaluation von Replikationsverfahren, der sowohl statische als auch unstrukturierte und strukturierte homogen-dynamische und darüber hinaus heterogen-dynamische Replikationsverfahren unterstützt. Verschiedene Replikationsverfahren werden im Systemmodell abgebildet, indem lediglich ihre Spezifikation ausgetauscht wird. Das Systemmodell erlaubt die Evaluation weiterer Qualitätsmaße neben der Operationsverfügbarkeit, wie z.B. der Operationskosten, sowohl für die Schreiboperation als auch für die Leseoperation.

Contents

1 Introduction

In the past decades, computer systems such as banking cash machine networks, networked business systems, or Internet services have become pervasive and gained significant importance in our daily private and business life. The flip side of the coin is computer systems not only having caused economic damage but also failures that lead to loss of life [Neumann, 1994]. Thus, a key concern is the trustworthiness of such systems with respect to safety, security, privacy, performance, correctness, and availability. In particular availability and correctness as the probability that a system is operable at a given time and provides the intended service is of utmost importance.

Replication Replication is a commonly used and well-established concept to improve the availability of systems whose components are subject to failures. Therefore, it is an important key concept to construct dependable and trustworthy systems. A prominent example of replication is *triple modular redundancy* [von Neumann, 1956]. Instead of relying on one component to deliver a potentially mission-critical service such as the altitude measurement of an airplane, the system consists of three such components. The three components must reach consensus on the airplane's altitude with the deciding majority being two out of the three independent components such that at least two components (must) agree on the altitude. Because of the redundancy in components and the agreement protocol, the failure or misbehavior of one component is compensated, provided that at any time, at least two components are not failed and therefore behave correctly. Given a sufficiently high individual component availability, the availability of this system is higher than the availability of a system relying on one single component.

The concept of fault tolerance to achieve increased availability by using replication inheres two facets, namely redundancy in components and a coordination protocol managing the multiple redundant components.

Applied to distributed computer systems, replication is used to increase the read and write operation availability on critical data objects, to improve the read and write operation efficiency, and to balance the workload in the system. A distributed computer system consists of several autonomously operating processing entities termed *processes*. Each process manages a local copy of the data object, called *replica*, its associated version number, and operation-specific locks. The individual processes are interconnected by a communication network and interact with each other by sending and receiving messages via the communication network. Due to the redundancy in replicas, read and write operations on the replicated data object remain available despite the presence of certain faults in the distributed system that are caused by process or communication link failures. Besides, having multiple replicas offers a choice on which replicas to perform an operation and thereby allows a process to execute operations on geographically nearby located replicas or even on its own local replica.

Data Consistency   To obtain meaningful results in the presence of interleaving or overlapping operations, a notion of operation execution correctness and data consistency among the replicas must be specified and guaranteed by the system. The consistency notion determines what values returned by read operations are acceptable. This specification must be strong enough to be useful and weak enough to be implemented efficiently. *Sequential consistency* [Lamport, 1979], for example, is a strong consistency notion as it requires (1) the total ordering of write operations as well as of read and write operations and it requires (2) read operations to return the value written by the "last" write operation.

Ensuring such a strong consistency notion demands great efforts in coordination and agreement among the processes. Weaker consistency notions relax these strong requirements. They are more permissive with respect to the ordering of operations and differ in the definition of the "last" write operation whose written value is to return by a successive read operation. *Causal consistency* [Ahamad, Burns et al., 1991; Ahamad, Neiger et al., 1995], as an example of a weak(er) consistency notion, requires the total ordering of operations that are potentially causally related whereas causally unrelated operations may be seen in a different order by different processes. Two operations are causally related if the "latter" operation reads or writes a value that potentially depends on knowledge about the value read or written by the "former" operation.

In general, weak consistency notions allow to provide a higher operation availability (at a lower degree of consistency) than strong consistency notions because of having less coordination and agreement demands. Unfortunately, weak consistency notions are not suited for every application scenario as their semantics must match the application's consistency requirements. For example, if an application merely requires a read operation to return the value written by one of the last few write operations, then a weak consistency notion may be a suitable candidate. In contrast, strong consistency notions have the advantage of being generally applicable to any application scenario as they define a more general consistency semantics.

Quorum Systems   A prominent way to ensure sequential consistency is to use locks and quorum systems. A *quorum system* is a tuple of a read and a write quorum set – each one being a set of subsets of the set of processes – whose elements are called *read quorums* and *write quorums*, respectively. A quorum system is constructed such that every write quorum intersects with every other write quorum and with every read quorum in at least one process while read quorums need not to intersect. A read (write) operation is performed in two steps by a process called operation *coordinator* as follows. First, the coordinator queries the processes of a read (write) quorum for their permission to execute the operation. A queried process grants permission, operation-specifically locks its replica, and responds with the replica's version number only if it is not write-locked (neither read- nor write-locked) for a concurrent operation execution. If not all the quorum's processes comply – because some of them are locked for a concurrent conflicting operation or have failed – then the complying processes' replicas are unlocked and another quorum's processes are queried for their permission alternatively. Eventually, either all operation-specific quorums are negatively probed and the coordinator aborts the operation execution, that is, the operation is not available, or the operation is *available* as a quorum of complying processes is found. Second, in case of a write operation, the new replica value is written to all the locked replicas, their version numbers are set to a new global maximum (that is, to the by one incremented highest version number reported in the first step), and finally the replicas are unlocked. In case of a read operation, the replica value is read from one of the replicas having the highest version number and the replica read locks of those processes not participating in a concurrent read operation are released. Due to the quorum system intersection property and in compliance with sequential consistency, write operations and read and write operations are performed mutually exclusive while read operations are allowed to be executed concurrently. Concurrent read operations are permitted since read quorums do not need to intersect and, in this operation execution protocol, concurrent read operations are also allowed to be performed with the same read quorum. Note that by the latter, the level of concurrency for read operations is increased at the cost of a higher risk of write operation starvation due to interleaving read operations.

Besides ensuring sequential consistency, quorum systems are able to correctly cope with network partitioning caused by communication link failures. If a network is partitioned, the set of processes is separated into partitions such that interprocess communication within a partition is possible while interprocess communication among partitions is not possible. Due to the mutual exclusion of write operations, there is always at most one partition in which the write operation is available. If the write operation is available in a partition, the read operation may only be available in the same partition. Since every read quorum intersects in at least one process with the available write quorum(s), the read operation cannot be available in other partitions as interprocess communication among partitions is not possible. If there is no partition in which the write operation is available, then there may be (multiple) partitions in which the read operation is available as read quorums need not to intersect. In either case, sequential consistency is preserved.

Data Replication Schemes Choosing a quorum system implies choosing a trade-off between different qualities such as load, capacity, and availability [Naor and Wool, 1998], scalability and operation costs [Jiménez-Peris, Patiño-Martínez et al., 2003]. For example, in order to increase the probability of finding an available write quorum and being low-cost in terms of the number of messages needed to perform the write operation, write quorums should consist of few processes. On the other hand, write quorums should contain many processes and thereby synchronize many replicas in order to decrease the minimal read quorum cardinality and read operation costs and to increase the probability of finding an available read quorum. Because of this trade-off, there is no single quorum system construction scheme that is best-suited for every application scenario. Hence, a plethora of schemes to construct quorum systems has been proposed that can be categorized into *unstructured* and *structured* data replication schemes.

Unstructured data replication schemes use combinatorics and minimal quorum cardinalities to specify quorum systems. Majority Consensus Voting [Thomas, 1979], for example, requires read quorums to consist of $\lceil n/2 \rceil$ processes and write quorums to contain $\lceil (n+1)/2 \rceil$ processes for a system comprising n processes. Due to such a threshold-based quorum specification, every process is equally suited for being in a particular read or write quorum. Unstructured approaches suffer from high operation costs and face scalability problems because of linearly increasing quorum cardinalities in the number of processes. On the other hand, as long as the number of non-failed processes resembles at least the minimal quorum cardinality, an arbitrary set of process failures can be tolerated, explaining the usually good process failure resilience of unstructured data replication schemes.

Structured data replication schemes impose a logical structure on the set of processes and use structural properties to specify quorum systems. The structured Grid Protocol [Cheung, Ammar et al., 1990], for example, arranges processes in a logical rectangular $k \times j$ grid having k columns and j rows for a system comprising $k \cdot j = n$ processes. A read quorum consists of one process from each column while a write quorum consists of all processes from a complete column plus one process from each column to meet the quorum system intersection property. Further examples of logical structures to arrange processes in are trees [Agrawal and El Abbadi, 1990], finite projective planes [Maekawa, 1985], and acyclic graphs [Theel, 1993b]. As a result of using logical structures, structured data replication schemes tolerate structure-specific process failure sets. Attributed to the selective nature of which processes may form a quorum, structured data replication schemes are usually not as resilient to process failures as unstructured schemes, particularly if the redundancy in processes (replicas) is close to exhaustion. On the other hand, exploiting logical structure properties to specify quorum systems usually results in sub-linear operation costs in the number of processes and thereby in a better scalability than provided by unstructured data replication schemes.

Dynamic Data Replication Schemes The aforementioned unstructured and structured data replication schemes are *static* in the sense that they use an immutable and a priori defined quorum system that remains in use for the entire lifetime of the system. Static data replication schemes have an upper bound on operation availability because of a symmetry constraint among the read and write operation availability graphs [Theel and Pagnia, 1998]. They cannot react to process failures beyond a scheme-specific threshold of processes. For example, the write operation of a system using the unstructured static Majority Consensus Voting with n processes becomes unavailable if $\lceil n/2 \rceil$ processes have failed. In contrast, *dynamic* data replication schemes can adapt the quorum system and thus can react to process failures at run-time. Whenever a process failure is detected, the quorum system is adapted – if possible – while maintaining the quorum system intersection property such that failed processes no longer partici-pate in any read or write quorum. Conversely, upon a process' recovery, the quorum system is adapted – if possible – to reintegrate the recovered process. Due to the dynamic adaptation mechanism, read and write op-erations remain available in cases static data replication schemes already had to cease operation. Although there are some cases in which the op-posite holds true [Jajodia and Mutchler, 1990], dynamic data replication schemes usually provide increased operation availabilities. Examples of dy-namic data replication schemes are the Dynamic Grid Protocol [Rabinovich and Lazowska, 1992b], the Dynamic Tree Quorum Protocol [Rabinovich and Lazowska, 1992a], and Dynamic Voting [Jajodia and Mutchler, 1990] – the dynamic counterpart of the unstructured static Majority Consensus Voting.

The dynamic switching among quorum systems requires some coordina-tion and agreement in itself to ensure that operations are performed ex-clusively with quorums of the current quorum system. Otherwise, there may exist disjoint quorum systems allowing conflicting operations, that is, (multiple) write operations or read and write operations, to be executed con-currently in violation of sequential consistency. One such concept ensuring a consistent quorum system transition is the concept of *epochs* [Rabinovich and Lazowska, 1992b]. An epoch is a set of processes that have a local copy of the same quorum system. In order to easily distinguish epochs, each process manages an epoch (version) number in addition to the replica, its version number, the operation-specific locks, and a local copy of the quorum system. The set of processes having the highest epoch number constitutes the current epoch and each of those processes has the current quorum sys-tem. Sequential consistency is guaranteed if operations are performed with exclusively using quorums of the current epoch's quorum system. The tran-sition to a new epoch requires the agreement and write-locking of all pro-cesses contained in a write quorum of the current epoch's quorum system as well as of all processes contained in a write quorum of the new epoch's quorum system. Then, the new quorum system is disseminated to all pro-cesses contained in the union of the two write quorums, their epoch numbers are set to a new global maximum, and their replicas' value is updated if nec-essary. Finally, the write locks are released and the epoch change operation is completed. Because of the quorum system intersection property, suffi-ciently many processes have learned about the new epoch to ensure that at least one process in every quorum of the old and the new epoch's quorum system knows the new quorum system. If a process of an old epoch initiates an operation with using a quorum of an old quorum system, this process learns about a newer epoch and a newer quorum system since at least one of the quorum's processes is in a newer epoch and has a higher epoch number. Then, the process aborts the operation execution and updates its quorum system and epoch number from a quorum's process of the highest epoch after which it restarts the operation, then using a quorum of the current or of a newer but still old epoch's quorum system. In the latter case, the process again learns about a newer epoch and a newer quorum system until it eventually has the globally highest epoch number and uses a quorum of the current epoch's quorum system.

Conceptually, a dynamic data replication scheme can be seen as a set of static data replication schemes, each specifying the quorum system for a particular subset of the set of processes. Among these quorum systems is consistently switched, for example, in response to a detected process failure, such that the quorum system for the subset of processes that reflects the set of currently non-failed processes becomes the current quorum system. Consider, for example, a system using Dynamic Voting with three processes p_1, p_2, and p_3 resulting in a set of seven quorum systems, each complying to the unstructured static Majority Consensus Voting for a different subset of processes. More specifically, with $\mathcal{Q}_R$ denoting a read quorum set and $\mathcal{Q}_W$ denoting a write quorum set, the set of seven quorum systems consists of one quorum system for no process being failed, namely

$$\mathcal{Q}_R = \mathcal{Q}_W = \{\{p_1, p_2\}, \{p_1, p_3\}, \{p_2, p_3\}\},$$

three quorum systems for one process being failed, namely

$$\mathcal{Q}_W = \{\{p_1, p_2\}\} \text{ and } \mathcal{Q}_R = \{\{p_1\}, \{p_2\}\} \text{ for process } p_3,$$
$$\mathcal{Q}_W = \{\{p_1, p_3\}\} \text{ and } \mathcal{Q}_R = \{\{p_1\}, \{p_3\}\} \text{ for process } p_2, \text{ and}$$
$$\mathcal{Q}_W = \{\{p_2, p_3\}\} \text{ and } \mathcal{Q}_R = \{\{p_2\}, \{p_3\}\} \text{ for process } p_1, \text{ and}$$

three quorum systems for two processes being failed, namely

$$\mathcal{Q}_R = \mathcal{Q}_W = \{\{p_1\}\} \text{ for processes } p_2 \text{ and } p_3,$$
$$\mathcal{Q}_R = \mathcal{Q}_W = \{\{p_2\}\} \text{ for processes } p_1 \text{ and } p_3, \text{ and}$$
$$\mathcal{Q}_R = \mathcal{Q}_W = \{\{p_3\}\} \text{ for processes } p_1 \text{ and } p_2.$$

Each subset of the set of static data replication schemes that determines the quorum systems for a particular number n' of processes describes a *stage* n' of the dynamics with $1 \leq n' \leq n$ and n being the total number of processes in the system.

For almost all dynamic data replication schemes, the maximal number of processes is predetermined at design-time. Conceptually, it is not possible to integrate new processes into the data replication scheme at run-time. Although for some dynamic data replication schemes such as for Dynamic

Voting there do exist add-on protocols that allow the integration of new processes at run-time [Jajodia and Mutchler, 1990], these protocols are scheme-specific and thus are not applicable to other data replication schemes. As modern distributed systems like peer-to-peer systems are highly dynamic in nature with processes joining and deliberately departing from the system at run-time, this restriction hinders the general application of quorum-based data replication schemes to such dynamic environments.

Homogeneous and Heterogeneous Dynamic Data Replication Schemes Traditional dynamic data replication schemes are *homogeneous* in the sense that a single scheme-inherent quorum system construction scheme is used homogeneously at all stages of the dynamics to determine the quorum systems. In case of Dynamic Voting, for example, the quorum systems for every stage $1 \leq n' \leq n$ of the dynamics are built in a Majority Consensus Voting-manner according to the rule that write quorums consist of $\lceil (n'+1)/2 \rceil$ processes and read quorums consist of $\lceil n'/2 \rceil$ processes. In the same sense as there is no single data replication scheme superior for every application scenario, there is also none superior for every stage of the dynamics: While unstructured data replication schemes face scalability problems with increasing numbers of processes, structured data replication schemes can only unleash their full potential if the underlying logical structure the processes are arranged in is fully or at least mostly populated by processes. Thus, homogeneity poses a limitation on the choice of an appropriate data replication scheme for a specific application scenario. Heterogeneous dynamic data replication schemes [Storm, 2006; Storm and Theel, 2006] overcome this restriction as they allow different quorum system construction schemes to be utilized for different stages of the dynamics. Hence, the data replication scheme-specific deficiencies can be countered by employing the respective best-option structured or unstructured static data replication scheme per stage of the dynamics for a concrete application scenario. This flexibility allows to realize fine-grained trade-offs between quality measures such as, for example, operation availability and operation costs in terms of the number of messages required to effectuate a quorum. As illustrated in Figure 1.1, heterogeneous dynamic data replication schemes introduce a third dimension to the data replication scheme design space that is spawned by static and dynamic, unstructured and structured, and homogeneous and heterogeneous data replication schemes. Note that static data replication schemes cannot be heterogeneous as they use a single quorum system. Also note that while the design space of homogeneous dynamic

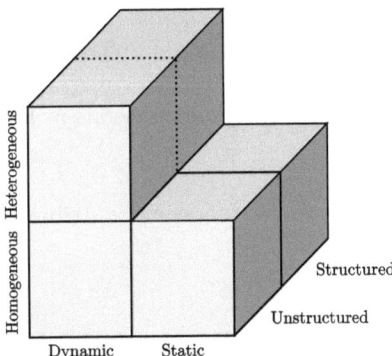

Figure 1.1: Data Replication Scheme Design Space

data replication schemes is segmented into structured and unstructured data replication schemes, it is not strictly segmented for heterogeneous schemes: Although there are heterogeneous dynamic (un)structured data replication schemes – namely those that exclusively use different (un)structured quorum system construction schemes – a strict separation of the heterogeneous dynamic data replication scheme design space into structured and unstructured schemes is inappropriate since a single heterogeneous dynamic data replication scheme can also be a blend of both.

Unfortunately, existing frameworks that support heterogeneous dynamic data replication schemes [Storm, 2006; Storm and Theel, 2006] are reliant on an actual implementation of the quorum system construction schemes underlying the static data replication schemes used in the different stages of the dynamics. Hence, the adoption to changing application scenarios or the integration of new static data replication schemes involves modifying the framework's code which may be tedious and costly but certainly is an error-prone task.

The choice of a particular data replication scheme for a specific application scenario – and thus a particular trade-off between quality measures – needs a careful evaluation as it has a strong impact on the performance and dependability of the system. Let aside simulation-based approaches, there are approaches to the analytical quality measure evaluation of static data replication schemes via calculating combinatorial formulas, for example, by Koch [1994], and there are approaches to the analytical evaluation of (some) unstructured homogeneous dynamic data replication schemes [Chen and Wang, 1996a,b,c; Chen, Wang et al., 2004a; Dugan and Ciardo, 1989; Jajodia and Mutchler, 1990; Pâris, 1986a; Wang, Chen et al., 2000]. However, there are none for structured homogeneous or heterogeneous dynamic data replication schemes.

These shortcomings motivate the following contributions.

Contributions

Uniform Specification of Data Replication Schemes A specification formalism allows to *specify* data replication schemes instead of having to implement them. For example, General Structured Voting [Theel, 1993a,b] and its dynamic counterpart [Theel and Strauß, 1998] allow data replication schemes to be specified in a visual graph-based manner, fostering an improved human comprehension of quorum system structures. The graphs are interpreted by a universal algorithm that outputs either the quorum system or a single operation-specific quorum. Another specification formalism example is Multidimensional Voting [Ahamad, Ammar et al., 1990, 1991] in which a quorum system is specified via a matrix of natural numbers that relates processes (rows) to vote dimensions (columns). An operation-specific quorum is the union of processes resulting from a successful threshold voting performed within and over the columns of the matrix.

The first contribution of this thesis that is presented in Chapter 3 is a uniform approach to the specification of quorum-based data replication schemes that refines and improves on the concepts introduced by General Structured Voting [Theel, 1993a,b]. This approach is universal in the sense that unstructured and structured static as well as homogeneous and heterogeneous dynamic data replication schemes are supported. Furthermore, it enables handling an unbounded number of processes at run-time in a uniform and convenient manner. As to be illustrated in Section 3.1, the aforementioned approaches are either limited to static data replication schemes [Ahamad, Ammar et al., 1990, 1991; Theel, 1993a,b] or to homogeneous dynamic data replication schemes having a fixed upper bound on the number of processes [Theel and Strauß, 1998].

Analytical Evaluation of Data Replication Schemes Finding and selecting an appropriate data replication scheme for a specific application scenario – and thus a specific trade-off between quality measures – is an important task. It is a crucial decision with respect to the performance and dependability of the distributed system and therefore needs to be carefully evaluated. Exploring the data replication scheme design space and evaluating the schemes found by means of simulation-based methods suffers from a huge time complexity for reaching a sufficiently high accuracy of results – or accepts inaccuracies traded for less time complexity. Contrarily, methods based on stochastic analysis are fast and accurate. However, this comes at the price of a higher degree of abstraction in the analytical system model: An analytical model which is as detailed as a simulation model is in general not tractable due to exponential time and space requirements. Of course, higher abstraction bears the risk of oversimplification. Thus, the analytical system model must be as precise as necessary and as abstract as possible for it to be solvable and to provide meaningful answers to the questions asked to the model.

Static data replication schemes can be modeled by and are easily analyzed via calculating combinatorial formulas (given some simplifying assumptions such as perfect channels). Modeling and analyzing dynamic data replication schemes is by far more difficult due to the additional complexity introduced by the dynamics. It needs a careful crafting of the system model for it to remain tractable at all. As to be discussed in Section 4.2, existing approaches to analytically evaluate dynamic data replication schemes by Chen and Wang [1996a,b,c]; Chen, Wang et al. [2004a]; Dugan and Ciardo [1989]; Jajodia and Mutchler [1990]; Wang, Chen et al. [2000], and Pâris [1986a] are restricted to unstructured homogeneous dynamic data replication schemes in terms of Dynamic Voting and variants thereof. Therefore, in each of these system models (1) only one type of quorum system construction scheme must be modeled that is homogeneously utilized at every stage of the dynamics and (2) logical structures are not used which is why process identities can be neglected as all processes are considered equivalent. As a result, the system models are kept small and tractable but they are also limited to a very specific subclass of unstructured homogeneous dynamic data replication schemes. All these approaches are tailored towards a particular data replication scheme such that the respective system models are inapplicable to the evaluation of other schemes. Besides, they consider no quality measures other than operation availability and its closely related measure reliability for the write operation only.

The second contribution that is presented in Chapter 4 of this thesis is a general and comprehensive approach to the analytical evaluation of quorum-based data replication schemes in terms of a flexible and modular system model. The system model is a compound of modules, each modeling a particular aspect such as the behavior of a process, the execution of operations, or a quorum system, the latter based on concepts introduced in Chapter 3. Simply by varying the quorum system modules, unstructured and structured static as well as homogeneous and heterogeneous dynamic data replication schemes are reflected in the system model. A data replication scheme always implements a trade-off between various quality measures and this trade-off needs to be evaluated in entirety in order to enable a fair and thorough comparison with other schemes. Besides operation availability and its related measure reliability, the system model allows other quality measures such as operation costs in terms of the number of messages required to effectuate a quorum to be evaluated for the read operation as well as for the write operation.

In summary, the main contributions of this thesis are:

(1) A uniform specification formalism for quorum-based data replication schemes that supports unstructured and structured static as well as homogeneous and heterogeneous dynamic data replication schemes. Furthermore, it enables handling an unbounded number of processes at run-time in a uniform and convenient manner.

(2) A general and flexible system model that supports the analytical quality measure evaluation of any quorum-based data replication scheme expressible via the uniform data replication scheme specification formalism. The system model allows to evaluate operation availability and other quality measures such as operation costs for the read as well as for the write operation.

2 Fault Tolerance in Distributed Computing

A distributed system consists of several independent processing components that interact with each other via an interconnecting communication link network consisting of communication components. Distributed computing refers to the algorithmic controlling of the distributed system's processing components by means of a distributed program in order to reach a collective goal, that is, to provide a certain service. Unfortunately, the components of literally every system are naturally imperfect and therefore prone to failures that may render the system unable to provide the service. In order to be able to tolerate the failure of some components, that is, to keep the service available despite these failures, the system must be equipped with redundancy in space and time. The former refers to redundant components that take over the part played by failed components. The latter refers to the additional overhead required to manage these components. Fault-tolerant distributed computing refers to the algorithmic controlling of the distributed system's components to provide the desired service despite the presence of certain failures in the system by exploiting redundancy in space and time. Of course, the failure of all the system's components cannot be coped with, but the failure of some of the components can be successfully tolerated. The more failures can be tolerated, the higher is the resilience to failures and the dependability of the distributed system in general.

This chapter introduces the fundamentals of fault-tolerant distributed computing as required for quorum-based data replication. The system model is introduced in the next Section 2.1. In particular, the communication model, the failure model, the dynamics model, and the timing model alongside with their specific assumptions are discussed. Regarding data replication, the consistency notion guaranteed by a data replication mechanism is a distinguishing aspect and is the concern of Section 2.2. Subsequently, quorum systems as a means to realize mutual exclusion and to ensure sequential consistency in distributed systems are presented in Section 2.3. In Section 2.4, different quality measures for quorum systems are discussed. Quorum-based data replication schemes are introduced in Section 2.5. In particular, data replication schemes ranging from static over dynamic schemes and their particular concepts to heterogeneous dynamic data replication schemes are presented. Finally, a summary concludes this introductory chapter on the fundamentals of fault-tolerant distributed computing.

2.1 System Model

Due to the ever increasing complexity of real-world distributed systems, an abstraction in terms of a system model is essential to develop and evaluate these systems. An evaluation or reasoning on the real-world system itself, respectively, on a model that is as detailed as the real-world system, is often computationally too complex to be feasible – if possible at all. A model is an abstract view on a system and concentrates on its relevant aspects while hiding the – for the purpose of the model – unimportant details. Of course, an abstraction bears the risk of oversimplification. Thus, a good model must be *accurate* and *tractable* [Schneider, 1993a]. A model is accurate if evaluation results derived from the model also hold for the real-word system. It is tractable if evaluations based on the model are possible at all. Models that are either not accurate or not tractable or even both are useless as they give invalid results concerning the real-world system or do not allow to obtain any results at all.

The major concerns in modeling a distributed system are the communication model, the failure model, the dynamics model, and the timing model. The communication model describes how the components of a distributed system interact. The failure model describes which failures may occur in the system, how many of them occur, and also their severity, for example, if components just stop working or may exhibit arbitrary, even malicious behavior. The dynamics model describes the evolution of the distributed system in terms of the number of components in the system over time. Finally, the timing model relates events in the system to the evolution of time, for example, by defining upper bounds on computation time.

2.1.1 Communication Model

In reference to Lamport and Lynch [1991], a distributed system is modeled via a *process model* representing the system by the concurrent execution of a sequential program on several processing components that cooperate with each other to perform some common task. A *process* is such a processing component in terms of an active computing entity such as, for example, a workstation's central processing unit, an operating system process, or a mobile device that executes a sequential program. Cooperation requires communication and coordination among the processes. Processes communicate with each other via sending and receiving messages over *channels*. A channel is a *logical* communication component that pairwise interconnects two processes. It abstracts from the particularities of the underlying physical communication link network consisting of physical communication components such as cables, routers, and switches. Communication via message passing is commonly considered to be the most general type of interprocess communication. For example, Lamport and Lynch [1991] consider a model to be a distributed system model only if its communication can be implemented via message passing. Other types of interprocess communication such as distributed shared memory or remote procedure calls can be implemented via message passing.

Formally, a distributed system model is a tuple consisting of a set of processes $P = \{p_1, \ldots, p_n\}$, $n > 1$, and a set of channels $C = \{c_1, \ldots, c_m\}$, $m \geq 1$, that pairwise interconnect the processes. Henceforth, the term component is used in the context of the system model to refer to processes and channels together if not explicitly stated otherwise.

Processes Each process has a globally unique identity, manages some variables, and sequentially executes a local program that operates on these variables. Examples of the variables a process manages are (the local copy of) the replica, its version number, the read and write operation locks, and the read lock counter indicating when to release the read lock if concurrent read operations are being performed.

The state of a process consists of an internal part and an external part, both defined by the values of some of the process' variables. The external part describes the "visible" behavior of a process that can be observed by other processes or an external observer of the system. The internal part is process-local and hidden from external observation. An example of the former is the version number of a process' replica or the replica data itself. An example of the latter is the read lock counter.

An instruction of the local program a process executes is either an internal action, that is, a computation on variables resulting in a state change, or a communication action, that is, sending or receiving messages. Instructions are assumed to be *atomic*, that is, indivisibly executed by the underlying hardware such that an instruction is either performed completely or not at all.

Channels   A channel, as illustrated in Figure 2.1, is a logical communication link between two processes. Channels are assumed to be unique, meaning that there must not be two channels connecting the same two processes. Two processes $p_i, p_j \in P$ can directly communicate with one another by sending and receiving messages if there is a channel connecting these two processes. If there exists no direct communication channel between two processes, they cannot communicate directly but may communicate indirectly by the help of other mediating processes. Assuming there is no process

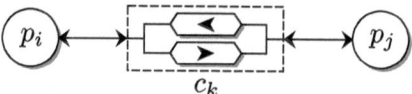

Figure 2.1: Bidirectional Channel c_k Interconnecting the Two Processes p_i and p_j

that is isolated, that is, not every other process can (in)directly communicate with this process, every process can directly or indirectly communicate with every other process. Seen on a more abstract level and modeling indirect communication by a channel that abstracts from the indirection, the set of processes is fully connected.

Channel Message Buffering   A channel c_k connecting two processes $p_i, p_j \in P$ buffers the messages it receives from the source process p_i (p_j) in an internal process-specific message queue and delivers the queued messages to the destination process p_j (p_i) according to some message dispatching policy, for example, in a first-in-first-out (FIFO) manner.

   The state of a channel is defined by the state of its message queue, that is, the sequence of yet undelivered messages. The size of the message queue can either be finite or infinite. If it is infinite, a process can always send messages to the channel without ever being hindered, that is, the sending process never blocks. Such a channel is called an *non-blocking channel*. If a non-blocking channel's message queue is empty, a process trying to receive a message from the channel may block until a new message arrives and is delivered by the channel, thereby unblocking the waiting process. Without the receive-blocking semantics, a process can query the channel for new messages, and, if there is a new message, receive it, or, if there is no new message, continue its local processing. Note that the blocking semantics can be emulated via encapsulating the query in a communication instruction in terms of a loop that is exited only if a new message is received by the process. Such an instruction can be considered a communication instruction since no local computation contributing to its progress is involved. These two behaviors are semantically equivalent since instructions are assumed to be atomic.

A channel that is not equipped with an infinite message buffer but instead has a finite-sized message queue may block a sending process in case the message queue is full until a message is delivered such that the new message can be enqueued. Such channels are called *(blocking) bounded-buffer channels*. Channels having a message queue of size zero, that is, having effectively no message queue, are termed *blocking channels*: A sending process is always blocked until the message is delivered by the channel and subsequently received by the destination process whereupon the sender is unblocked. Using blocking channels, communication marks a synchronization point of the two processes interconnected by a blocking channel.

Reliable Channels   Channels can be *reliable* or *unreliable* [Lynch, 1996]. Intuitively, a reliable channel does not lose, corrupt, or create new messages. A reliable channel is called a reliable FIFO channel if it delivers messages in the order they were sent. More specifically, a reliable FIFO channel is characterized by the following attributes:

NO MESSAGE CREATION AND DUPLICATION.   Every message delivered to a receiver was sent by some sender and is delivered at most once.

RELIABLE DELIVERY.   Every message sent by a sender is eventually delivered to the receiver.

FIFO ORDER.   Messages are delivered to the receiver in the order they were sent by the sender.

Whether a channel adheres to these attributes or not strongly depends on the failure model and failure assumptions made for the system that are discussed in the next section. Note that, if a process receives messages from several other processes, respectively, from their interconnecting reliable FIFO channels, it is unspecified in which ordering the process will get and acknowledge the messages from the other processes.

Henceforth, the terms reliable channel and reliable FIFO channel are used synonymously.

Topology of a Distributed System   The topology of a distributed system can be represented by an undirected graph when considering the set of processes as the graph's nodes and the set of channels as the graph's edges. Three exemplary topologies of a distributed system comprising eight processes are shown in Figure 2.2. In Figure 2.2 (a), a *fully connected* topology with $1/2 \cdot (8^2 - 8) = 28$ channels is shown in which every two processes can directly communicate with each other. In the *ring* topology with eight channels as shown in Figure 2.2 (b), non-neighboring processes, that is, processes not interconnected by a channel, need at least one mediating process to communicate with each other. The topology shown in Figure 2.2 (c) is a blend of both in which direct as well as indirect communication is required for a process to communicate with every other process.

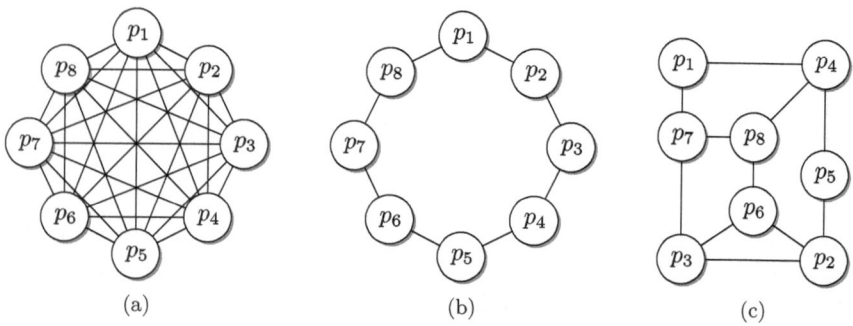

Figure 2.2: Exemplary Fully Connected Topology (a), Ring Topology (b), and Ethernet Topology (c) of a Distributed System with Eight Processes

Distributed Program Execution   Conceptually, a distributed system can be represented by a state machine as being a tuple of (1) the state space of its components, that is, the compound individual state spaces of the processes and channels, (2) an initial state, and (3) a state transition relation defined by the distributed program. A state transition may affect the state of more than one component if it follows *non-interleaving seman-tics*. Otherwise, it follows *interleaving semantics* and is restricted to alter the state of a single component only. Depending on the level of abstraction and fine-grain atomicity, non-interleaving semantics can be implemented by interleaving semantics [Abadi and Lamport, 1995]. The subtle implications of choosing one over the other are discussed in Section 4.3.1.

In reference to Alpern and Schneider [1985], a distributed computation, an execution of a distributed program, or simply a *run* of a distributed system is an infinite sequence of states, starting from the initial state and with subsequent states resulting from state transitions of the system. A run represents one possible execution of the system. The notion of runs also covers terminating computations – that are characterized by a finite sequence of states – via repeating the final state indefinitely. A *property* is a set of runs of the distributed system. Note that the set of all runs a distributed system may show – and by which it is completely characterized – is itself a property of the system. Intuitively, the runs that form a property have a certain characteristics in common, meaning that some predicate holds for all runs of a property.

Safety and Liveness Two important system properties are *safety* and *liveness* [Alpern and Schneider, 1985; Lamport, 1977]. Informally, safety states that something "bad" never happens while liveness states that something "good" must eventually happen.

A safety property is, for example, a distributed program's deadlock-freeness. A run is called safe if there is no state in this run in which the "bad" thing in terms of a deadlock happens. A system is called safe if all runs of the system are safe. A safety property must always hold in every state of a safe system.

A liveness property is, for example, starvation-freedom which means that a process makes progress infinitely often. A run is called live if for every state in this run there is a successive state that is eventually reached in a finite number of state transitions and in which the "good" thing in terms of making progress happens. A system is called live if all runs of the system are live. Liveness expresses a notion of progress in the execution of a distributed program.

The system model introduced so far has no notion of failures. The next section describes how process and channel failures are reflected in the system model and discusses the specifics of failures, that is, how a failed component behaves, how many (simultaneous) component failures may occur in a run of the distributed system, and in what state a failed component will be upon recovery from a failure.

2.1.2 Failure Model

Processes as well as the channels interconnecting them, respectively, the processes' hardware and the physical communication components underlying a channel, are naturally subject to failures. A component is *non-failed* if it behaves according to its specification, that is, the precise definition of the (intended) component's behavior. Otherwise, if it deviates from its specified behavior, it has *failed*. A component that does not fail in a run is called *correct* with respect to this run. Otherwise, it is termed *faulty* for the run. Initially, all components of the distributed system are assumed to be non-failed.

Failure-Extended Component State Space   A system changes its state as a result of normal system operation and failure events [Cristian, 1985]. Thus, the failure of a component can be represented by a *failure state transition* that occurs when the component starts to misbehave with respect to its specification. A failed component may be allowed to recover from its failure. The recovery of a failed component is represented by a *recovery state transition* that occurs when the component resumes to behave according to its specification. In order to represent a component's state of being failed or non-failed, its state space is enlarged by introducing a virtual boolean *failure variable* that is set while the component is failed and unset otherwise. The so enlarged component's state space, respectively, the global state space enlarged by the individual components' virtual failure variables, is called *failure-extended* state space. Note that since the failure variable describes a "visible" behavior of a component, it is associated with the external part of the component's state and can be observed by (other) processes or an external observer of the system.

While all state transitions contribute to the *evolution* of the distributed computation, state transitions that are neither failure nor recovery transitions contribute to the *progress* of the distributed computation.

Fault, Error, and Failure   Following the definitions of Avižienis, Laprie et al. [2004] and transposing the notion of a failed component to the system level, a system *failure* has occurred whenever the system starts to misbehave with respect to its specification. An *error* is that part of the system state that may cause a subsequent system failure, that is, there may exist a sequence of state transitions resulting in a system failure. Note that the presence of an error must not necessarily result in a system failure. Errors are part of the system state in terms of the system's data and are therefore potentially observable and detectable. The cause of an error is a *fault*. The presence of faults in the system does not necessarily imply the manifestation of errors as a fault may or may not generate an error. The inverse, however, holds: the presence of an error in the system state implies the presence of a fault in the system.

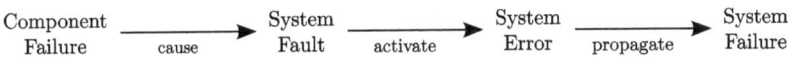

Figure 2.3: Dependency among Fault, Error, and Failure

As an example of the dependencies among fault, error, and failure, consider the failure of one of the distributed system's components and this component failure to cause a fault in the system as illustrated in Figure 2.3. This fault is activated resulting in an error. The error may propagate and cause a system failure.

Redundancy and Fault-Tolerant Systems   Intuitively, for being able to tolerate the failure of some components of the distributed system, it must be equipped with extra components that take over the function of failed components. This intuition is captured by the notion of *redundancy*.

More specifically, *redundancy in space* means to equip a system with more components than needed to provide its service in the failure-free case. Hence, the system state space is enlarged by additional and functionally meaningful states that are not needed if failures do not occur. Without redundancy in space, that is, the distributed system is equipped with no more components than required, every state of the distributed system must be visited in every possible run of the distributed system [Gärtner, 1999].

Redundancy in time refers to additional and functionally meaningful work done by the system that is not needed in the failure-free case. The extra state transitions introduced are used, for example, to manage the redundant components or to do redundant computation in the line of triple modular redundancy [von Neumann, 1956]. Without redundancy in time, every transition must be eventually executed in all possible executions of the distributed system [Gärtner, 1999].

A system is *fault-tolerant* if it can provide its service despite the presence of certain faults in the system by using redundancy. The objective of *fault tolerance* is to avoid a system failure even in the presence of faults. Thus, redundancy is the key to fault tolerance as there can be no fault tolerance without redundancy. The inverse, however, does not hold: redundancy alone does not provide fault tolerance.

With respect to data replication, redundancy in space is impersonated by multiple processes each managing a local copy of the replicated data object and its associated metadata (cf. Section 2.1.1). Redundancy in time is embodied in the protocol to execute read and write operations on (some of) the multiple processes' local copy of the replicated data object (cf. Section 2.3).

Classes of Fault Tolerance According to Arora and Gouda [1993], Arora and Kulkarni [1998a,b], and Gärtner [1999], three types of fault tolerance can be distinguished, namely masking, fail-safe, and non-masking fault tolerance.

Masking fault tolerance is the most desirable type of fault tolerance as failures are tolerated transparently, meaning they are not observable from outside the system. Safety and liveness properties always hold and are never violated. As it is the strictest variant of fault tolerance, it is therefore also the most costly. Examples of masking fault tolerance are triple modular redundancy [von Neumann, 1956] and quorum-based data replication (cf. Section 2.5).

Fail-safe fault tolerance guarantees safety but not liveness. A system may stop in a particular state without making further progress (that is, the system is halted) but this stopping state is safe [Kulkarni and Ebnenasir, 2002].

Complementary to fail-safe fault tolerance is *non-masking* fault tolerance that guarantees liveness but not safety. Faults may be observable from outside the system, thereby violating safety, but the system is guaranteed to make progress. An example of non-masking fault tolerance is self-stabilization surveyed by Schneider [1993b] where safety eventually always holds once the last error has occurred.

No system built from imperfect components can tolerate arbitrary many or severe component failures. Thus, a decision which component failures and how many of them should be tolerated by a system must be made. The result is a failure model that precisely describes the failures a system is specified for and assumed to tolerate. In reference to Echtle [1990], the formalization of failure assumptions is separated into *functional* and *structural* failure models.

Functional Failure Model

A functional failure model specifies what behavior a failed component may exhibit and thus defines the semantics of failures that are to be tolerated by a system. Cristian, Aghili et al. [1995] identify the failure classes of *crash*, *omission*, *timing*, and *byzantine* failures, ordered by hierarchical inclusion according to their severity as illustrated in Figure 2.4. A failure class includes another if the behavior of a failed component in the latter is also possible in the former failure class. For example, the timing failure class is included in the byzantine failure class, but not in the omission failure class.

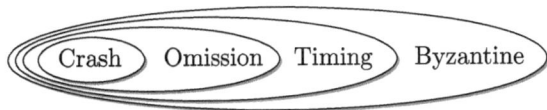

Figure 2.4: Hierarchical Ordering of Functional Failure Classes [Jalote, 1994]

Crash Failure   A component that fails according to the failure semantics of the *crash failure* class either behaves correctly according to its specification or has crashed, meaning it has halted and stopped to make any progress. Cristian [1991] further distinguishes the crash failure class depending on the state of a failed component after its recovery.

If a failed component is restarted from its initial state after recovery – that is not dependent on the progress the component has made while being non-failed – an *amnesia-crash* of the component has happened. The recovered component is not aware of its former failure as it cannot distinguish between having failed and subsequently being repaired or having just started from its initial state. An amnesia-crash failure may render a reliable channel an unreliable channel as the channel's message buffer is reset to its initial (empty) state such that possibly enqueued messages are lost and are never delivered, thereby violating the reliable delivery requirement.

A *partial-amnesia-crash* failure has occurred if upon recovery some parts of the component's state are reset to the initial state while others resemble the state from before the failure.

If a failed component restarts in the state it was in before its failure, then it has suffered a *pause-crash* failure. Note that pause-crash failures and partial-amnesia-crash failures require the state of a component to be conserved upon failure for the purpose of being restored upon recovery, for example, by employing stable storage [Lampson, 1981; Lampson and Sturgis, 1979]. As additional recovery steps must be taken, that is, restoring the state from stable storage, a recovering component is aware of the fact of having failed.

A *halting-crash* failure has occurred if a crash-failed component never recovers and remains failed indefinitely.

Henceforth, the term crash failure is identified with pause-crash failure if not explicitly stated otherwise.

Omission Failure   If an otherwise non-failed process or channel fails to execute one or more instructions of its local program, respectively, fails to deliver one or more messages, then it has suffered an *omission failure*. An omission failure renders a reliable channel an unreliable channel as it loses one or more messages, that is, deletes them from the message buffer, thereby violating the reliable delivery requirement.

If an omission-failed process always fails to execute instructions, that is, it does not make any progress, then it has halting-crash-failed. Alike, a channel that always neither receives nor delivers messages has halting-crash-failed.

Timing Failure   A *timing failure* has occurred if a component functions correctly but does so untimely, that is, outside of the specified expected time frame. Components that have failed according to the failure semantics of the timing failure class respond either too early, too late, or even not at all. The latter resembles an omission failure.

Byzantine Failure   A component that fails according to the failure semantics of the *byzantine failure* class may exhibit arbitrary behavior while being failed, which includes correct as well as unusual or even malicious behavior. Therefore, byzantine-failed components are also called *fail-un-controlled* components [Lamport, Shostak et al., 1982]. A byzantine-failed component may generate arbitrary errors in both, the time and value domain of data [Powell, 1992], allowing the byzantine-failed component to consciously sabotage the distributed computation. Note that a byzantine-failed component may also decide to mimic the failure behaviors of the crash, omission, and timing failure classes.

In addition to specifying what behavior a failed component may exhibit, the specification of which and how many components may fail is mandatory. This is realized by a *structural* failure model as described next.

Structural Failure Model

A structural failure model describes (1) the type of components, (2) how many of them, and (3) which components may fail in a run of the distributed system. If only processes are subject to failures while channels are perfect, the structural failure model is said to be a *process failure model*. Conversely, if processes are perfect and channels are subject to failures, the structural failure model is a *channel failure model*. If both, processes and the channels interconnecting them are subject to failures in a run, the structural failure model is a *combined failure model*.

The set of failed components in a run is termed the *failure scenario* for this run.

Threshold-Based Structural Failure Model A simple example of a structural failure model is the so-called *threshold model* [Chandra and Toueg, 1996; Fischer, Lynch et al., 1985] specifying that at most t out of n components with $t \leq n$ may fail in a run. For example, consider a system consisting of three processes p_1, p_2, p_3 that are interconnected by perfect channels and a structural failure specification stating that at most one process may fail in a run. This failure scenario is precisely described by a threshold model with a threshold of $t = 1$. Assume that, due to knowledge about the concrete application scenario, the original failure specification is refined to also include the case that p_1 and p_2 may fail in a run. This refined failure specification cannot be precisely described by a threshold model. It is not possible to specify the additional failure scenario of p_1 and p_2 failing without raising the threshold to $t = 2$, thereby also specifying the failure scenarios of p_1, p_3 and p_2, p_3 failing in a run. Threshold models easily under- or overspecify the failures a system has to face: Either a failure scenario that may occur is not specified or a failure scenario that may not occur is specified and unnecessarily respected in the structural failure model. Hence, a threshold model specifies the possible failure of arbitrary subsets of the set of components whose cardinality is less than or equal to t.

Set-Based Structural Failure Models Set-based structural failure models such as, for example, *adversary structures* [Hirt and Maurer, 1997] or *DiDep* [Warns, 2009], allow a more fine-grained and more detailed structural failure specification by means of sets of subsets of components that may fail in a run. Such set-based structural failure models strictly generalize threshold models as those can be represented by sets of subsets of components. Revisiting the above example, the set-based structural failure model $\{\emptyset, \{p_1\}, \{p_2\}, \{p_3\}, \{p_1, p_2\}\}$ stating that either no process, exactly one process, or only p_1 and p_2 may fail in a run precisely describes the refined failure specification.

Moreover, set-based structural failure models can describe dependencies among component failures that threshold models cannot. For example, in the set-based structural failure model given above, the failure of p_1 and p_2 prevents the failure of p_3 in the same run. Assuming process p_1 cannot fail on its own, that is, the structural failure model becomes $\{\emptyset, \{p_2\}, \{p_3\}, \{p_1, p_2\}\}$, then its failure also prevents the failure of p_3 but enforces the failure of p_2 in the same run. Informally, an independent component failure does neither prevent nor enforce the failure of other components. The structural failure model in which the three processes p_1, p_2, p_3 may fail independently is $\{\emptyset, \{p_1\}, \{p_2\}, \{p_3\}, \{p_1, p_2\}, \{p_1, p_3\}, \{p_2, p_3\}, \{p_1, p_2, p_3\}\}$.

Assumption Coverage Albeit a careful structural failure specification, the risk of underspecifying the extent of failures remains. This risk is expressed by the notion of *assumption coverage* [Powell, 1992] as the probability that no more than the specified failure scenarios will occur. The assumption coverage is generally less than 1 since some failure scenarios may be left unspecified, either intentionally or unintended. If all potential failure scenarios were specified in the structural failure model, the model may be of no use as it is too complex, respectively, describes too severe failure scenarios for a system to tolerate. For example, the failure of all components of the system may be specified in the structural failure model but this failure scenario cannot be tolerated by any system that is built from imperfect components – at least not if the components are failed for a longer period of time.

Network Partitioning The failure of channels changes the topology of the distributed system and thereby has an impact on communication among the processes. This in return affects the progress of the distributed computation. For example, if the two channels in the ring topology shown in Figure 2.2 (b) that connect p_1 and p_2 and p_5 and p_6 fail, the network is split into two *partitions*. While inter-partition communication is rendered impossible, intra-partition communication among processes is not affected. If the two channels have suffered a halting-crash and thus are failed permanently, then the system has permanently failed given that the processes of both partitions must cooperate for the distributed computation to make progress. If, on the other hand, the failed channels eventually recover, then the distributed computation's progress is not rendered impossible but is merely delayed until at least one of the failed channels recovers – and no intermittent failures have occurred – such that the partitions are rejoined.

The next section extends the communication model introduced so far to support processes arriving at and departing from the distributed system at run-time.

2.1.3 Dynamics Model

The communication model introduced so far is a *static* model meaning that the set of processes and channels is a priori defined and remains fixed for the entire lifetime of the distributed system. Such a static model is insufficient to model dynamic distributed systems such as, for example, peer-to-peer systems or mobile ad-hoc networks. These systems are highly dynamic in nature with processes arriving at and deliberately departing from the system at run-time. As a result, the topology in suchlike systems changes over time as arriving processes introduce new channels and channels connecting to departing processes must be removed from the topology. For the communication model to be able to also cover such dynamic systems, it must be capable of reflecting these topology changes at run-time. Unfortunately, there are yet no commonly agreed "standard" dynamic communication models as it is the case for static communication models.

Global Static Communication Model   A rather simple first approach to a dynamic communication model is to a priori specify the communication model to include any topology potentially occurring at run-time and marking the initially not active channels and processes as "failed". Whenever a process "arrives" at the system, the process and its connecting channels are already present in the communication model and get "recovered". Upon a deliberate "departure" of a process, the process and its connecting channels are treated as having failed. For this model, the previously made assumption that all components are initially non-failed must obviously be revoked.

Although being a viable solution to model a dynamic distributed system (in terms of a single static communication model), this approach has a severe drawback: The solution confuses the two separate dimensions of normal dynamics and failure-induced dynamics as both are modeled by the same means, namely by the failure dynamics. Without further ado, it is not possible to distinguish departed processes from failed ones. However, knowing whether a process has failed or deliberately departed from the system may have an impact on the reconfiguration decision to be made.

Dynamic Communication Model as Sequencing Static Models A solution that avoids the confusion of normal dynamics and failure dynamics is to consider the communication model itself as being dynamic. Essentially, the set of processes and channels must not be static and a priori fixed but can instead evolve over time to reflect arriving and departing processes. If a new process arrives at the system, it must be joined with the set of processes and at least one channel connecting the new process to an already established process must be added to the set of channels such that the new process can directly or indirectly communicate with other processes. Subsequently, the state transition relation must be adapted to incorporate new state transitions for the new process and its connecting channel(s). Conversely, whenever a process deliberately departs from the system, the process and its connecting channels must be removed from the set of processes and the set of channels, respectively. Finally, the state transition relation must be adapted to no longer include any transitions involving the departed process or its connecting channel(s).

Conceptionally, such a dynamic communication model can be seen as a set of static communication models among which is transitioned upon a process arrival or departure, starting from a distinguished initial static model. Whenever processes arrive or depart from the system, a transition from the current static communication model to one of its subsequent static communication models is taken. Each of these subsequent models has an *initial state* defined by one of the current communication model's *transition states* plus the states due to newly arrived processes and their interconnecting channels and minus the states of departed processes and their channels. A transition state is modeled as a final state of a static communication model. A final state of the system, that is, a terminating system state, is modeled by repeating this final state in the respective static communication model indefinitely. As for the first approach, the assumption that all components are initially non-failed must be revoked since a subsequent static communication model may inherit failed components from its preceding static communication model. The notion of a run can be applied to the dynamic communication model as being the sequential concatenation of the individual static communication model runs in the order the static communication models were transitioned to, starting with the initial static communication model.

A dynamic communication model can be represented as a directed graph of static communication models having a distinguished root node model whose initial state represents the initial state of the system as illustrated in Figure 2.5. This exemplary dynamic communication model consists of

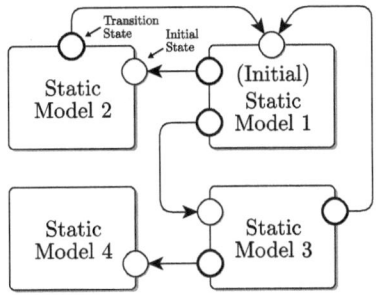

Figure 2.5: Dynamic Communication Model as Sequencing Static Models

four static communication models with the model 1 being the initial static communication model. The static models 1, 2, and 3 form a cycle in the graph, meaning that it may be indefinitely transitioned among these models – given that no system end state is present and transitioned to in one of the models. The static communication model 4 is a leaf node in the graph having no subsequent static communication models. Once transitioned to this static communication model, forever no process will arrive at or depart from the system and thus no transition to a subsequent static communication model occurs.

Proving safety and in particular liveness properties becomes more ambitious in a suchlike modeled dynamic distributed system. For proving safety, it must provably hold in all states of each static communication model. Considering liveness and depending on the specific distributed program, a non-trivial liveness property may require to impose restrictions on the transitioning among static communication models with respect to the residence time in each model. For example, the forevermore rapid switching among two static communication models in an alternating manner may hinder the distributed system from making progress because of the need for constant reconfiguration in terms of the integration and disintegration of processes (and their interconnecting channels), thereby violating liveness. Unfortunately, proving the liveness property for every static communication model individually is not sufficient.

While this model separates the dimensions of normal dynamics and failure dynamics, it requires a multitude of static communication models to reflect the dynamics in processes of the system. This problem may be relieved by allowing static communication models to have multiple initial states and a more sophisticated state transition relation such that each model represents the static communication model for a particular number of processes rather than for a particular subset of the set of processes. Then, the number of required static communication models is bounded by the overall total number of processes in the system. However, an optimization in this respect is beyond the scope of this thesis and remains future work.

Both dynamic communication models instrument static communication models to describe the dynamics in the number of processes. Therefore, existing approaches to evaluate distributed systems that rely on static communication models are applicable with no or minor modifications to these two dynamic communication models. Using the latter model, however, requires to combine the individual results obtained for every static communication model in order to obtain a result for the overall system.

The system model introduced so far is time-free, that is, it has no notion of time or duration associated to state transitions and thus makes no assumptions about the passage of (real-)time while the evolution of the distributed computation. However, time is an important aspect of a distributed system concerning, for example, failure detection and performance in terms of the distributed computation's speed of progress.

2.1.4 Timing Model

The timing model describes timing assumptions in a distributed system regarding, for example, the individual processes' processing speed or message delivery delays related to the passage of (real-)time. Next, the *time-synchronous* and subsequently the *time-asynchronous* models along with their timing assumptions' effect on failure detection and coordination are presented. Thereafter, an intermediate model with respect to the timing assumptions' strength, the *timed asynchronous* system model, is sketched.

Time-Synchronous Systems

In purely *time-synchronous systems*, the individual processing speeds of the *time-synchronous processes* and the message propagation times of the *time-synchronous channels* have a known upper bound.

Failure Detection In a time-synchronous system and assuming that channels do not fail, timeouts can be used to reliably detect crash-failed processes: It can be safely assumed that a process has crash-failed whenever it does not respond within an upper-bounded period of time. A perfect process failure detector is easily implementable, and, therefore, coordination problems such as the consensus problem [Fetzer and Cristian, 1995; Fischer, Lynch et al., 1985], that is, reaching the agreement of all processes on a common value, or leader election [García-Molina, 1982; Stoller, 2000] are easily solvable and implementable. Furthermore, timeliness assumptions such as an algorithm terminating within a given period of time can be validly stated for a time-synchronous system. However, if channels are not perfect and may crash-fail, then the failure of a process cannot be distinguished from the failure of the channels connecting this process to other processes.

Process Step-Lock Synchrony Exploiting the fact of a known upper bound on the individual processing speeds, realtime can be partitioned into consecutive phases or *rounds*, each being of the length defined by the largest upper bound, that is, the slowest processing speed. Time-synchronous processes follow *step-lock* semantics, meaning that each process performs exactly one step, respectively, state transition in a round. A round is complete when every process has executed its single step. Thereafter, a new subsequent round begins in which the processes again take exactly one step, and so forth. This notion allows processes to have different processing speeds, but they all make progress in a coordinated fashion.

Note that systems are usually seen from the processes' point of view and messages sent in a round are assumed to be delivered in the same round such that the processes can compute with their received messages' information in the subsequent round. On a lower level of abstraction, this assumption can be conceptually met by introducing alternating rounds of communication in terms of message propagation and computation.

Time-synchronous systems are desirable from the algorithm designer's perspective as distributed programs are easier to design if processes work in step-lock synchrony. However, the upper bounds on message propagation times and processing speeds must hold in the real world a distributed system is deployed in, that is, they must not be violated by too long message propagation times or too slow processing speeds. This may not always be the case, for example, if relying on the Internet for communication which has arbitrary message delivery delays because of its routing infrastructure.

Time-Asynchronous Systems

In contrast to time-synchronous systems, a *time-asynchronous system* literally makes no assumptions about the timing behavior of its *time-asynchronous processes* and *time-asynchronous channels*. Specifically, the processes' individual processing speeds, their relative processing speed difference, and the channels' message delivery times are assumed to be arbitrary (but finite) and cannot be determined. It is therefore undecidable whether a process has halting-crash-failed or is merely slow at computation, even if perfect channels are assumed. As a result, coordination problems that are easily solvable in time-synchronous systems are either hard to implement or even not solvable at all in time-asynchronous systems. For example, as shown by Fischer, Lynch et al. [1985], the consensus problem is not deterministically solvable in the sense that the consensus algorithm always terminates, even in the presence of only one halting-crash-failed process. An indefinitely slow process may hinder the algorithm from terminating and this slowness cannot be distinguished from the process having halting-crash-failed. However, the consensus problem is probabilistically solvable in time-asynchronous systems as long as a majority of processes are correct [Ben-Or, 1983]. Alike, problems that are not deterministically solvable in time-asynchronous systems often have a probabilistic solution.

Failure Detection A problem similar to reaching consensus is failure detection in time-asynchronous systems. In order to tackle failure detection (and to separate the concerns of algorithm design and failure detection) the *failure detector* abstraction has been introduced by Chandra and Toueg [1996]. A failure detector is in essence an oracle that can be queried about processes it suspects to have failed. Each process is equipped with a local failure detector. The (local) failure detectors communicate with each other to provide the failure detection service. Because such a service is not implementable in a time-asynchronous system, assuming a failure detector service weakens the pure asynchrony assumption and effectively introduces a certain degree of synchrony to the timing model.

Failure detection, even in weakened time-asynchronous environments, is unreliable and based on observation such as on observed message propagation times and on indirect information such as the failure suspicion of other failure detectors. Thus, different (local) failure detectors may have a different suspicion of failed processes. For a failure detector to provide useful information that is beneficially exploitable by the distributed program, it must give some guarantees about its quality-of-service that are expressed by the notions of *completeness* and *accuracy*. A failure detector is *complete* if every failed process is suspected. It is *accurate* if no correct process is suspected. Completeness and accuracy can be further classified in the range from strong to weak completeness, respectively, from strong to weak accuracy. A failure detector is *strongly complete* if every failed process is eventually suspected by every correct process' failure detector and remains suspected thereafter. It is *weakly complete* if every failed process is eventually suspected by at least one correct process' failure detector and remains suspected thereafter. In reference to the eventual suspicion of failed processes, completeness is a liveness property while accuracy is a safety property: A failure detector is *strongly accurate* if no correct process is ever suspected of having failed. It is *weakly accurate* if there is at least one correct process that is never suspected.

A failure detector that is strongly complete and strongly accurate is a *perfect failure detector*. A perfect failure detector cannot be implemented even in a reasonably weakened time-asynchronous system as its properties are too strong. Fortunately, weaker failure detectors can be successfully employed to solve coordination problems in weakened time-asynchronous systems: The consensus problem, for example, can be solved by the help of a *strong failure detector* which is strongly complete but only weakly accurate. Even weaker failure detectors are the *eventually perfect* and *eventually strong* failure detectors that are both strongly complete but only eventually strongly accurate, respectively, eventually weakly accurate. Besides these failure detectors due to Chandra and Toueg [1996], a variety of failure detectors such as the *trusting failure detector* [Delporte-Gallet, Fauconnier et al., 2005] that are tailored towards specific problems have been proposed. The trusting failure detector is the weakest failure detector for solving the fault-tolerant mutual exclusion problem.

Process Step-Lock Synchrony Also because of the absence of timing assumptions in time-asynchronous systems, no bounded period of time that

represents a round can be found. Nonetheless, with the help of round synchronization protocols such as the *asynchronous bounded delay synchronizer*
[Chou, Cidon et al., 1990], a step-lock semantics can be implemented with
time-asynchronous processes. This is, however, only possible under certain asynchrony-restricting conditions whereby the asynchrony assumption
is effectively weakened and a certain degree of synchrony is implicitly introduced to the timing model: The asynchronous bounded delay synchronizer
requires processes to have sufficiently precise physical clocks and message
propagation times to have a known upper bound, thereby effectively requiring time-synchronous channels. Such a system is a special instance of a
weakened time-asynchronous system. Depending on the degree of synchrony
(implicitly) introduced, a time-asynchronous system can be gradually transformed into a time-synchronous system – in which coordination problems
are easily solvable. Therefore, the degree of synchrony introduced must be
reasonably minimal, meaning sufficient and necessary to solve the problem
at hand.

Albeit these problems, the (weakened) time-asynchronous timing model is
a good timing model choice for developing distributed systems. Since it
does not have as high demands on the real world the distributed system
is deployed in as the time-synchronous timing model has, systems developed for this timing model are applicable to a wider range of real-world
application scenarios.

Timed Asynchronous Systems

In between the two extremes of time-synchronous and time-asynchronous
timing models, there are intermediate weakened time-asynchronous timing
models such as the *timed asynchronous model* [Cristian and Fetzer, 1998].
This timing model is generally time-asynchronous but assumes "stable" pe-
riods of time in which an upper bound on communication delay exists such
that the system is effectively time-synchronous for a limited period of time.
The timed asynchronous model allows a perfect failure detection [Fetzer,
2003] if processes can measure time intervals with a known error and are
equipped with a hardware watchdog that crashes a process on purpose when
not being updated in its regular update interval.

After having introduced the fundamentals of the system model, the next section elaborates on some notions of data consistency a system may provide.

2.2 Data Consistency

Computing refers to and involves processing of data. In a centralized computing environment, a single process manages some local data stored in local memory and exclusively operates on this local data according to its local program. Because of the sequential execution of local operations, there is no interleaving or overlapping of read and write operations on the local data and the local memory has the register property [Misra, 1986]: Read operations return the value written by the most recent write operation and the value returned by a read operation must have been written by a write operation beforehand.

In a distributed computing environment, each process has some local data and locally operates on it. In order to enable the processes to cooperatively perform a common task, they communicate and exchange information, meaning they (indirectly) read and write other processes' data. The register property found in centralized computing environments is a desirable semantics also in distributed systems. Unfortunately, due to the distributed nature, a read operation may not always return the value most recently written by a write operation. For example, due to channel latency and message propagation delay, a process that performs a read operation might not be aware of a meanwhile executed write operation – which then constitutes the most recent write operation – and returns a stale value that potentially does not match the most recently written value. Such a behavior may violate the intuition of correctness.

Consistency Criterion   The meaning of correctness and the correct ordering of operations is expressed by a *consistency criterion*. It specifies what guarantees are provided about the value returned by a read operation. A consistency criterion that is never compromised is a safety property of the system. In contrast to concurrency control theory [Bernstein, Hadzilacos et al., 1987] employed in the context of database systems and dealing with the serialization of transactions as an aggregation of many operations, a consistency criterion – as used here – refers to a sequence of read and write operations. The relation of consistency criteria and concurrency control mechanisms becomes apparent if assuming transactions to consist of a single read or write operation finalized by a commit statement. Then, both concepts are semantically equivalent.

Two conflicting goals of a consistency criterion are (1) to be strong enough to be useful and (2) to be weak enough to be implemented efficiently. The strength of a consistency criterion refers to its demands regarding operation ordering and real-time constraints. Generally, systems using weaker consistency criteria are implementable more efficiently because of less restrictions. Next, some necessary definitions for reasoning about consistency criteria are introduced.

Operation Execution   A process performs read and write operations on a global data object x according to its local program. An operation is an atomically executed composite of lower-level operations such as memory access and communication. Therefore, the execution of an operation is not finalized immediately on the realtime instant it is invoked but instead needs some time to take effect. A read operation on the data object x invoked by a process p_i at the realtime instant t and completed at the realtime instant $t' = t + \delta$ is denoted by $R_{p_i}(x = u)_{[t,t']}$ where u is the value of the data object x read by this operation. The time interval $[t, t']$ is called the *execution interval*. Alike, a write operation performed by a process p_i on the data object x is denoted by $W_{p_i}(x := v)_{[t,t']}$ where v represents the value written to the data object x by this operation.

For convenience, it is assumed that all values written are distinct such that write operations can be distinguished by their written values and read operations can be associated with specific write operations if the written and read values are identical. This assumption can be realized by encoding the actual value to be written and the write operation instance into a joint value which is associated with the write operation, that is, written by the write operation.

History and Ordering of Operations   The sequence of read and write operations performed by a process in a run is called its *process-local history*. It is always totally ordered because processes execute a sequential local program. The ordering of operations in the process-local history is called the *process order* of operations. An operation *precedes* another operation if it is completed before the other operation is invoked. Since the process-local history is totally ordered, each operation precedes those operations that appear later in the history.

The union of all process-local histories forms the *global history*. In a global history, there may be operations of distinct processes for which neither operation precedes the other operations. Such operations are called *concurrent operations*. A global history is a *sequential history* if it does not contain concurrent operations, that is, it is totally ordered. Otherwise, the history is partially ordered and is termed *concurrent history*.

A read operation *reads-from* a write operation if it returns the value written by the write operation. It is a *legal* read operation if it reads-from the "most recent" write operation. In a sequential history, this is the last write operation in the totally ordered sequence of operations that precedes the read operation, that is, there is no intermittent write operation that has written a different value. In presence of concurrent write operations, it is not as obvious which write operation is the most recent because write operations may interleave or overlap. For being able to nonetheless define the most recent write operation, concurrent operations are arbitrated and totally ordered by selecting a time point in the operation execution interval at which an operation "takes effect". As point events are not allowed to coincide [Lamport, 1986], this arbitration establishes a total order on operations such that a respective most recent write operation can be identified.

Based on these definitions, the consistency criteria *static atomic consistency* [Misra, 1986], also referred to as *strict consistency*, and *sequential consistency* [Lamport, 1979] are introduced next.

Strict Consistency

The strongest and likely most intuitive consistency criterion is *static atomic consistency* [Misra, 1986], also called *strict consistency*. The adjective "static" stems from the definition of the time instant an operation takes effect: Read operations take effect at the time instant of their invocation while write operations take effect upon their completion.

A run of a distributed system is strictly consistent if its global history resembles some sequential history (1) that is defined on the same set of operations, (2) that has the same process order relation, (3) that has the same reads-from relation and all read operations are legal, and (4) in which the ordering of operations reflects their real-time ordering. If for each run of the distributed system such a sequential history is constructible, then the distributed system complies to strict consistency.

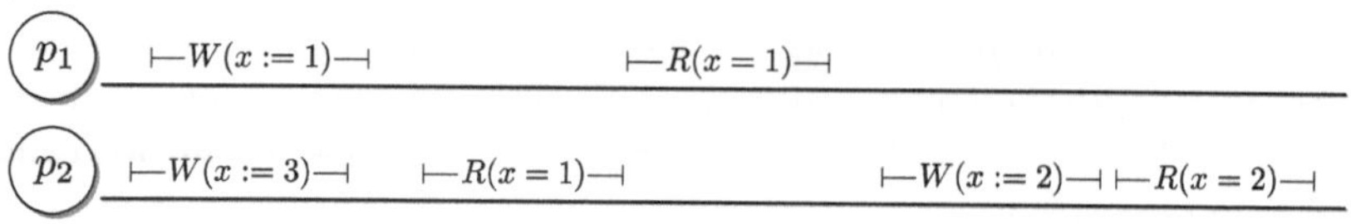

Figure 2.6: Illustration of Strict Consistency. (Real-)Time Progress is from
            Left to Right. Operation Execution Intervals are Indicated by In-
            terval Markers

For example, in Figure 2.6, the processes p_1 and p_2 perform read and
write operations on a data object x which is initially set to 0. Specifically, process p_1 executes a write operation $W_{p_1}(x := 1)$ and a read operation $R_{p_1}(x = 1)$ while process p_2 executes the operations $W_{p_2}(x := 3)$,
$R_{p_2}(x = 1)$, $W_{p_2}(x := 2)$, and $R_{p_2}(x = 2)$. In this figure, (real-)time progress is from left to right and operation execution intervals are indicated by
interval markers. This run is strict consistent as its global history resembles
the sequential history
$$H = \langle\, W_{p_2}(x := 3),\, W_{p_1}(x := 1),\, R_{p_2}(x = 1),\, R_{p_1}(x = 1),$$
$$W_{p_2}(x := 2),\, R_{p_2}(x = 2)\, \rangle$$
that fulfills the conditions stated above.

Strict consistency is – due to its reference to realtime – a too strong consistency criterion that cannot be implemented efficiently. Next, a weaker
consistency criterion without reference to realtime is presented.

Sequential Consistency

Sequential consistency [Lamport, 1979] is a consistency criterion without
reference to realtime and is therefore weaker than strict consistency. Specifically, sequential consistency does not require the ordering of operations in
the global history to resemble their real-time ordering but only the process
order of operations. Informally, the precise timing of operations in the global
history is of no importance while the process order and the reads-from relation must be satisfied and all read operations must be legal.

A run of a distributed system is sequentially consistent if its global history
resembles some sequential history (1) that is defined on the same set of
operations, (2) that has the same process order relation, and (3) that has
the same reads-from relation and all read operations are legal. If for each
run of the distributed system such a sequential history is constructible, then
the distributed system complies to sequential consistency.

There are weaker consistency criteria than sequential consistency such as *causal consistency* [Ahamad, Burns et al., 1991; Ahamad, Neiger et al., 1995]. A global history is causally consistent if each process-local history joined with the other processes' process-local histories – restricted to write operations only – is sequentially consistent [Ahamad, Neiger et al., 1995]. Informally, while sequential consistency requires all processes to "agree" on the same order of operations, causal consistency allows processes to "disagree" on the order of concurrent write operations.

Consistency criteria such as causal consistency are not generally applicable as it depends on the concrete application scenario whether the consistency guarantees provided are reasonable in the application scenario's context or not. Sequential consistency is weak enough to be implemented efficiently (as shown in the next section) and strong enough to be independent of a specific application scenario context and, therefore, generally applicable. This fact qualifies sequential consistency as a prominent and widely used consistency criterion.

It has been shown to be a NP-complete problem to decide if a run's global history is sequentially consistent [Taylor, 1983]. Therefore, it is not feasible to test upon every operation invocation if this operation's execution does not violate sequential consistency and can therefore be safely performed or if it must be rescheduled to some other time instant, if not aborted at all. Instead, an operation execution must be forced to comply to sequential consistency by appropriate means. A prominent and well-known means to enforce sequential consistency is by locks and quorum systems as introduced next.

2.3 Quorum Systems

Enforcing sequential consistency requires coordination among the processes such that write operations and read and write operations are performed mutually exclusive while read operations may be performed concurrently. Write operations are *competitive* [Barbara and García-Molina, 1986a] in the sense that they are in conflict with each other and must be coordinated. Read operations are *non-competitive* [Barbara and García-Molina, 1986a] and not in conflict with each other but are competitive to write operations with which they are in conflict and must be coordinated.

Quorum, Quorum Set, and Quorum System A process that wants to perform an operation – henceforth termed *coordinator* – must cooperate with specific other processes and is only allowed to execute the operation with permission from these other processes. A process grants its permission if it has not granted permission to a concurrent competitive operation execution. Only after the operation is completed, the process may grant its permission to another operation execution. The set of processes a coordinator has to cooperate with is called a *quorum*. Multiple quorums form a *quorum set*.

Definition 2.1 (Quorum, Quorum Set) A *quorum* Q is a non-empty subset of the set of processes P, that is, $Q \subseteq P$ and $Q \neq \emptyset$.

A *quorum set* $\mathcal{Q} \subseteq 2^P$ (with 2^P being the power set of the set of processes) is a non-empty set of quorums $\mathcal{Q} = \{Q_1, \ldots, Q_m\}$, $m > 0$, such that no quorum $Q_i \in \mathcal{Q}$ is a subset of another quorum $Q_j \in \mathcal{Q}$ for $i \neq j$, formally $\forall Q_i, Q_j \in \mathcal{Q}, i \neq j : Q_i \not\subset Q_j$.

A quorum set $\mathcal{Q}$ is an *intersecting* quorum set, also referred to as a *coterie* [García-Molina and Barbara, 1985], if every quorum intersects with every other quorum in at least one process, formally $\forall Q_i, Q_j \in \mathcal{Q}, i \neq j : Q_i \cap Q_j \neq \emptyset$.

By using an intersecting quorum set for coordination, at any time, at most one coordinator has the permission from all processes of a quorum and can execute an operation. Hence, competitive (and non-competitive) operations are performed mutually exclusive and sequential consistency is enforced. However, the mutual exclusion of non-competitive read operations is an unnecessary restriction since performing read operations concurrently does not sacrifice sequential consistency. Allowing concurrent read operations may result in an increased overall throughput of the system in terms of the number of (read) operations that can be executed in a given period of time. Therefore, a *quorum system* that consists of a read and a write quorum set is needed, both constructed such that non-competitive read operations may be performed concurrently while the concurrent execution of competitive operations is prohibited.

Definition 2.2 (Quorum System) A *quorum system* is a tuple $(\mathcal{Q}_W, \mathcal{Q}_R)$ consisting of the *write quorum set* $\mathcal{Q}_W$ which is an intersecting quorum set that is used to perform write operations and the *read quorum set* $\mathcal{Q}_R$ which is a (not necessarily intersecting) quorum set that is used to perform read operations. Both are constructed such that every write quorum intersects with every other write quorum and with every read quorum in at least one process whereas two read quorums need not to intersect, formally $\forall Q_i, Q_j \in \mathcal{Q}_W, i \neq j : Q_i \cap Q_j \neq \emptyset$ and $\forall Q_i \in \mathcal{Q}_W, Q_j \in \mathcal{Q}_R : Q_i \cap Q_j \neq \emptyset$.

Due to the quorum system intersection property, competitive operations cannot be performed concurrently while non-competitive (read) operations may be executed concurrently since read quorums do not need to intersect. Also, as every read quorum intersects with every write quorum, the value written by the most recent write operation can be returned by successive read operations since at least one process of every read quorum has participated in the most recent write operation's quorum. Hence, using quorum systems for coordination is an appropriate means to enforce sequential consistency.

Next, the data structures each process manages and the steps a coordinator has to perform in order to execute an operation on a replicated data object (*replica*) are presented in detail.

Operation Execution Protocol   Each process has a local copy of the quorum system in terms of an encoding of the read and write quorum sets as well as a local copy of the replica. Associated to the local replica copy are a replica version number, a write lock, a read lock, and a read lock counter. Initially, the replica data and its version number are set to some common value for all processes, the locks are not set, and the read lock counter is set to zero. The write lock is an *exclusive write lock* meaning that a write-locked replica cannot be locked for concurrent competitive read or write operations. The read lock is a *shared-exclusive read lock* meaning that a read-locked replica cannot be locked for concurrent competitive write operations but concurrent non-competitive read operations may share a set read lock. The number of read operations sharing a read lock is kept track of by the read lock counter. A read (write) operation is performed in two steps, namely (1) quorum probing and replica locking and (2) the actual operation execution, as follows:

STEP 1 (QUORUM PROBING AND REPLICA LOCKING)

The coordinator selects a read (write) quorum from the read (write) quorum set and *probes* the processes of the chosen quorum, that is, queries them for their permission to execute the read (write) operation. A probed process grants its permission if it has not granted permission to the execution of a concurrent competitive operation as indicated by the state of its locks: If neither lock is set, the process read-locks (write-locks) its replica and responds with its permission and the replica version number to the coordinator. If the read lock is set and the coordinator wants to perform a read operation, the process increases its read lock counter and responds with its permission and the replica version number to the coordinator. If the coordinator wants to perform a read (write) operation and the write lock (read lock or write lock) is set, the process responds with its replica version number to the coordinator but does not grant its permission to the operation execution.

If the coordinator got permission from all processes of the chosen quorum, then the quorum is *available* and the coordinator continues with ↑Step 2. Otherwise, at least one process has not granted its permission because it is locked for a concurrent competitive operation and *refuses* to cooperate or it has failed. The coordinator instructs the processes that have granted their permission to operation-specifically unlock their replicas. While a replica's write lock is unconditionally released, a replica's read lock is only released if the read lock counter is zero after having decremented it. Then, by repeating ↑Step 1, the coordinator chooses an alternative quorum which is subsequently probed.

Eventually, either a quorum of processes that unanimously permit the operation execution is found or all operation-specific quorums are negatively probed and the coordinator must abort the operation execution, that is, the operation is not available.

STEP 2 (OPERATION EXECUTION)

In case of a write operation, the coordinator instructs the processes of the write quorum (1) to write the new replica value to their replicas, (2) to set their replica version number to a new global maximum, that is, to the by one incremented highest version number reported to the coordinator in Step 1, and (3) to finally unlock their write locks.

In case of a read operation, the coordinator (1) reads the replica value from one of the read quorum's processes managing a replica with the highest version number as reported to the coordinator in Step 1 and (2) instructs the read quorum's processes to unlock their read locks, that is, to release the read lock if the read lock counter is zero after having decremented it.

There are some assumptions and issues in this operation execution protocol that are discussed next. Specifically, interleaving read operations may starve out the write operation, failures are assumed to be detectable, quorum probing is dependent on the type of channels, and finally, the order of probing quorums is unspecified.

Write Operation Starvation Read quorums are not required to intersect such that interleaved read operations may be performed with disjoint read quorums even if the read lock is assumed to be an exclusive lock. With a shared-exclusive read lock and because of the read lock counter mechanism, a process may grant permission to multiple concurrent or interleaving read operations, resulting in an increased concurrency of the read operation as the process may participate in multiple and not necessarily disjoint read quorums simultaneously.

Allowing the interleaved execution of read operations may result in starvation of the write operation: No write quorum's replicas can be write-locked while read operations are being executed such that an infinite sequence of interleaved read operations may starve out the write operation. The read lock counter mechanism amplifies this effect as a write operation-starving infinite read operation sequence is not only possible with (some) disjoint read quorums but also with an intersecting read quorum set.

This effect can be mitigated while not generally avoided by extending the operation execution protocol such that a process having a read-locked replica does not grant its permission to further interleaving read operations after being unsuccessfully probed for a write operation. Eventually, all processes of a deemed write quorum have released their read locks since their read lock counter has reached zero. If meanwhile none of these then read-unlocked processes grants permission to another read operation, read and write operation coordinators can race for the operation-specific lock to be granted.

Another option is to impose an upper bound on the number of read operations a process grants permission to while its read lock is set. If this upper bound is reached, then no further read operations are granted permission to until eventually the process' read lock counter reaches zero and its read lock is released. If the then read-unlocked processes incidentally do not grant permission to another read operation, some processes forming a write quorum are probably not locked such that a write operation coordinator can get their permission to execute the write operation. Note that setting the upper bound on concurrent read operations to one effectively disables the read lock counter mechanism such that interleaved read operations can be performed with disjoint read quorums only.

While both options do not generally avoid write operation starvation, there is at least a possibility of write operations being executed. To completely avoid write operation starvation, the concurrent execution of read operations must be prohibited by employing an intersecting read quorum set and using exclusive read locks to coordinate read operations such that they are performed mutually exclusive. However, concurrency and throughput of the read operation is negatively affected.

Failure Detection   The operation execution protocol requires failures to be detectable and to be distinguishable from mere slowness of processes in order to decide whether to wait for a probed process' answer or to probe an alternative quorum for permission in Step 1. Even if assuming perfect channels, this failure detection requirement is not met in time-asynchronous systems as discussed in Section 2.1.4. Therefore, in order to implement the above operation execution protocol, either a less strict timing model such as the *timed asynchronous model* [Cristian and Fetzer, 1998] in which reliable failure detection is possible [Fetzer, 2003] must be employed, or the system must be equipped with an appropriate failure detector such as the *trusting failure detector* [Delporte-Gallet, Fauconnier et al., 2005] which is the weakest failure detector to solve the mutual exclusion problem (whereby effectively a weaker timing model is introduced). Note that instead of a reliable failure detection, a suspicion of process failures is sufficient if it can be tolerated that a coordinator may falsely suspect processes to have failed and therefore may have to abort the operation execution albeit a quorum of non-failed processes is actually available.

Furthermore, a quorum's processes are not allowed to fail while the operation is being executed. This restriction can be addressed by integrating a (non-blocking) commit protocol [Skeen, 1981] into the operation execution protocol.

Quorum Probing   The coordinator has to decide according to a *quorum probing strategy* in which order to probe the operation-specific quorums for finding an available quorum to perform the operation with or to reveal that no such quorum (currently) exists. While probing quorums, the coordinator exploits the learned information about failed or refusing processes for choosing the next worth to be probed quorum that does not contain such processes. If additional knowledge in terms of a structural failure model that can express failure dependencies and failure propagation is given, this knowledge can be used to further reduce the number of remaining quorums to probe [Warns, Storm et al., 2009].

The process of quorum probing is influenced by the type of channels. If assuming blocking channels with which a process sending a message is blocked until the message is delivered to and received by its destination process, then a quorum's processes are probed iteratively one after another in a unicast manner. The coordinator sequentially sends an operation execution permission request message to each process in the selected operation-specific quorum and blocks until it receives the process' answer. If a probed process does not grant its permission or has detectably failed, then this quorum's probing can be prematurely aborted and one of the remaining quorums, if any, can be probed.

Otherwise, if non-blocking channels are assumed, then the quorum's processes may be probed concurrently in a multicast manner. The coordinator sequentially sends operation execution permission request messages to the quorum's processes without being blocked and collects the processes' answers after having sent all permission request messages. While an optimization in the number of messages by prematurely aborting the quorum probing upon a detected process failure as for blocking channels is not possible, concurrently probing processes has less latency.

A quorum set does not have an ordering defined on its quorums. Thus, any not yet unsuccessfully probed quorum that does not contain known to be failed or refusing processes is equally suited for being probed (next).

Ordering Quorum Sets Probing quorums in a specific ordering that is not only induced by the learned information about failed or refusing processes but also driven by an ordering imposed on the quorum set itself can be reasonable, for example, if a quorum set can be (partially) ordered by its quorums' cardinality. Probing the quorums in ascending order on their cardinality allows for a graceful degradation in terms of the number of messages required to find an available quorum as it gradually increases with failed or refusing processes found in a quorum. Such an ordering cannot be expressed by a quorum set but by a sequence of quorum sets whereby an ordering on the quorums is established: Quorums within the same quorum set are partially ordered while quorums of different quorum sets are totally ordered. Such a sequence is called *quorum sequence*. Resuming the above example, the according quorum sequence consists of quorum sets that are populated by quorums of a particular cardinality by which the quorum sequence is ordered such that its first quorum set's quorums have the smallest cardinality. The quorum probing strategy is obliged to follow this quorum ordering but may skip quorums based on learned information about failed or refusing processes.

An alternative representation for quorum sequences is obtained by associating a quorum set $\mathcal{Q} = \{Q_1, \ldots, Q_n\}$ with a dedicated quorum ordering function $\varphi : \mathcal{Q} \to \mathbb{N}$ that maps quorums to not necessarily distinct natural numbers such that the ordering relation $Q_i \leq Q_j \Leftrightarrow \varphi(Q_i) \leq \varphi(Q_j)$ defines a total order on equivalence classes in each of which the quorums are unordered. Quorums are probed in an ordering as defined by the total ordering on the equivalence classes in each of which quorums can be probed in any order. Conceptually, a quorum set as defined above can be seen as a quorum set with a quorum ordering function $\varphi(Q) = 1$ for all $Q \in \mathcal{Q}$ such that the quorums can be probed in any order.

Henceforth, quorum sets are assumed to be associated with a quorum ordering function which is, however, hereafter not explicitly stated if the ordering of quorums is obvious from the context or if it is of no importance to the specific rationale at hand.

Quorum systems are a versatile means to realize coordination in distributed systems. For example, quorum systems in the form of *byzantine quorum systems* [Malkhi and Reiter, 1998] can be employed to cope with byzantine process failures (cf. Section 2.1.2), that is, with processes failing according to a failure model in which failed processes may behave arbitrarily and even malicious such that they may viciously try to sabotage sequential consistency: A process may behave as specified except that it omits updating its replica value upon write operations such that a subsequent read operation including this malicious process in its quorum may read from this process and return an outdated value. By having a (minimal) quorum system intersection in exactly one process, such a malicious process cannot be exposed. Therefore, byzantine quorum systems require quorums to intersect in $2 \cdot f + 1$ processes for tolerating f byzantine process failures. With the help of the – assumed to be correct – $f + 1$ processes, the byzantine-failed processes can be detected. While the presented operation execution protocol in this form is not ready to be employed for byzantine process failures, it may be extended in this respect to uncover byzantine-failed processes.

Apart from being applicable to tolerate byzantine process failures, quorum systems also correctly cope with network partitioning without sacrificing sequential consistency. Recall that a network partitioning due to processes or channels having failed results in a separation of the processes into partitions until some failed components recover such that the partitions rejoin. While the network is partitioned, inter-partition communication is not possible while intra-partition communication is not affected. Using quorum systems, a write quorum is available in at most one partition due to the quorum system intersection property. If the write operation is available in a partition, then it is not available in any other partition as no write quorum can be formed in any of these write operation-defunct partitions. A read operation, however, may be available in more than one partition but only under the premise that the write operation is not available in any partition. Hence, sequential consistency is preserved even in the presence of network partitioning.

Beyond the broad classification of quorum sets into intersecting and non-intersecting quorum sets, a more fine-grained classification is presented next.

Quorum Set Classes

As illustrated in Figure 2.7, four classes of quorum sets can be distinguished, namely (1) (general) quorum sets, (2) intersecting quorum sets, (3) *vote-assignable* intersecting quorum sets, and (4) *non-dominated* intersecting quorum sets.

The most general class of quorum sets contains all sets of quorums under a particular universe of processes. Read quorums can be of this class because they need not to mutually intersect. Note that the class of general quorum sets also includes vote-assignable non-intersecting quorum sets which, however, are not explicitly distinguished here.

A proper subclass of general quorum sets is the class of intersecting quorum sets that – in contrast to general quorum sets – has the property

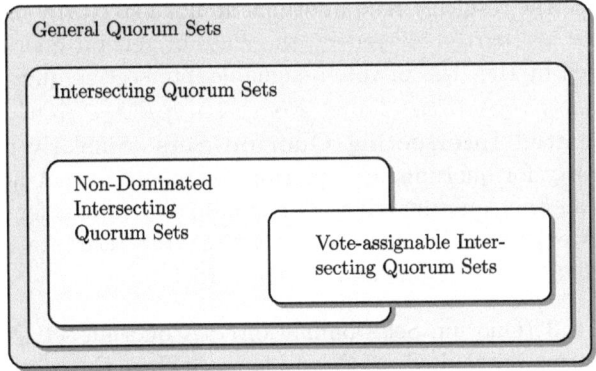

Figure 2.7: Illustration of Quorum Set Classes

of mutual quorum intersection. Write quorums are of this class to ensure
the mutual exclusion of write operations. Note that, although not required,
read quorums may also be intersecting quorum sets.

Both, the classes of vote-assignable intersecting quorum sets and non-
dominated intersecting quorum sets are proper subclasses of the class of
intersecting quorum sets while they are neither disjoint nor in a proper
part-of relation with each other.

Next, vote-assignable intersecting quorum sets and non-dominated intersecting quorum sets are introduced after which examples of their interrela-
tion are presented.

Vote-Assignable Intersecting Quorum Sets   Vote-assignable intersecting quorum sets have been introduced by Gifford [1979] who proposed
to equip processes with an individual vote being a natural number (greater
than zero) and to constrain quorums to consist of a number of processes
whose accumulated votes exceed a certain threshold of votes. This threshold is defined such that in each quorum, the processes' accumulated votes
are more than half the sum of votes assigned to all processes in the system.
Then, for any two quorums, the sum of both their processes' votes exceeds
the accumulated votes assigned to all processes in the system and the two
quorums intersect in at least one process.

Note that vote assignment can also be used to define read quorums by
defining a read operation threshold such that the sum of the read and the
write operation thresholds exceeds the sum of votes assigned to all processes
in the system. Then, read and write quorums intersect in at least one
process. Since the resulting read quorums do not necessarily intersect with
another, they are partly covered by the class of general quorum sets and
partly covered by the class of vote-assignable intersecting quorum sets.

Non-Dominated Intersecting Quorum Sets   Similarly to the minimality property for quorums in a quorum set requiring that no quorum is
a subset of another quorum, there is a minimality notion for intersecting
quorum sets expressed by quorum set *domination* [Barbara and García-
Molina, 1986a; García-Molina and Barbara, 1985]:

Definition 2.3 (Quorum Set Domination)   A quorum set Q_1 *dominates*
another quorum set Q_2 if $Q_1 \neq Q_2$ and for each $Q_j \in Q_2$ there is a $Q_i \in Q_1$
such that $Q_i \subseteq Q_j$. A quorum set for which no dominating quorum set

exists is called a *non-dominated* quorum set. Otherwise, it is called a *dominated* quorum set.

Non-dominated intersecting quorum sets are preferable to dominated ones as they have at least one quorum with a smaller cardinality. Hence, a coordinator has to acquire the permission of fewer processes resulting in less communication and a better resilience to process failures since fewer processes are required to cooperate. For example, consider for a system consisting of six processes $P = \{p_1, \ldots, p_6\}$ the intersecting quorum set $\mathcal{Q}_1 = \{\{p_1, p_2\}, \{p_1, p_5\}, \{p_2, p_5\}\}$ and the intersecting quorum set $\mathcal{Q}_2 = \{\{p_1, p_2, p_3\}, \{p_1, p_4, p_5\}, \{p_2, p_5, p_6\}\}$. Clearly, the quorum set $\mathcal{Q}_2$ is dominated by the quorum set $\mathcal{Q}_1$.

Quorum set domination is also defined for non-intersecting (general) quorum sets. However, the notion of domination for these quorum sets is only really meaningful if considered in conjunction with the read and write quorum set intersection requirement in a quorum system. Otherwise, a dominating quorum set can be found by reducing each quorum of a quorum set to one of its processes. This process is preferably chosen such that it is contained in – and thereby represents – multiple quorums of the dominated quorum set.

Relation of Vote-Assignable and Non-Dominated Intersecting Quorum Sets As illustrated in Figure 2.7, there are (1) non-dominated intersecting quorum sets that are not expressible via vote-assignable intersecting quorum sets, there are (2) vote-assignable intersecting quorum sets that correspond to a non-dominated intersecting quorum set, and there are (3) vote-assignable intersecting quorum sets that are dominated.

An example of a non-dominated intersecting quorum set that is not expressible by a vote assignment is $\mathcal{Q} = \{\{p_1, p_2\}, \{p_1, p_3, p_4\}, \{p_1, p_3, p_5\}, \{p_1, p_4, p_6\}, \{p_1, p_5, p_6\}, \{p_2, p_3, p_6\}, \{p_2, p_4, p_5\}\}$ for a system with six processes $P = \{p_1, \ldots, p_6\}$ [García-Molina and Barbara, 1985].

An example of a vote-assignable intersecting quorum set that corresponds to a non-dominated intersecting quorum set is the quorum set $\mathcal{Q} = \{\{p_1, p_2\}, \{p_1, p_3\}, \{p_2, p_3\}\}$ for a system with the three processes $P = \{p_1, p_2, p_3\}$. This non-dominated intersecting quorum set corresponds to a uniform vote assignment of 1 to each process and a threshold of two votes.

Finally, there are vote-assignable intersecting quorum sets that are dominated. For example, consider the quorum set $\mathcal{Q}_1 = \{\{p_1, p_2, p_3\}, \{p_1, p_2, p_4\}, \{p_1, p_3, p_4\}, \{p_2, p_3, p_4\}\}$ for a system with four processes

$P = \{p_1, \ldots, p_4\}$ resulting from each process having a vote of one and the threshold being set to three votes. This quorum set is dominated by $\mathcal{Q}_2 = \{\{p_1, p_2\}, \{p_1, p_3\}, \{p_1, p_4\}, \{p_2, p_3, p_4\}\}$ [Barbara and García-Molina, 1986a].

For systems with less than six processes, there is a vote-assignable intersecting quorum set for each non-dominated intersecting quorum set as has been pointed out by García-Molina and Barbara [1985]. For systems with more than five processes, there are more intersecting quorum sets than representable by vote assignments [García-Molina and Barbara, 1985].

Non-domination is a (boolean) quality indicator for quorum sets as non-dominated ones are preferable to dominated ones. Alike, there are many quality measures for quorum sets and quorum systems such as, for example, operation availability, load, and capacity [Naor and Wool, 1998]. A selection of prominent quality measures for quorum sets and quorum systems is presented next.

2.4 Quality Measures for Quorum Systems

Quality measures allow to distinguish and to compare quorum sets and quorum systems with respect to their specific qualities. A simple quality measure is, for example, the *quorum cardinality* that determines the number of processes in a quorum and thus the number of messages required to perform an operation with this quorum. Using this measure to distinguish quorum sets, quorum sets with overall smaller quorum cardinalities are preferred over ones having larger quorum cardinalities, thereby resulting in fewer messages to be sent for performing operations.

The construction of a quorum system's read quorum set optimizing for this quality measure results – in the extreme case – in each read quorum consisting of exactly one distinct process of the system. This read quorum set is optimal with respect to the quorum cardinality quality measure. Since each write quorum has to intersect with every read quorum (and with every other write quorum) the only possible write quorum for this read quorum set consists of all processes of the system. This write quorum set has the worst quorum cardinality quality. Moreover, it cannot tolerate even a single process failure upon which the write quorum is not available and the write operation cannot be performed. A read quorum, on the other hand, is available as long as not all processes have failed.

In this example, the quorum cardinality quality and the quorum availability of the write quorum set is balanced in favor of optimal quorum
cardinality quality and quorum availability of the read quorum set. Such
a balancing is called a *trade-off* which is a relation between quality measures such that a change in one measure affects other measures. Note that
a trade-off in favor of one measure must not necessarily have a negative impact on all other measures as illustrated for the quorum cardinality quality
and the quorum availability of the read quorum set. On the other hand,
it also must not necessarily have a positive impact on all other measures
as shown for the quorum cardinality quality and the quorum availability of
the write quorum set. Thus, choosing a particular quorum system always
incorporates choosing a particular trade-off between quality measures of its
read and write quorum set.

Quorum system quality measures can be roughly categorized into *structural* and *operational* measures. Structural quality measures relate a quorum system's quality to its structural characteristics as being a tuple of
two sets of subsets of the set of processes and are independent of the assumed communication, failure, and timing model. For example, quorum
cardinality and non-domination are structural quality measures.

Operational quality measures relate a quorum system's quality to its characteristics at run-time which is dependent on the assumed timing, communication, and failure model and mediately also on structural quality measures. For example, the time complexity of performing operations, and,
derived therefrom, the number of operations that can be performed in a
specific period of time, known as *throughput*, is an operational measure.
Such measures relating a quorum system's quality to the passage of time
are directly dependent on the assumed timing model and, consequently,
their expressiveness is tightly coupled to the timing model: the less syn-
chronous a system is, the less meaningful are such performance-related operational quality measures. The operational quality of a quorum system is
significantly influenced by the communication model in terms of the system's network topology. For example, Papadimitriou and Sideri [1991] have
studied the problem of finding an optimal available vote-assignable intersecting quorum set for a given network topology and given process weights.
Diks, Kranakis et al. [1994] have shown that there are network topologies
for which an optimal intersecting quorum set is not vote-assignable. Both
assume independent process failures and channels to be perfect. Hence,
the assumed failure model for processes and channels is also an important

factor to a quorum system's operational quality. For example, network partitioning due to channel or process failures may lead to quorums being not available because the quorum's processes – although being non-failed – cannot communicate with each other and are therefore unable to cooperate. The impact of network partitioning has been studied, for example, by Pâris [1991] and Barbara and García-Molina [1986b].

Next, a selection of prominent quality measures grouped by similarity is presented, namely
- availability,
- reliability, node and edge vulnerability,
- load,
- capacity, throughput, mean time to respond,
- message complexity, average message overhead, probe complexity, cost of failures, and
- scalability.

Since most quality measures are operational measures, henceforth only pure structural measures are explicitly indicated.

Availability An operation can be performed whenever an operation-specific quorum is available, that is, whenever (1) an operation-specific quorum of non-failed processes can be found and (2) this quorum's processes unanimously grant their permission to perform the operation. In analogy to Trivedi [2002], the probability of successfully finding an available operation-specific quorum at a time instant t is termed *point operation availability*. The point operation availability depends on (1) the individual *point process availability* of the quorum's processes which is the probability that a process has not failed but is operational at time t and on (2) the individual processes' locking state. Often, the interest in process or operation availability is not limited to specific time instants but is in the availability after a sufficiently long time has elapsed, that is, when a *steady state* is reached. The limiting or *steady-state operation availability*, in short *operation availability*, is the limiting value of point operation availability when the value of time approaches infinity. Accordingly, *process availability* is the limiting value of point process availability when the value of time approaches infinity.

The individual processes' process availability has a significant impact on operation availability: highly (lowly) available processes increase (decrease) the probability of finding a quorum of non-failed processes that can then be queried for their permission to perform an operation. For intersecting quorum sets and under the premises of (1) a fully connected topology with perfect channels, (2) independent process failures, and (3) a uniform process availability lower than 0.5, the best option in terms of operation availability is to use a quorum set with a single quorum consisting of a single process whereas the worst option is to choose a vote-assignable intersecting quorum set with a uniform vote assignment [Diks, Kranakis et al., 1994; Wool and Peleg, 1995]. With a uniform process availability higher than 0.5, the formerly best option becomes the worst option and vice versa [Diks, Kranakis et al., 1994; Wool and Peleg, 1995]. With a uniform process availability of 0.5, any non-dominated intersecting quorum set provides an operation availability of 0.5 while the operation availability provided by a dominated intersecting quorum set is strictly lower than 0.5 [Wool and Peleg, 1995]. Non-dominated intersecting quorum sets provide strictly higher operation availability than dominated intersecting quorum sets [Wool and Peleg, 1995].

Again assuming a fully connected topology with perfect channels, independent process failures, and a uniform process availability, there is a rotational symmetry around the point 0.5 in the availability graph of non-dominated intersecting quorum sets [Wool and Peleg, 1995]. This finding has been extended and generalized by Theel and Pagnia [1998]: The optimal read operation availability graph is symmetric around the point 0.5 to a given write operation availability graph such that there is an upper bound on read operation availability that depends on the write operation availability, and vice versa.

Reliability   The measure of availability assumes a functional failure model in which processes may fail and failed processes may recover from being failed. Otherwise, if processes may fail but not recover from their failure, process availability is equivalent to *process reliability* which is the probability that an initially non-failed process does not fail until some time instant t [Trivedi, 2002]. Analogously, *operation reliability* is the probability that an initially available operation remains available until some time instant t. Thereafter, no further operations can be performed since every quorum contains at least one failed process. Note that this state is always eventually reached under a functional failure model such as the halting-crash functional failure model in which processes may fail but not recover from their failure.

Related to reliability – and also assuming a halting-failed functional failure model – are the measures of *node vulnerability* and *edge vulnerability*

[Barbara and García-Molina, 1986b] which denote the minimal number of halting-failed processes or channels that results in a halted state of the system.

Load   Intuitively, *(process) load* [Naor and Wool, 1998] is a measure of how fairly balanced the amount of computational work imposed on a process by the quorum probing strategy choosing quorums containing this process is spread among the processes. If the quorum probing strategy tends to use a particular quorum whenever possible, then the processes contained in this quorum have to cope with a much higher individual computational work compared to the other processes. The individual process load is the probability that the quorum probing strategy chooses a quorum including this process. The system load is the maximum of the individual process loads, that is, the process load posed on those processes most affected by the quorum probing strategy selecting quorums which contain these processes.

Another definition of load due to Holzman, Marcus et al. [1997] is by the ratio of the least frequently selected quorum and the most selected one. Accordingly, a quorum system is perfectly load balanced if all processes are equally employed for performing operations.

Capacity, Throughput, and Mean Time to Respond   *Capacity* [Naor and Wool, 1998; Rangarajan, Jalote et al., 1993] is the maximal quorum access rate a quorum system can handle in a bounded period of time and is synonymous to the *throughput* allowed by the quorum system. It is a compound measure of availability and communication, respectively, processing time overhead: A highly available quorum system spending too much time on performing internal data management operations leaves less time to perform read and write operations, thereby offering a degraded capacity. On the other hand, a communication-efficient system having unreliable – in terms of frequently unavailable – processes also offers low capacity since operations are frequently unavailable because of too many processes having failed.

Related to capacity is the measure of *mean time to respond* [Qureshi and Sanders, 1995] defining operation availability and mean time to respond for (write) operations as a function that is dependent on the number of processes. The computational workload of the system negatively affects operation availability by a high process workload hindering processes from granting permission to execute operations.

Message Complexity, Average Message Overhead, Probe Complexity, Cost of Failures   A simple measure to quantify the cost of performing operations is by the structural measure of *quorum cardinality* that determines the number of processes in a quorum and thus the number of messages required to perform an operation with this quorum. Since quorum cardinality is specific to a single quorum, this measure has to be extended to all quorums of a quorum set for it to have a meaning for quorum sets. A quorum set's *(structural) message complexity* quality measure may be defined, for example, by the smallest quorum cardinality of all its quorums. However, this measure is unfair as it accounts the quality of possibly only a single quorum for the quality of the whole quorum set. A more fair – and henceforth used – measure of a quorum set's message complexity is by the arithmetic mean of its quorum cardinalities such that a quorum set's overall quality instead of the quality of a single or a few of its quorums is decisive.

A closely related measure is the *average message complexity* or *average message overhead* [Saha, Rangarajan et al., 1996] in terms of the average number of messages required to find an available quorum or to reveal that no such quorum (currently) exists. In contrast to message complexity, it is not a pure structural measure on (average) quorum cardinalities but also considers the individual processes' availability. Therefore, it can be seen as a compound measure of process availability and quorum cardinality.

Probe complexity [Hassin and Peleg, 2006; Peleg and Wool, 2002] is a measure of how many processes must be probed – and thereby how many messages must be sent – in the worst case until either an available quorum to perform the operation with is found or it is revealed that the operation is not available as no available quorum exists.

Related to probe complexity is the measure of the *cost of failures* [Bazzi, 2000]. Intuitively, it is a measure of the additional number of processes that need to be contacted – and thus the additional number of messages to be sent – when process failures are detected during quorum probing.

Scalability   Finally, *scalability* is a measure of how well a specific quorum system construction can maintain qualities when managing varying numbers of processes. Ideally, the more processes participate in a quorum system, the more balanced the load is among the processes and the more operation availability is increased.

Scalability is in a sense a "meta-measure" of quorum system quality since it quantifies the quality of a specific quorum system construction for varying numbers of processes instead of quantifying the quality of one particular quorum system having a fixed number of processes.

Choosing a quorum system implies choosing a particular trade-off between different qualities. Because of this quorum system-specific trade-off and highly varying application scenario quality demands, there is no single quorum system that is best-suited for every application scenario. The next section introduces data replication schemes as a means to construct quorum systems having a specifically balanced trade-off between particular quality measures.

2.5 Data Replication Schemes

A data replication scheme can be seen as a quorum system construction directive for quorum systems having a specific trade-off between different qualities. In this sense, requiring read quorums to consist of $\lceil n/2 \rceil$ processes and write quorums to consist of $\lceil (n+1)/2 \rceil$ processes for a system comprising n processes constitutes a particular data replication scheme known as *Majority Consensus Voting* [Thomas, 1979].

Duality of Data Replication Schemes and Structural Failure Models   A quorum system implicitly expresses a structural failure model that defines the process failures the quorum system can successfully tolerate. For example, consider for three processes $P = \{p_1, p_2, p_3\}$ a quorum system with the quorum set $\mathcal{Q} = \{\{p_1, p_2\}, \{p_1, p_3\}, \{p_2, p_3\}\}$ that is used for the read as well as for the write operation. This quorum system tolerates the failure of none or exactly one process as expressed in the implicitly specified structural failure model $\{\emptyset, \{p_3\}, \{p_2\}, \{p_1\}\}$. If this structural failure model precisely describes the process failure scenarios that may occur in a run of the distributed system, the quorum system is *perfectly available*, that is, there is an available quorum for any assumed failure scenario. This duality of quorum systems and structural failure models can be exploited to construct quorum systems from a given structural failure model [Junqueira and Marzullo, 2005a,b; Malkhi and Reiter, 1997; Storm and Warns, 2008]. Unfortunately, such approaches are reliant on the structural failure model given and are therefore not applicable in absence of this information. Hence, a plethora of generally applicable quorum-based data replication schemes not relying on specific additional information has been proposed, each directed at a different scheme-specific trade-off between quality measures. Prominent examples that are presented in the following are the Read One Write All Protocol [Bernstein, Hadzilacos et al., 1987], Majority Consensus Voting [Thomas, 1979], Weighted Voting [Gifford, 1979], the Tree Quorum Protocol [Agrawal and El Abbadi, 1990], the Grid Protocol [Cheung, Ammar et al., 1990], the Triangular Lattice Protocol [Wu and Belford, 1992], and the Triangular Grid Protocol [Cheng-Hong and Jer-Tsang, 1998; Kuo and Huang, 1997].

Unstructured and Structured Data Replication Schemes   The various generally applicable data replication schemes can be coarsely categorized into *unstructured* and *structured* data replication schemes [Theel, 1993a].

Unstructured data replication schemes such as Majority Consensus Voting [Thomas, 1979] use combinatorics and minimal quorum cardinalities to construct quorum systems. Any process is equally suited for being in a particular quorum since not some specific processes but a number of processes constitute a quorum. Such approaches suffer from high message complexity and face scalability problems because of linearly increasing quorum cardinalities in the number of processes. On the other hand, as long as the number of non-failed processes resembles at least the minimal quorum cardinality, an arbitrary set of process failures can be tolerated.

In contrast, structured data replication schemes such as the Grid Protocol [Cheung, Ammar et al., 1990] impose a logical structure on the set of processes and use structural properties to specify quorum systems. The Grid Protocol logically arranges the processes in a rectangular grid and defines a read quorum to contain one process from each column of the grid while a write quorum must additionally contain all processes of a single column to meet the quorum system intersection property. As a result of using logical structures, structured data replication schemes usually have a sub-linear message complexity in the number of processes and tolerate structure-specific process failure sets.

Static and Dynamic Data Replication Schemes   Systems employing one of the aforementioned unstructured or structured data replication schemes are said to use a *static* data replication scheme in terms of an immutable and a priori defined quorum system. At design-time, the projected maximal number of processes and their identities are known. The system is equipped with a single quorum system reflecting this set of processes and this single quorum system remains in use for the entire lifetime of the system. As a consequence, the (implicitly defined) structural failure model also does not change over time.

Unfortunately, static data replication schemes – regardless of being structured or unstructured – have an upper bound on operation availabilities because of a symmetry constraint among the read and write operation availability graphs [Theel and Pagnia, 1998] as they cannot react to process failures beyond a scheme-specific threshold. In contrast, *dynamic* data replication schemes can switch among quorum systems in order to adapt to failures. Whenever a process failure is detected and a quorum system switching is possible, the quorum system is switched to one in which the failed process does not participate in any read or write quorum. Conversely, upon a process' recovery and given that a quorum system switching is possible, the quorum system is switched to one containing the recovered process in order to reintegrate it. By switching quorum systems, operations usually remain available in cases where static data replication schemes cannot maintain operation availability because they tolerate only limited scheme-specific failure scenarios. Although there are some cases in which the opposite holds true [Jajodia and Mutchler, 1990], dynamic data replication schemes usually provide increased operation availabilities at the expense of slightly higher costs caused by quorum system switching. Examples of dynamic data replication schemes are the Dynamic Grid Protocol [Rabinovich and Lazowska, 1992b], the Dynamic Tree Quorum Protocol [Rabinovich and Lazowska, 1992a], and Dynamic Voting [Jajodia and Mutchler, 1990] – the dynamic counterpart of the unstructured static Majority Consensus Voting.

Next, a selection of generally applicable data replication schemes is surveyed. First, unstructured and subsequently structured static approaches are presented, followed by the introduction of dynamic data replication schemes in the next section.

2.5.1 Static Data Replication Schemes

In this section, a variety of static data replication schemes are surveyed. First, unstructured data replication schemes are presented, namely
- the Read One Write All Protocol [Bernstein, Hadzilacos et al., 1987],
- Majority Consensus Voting [Thomas, 1979], and
- Weighted Voting [Gifford, 1979].

Subsequently, structured data replication schemes in terms of
- the Tree Quorum Protocol [Agrawal and El Abbadi, 1990] and
- three grid-based data replication schemes being
  - the Grid Protocol [Cheung, Ammar et al., 1990],
  - the Triangular Lattice Protocol [Wu and Belford, 1992], and
  - the Triangular Grid Protocol [Cheng-Hong and Jer-Tsang, 1998; Kuo and Huang, 1997]

are introduced.

Read One Write All Protocol

The probably most intuitive and simplest data replication scheme is the unstructured *Read One Write All Protocol* [Bernstein, Hadzilacos et al., 1987]. The write quorum set consists of a single quorum that contains all n processes in the system while the read quorum set consists of n quorums, each comprising a distinct single process. This construction obviously satisfies the quorum system intersection property. On one hand, the write operation requires all processes in the system to participate in the operation execution and thus does not tolerate even a single process or channel failure which results in some processes being unavailable or not reachable by other processes via the network. On the other hand, having read quorums of cardinality one allows to perform local read operations without the involvement of other processes. Clearly, the Read One Write All Protocol is strictly balanced towards the read operation in all aspects. It is a good candidate for application scenarios in which read operations are by far more frequent than write operations and in which read operation availability is of utmost importance.

In order to improve on the write operation availability, the *Read One Write All Available Protocol* has been proposed [Bernstein, Hadzilacos et al., 1987]. In this scheme, write operations are performed on all *available* processes of the single write quorum, that is, on all non-failed processes, as opposed to all processes as required by the Read One Write All Protocol. As a consequence, a formerly failed process may return a stale replica value if it performs a (local) read operation upon its recovery and a write operation has been executed while this process was failed. Therefore, upon recovery, the process must be aware of having failed and must execute a scheme-specific recovery protocol to update its replica prior to executing regular operations. Jiménez-Peris, Patiño-Martínez et al. [2001, 2003] consider the Read One Write All Available Protocol to be the best choice for a range of cluster computing applications with its specific communication network infrastructure and network topologies.

Voting Protocols

Voting protocols such as *Weighted Voting* [Gifford, 1979] and *Majority Consensus Voting* [Thomas, 1979] specify quorum systems via assigning votes in terms of natural numbers to processes and require a quorum to consist of a number of processes whose accumulated votes exceed a certain operation-specific threshold of votes.

Majority Consensus Voting *Majority Consensus Voting* [Thomas, 1979] uniformly assigns each process a vote of 1. The read quorum threshold of votes is $\lceil n/2 \rceil$ and the write quorum threshold of votes is $\lceil (n+1)/2 \rceil$ for a total of n votes and processes in the system. As $\lceil n/2 \rceil + \lceil (n+1)/2 \rceil > n$ and $2 \cdot \lceil (n+1)/2 \rceil > n$, the quorum system intersection property is satisfied. The primary objective of Majority Consensus Voting is to evenly balance quality measures for the read and the write quorum set. It defines no quorum probing ordering on quorum sets and, therefore, the computational work induced on the processes by the quorum probing strategy can be balanced among them. Because of the quorum system specification via vote thresholds, any process is equally suited for being in a particular quorum since not some specific processes but a number of processes constitute a quorum. Therefore, Majority Consensus Voting is highly resilient to process failures since as long as the number of non-failed processes satisfies at least the minimal votes required for a read or a write quorum, an arbitrary set of process failures can be tolerated. As a result, Majority Consensus Voting provides very high operation availability for both, the read and the write operation, given that the individual processes' availability exceeds 0.5. However, quorum cardinalities increase linearly in the number of processes, thereby resulting in only linear scalability, for example, in reference to message complexity.

Weighted Voting *Weighted Voting* [Gifford, 1979] generalizes Majority Consensus Voting by allowing the assignment of an individual number of votes to processes, thereby rendering Majority Consensus Voting with its uniform vote assignment a special case of Weighted Voting. It is therefore dedicated to be used if process availabilities are not uniform but are divergent since processes with a high availability can be prioritized over processes with a low availability by assigning them more votes, thereby potentially increasing operation availability. Also, the computational work induced by the quorum probing strategy can be posed on computationally more powerful processes by equipping them with more votes than less powerful processes are equipped with. For example, in terms of message complexity, it is desirable for the quorum selection strategy to favor quorums having small cardinalities, resulting in those processes having many votes to be more often selected for participating in an operation execution than other processes having fewer votes, simply because the vote threshold is reached with fewer processes if those provide many votes. However, finding an appropriate vote assignment is not a trivial problem [Barbara and García-Molina, 1986b; Cheung, Ahamad et al., 1989; Papadimitriou and Sideri, 1991]. Depending on the particular vote assignment, quorum cardinalities may increase linearly in the number of processes, thereby resulting in scalability issues as it is the case for Majority Consensus Voting.

Voting Protocols are optimal with respect to read and write operation availability in fully connected network topologies with perfect channels if assuming a process availability of at least 0.5 and process failures to be independent [Obradovic and Berman, 1990].

Next, structured static data replication schemes are presented with the first being the Tree Quorum Protocol [Agrawal and El Abbadi, 1990], followed by the Grid Protocol [Cheung, Ammar et al., 1990], the Triangular Lattice Protocol [Wu and Belford, 1992], and the Triangular Grid Protocol [Cheng-Hong and Jer-Tsang, 1998; Kuo and Huang, 1997].

Tree Quorum Protocol

The structured *Tree Quorum Protocol* [Agrawal and El Abbadi, 1990] logically arranges the processes in a tree structure as illustrated in Figure 2.8 (a) by an example having 13 processes. A read quorum is derived from the tree structure by interpreting it as follows. Initially, the read quorum consists of

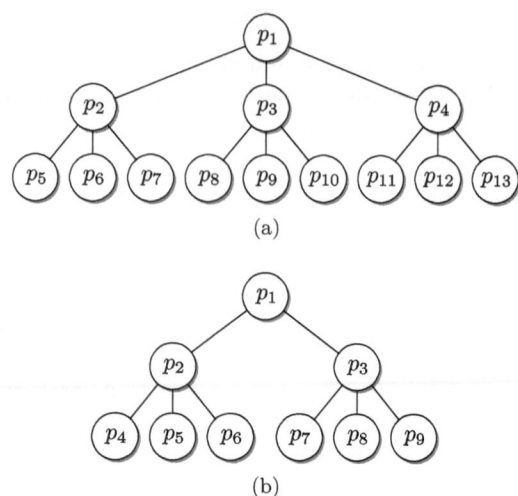

Figure 2.8: Logical Processes Layout of the Original Tree Quorum Protocol with 13 Processes (a) and the Generalized Tree Quorum Protocol with Nine Processes (b)

the root node process on level zero of the tree. If this process has failed, then it is substituted by a preferably non-failed majority of its child processes on level one of the tree. For each failed process in the chosen majority, this failed process is again substituted by a preferably non-failed majority of its child processes on level two of the tree, and so forth. The traversal stops if (1) a set of non-failed processes has been assembled that constitutes the read quorum or if (2) a failed process cannot be substituted by a majority of its child processes, either because the failed process is a leaf node process or too many of its child processes have also failed. In this case and if non-failed substitute processes have been chosen preferably, no read quorum is available. For example, with the processes p_1 and p_3 having failed in Figure 2.8 (a), the set $\{p_2, p_4\}$ is a valid read quorum. If additionally the process p_4 has failed, the set $\{p_2, p_{11}, p_{12}\}$ is a valid read quorum. Note that the Tree Quorum Protocol defines an ordering on the read quorums and thus a mandatory quorum probing order for the read operation.

A write quorum consists of the root node process plus a majority of its child processes plus a majority of their respective child processes, and so forth. For example, the set $\{p_1, p_2, p_3, p_5, p_6, p_8, p_9\}$ is a valid write quorum of the Tree Quorum Protocol with 13 processes as illustrated in Figure 2.8 (a).

Note that quorum systems complying to the Tree Quorum Protocol cannot be expressed by vote-assignable quorum sets [Agrawal and El Abbadi, 1990].

The Tree Quorum Protocol requires the logical tree to be of height h and of degree $2 \cdot d + 1$ with $d > 0$, that is, the number of levels (counting from zero) in the tree is h and each node has $2 \cdot d + 1 \geq 3$ child nodes. Furthermore, the tree is required to be complete, that is, each node has to have exactly $2 \cdot d + 1$ child nodes. As a result, the Tree Quorum Protocol is defined for specific numbers of processes only, namely for numbers of processes matching $\sum_{i=0}^{h} (2 \cdot d + 1)^i$. For example, for ternary trees with $d = 1$, the Tree Quorum Protocol is only defined for numbers of processes matching $1, 4, 13, 40$, and so forth.

The restriction to complete trees has later been relieved by the *Generalized Tree Quorum Protocol* [Agrawal and El Abbadi, 1992] that allows incomplete trees with a degree of $d' \geq 2$ in which each node has at most d' instead of exactly $2 \cdot d + 1$ child nodes. The minimal degree $d' = 2$ results in a binary tree and is the lowest degree to provide reasonable tree structures. Figure 2.8 (b) illustrates the Generalized Tree Quorum Protocol with nine processes that cannot be modeled by the original Tree Quorum Protocol. The quorum specification of the original Tree Quorum Protocol applies unaltered to the Generalized Tree Quorum Protocol. For example, in Figure 2.8 (b), a valid write quorum is $\{p_1, p_2, p_3, p_4, p_5, p_7, p_8\}$ and a valid read quorum in case the root node has failed is $\{p_2, p_3\}$.

The Tree Quorum Protocol has the desirable property of *graceful degradation* for the read operation. Read operation costs in terms of message complexity are minimal in the failure-free case and increase gracefully in the presence of failures. Unfortunately, this is not true for the write operation as the root node process is included in every write quorum, rendering the write operation unavailable if the root node process has failed. Because of the prominent root node, the write operation availability cannot exceed the process availability of the tree's root node process. Therefore, the Tree Quorum Protocol is – like the Read One Write All Protocol – suited for application scenarios in which read operations are much more frequent than write operations and in which read operation availability is more important than write operation availability. Compared to the Read One Write All Protocol, the original Tree Quorum Protocol has a lower message complexity for the write operation: The Read One Write All Protocol requires n processes for a write quorum whereas the original Tree Quorum Protocol requires $1/\mathrm{d} \cdot ((d + 1)^{h+1} - 1) < n$ processes [Agrawal and El Abbadi, 1990]. While the write operation message complexity of the Generalized Tree Quorum Protocol with binary trees is identical to the Read One Write All Protocol, it is lower for at least ternary trees. The Tree Quorum Protocol has a higher read operation message complexity than the Read One Write All Protocol: While the read quorums of the Read One Write All Protocol have a cardinality of 1, the cardinalities vary between 1 and $(d + 1)^h$ for the original Tree Quorum Protocol [Agrawal and El Abbadi, 1990].

An optimization circumventing the root node sensitivity for write operations is to require a quorum to consist of a majority of processes in each level and over a majority of levels for both, the read and the write operation. Then, however, the read operation's graceful degradation property is partially traded-off for higher write operation availability.

Next, three structured static data replication schemes logically arranging the processes in grid-structures are presented.

Grid-Based Protocols

Grid-based data replication schemes impose a logical grid structure on the processes and use structural properties to specify the quorum system. Three such grid-based data replication schemes, namely the Grid Protocol [Cheung, Ammar et al., 1990], the Triangular Lattice Protocol [Wu and Belford, 1992], and the Triangular Grid Protocol [Cheng-Hong and Jer-Tsang, 1998; Kuo and Huang, 1997], are presented next.

The Grid Protocol The structured *Grid Protocol* [Cheung, Ammar et al., 1990] arranges the processes in a logical rectangular $k \times j$ grid with $k \cdot j = n$ for a system comprising n processes where k is the number of columns and j is the number of rows in the grid. Figure 2.9 shows the logical 3×3 grid for a system consisting of nine processes. A horizontal crossing of the grid from the leftmost column to the rightmost column is termed a *column cover*, in short *C-Cover*. A vertical crossing of the grid from the topmost row to the bottommost row exclusively following vertical edges such that it includes all processes of a single column is referenced to as a *complete column cover*, in short *CC-Cover*. For example, the process set $\{p_3, p_6, p_9\}$ forms a CC-Cover and the process set $\{p_1, p_5, p_6\}$ represents a C-Cover in Figure 2.9.

In the original Grid Protocol [Cheung, Ammar et al., 1990], a read quorum consists of one process from each column (C-Cover) while a write quorum

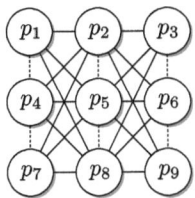

Figure 2.9: Logical Processes Layout of the 3×3 Grid Protocol [Theel and Pagnia-Koch, 1995]

requires both, a C-Cover and additionally a CC-Cover to meet the quorum system intersection property. The read and write operation availability graphs of the original Grid Protocol are not symmetric and thus are not optimal [Theel and Pagnia, 1998]. The optimized version of the Grid Protocol [Kumar, Rabinovich et al., 1993; Neilsen, 1992; Theel and Pagnia-Koch, 1995] additionally allows a read quorum to be a CC-Cover. This seemingly minor enhancement increases the probability of finding a read quorum and thus increases read operation availability while not decreasing write operation availability: If a complete column of processes has failed, the original Grid Protocol cannot form a C-Cover – which constitutes a read quorum – and thus the read operation is not available. The optimized version, however, can use another complete column (CC-Cover) of non-failed processes as read quorum and the read operation remains available. The optimized Grid Protocol has point-symmetric read and write operation availability graphs and therefore is optimal [Theel and Pagnia, 1998].

Furthermore, the original Grid Protocol is defined for fully populated grids only with the number of processes n calculating to $n = k \cdot j$. If the number of processes n is prime, the Grid Protocol degenerates to the Read One Write All Protocol for $k = 1$ or requires all n processes for the read as well as for the write operation if $j = 1$. With the exception of these extremes, Grid Protocol quorum systems cannot be expressed via vote assignments [Cheung, Ammar et al., 1990]. The original Grid Protocol's restriction to fully populated grids has later been overcome [Kumar, Rabinovich et al., 1993] by choosing k and j for a number of processes n such that $(k - 1) \cdot j < n \leq k \cdot j$ and introducing $k \cdot j - n$ unpopulated places into the grid in order to maintain the rectangular grid structure. The unpopulated places serve structure-preserving purposes only and are treated as being populated by processes that have permanently failed.

Triangular Lattice Protocol   Another structured grid-based protocol is the *Triangular Lattice Protocol* [Wu and Belford, 1992] as shown for nine processes in Figure 2.10. In the style of the Grid Protocol nomenclature, a horizontal crossing of the lattice structure is termed an *H-Cover* and a vertical crossing is called a *V-Cover*. In contrast to the Grid Protocol that poses no restriction on which processes form a horizontal path as long as one process from each column is involved, the Triangular Lattice Protocol restricts the processes permitted in a horizontal path. For each process and its successive process in a horizontal path, the successive process is either its left-adjacent, right-adjacent, upwards-adjacent, downwards-adjacent, right downwards diagonal-adjacent, or left upwards diagonal-adjacent process in the lattice structure. Also in contrast to the Grid Protocol, a vertical crossing of the lattice from the topmost row to the bottommost row must not only follow vertical edges. Instead, the same rules as for horizontal paths apply to each process and its successive process in a vertical path.

A read quorum either consists of processes on a horizontal path from the leftmost column to the rightmost column of the lattice (H-Cover) or of processes on a vertical path from the topmost row to the bottommost row of the lattice (V-Cover). A write quorum requires both, the processes of a horizontal and a vertical crossing of the lattice. For example, in the logical lattice structure in Figure 2.10, the process set $\{p_4, p_5, p_9\}$ is an H-Cover and the process set $\{p_1, p_5, p_8\}$ is a V-Cover. If existent, the diagonal path in a lattice – the process set $\{p_1, p_5, p_9\}$ in the figure – is a V-Cover as well as an H-Cover and can be used to perform read as well as write operations. By using this process set as write quorum, only three instead of five processes are required to cooperate for the write operation.

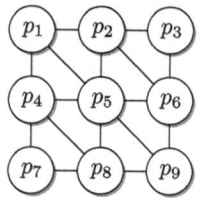

Figure 2.10: Logical Processes Layout of the 3×3 Triangular Lattice Protocol

The Triangular Lattice Protocol construction is *complete* [Theel and Pagnia-Koch, 1995] in the sense that adding an edge to the structure violates the quorum system intersection property. For example, introducing an edge connecting p_2 and p_4 in Figure 2.10 results in a possible vertical and horizontal crossing not having a process in common, namely by the vertical path consisting of the processes p_2, p_4, p_7 and the horizontal path consisting of p_1, p_5, p_6.

The weak point of the Grid Protocol is its requirement for a complete column of processes (CC-Cover) for write quorums. Consider, for example, the processes p_1, p_5, and p_3 – that represent a C-Cover – having failed in the 3×3 logical grid structure shown in Figure 2.11 (a). While an alternative C-Cover, for example, $\{p_4, p_2, p_6\}$, can be formed and the read operation is available, the write operation is unavailable because no column consisting of non-failed processes only exists. In this failure scenario, the 3×3 Triangular Lattice Protocol as shown in Figure 2.11 (b) is able to form read quorums and a write quorum. A read quorum is, amongst others, the horizontal path containing the processes p_4, p_8, p_9 while the single write quorum must contain the processes p_2, p_6, p_9 that form the only vertical path left.

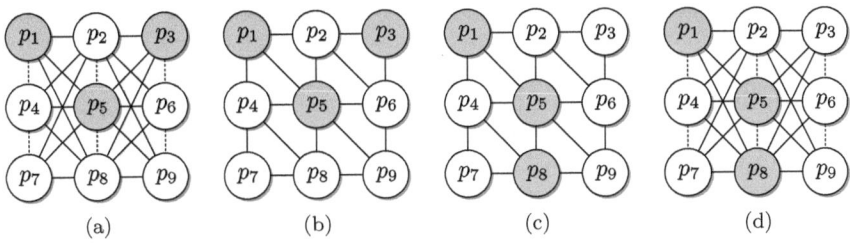

Figure 2.11: The 3×3 Grid Protocol (a), (d), and the 3×3 Triangular Lattice Protocol (b), (c), with Failed Processes shown Shaded

The weak point of the Triangular Lattice Protocol is its requirement for successive processes in a path to be in specific positions in the logical triangular lattice structure. For example, consider the process set $\{p_1, p_5, p_8\}$ having failed in Figure 2.11 (c). The Triangular Lattice Protocol is able to form a vertical crossing but no horizontal crossing. Thus, the read operation is available but the write operation is not. Using the Grid Protocol as shown in Figure 2.11 (d), both operations are available in this failure scenario.

The primary objective of both, the (optimized) Grid Protocol and the Triangular Lattice Protocol, is to be "good" with respect to quality measures for both operations, however with a bias towards the read operation. In contrast to Majority Consensus Voting seeking the same objective, the grid-based protocols have a lower message complexity. For example, the 3×3

Grid Protocol as well as the 3×3 Triangular Lattice Protocol, each with
nine processes as illustrated in Figures 2.9 and 2.10, require three processes
for a read quorum and – with the exception of the diagonal path for the
Triangular Lattice Protocol – five processes for a write quorum whereas Majority Consensus Voting with nine processes requires five processes for both
operation quorums. Including the diagonal path, the Triangular Lattice
Protocol allows for a minimal write quorum cardinality of three processes.
With increasing the number of processes, the better scalability of the structured grid-based data replication schemes in terms of message complexity
becomes more apparent: Excluding the diagonal path for the Triangular
Lattice Protocol, the 4×4 Grid Protocol as well as the 4×4 Triangular
Lattice Protocol, both with 16 processes, require read quorums to consist
of four and write quorums to consist of seven processes whereas Majority
Consensus Voting requires nine and eight processes, respectively.

On the other hand, the Grid Protocol and the Triangular Lattice Protocol – as being structured data replication schemes – are more vulnerable to
process failures than the unstructured Majority Consensus Voting. They
tolerate the failure of specific sets of processes rather than a specific number of process failures. For example, upon the failure of some processes
constituting a CC-Cover or a V-Cover, say, the process set $\{p_3, p_6, p_9\}$ in
Figure 2.9 and Figure 2.10, the write operation becomes unavailable. Majority Consensus Voting with nine processes can tolerate up to four arbitrary
processes failing and the write operation still remains available.

Triangular Grid Protocol   A third example of a grid-based protocol is
the *Triangular Grid Protocol* [Cheng-Hong and Jer-Tsang, 1998] which is
also known as the *Y-Quorums Protocol* [Kuo and Huang, 1997]. It arranges
the processes in a logical tree-like structure in which each non-leaf node has
two child nodes that are interconnected and each two adjacent nodes on
the same level have a common preceding node (with the exception of the
root node having none). An example of a logical triangular grid layout with
six and ten processes is shown in Figure 2.12 (a) and 2.12 (b), respectively.
Processes in the three corners of a logical triangular grid are termed *corner
nodes*, processes on the three border lines connecting the corner nodes are
called *boundary nodes*, and all other processes are referenced to by *inner
nodes*. A path in a triangular grid which includes at least one boundary
node from each of the triangular grid's three sides is called a *valid path*.
Note that a corner node accounts for two border lines and thus for two
boundary nodes.

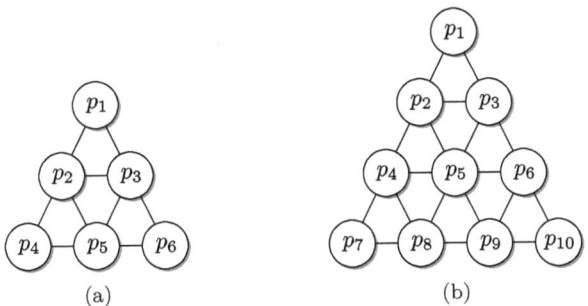

Figure 2.12: Logical Processes Layout of the Triangular Grid Protocol with Six
Processes (a) and Ten Processes (b)

In contrast to the above presented grid-based protocols, the Triangular Grid Protocol does not differentiate between read and write quorum sets and, therefore, its primary application is mutual exclusion. A valid path is a quorum that can either be used for a read or a write operation as the write quorum set is identical to the read quorum set. For example, in the triangular grid shown in Figure 2.12 (a), the process set $\{p_4, p_5, p_3\}$ is a valid quorum. In Figure 2.12 (b), the processes p_1, p_3, p_6, and p_{10} including the two corner nodes p_1 and p_{10} form a valid quorum as well as the processes p_4, p_8, p_5, and p_6 not including a corner node.

The minimal path length and thus minimal quorum cardinality in a triangular grid with height h (counting from one) is h processes. The total number of minimal quorums is $((h-1)^2 + (h-1) + 4) \cdot 2^{(h-1)-1}$ [Cheng-Hong and Jer-Tsang, 1998]. The number of processes in a (fully populated) triangular grid is dependent on its height and calculates to $n = h \cdot (h+1)/2$. Like for the Grid Protocol, the specification of a quorum system with a number of processes not matching $h \cdot (h+1)/2$ is realized by introducing a number of unpopulated places in the triangular grid in order to maintain the logical structure. Note that the number of unpopulated places is always less than $h-1$ or, more precisely, in between $h \cdot (h-1)/2$ and $h \cdot (h+1)/2$, as otherwise the triangular grid can be reorganized into a logical structure having fewer unpopulated places.

As a consequence of having identical read and write quorum sets, the Triangular Grid Protocol is actually equally good with respect to quality measures for both operations. Compared to Majority Consensus Voting that also has identical read and write quorum sets for odd numbers of processes and – with respect to quorum cardinality – nearly identical quorum sets for even numbers of processes, the Triangular Grid Protocol has a lower message complexity because it is a structured data replication scheme exploiting logical triangular grid structures to specify quorum systems. For example, the message complexity of Majority Consensus Voting with ten processes is five for the read and six for the write operation while the Triangular Grid Protocol has a message complexity of four (for both operations). Likewise to the other structured data replication schemes, the better scalability of the Triangular Grid Protocol over unstructured data replication schemes in terms of message complexity becomes more apparent with increasing numbers of processes: For example, with 55 processes, the Triangular Grid Protocol requires ten processes for a read or write quorum whereas Majority Consensus Voting requires 28 processes for a read quorum as well as for a write quorum. Compared to the Grid Protocol, the Triangular Grid Protocol has a higher message complexity for the read operation but a lower message complexity for the write operation. For example, for six processes, the Triangular Grid Protocol requires three processes for a (read or write) quorum while the Grid Protocol requires four processes for a write quorum and at least two processes for a read quorum. For 20 processes with the bottom-right corner unpopulated, the Triangular Grid Protocol requires minimally five and generally six processes while the Grid Protocol requires eight processes for a write quorum and minimally four processes for a read quorum.

Like the other structured data replication schemes, the Triangular Grid Protocol tolerates specific sets of process failures. Therefore, it is more vulnerable to process failures than the unstructured Majority Consensus Voting that tolerates a specific number of arbitrary process failures. For example, the failure of the four processes p_1, p_2, p_5 and p_8 in Figure 2.12 (b) renders the read and the write operation unavailable while Majority Consensus Voting with ten processes can tolerate five arbitrary process failures for the read operation and four arbitrary process failures for the write operation.

All static data replication schemes – regardless of being structured or unstructured – have an upper bound on operation availability because of a point-symmetry constraint among the read and write operation availability graphs [Theel and Pagnia, 1998] as they cannot react to process failures beyond a scheme-specific threshold. The next section introduces *dynamic* data replication schemes that can switch among quorum systems in order to adapt to failures, thereby usually providing increased operation availabilities at the expense of slightly higher costs caused by quorum system switching.

2.5.2 Dynamic Data Replication Schemes

Employing a dynamic data replication scheme enables the adaptation of the quorum system, respectively, allows to switch among quorum systems at run-time. Conceptually, a dynamic data replication scheme is a set of static data replication schemes – each representing the quorum system for a particular subset of the set of processes – among which the system may switch at run-time. Each subset of the set of static data replication schemes that determines the quorum systems for a particular number n' of processes describes a *stage* n' of the dynamics with $1 \leq n' \leq n$ and n being the total number of processes in the system. The quorum systems in a particular stage n' of the dynamics all consider n' processes but each set of processes is distinct with respect to the participating processes' identities. Data structure-wise, a dynamic data replication scheme is essentially an associative array relating each subset of the set of processes to a quorum system that is to be used for this subset of processes.

By switching quorum systems in response to process failures, operations usually remain available in cases where static data replication schemes cannot maintain operation availability because they tolerate only limited scheme-specific failure scenarios. For example, if there are failure scenarios specified in the structural failure model that are too severe for a static data replication scheme to tolerate, a dynamic data replication scheme may maintain operation availability: According to the respective currently faced failure scenario, the system switches among the set of static data replication schemes and thereby tolerates such failure scenarios [Storm and Warns, 2008].

In absence of an explicitly specified structural failure model, an implicit structural failure model is induced by the chosen static data replication scheme because of the duality of quorum systems and structural failure models. This implicit structural failure model may, however, be under specified and therefore does not reflect the extent and severity of failures possible. In such cases, using a dynamic data replication scheme creates the necessary flexibility of dynamically reacting to failures beyond the implicitly specified failure scenarios.

As an illustrating example, consider the static Majority Consensus Voting with four processes $P = \{p_1, \dots, p_4\}$ resulting in the write quorum set $\mathcal{Q}_{W_4} = \{\{p_1, p_2, p_3\}, \{p_1, p_2, p_4\}, \{p_1, p_3, p_4\}, \{p_2, p_3, p_4\}\}$ and the read quorum set $\mathcal{Q}_{R_4} = \{\{p_1, p_2\}, \{p_1, p_3\}, \{p_1, p_4\}, \{p_2, p_3\}, \{p_2, p_4\}, \{p_3, p_4\}\}$. This quorum system tolerates one process failure for the write operation and two process failures for the read operation. The implicit structural failure model expressed by this quorum system is $\{\emptyset, \{p_1\}, \{p_2\}, \{p_3\}, \{p_4\}\}$ for the write operation and $\{\emptyset, \{p_1\}, \{p_2\}, \{p_3\}, \{p_4\}, \{p_3, p_4\}, \{p_2, p_4\}, \{p_2, p_3\}, \{p_1, p_4\}, \{p_1, p_3\}, \{p_1, p_2\}\}$ for the read operation. Initially, no process has failed and the read as well as the write operation is available. Then a process fails, for example, process p_1. Both operations remain available as there is a read as well as a write quorum not containing process p_1. Then, another process fails, for example, process p_2. As a result, the write operation becomes unavailable. The read operation is still available using the quorum $\{p_3, p_4\}$.

In contrast, adapting the quorum system upon the failure of process p_1 to a quorum system complying to Majority Consensus Voting with the three non-failed processes, namely to $\mathcal{Q}_{R_3} = \mathcal{Q}_{W_3} = \{\{p_2, p_3\}, \{p_2, p_4\}, \{p_3, p_4\}\}$, avoids the unavailability of the write operation when in addition process p_2 fails as the write quorum $\{p_3, p_4\}$ of $\mathcal{Q}_{W_3}$ is still available. Thus, because of the quorum system switching, the write operation remains available in the presence of two process failures, a failure scenario the static Majority Consensus Voting with four processes is not able to tolerate.

Although there are some cases in which the opposite holds true [Jajodia and Mutchler, 1990], dynamic data replication schemes usually provide increased operation availabilities. Also, quorum system reconfiguration may improve on quality measures like probe complexity in the presence of failures.

Next, the concept of *epochs* [Rabinovich and Lazowska, 1992b] for consistently switching among quorum systems is presented.

Switching Quorum Systems   If done in a naive manner, switching quorum systems may sacrifice sequential consistency. Continuing the above example, assume process p_1 fails and the quorum system is adapted. Some write operations are performed using quorums of $\mathcal{Q}_{W_3}$ such that the processes p_2, p_3, and p_4 have a higher replica version number than process p_1. Then, process p_2 fails but the quorum system is not adapted. Subsequently, the processes p_3 and p_4 perform a write operation using a write quorum of $\mathcal{Q}_{W_3}$ such that their replicas have a higher replica version number than p_2's replica which in turn has a higher version number than p_1's replica. Then, the processes p_1 and p_2 recover. Process p_1 is not aware of the quorum system switch and executes a read operation with the read quorum

$\{p_1, p_2\}$ of $\mathcal{Q}_{R_4}$, thereby learning that p_2 has a higher replica version number such that it reads the value of p_2's replica. Clearly, the read operation does not return the value last written and violates sequential consistency. Thus, in order to guarantee sequential consistency, it must be ensured that (1) for safety, no operation is executed using a quorum of an outdated quorum system, and (2) for liveness, any coordinator process attempting to perform an operation either already knows or eventually learns about the current quorum system (assuming a functional failure model in which processes may recover from their failure).

A quorum system as stored on the processes is data. Hence, a quorum system can be seen as the data of a replicated data object and can therefore be consistently managed using the same means as for managing the "real" replica data, namely by using the same quorum system. This observation is manifested in the concept of *epochs* [Rabinovich and Lazowska, 1992b] for consistently switching quorum systems in a decentralized manner. Every process manages an additional variable termed *epoch number* which is initially set to zero, meaning that all processes are in the same epoch zero and know the initial quorum system. A so-called *epoch change* operation consistently switches from the current to a new quorum system. Intuitively, it is a write operation as described in Section 2.3 that does not (only) write the replica value but (also) the "quorum system value" with the epoch number being its associated version number. More specifically, an epoch change operation is performed by (1) writing the new quorum system to the union of a write quorum of the current quorum system and a write quorum of the new quorum system, (2) setting the epoch number of each process in either of the two write quorums to a new global maximum, and (3) writing the current replica value to the replica of each process in the two write quorums' union including the update of its replica version number to the current global maximal replica version number. Note that the latter is only required for processes having an outdated replica. The new global maximal epoch number is identified similar to the global maximal replica version number as described in the operation execution protocol in Section 2.3. If a write quorum of the current quorum system or a write quorum of the new quorum system or both quorums cannot be formed, then the epoch change operation must be aborted.

Switching quorum systems via the epoch change operation preserves sequential consistency: Because of the quorum system intersection property, there is at least one process in every read and write quorum of the old quorum system – and obviously also of the new quorum system – knowing this new quorum system. Thus, by querying the epoch number in addition to the replica version number during the course of quorum probing, any coordinator process attempting to perform an operation either already knows the new quorum system or learns about a newer quorum system by comparing its epoch number with those of the other quorum's processes. If a coordinator process learns about a newer quorum system while probing a quorum, that is, it has not participated in at least one of the last epoch change operation's two write quorums, it must cancel the operation execution and must update its quorum system and epoch number from one of the quorum's processes having the highest epoch number prior to trying to perform the operation again. Then, the coordinator process may again learn about a newer quorum system and again has to cancel the operation execution and has to update its quorum system and epoch number. Eventually, the coordinator process has the globally highest epoch number and uses a quorum of the newest quorum system to perform the operation. Note that the coordinator process may already be considered in a newer quorum system which it however does not yet know as it was in neither one of the corresponding epoch change operation's two write quorums. Also note that processes in a probed quorum not knowing the new(er) quorum system are revealed during quorum probing and may be updated by the coordinator process.

A concept similar to epochs, called *generations*, has been introduced by Gifford [1979] to adapt vote assignments in Weighted Voting in order to cope with changing application scenario needs. It also requires a write quorum of the old and a write quorum of the new quorum system to cooperate.

Both concepts require a relation of the new current quorum system to the then outdated old quorum system by demanding the new quorum system to be established on the union of a write quorum of the old and a write quorum of the new quorum system. This relation ensures that the new and the old quorum system are not disjoint, thereby in conjunction with the previous discussion satisfying the above stated safety requirement. But, because of the quorum system switching mechanism relying on write quorums, it directly interferes and conflicts with regular operations. Regular read and write operations cannot be performed and are thus not available while switching quorum systems. A locked write quorum constitutes a global lock on the system with respect to performing concurrent operations, thereby guaranteeing the installment of the new quorum system to be performed mutually exclusive to other operations. In this sense, quorum system switching via the concepts of epochs or generations is a global reconfiguration mechanism. To mitigate the global locking handicap, the quorum switch operation coordinator may "piggy-back" a regular read or write operation on such an operation. In case of a read operation, it reads the replica value from some process of either write quorum used for the quorum switch operation after it has been completed. In case of a write operation, the replica value written to each process in the two write quorums' union is not the current replica value but a new replica value, followed by setting the replica version numbers of the processes in either write quorum to a new global maximum.

Switching quorum systems is an expensive operation in terms of requiring the cooperation of two write quorums' processes. Therefore, it is usually assumed to be infrequent compared to regular read and write operations and the unavailability of operations due to the global locking while switching quorum systems is accepted. However, there are other approaches to quorum system switching that decouple the switching mechanism from the quorum system used to perform regular operations by providing a concurrently executed quorum system switching service.

For example, Yu and Vahdat [2005] use the concept of *leases* [Gray and Cheriton, 1989]. Basically, a lease is a license to perform read or write operations that is valid for a limited period of time after which it expires and becomes invalid. A process may only perform operations if it has a valid lease, that is, after having applied for and being granted a lease on the quorum system by a *lease manager*. Whenever a quorum system switching is required, no further leases are granted by the lease manager. Eventually, all leases have expired, resulting in read and write operations being unavailable. Then, the lease manager installs the new quorum system on the processes that were previously granted a lease and serves their subsequent requests for new leases on the new quorum system. Thus, all processes having a non-expired lease know the current quorum system. In this approach, the old and the new quorum system need not to be related. However, it is – like the concepts of epochs and generations – a global reconfiguration mechanism and requires the mutual exclusion of regular operations and the quorum system switching operation.

As another example, Englert and Shvartsman [2000] proposed to use *intermediate quorum systems*, that is, the accumulated union of old and new quorum systems, as long as eventually a consolidated quorum system is installed on the processes by a coordinating process. The eventual quorum system installment is done concurrently to regular read and write operations and thus does not render them unavailable during reconfiguration. However, quorum cardinalities in the intermediate quorum system grow large, thereby resulting in quality-of-service degradation, for example, with respect to the messages required to effectuate a quorum. Like the former approach using leases, the old and the new quorum system need not to be related. However, using intermediate quorum systems does not require a global locking unlike the concepts of leases, epochs, and generations.

Henceforth, the concept of epochs is assumed to be used for quorum system switching due to its conceptual simplicity. Note that, however, the concepts and methods developed in the remainder of this thesis are in general independent of the quorum system switching mechanism and can as well be implemented using other concepts than epochs.

Next, heterogeneous dynamic data replication schemes as a result of two traditional dynamic data replication schemes' shortcomings in terms of (1) their homogeneity and (2) their boundedness in the number of processes manageable at run-time are briefly sketched to motivate the need for the concepts and methods to be introduced in the next chapter. The underlying concepts of heterogeneous dynamic data replication schemes are examined more closely in the following Chapter 3.

Heterogeneous Dynamic Data Replication Schemes   Traditional dynamic data replication schemes such as the Dynamic Grid Protocol [Rabinovich and Lazowska, 1992b], the Dynamic Tree Quorum Protocol [Rabinovich and Lazowska, 1992a], and Dynamic Voting [Jajodia and Mutchler, 1990] – being the dynamic counterpart of the unstructured static Majority Consensus Voting – are *homogeneous* in the sense that the same scheme-inherent quorum system construction rules in terms of a static data replication scheme are homogeneously used to construct the set of quorum systems to switch among. In case of Dynamic Voting, for example, every quorum system is built in a Majority Consensus Voting-manner according to the rule that every read quorum consists of $\lceil n'/2 \rceil$ processes and every write quorum consists of $\lceil (n'+1)/2 \rceil$ processes for each subset of the set of processes with cardinality n', that is, each stage n' of the dynamics $1 \leq n' \leq n = |P|$. In the same sense as there is no single data replication scheme superior for every application scenario, there is also none superior for every stage of the dynamics: Unstructured data replication schemes face scalability problems with increasing numbers of processes while structured data replication schemes can only unleash their full potential if the underlying logical structure the processes are arranged in is fully or at least mostly populated by processes. Thus, homogeneity poses a limitation on the choice of an appropriate data replication scheme for a concrete application scenario.

Heterogeneous dynamic data replication schemes [Storm, 2006; Storm and Theel, 2006] overcome this limitation by allowing different quorum system construction rules (in terms of a different static data replication scheme) to be utilized per stage of the dynamics. Hence, the scheme-specific deficiencies can be countered by employing the respective best-option structured or unstructured static data replication scheme per stage of the dynamics for a concrete application scenario. Because of being capable to employ *any* static data replication scheme per stage of the dynamics – including those not having a vote-assignable counterpart such as the Grid Protocol – heterogeneous dynamic data replication schemes are clearly more flexible than any homogeneous dynamic data replication scheme – including those ones having the ability to dynamically reassign votes. This flexibility allows to realize fine-grained trade-offs between quality measures such as, for example, operation availability and operation costs in terms of the number of messages required to effectuate a quorum and thereby allows to match an application's needs more closely than possible with traditional homogeneous dynamic data replication schemes. As illustrated in Figure 2.13, heterogeneous dynamic data replication schemes introduce a third dimension to the data replication scheme design space that is spawned by static and dynamic, unstructured and structured, and homogeneous and heterogeneous data replication schemes. Note that static data replication schemes cannot

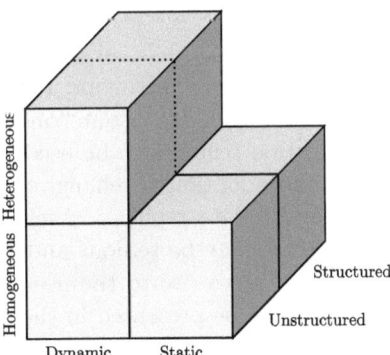

Figure 2.13: Data Replication Scheme Design Space

be heterogeneous as they define a single static quorum system. Also note that, in contrast to homogeneous dynamic data replication schemes, the design space of heterogeneous dynamic data replication schemes is not strictly segmented into structured and unstructured schemes: While there are heterogeneous dynamic (un)structured data replication schemes – namely those that exclusively use different (un)structured quorum system construction rules – a strict separation of the heterogeneous dynamic data replication scheme design space into structured and unstructured schemes is inappropriate as a single heterogeneous dynamic data replication scheme can also be a blend of both.

In addition to the restriction to homogeneity, almost all traditional dynamic data replication schemes have a static upper bound on the number of processes manageable at run-time. The maximal number of processes supported is predetermined at design-time and remains fixed at run-time such that it is not possible to integrate new processes into the data replication scheme at run-time. For those schemes for which a mechanism to integrate new processes at run-time does exist, as, for example, for Dynamic Voting [Jajodia and Mutchler, 1990], the mechanisms are scheme-specific and are thus not applicable to other data replication schemes. This restriction hinders the general application of quorum-based data replication schemes to dynamic environments such as ad-hoc or peer-to-peer networks in which processes join and deliberately leave the system at run-time. In contrast, heterogeneous dynamic data replication schemes not only provide the flexibility of choosing the best-option static data replication scheme per stage of the dynamics but moreover allow to manage an arbitrary number of processes at run-time.

Unfortunately, existing frameworks that support heterogeneous dynamic data replication schemes [Storm, 2006; Storm and Theel, 2006] are reliant on an actual implementation of the quorum system construction rules complying to the static data replication schemes to be used in the different stages of the dynamics. Hence, the adoption to changing application scenarios or the integration of new static data replication schemes involves modifying the framework's code which may be tedious and costly but certainly is an error-prone task. This fact gives rise to the need for a quorum system specification formalism that is to be presented in the next chapter. From a given specification, operation-specific quorums can be derived by interpreting the specification at run-time. By this means, data replication schemes can be *configured* via the specification formalism rather than having to be

implemented. Besides, using a specification formalism is much more convenient and flexible than adopting an implementation. Such a quorum system
specification formalism must be flexible enough to (1) support static and dynamic, structured and unstructured, homogeneous and heterogeneous data
replication schemes and to (2) express quorum systems with a variable and
not upper-bounded number of processes at run-time.

2.6 Summary

Fault-tolerant distributed systems are a complex matter. This chapter has
introduced some selected aspects of distributed systems that are related
to quorum-based data replication. First, the communication model and
its terminology has been introduced and, based thereon, failure, dynamics,
and timing models have been presented alongside with their specific subtle
implications. Subsequently, data consistency as a measure of operation correctness has been discussed, followed by the introduction of quorum systems
whose employment ensures a certain notion of consistency, namely sequential consistency which is a prominent consistency criterion due to its general
applicability. Hence, quorum systems have become a well-known and established means to realize distributed mutual exclusion and data replication.
Then, various quality measures for quorum systems have been presented
and, consecutively, some selected unstructured and structured data replication schemes have been illustrated alongside with their specific advantages
and disadvantages. As a result of the limited operation availability of static
(unstructured as well as structured) data replication schemes, the concept
of dynamic data replication schemes has been presented. Motivated by the
limited variability of traditional dynamic data replication schemes in terms
of the number of processes manageable at run-time and their inability to
support different quorum system construction rules per stage of the dynamics, heterogeneous dynamic data replication schemes that are not subject to
those restrictions have been briefly sketched.

The next chapter revisits and improves on the ideas and concepts of heterogeneous dynamic data replication schemes. In particular, a specification
formalism for arbitrary quorum-based data replication schemes that is also
able to express quorum systems for an unbounded number of processes at
run-time is presented.

3 Specification of Quorum Systems

Quorum-based data replication schemes are specified via two sets of subsets of the set of processes: The write quorum set's quorums are used to perform write operations and the read quorum set's quorums are used to perform read operations. These two sets are constructed such that every two write quorums intersect in at least one process and every write quorum intersects with every read quorum in at least one process. Two read quorums need not to intersect. The deployment of a quorum-based data replication scheme requires a representation of the quorum system in terms of an encoding to be stored on each process in the system.

Explicit Quorum System Encoding An explicit quorum system encoding, that is, storing the plain enumeration of all quorums, is very space-consuming. Consider, for example, the unstructured static Majority Consensus Voting [Thomas, 1979] with eight processes. A read quorum consists of four processes, resulting in a total read quorum set cardinality of 70 quorums. The write quorum set consists of 56 quorums with each quorum having five processes. Doubling the number of processes to 16 processes results in a read quorum set cardinality of 12, 870 quorums with each quorum having eight processes, and a write quorum set cardinality of 11, 440 quorums with each quorum consisting of nine processes. The read quorum set cardinality increased by factor 183.86 and the write quorum set cardinality increased by factor 204.29. Assuming that 12 bytes are needed to encode each process' identity, for example, to encode its IP address, the write quorum set needs 1206.56 kilobytes and the read quorum set needs 1357.38 kilobytes. In total, 2563.95 kilobytes are required on each process of the system to store the quorum system of the *static* Majority Consensus Voting with a fixed number of 16 processes.

A *dynamic* data replication scheme requires one quorum system for each combination of non-failed processes in order to be prepared for any failure scenario potentially occurring at run-time. Hence, $\sum_{k=1}^{n} \binom{n}{k} = 2^n - 1$ quorum systems are needed for a system comprising n processes, namely

$\binom{n}{n}$ quorum system for no process being failed,

$\binom{n}{n-1}$ quorum systems for one process being failed,

$\binom{n}{n-2}$ quorum systems for two processes being failed, and so forth.

For example, with 16 processes in a system, $2^{16} - 1 = 65535$ quorum systems are required. An a priori explicit encoding of quorum systems is thus problematic from the implementation perspective due to its exponential space requirement.

Implicit Quorum System Encoding An implicit quorum system encoding alleviates the exponential space requirement problem by not explicitly encoding a quorum system but instead its construction rules. The quorum system construction rules of a specific data replication scheme can be encoded, for example, in an explicitly stated quorum system construction algorithm which yields individual operation-specific quorums *on request*. For example, such an algorithm obeying the rule that read quorums consist of $\lceil n/2 \rceil$ processes and write quorums consist of $\lceil (n+1)/2 \rceil$ processes generates operation-specific quorums complying to Majority Consensus Voting for n processes. A coordinator process derives an initial operation-specific quorum from the implicit quorum system encoding and then probes it. In case the quorum is not available, another quorum is derived from the implicit quorum system encoding and subsequently probed. Eventually, either an available quorum has been found or all operation-specific quorums are derived and negatively probed such that the operation is not available. Only if approaching the latter case, that is, if very many operation-specific quorums must be derived and are negatively probed, exponential time is required. Otherwise, and this is assumed to be the usual case, only one or a few quorums must be derived such that the time complexity is much less than exponential.

Hence, the choice of using an implicit or explicit quorum system encoding requires to choose a trade-off between storage space and time required to derive quorums at run-time. While explicit quorum system encodings are strictly biased towards minimizing the latter (assuming a quorum lookup to be faster than a quorum derivation) and accept the exponential space requirement, implicit quorum system encodings are more balanced as they avoid the exponential space requirement and usually also avoid the exponential time requirement. Note that if a dynamic data replication scheme is used, the (explicit) implementation of a single or a multitude of quorum system construction algorithms is required, the latter in case of a heterogeneous dynamic data replication scheme.

A severe drawback of using implicit quorum system encodings in terms of quorum system construction algorithms becomes apparent if the application scenario demands to the data replication scheme evolve over time. Then, the algorithm implementations must be repeatedly and manually adapted – or even reimplemented if the application requirements deviate drastically – to match the new application scenario needs. The manual adaptation of the algorithms is a safety-critical and error-prone task that requires great expert knowledge. For example, simple programming errors like off-by-one errors in array indexing may lead to quorum sets being disjoint and thereby most likely to the violation of sequential consistency. Thus, the quorum system construction algorithms must be proven to be correct which is time-intensive and extremely costly. Apart from safety, quality measures may be negatively affected if the adapted quorum system construction algorithms are not particularly well-suited for the application scenario. Finding the specific best-option data replication scheme is a problem on its own and requires a thorough analysis of the data replication scheme candidates, which alone requires great expert knowledge. This problem is addressed in the next chapter.

Quorum System Specification The burden of adapting the quorum system construction algorithm implementations is relieved by a quorum system specification formalism in conjunction with a universal algorithm that interprets a given specification in order to derive an operation-specific quorum from it at run-time. By this means, data replication schemes can be *configured* (via the specification formalism) rather than having to be implemented or reimplemented. Instead of adapting the quorum system construction algorithm implementations, the data replication scheme is reconfigured simply by giving a new specification. Moreover, reconfiguration is easily realized at run-time whereas deploying a new implementation either requires to shut down the system (which negatively impacts operation availability) or requires great efforts to transition to the new implementation.

While expert knowledge is still required to design good data replication schemes, using a specification formalism is much more convenient and flexible than adapting an implementation. Besides, the data replication scheme designer can be supported in an automatic manner, for example, by sanity-checking if the specified data replication scheme honors sequential consistency or by an automated quality-of-service analysis for a given application scenario.

Every data replication scheme has its specific inherent quorum system construction rules and these rules are very different in nature. For example, the unstructured Majority Consensus Voting [Thomas, 1979] (cf. Section 2.5.1) uses minimal quorum cardinalities to construct quorum systems. Every read quorum consists of $\lceil n/2 \rceil$ processes and every write quorum consists of $\lceil (n+1)/2 \rceil$ processes for a total of n processes in the system. As another example, the structured (original) Grid Protocol [Cheung, Ammar et al., 1990] (cf. Section 2.5.1) imposes a logical rectangular grid structure on the set of processes and uses structural properties to specify quorum systems. In the original Grid Protocol, a read quorum must contain one process from each column of the grid while a write quorum must additionally contain the processes forming a complete column of the grid.

Because of the diversity in quorum system construction rules, a quorum system specification formalism must be able to uniformly express the inherent quorum system construction rules of the various data replication schemes. Moreover, it must be flexible enough to reflect homogeneous and heterogeneous dynamic as well as unstructured and structured static data replication schemes. Also, it must be able to express quorum systems for a variable and unbounded number of processes at run-time.

The remainder of this chapter is structured as follows. First, related work to implicitly represent and specify quorum systems is outlined in Section 3.1. Then, *tree-shaped voting structures* as a universal quorum system representation means in the form of semantics-enriched tree graphs are presented in Section 3.2. They serve the two purposes of (1) being the foundation for representing quorum systems in the system model to be presented in Chapter 4 and (2) being a unified specification language of the various data replication schemes' quorum system construction rules applied to particular numbers of processes. The latter is exploited by *voting structure shapes* that are introduced in Section 3.3. Basically, a voting structure shape is an abstraction from the number of processes encoded in tree-shaped voting structures complying to a particular static data replication scheme in terms of a composition graph steering the construction of tree-shaped voting structures complying to this particular static data replication scheme but for arbitrary numbers of processes. Based on voting structure shapes, homogeneous dynamic data replication schemes managing an arbitrary number of processes at run-time are realized. The additional support for heterogeneous dynamic data replication schemes is presented in Section 3.4 by introducing the specification formalism that employs voting structure shapes. Finally, Section 3.5 sketches future work and Section 3.6 summarizes this chapter.

3.1 Related Work

While a lot of effort has been spent on identifying particularly good data replication schemes for diverse application scenarios in terms of quorum system construction rules, far less work has been committed to research implicit quorum system encodings in terms of proposing quorum system specification formalisms. In some sense, a quorum system construction rule is itself an implicit representation of a quorum system that results from the application of this rule to a specific number of processes. A specification formalism must abstract from the specifics of a particular data replication scheme's quorum system construction rules and must provide a uniform specification means for quorum systems complying to the various data replication schemes.

Three such quorum system specification formalisms to be presented in the following are *Multidimensional Voting* [Ahamad, Ammar et al., 1990, 1991], *General Structured* Voting [Theel, 1993a,b], and its dynamic counterpart *Dynamic General Structured Voting* [Theel and Strauß, 1998]. Unfortunately, the former two are limited to static data replication schemes and, in contrast to General Structured Voting, Multidimensional Voting cannot express an ordering on quorum sets. The latter Dynamic General Structured Voting is restricted to homogeneous dynamic data replication schemes with a static and a priori determined upper bound on the number of processes. Therefore, albeit not being a pure specification formalism, the idea of *Voting Structure Generators* [Storm, 2006; Storm and Theel, 2006] that overcomes both these limitations is subsequently presented. It is a hybrid approach in terms of a combination of the General Structured Voting specification formalism with specific and explicitly stated quorum system construction algorithms. These algorithms generate implicit quorum system encodings in the syntax and semantics of General Structured Voting, each for a particular data replication scheme. The maximal number of processes manageable at run-time is not bounded because of the algorithms' ability to generate implicit quorum system encodings for any number of processes. Simply by allowing a different implicit quorum system encoding construction algorithm to be utilized per stage of the dynamics, the limitation to homogeneous dynamic data replication schemes is overcome and heterogeneous dynamic data replication schemes are realized.

Multidimensional Voting

Multidimensional Voting [Ahamad, Ammar et al., 1990, 1991] specifies a
quorum system via a $n \times k$ matrix of votes (in terms of non-negative natural numbers) with n rows representing the n processes in the system and
k columns representing the number of vote dimensions. A quorum is derived by performing a threshold voting within and over the columns of the
matrix, resulting in a set of columns with cardinality j, $1 \le j \le k$, in
each of which at least a number of processes satisfying the column-specific
vote threshold must grant permission to perform the operation. Given the
threshold votings have been successful, the actual quorum is the union of
those processes in the set of j columns that have granted their permission
to the operation execution.

For example, consider the structured static original Grid Protocol with
four processes $p_1, \ldots, p_4$ that are arranged in a logical rectangular 2×2 grid.
The processes p_1, p_2 form the left and the processes p_3, p_4 form the right
column of the grid. Recall that in the original Grid Protocol, a read quorum
consists of one process from each column (C-Cover) while a write quorum
additionally requires the processes of a complete column (CC-Cover). The
original Grid Protocol with four processes specified in terms of Multidimensional Voting is shown in Figure 3.1 (a) with the matrix' four rows
corresponding to the four processes in the ordering $p_1, \ldots, p_4$ from top to
bottom. According to their column affiliation in the logical grid structure,
the processes p_1 and p_2 are assigned one vote whereas the processes p_3 and
p_4 have zero votes in the left column (vote dimension). In the right vote
dimension, the processes p_1 and p_2 are assigned zero votes while the processes p_3 and p_4 each have one vote.

For a read quorum, that is, for a C-Cover, the minimal number of processes required to grant their permission within a vote dimension is one
process as reflected by the read quorum vote threshold $r = (1, 1)$. Since
at least one process from both vote dimensions is required for a C-Cover,
a voting over both vote dimensions must be conducted as expressed by
$MD_R = (2, 2)$, meaning that the respective read quorum vote threshold
must be satisfied in two out of the two vote dimensions.

For a write quorum's CC-Cover, the minimal number of processes required to grant their permission within a vote dimension is two processes as
reflected by the write quorum vote threshold $w = (2, 2)$. Since only one of
the two vote dimensions is required for a CC-Cover, a $MD_W = (1, 2)$ voting
is conducted, meaning that the respective write quorum vote threshold must

$$
\begin{array}{cc}
p_1 \\ p_2 \\ p_3 \\ p_4
\end{array}
\begin{pmatrix}
1 & 0 \\
1 & 0 \\
0 & 1 \\
0 & 1
\end{pmatrix}
\quad
\begin{array}{l}
r = (1,1) \\
w = (2,2)
\end{array}
\qquad\qquad
\begin{array}{cc}
p_1 \\ p_2 \\ p_3 \\ p_4
\end{array}
\begin{pmatrix}
1 \\
1 \\
1 \\
1
\end{pmatrix}
\quad
\begin{array}{l}
r = (2) \\
w = (3)
\end{array}
$$

$$
\begin{array}{cc}
MD_R = (2,2) & \qquad\qquad MD_R = (1,1) \\
MD_W = (1,2) & \qquad\qquad MD_W = (1,1) \\
\text{(a)} & \qquad\qquad \text{(b)}
\end{array}
$$

Figure 3.1: Multidimensional Voting Specification of the Original Grid Protocol (a) and Majority Consensus Voting (b), each with Four Processes

be satisfied in one out of the two vote dimensions. A write quorum, that consists of a CC-Cover and additionally a C-Cover, is the union of processes resulting from a $MD_W = (1, 2)$ and from a $MD_R = (2, 2)$ voting. The read and write quorum sets deducible from this specification of the original Grid Protocol are

$$
\mathcal{Q}_R = \{\{p_1, p_3\}, \{p_1, p_4\}, \{p_2, p_3\}, \{p_2, p_4\}\} \text{ and}
$$
$$
\mathcal{Q}_W = \{\{p_1, p_2, p_3\}, \{p_1, p_2, p_4\}, \{p_3, p_4, p_1\}, \{p_3, p_4, p_2\}\}.
$$

As a second example, consider the Multidimensional Voting specification of Majority Consensus Voting with four processes $p_1, \ldots, p_4$ as shown in Figure 3.1 (b). The vote matrix has four rows corresponding to the four processes – in the ordering $p_1, \ldots, p_4$ from top to bottom – and one column representing the single vote dimension. Majority Consensus Voting with four processes requires $\lceil 4/2 \rceil = 2$ processes for a read quorum and $\lceil 4+1/2 \rceil = 3$ processes for a write quorum. Hence, the read quorum vote threshold is $r = (2)$ and the vote threshold for write quorums is $w = (3)$. Since there is exactly one vote dimension, the threshold voting over and within the vote dimensions reduces to a threshold voting within the single vote dimension. Specifically, a $MD_R = (1, 1)$ voting must be conducted for a read quorum and a $MD_W = (1, 1)$ voting must be conducted for a write quorum. The resulting read and write quorum sets are

$$
\mathcal{Q}_R = \{\{p_1, p_3\}, \{p_1, p_4\}, \{p_2, p_3\}, \{p_2, p_4\}, \{p_1, p_2\}, \{p_3, p_4\}\} \text{ and}
$$
$$
\mathcal{Q}_W = \{\{p_1, p_2, p_3\}, \{p_1, p_2, p_4\}, \{p_3, p_4, p_1\}, \{p_3, p_4, p_2\}\}.
$$

Note that the formalism of Multidimensional Voting is restricted to the specification of quorum systems complying to static data replication schemes not defining an ordering on quorum sets. For example, the Tree Quorum Protocol [Agrawal and El Abbadi, 1990] (cf. Section 2.5.1) defines a partial order on (read) quorums and thereby an order in which to probe (read) quorums. Multidimensional Voting cannot express an ordering on quorums as it defines no order in which to perform the threshold voting over the vote dimensions: It requires a particular number rather than specific vote dimensions to satisfy the respective operation-specific vote thresholds.

A specification formalism that is not restricted in this respect but also limited to static data replication schemes, namely *General Structured Voting*, is presented next.

General Structured Voting

General Structured Voting [Theel, 1993a,b] specifies a quorum system via a rooted directed acyclic graph called *voting structure* as illustrated in Figure 3.2. A voting structure is interpreted by a general algorithm in order to derive an operation-specific quorum from it at run-time. The nodes in a voting structure are either *physical nodes* representing real processes managing replicas or are *virtual nodes* that serve for grouping physical and virtual nodes. For a simpler presentation, the latter virtual nodes are labeled V_i with $i = 1, 2, 3, \ldots$ and the former physical nodes are labeled p_j with $1 \leq j \leq n$ and n being the total number of processes in the system. Regardless of being a physical or a virtual node, each node is equipped with a vote in terms of a natural number (upper right index) and a pair of minimal votes to collect among its child nodes for a read or a write quorum (lower right index). Each node's minimal votes to collect per operation must be less than or equal to the sum of its child nodes' votes. Some data replication schemes such as the Tree Quorum Protocol define a partial order on quorum sets specifying the ordering in which to probe quorums. To specify such an ordering, that is, to specify which quorums are tried to be used prior to other ones, the directed edges of a voting structure can be annotated with operation-specific priorities reflecting this ordering. An edge priority of 1 represents the highest and the symbol ∞ denotes the lowest priority. A default edge priority of ∞ is assumed in absence of an explicitly stated priority.

Note that voting structures can specify the coordination of more than two operations. However, only the special case of two operations, namely the read and the write operation, is considered here.

The voting structures in Figure 3.2 specify the quorum systems of the Tree Quorum Protocol, the optimized Grid Protocol [Kumar, Rabinovich et al., 1993; Neilsen, 1992; Theel and Pagnia-Koch, 1995], and of Majority Consensus Voting, each with four processes. The traversal of a voting structure obeying the vote collection specification expressed by the minimal votes to collect among a node's child nodes and the edge priority-induced traversal ordering yields a set of nodes whose physical nodes' processes constitute an operation-specific quorum. The recursive algorithm to interpret voting structures in order to derive a quorum is as follows.

Starting with the root node, each node queries as many of its child nodes for their votes as needed to satisfy its minimal vote requirement for the read (write) operation while obeying the query ordering specified via edge priorities. A queried node casts its vote if the sum of votes casted by its

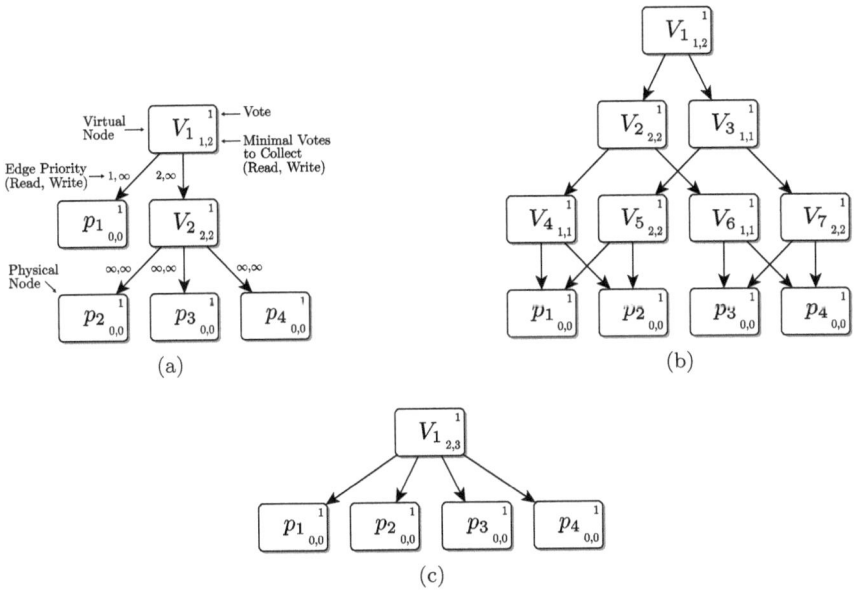

Figure 3.2: Voting Structures of Theel [1993a] for the Tree Quorum Protocol (a), the Optimized Grid Protocol (b), and Majority Consensus Voting (c), each with Four Processes

queried child nodes satisfies this node's minimal operation-specific vote requirement. If the queried node is a physical node, then, additionally, its associated process must not have failed and it must not have casted its vote for a concurrent competitive operation. If a queried node does not cast its vote, then the querying node chooses an alternative and not yet queried child node to query for its vote, again respecting the query ordering specified via edge priorities. If there are no alternative nodes left to query and the querying node's minimal operation-specific vote requirement cannot be satisfied, then it does not cast its vote to its father node. Eventually, the root node either has received sufficiently many votes and grants permission to execute the read (write) operation or must refuse to do so. In the former case, the read (write) operation is executed with a quorum consisting of those processes associated to the physical nodes that have casted their votes and for which their respective father nodes – if any – have also casted their votes. In the latter case, no read (write) quorum can be found and the operation is not available.

For example, the thorough interpretation of the Tree Quorum Protocol voting structure in Figure 3.2 (a) yields the partially ordered read and write quorum sets

$$\mathcal{Q}_R = \langle \{\{p_1\}\}, \{\{p_2, p_3\}, \{p_2, p_4\}, \{p_3, p_4\}\} \rangle \text{ and}$$
$$\mathcal{Q}_W = \langle \{\{p_1, p_2, p_3\}, \{p_1, p_2, p_4\}, \{p_1, p_3, p_4\}\} \rangle .$$

The read quorum set is ordered while the write quorums can be used in any order. The thorough interpretation of the optimized Grid Protocol voting structure in Figure 3.2 (b) yields the read and write quorum sets

$$\mathcal{Q}_R = \{\{p_1, p_3\}, \{p_1, p_4\}, \{p_2, p_3\}, \{p_2, p_4\}, \{p_1, p_2\}, \{p_3, p_4\}\} \text{ and}$$
$$\mathcal{Q}_W = \{\{p_1, p_2, p_3\}, \{p_1, p_2, p_4\}, \{p_3, p_4, p_1\}, \{p_3, p_4, p_2\}\},$$

both of which can be used in any order. The same quorum system results from the thorough interpretation of the Majority Consensus Voting voting structure with four processes shown in Figure 3.2 (c).

Next, the dynamic counterpart of General Structured Voting that introduces support for homogeneous dynamic data replication schemes with a fixed upper bound on the number of processes is presented.

Dynamic General Structured Voting

A voting structure represents the (partially ordered) quorum sets according to a specific data replication scheme and for a particular number of processes. It is therefore limited to express static data replication schemes only. The dynamic counterpart [Theel and Strauß, 1998] of General Structured Voting relieves this restriction and allows to specify homogeneous dynamic data replication schemes with a fixed upper bound on the number of processes. For an a priori known maximal number of processes n, a fixed template voting structure called *master voting structure* complying to some static data replication scheme is manually constructed at design-time. From the master voting structure, a so-called *current voting structure* is derived by applying a sequence of transformation rules (for details on the transformation refer to [Theel and Strauß, 1998] or Section 3.3.1). The current voting structure represents the quorum system for the current stage n' of the dynamics with $1 \leq n' \leq n$. Hence, the multiple quorum systems as required for a dynamic data replication scheme – that is, one quorum system for each combination of non-failed processes in order to be prepared for any failure scenario potentially occurring at run-time – are constructed by processing the master voting structure.

As an example, consider the Majority Consensus Voting voting structure with four processes shown in Figure 3.2 (c) as the master voting structure. Initially, no process is failed and the current voting structure resembles the master voting structure. Then, for example, process p_4 fails and its failure is detected by process p_2 as the coordinator of an operation execution. Process p_2 initiates and coordinates the upcoming epoch change operation: It derives the new quorum system not including process p_4 in terms of the new current voting structure from the master voting structure by removing the physical node corresponding to the failed process p_4 and its connection to the virtual node V_1. The minimal operation-specific vote requirements of the virtual node V_1 are adapted as Majority Consensus Voting with three processes requires two processes for a read as well as for a write quorum. This new current voting structure (and the current replica value) is disseminated to the other two processes p_1 and p_3 that form a write quorum of the new epoch and, in conjunction with p_2 itself, form a write quorum of the current epoch. Eventually, process p_4 recovers and initiates an epoch change operation to reintegrate itself into the quorum system. Since no process is failed, the new current voting structure resembles the master voting structure.

The master voting structure is actually a voting structure and hence complies to a specific static data replication scheme. Therefore, it determines and manifests at design-time (1) the maximal number n of processes manageable at run-time and (2) the homogeneous dynamic data replication scheme in terms of a single static data replication scheme's quorum system construction rules used to construct the quorum systems for all stages $1 \leq n' \leq n$ of the dynamics.

Next, the concept of *Voting Structure Generators* is presented. It is not a pure specification formalism but overcomes both these limitations.

Voting Structure Generators

Supporting an at design-time undetermined and at run-time variable and flexible number of processes requires the ability to dynamically generate (implicit) quorum system encodings for any number of processes at run-time. The concept of *Voting Structure Generators* [Storm, 2006; Storm and Theel, 2006] employs a number of explicitly stated voting structure construction algorithms that can generate voting structures for arbitrary numbers of processes at run-time, each for a specific data replication scheme whose inherent quorum system construction rules are embodied in the construction algorithm. Conceptually, an associative array as illustrated in Figure 3.3 relates a set of numbers of processes to a particular voting structure generator algorithm for which this algorithm generates voting structures. For numbers of processes to which no voting structure generator is explicitly associated, a *default voting structure generator* is specified to generate the voting structures. Whenever a quorum system switching is due, for example, because of a detected process failure, then the associative array is inspected for a voting structure generator that is associated with the number of processes in the new epoch, that is, in the new stage of the dynamics. If one is found, this voting structure generator is used to generate the quorum system in terms of a voting structure for the new epoch. If the array contains no such associated voting structure generator, then the default voting structure generator is chosen.

Homogeneous dynamic data replication schemes are specified, for example, by an empty associative array as illustrated in Figure 3.3 (a). The default Majority Consensus Voting voting structure generator is used for any number of processes, thereby specifying the homogeneous Dynamic Voting. Heterogeneous dynamic data replication schemes are realized, for example,

Number of Processes	Voting Structure Generator
∞	⊥
⋮	⊥
5	⊥
4	⊥
3	⊥
2	⊥
1	⊥
default	Majority Consensus Voting

(a)

Number of Processes	Voting Structure Generator
∞	⊥
⋮	⊥
5	⊥
4	Majority Consensus Voting
3	Majority Consensus Voting
2	⊥
1	⊥
default	Grid Protocol

(b)

Number of Processes	Voting Structure Generator
∞	⊥
⋮	⊥
5	⊥
4	Majority Consensus Voting
3	⊥
2	⊥
1	⊥
default	Void Generator

(c)

Number of Processes	Voting Structure Generator
∞	⊥
⋮	⊥
5	⊥
4	⊥
3	⊥
2	Void Generator
1	Void Generator
default	Majority Consensus Voting

(d)

Figure 3.3: Example Specifications of a Homogeneous Dynamic (a), a Heterogeneous Dynamic (b), a Static (c), and a Lower-Bounded Homogeneous Dynamic (d) Data Replication Scheme. No explicit Voting Structure Generator Association is denoted by ⊥

by specifying a default voting structure generator and stating distinct other voting structure generators for specific numbers of processes as illustrated in Figure 3.3 (b): Except for three and four processes being in the new epoch for which the Majority Consensus Voting voting structure generator is used, the default Grid Protocol voting structure generator is used for all (other) numbers of processes. Note that, for both specifications, the number of processes is not a priori bounded. To any number of processes, either an explicitly stated or the default voting structure generator is associated to generate the (implicit) quorum system encoding in terms of a voting structure at run-time.

A special *void voting structure generator* is used to restrict the dynamics and to support static data replication schemes. Conceptually, the void voting structure generator generates a voting structure that is identical to the one currently in use. Hence, a quorum system switching results in a transition from the current quorum system to the current quorum system, thereby effectively disabling the dynamics. For example, in Figure 3.3 (c), the static Majority Consensus Voting with four processes is specified by using the Majority Consensus Voting voting structure generator for four processes and the default void voting structure generator for all other numbers of processes. Assume that, initially, no process is failed such that the Majority Consensus Voting voting structure with four processes represents the current quorum system. Then, a process fails and its failure is detected during the course of an operation execution. The coordinator of the upcoming epoch change operation finds that the void voting structure generator is responsible for generating the new epoch's voting structure comprising the remaining three processes. Since the void voting structure generator would return the currently used Majority Consensus Voting voting structure with four processes, the coordinator may as well abort the epoch change operation. Hence, the default void voting structure generator prevents the transition to a new quorum system.

Apart from realizing support for static data replication schemes, the void voting structure generator can also be used to restrict the dynamics of dynamic data replication schemes. For example, Jajodia and Mutchler [1988] have proposed to limit the dynamics to numbers of processes exceeding two by using a combination of the static Majority Consensus Voting and a Dynamic Voting variant. Specifically, the latter is used for numbers of processes exceeding three and the former Majority Consensus Voting is used for exactly three processes while intentionally excluding quorum systems for one and two processes. As illustrated in Figure 3.3 (d), this specification can be realized by relating the void voting structure generator to numbers of processes matching one and two and otherwise using the default Majority Consensus Voting voting structure generator.

A verbatim implementation of the concept may result in the associative array relating numbers of processes to voting structure generators to grow indefinitely. Therefore, in an actual implementation as described in [Storm, 2006], the relation of voting structure generators to numbers of processes is realized by tagging voting structure generators: Each voting structure generator is tagged with a set of numbers of processes for which it is used to generate voting structures. Additionally, a voting structure generator can be associated with algorithmic expressions evaluating to a set of numbers of processes. Instead of looking up a voting structure generator in the associative array, the set of voting structure generators is searched for a voting structure generator that is tagged for a given number of processes. If none is found, then the default voting structure generator is used to construct the voting structure.

Summary of Related Work

The concept of Voting Structure Generators overcomes the limitations of Dynamic General Structured Voting which are (1) the restriction to homogeneous dynamic data replication schemes and (2) the restriction to an a priori determined upper bound on the number of processes manageable at run-time. However, its reliance on explicitly stated algorithms to construct the (implicit) quorum system encodings in terms of voting structures is a severe drawback of the concept: The algorithms must be actually implemented, one for each static data replication scheme intended to be used in a stage of the dynamics. Therefore, it is more an implementation rather than a specification approach.

Previous quorum system specification formalisms are either limited to static data replication schemes or are limited to homogeneous dynamic data replication schemes having a fixed upper bound on the number of processes manageable at run-time. Examples of the former are Multidimensional Voting [Ahamad, Ammar et al., 1990, 1991] and General Structured Voting [Theel, 1993a,b]. Dynamic General Structured Voting [Theel and Strauß, 1998] is an example of the latter. So far, there is no approach to the *specification* of data replication schemes that (1) supports static and dynamic, structured and unstructured, as well as homogeneous and heterogeneous data replication schemes and that (2) enables an arbitrary number of processes to be managed at run-time.

In the remainder of this chapter, a "meta quorum system specification formalism" called *voting structure shapes* is presented. Essentially, a voting structure shape is a specification formalism for a quorum system specification formalism, namely for *tree-shaped voting structures*. Tree-shaped voting structures are a quorum system specification formalism that is semantically equivalent to voting structures but based on simpler tree graphs. Each voting structure shape instance specifies a particular data replication scheme for an arbitrary number of processes, that is, a homogeneous dynamic data replication scheme without a maximal process number bound.

Analogously to Voting Structure Generators, heterogeneous dynamic data replication schemes are specified and implemented by relating different voting structure shapes to distinct numbers of processes. Static data replication schemes are supported as a special case.

In preparation to present voting structure shapes in Section 3.3, tree-shaped voting structures and their universality in expressing quorum systems are presented next.

3.2 Tree-Shaped Voting Structures

A *tree-shaped voting structure* is a tree graph whose leaf nodes represent real processes having replicas while its inner nodes serve grouping purposes. In the voting structure nomenclature, leaf nodes are physical nodes while inner nodes are virtual nodes. Like in voting structures, each node in a tree-shaped voting structure is equipped with a *vote* in terms of a natural number greater than zero, each node is assigned a *pair of minimal votes* to collect among its child nodes, and edges can be annotated with (non-default) *operation-specific priorities* to reflect a quorum probing ordering. In contrast to voting structures that are directed acyclic graphs, tree-shaped voting structures are tree graphs. The simpler graph structure of tree graphs allows the voting structure shape specification formalism for tree-shaped voting structures that is to be presented in Section 3.3 to remain simple. Besides, the fact of being tree graphs allows tree-shaped voting structures to be easily and automatically transformed into quorum system representations that are suited for the system model used for the analytical evaluation of data replication schemes as to be presented in Chapter 4.

Next, notations and definitions are introduced which are used to reason about graph structures in the remainder of this chapter. Based thereon, tree-shaped voting structures are defined.

Directed Graphs   A *directed graph* is a tuple (N, E) where $N \subset \mathcal{L}^*$ is the non-empty finite set of labeled nodes and $E \subseteq N \times \mathcal{L}^* \times N$ is the finite set of node-interconnecting labeled edges with $\mathcal{L}$ being a totally ordered non-empty set of labels and $\mathcal{L}^*$ being the set of all non-empty strings over labels in $\mathcal{L}$ that is also totally ordered. For any edge $e = (u, \ell, v) \in E$, the node u is the *source node* $\mathrm{src}(e) = u$, ℓ is the *label* $\mathrm{lab}(e) = \ell$, and the node v is the *destination node* $\mathrm{dst}(e) = v$ of the edge. Two edges $e_i, e_j \in E$ are equal (in the notation $e_i = e_j$), if their respective source nodes, destination nodes, and labels are equal. An edge $e_i \in E$ *prevails* another edge $e_j \in E$, denoted by $e_i \prec e_j$, if their source nodes are equal $(\text{src}(e_i) = \text{src}(e_j))$ and the label of e_i is less than the label of e_j $(\text{lab}(e_i) < \text{lab}(e_j))$, according to the total label ordering. A directed graph is *deterministically edge-labeled* if each node's leaving edges have distinct labels: $\forall e_i, e_j \in E$, $e_i \neq e_j$, $\text{src}(e_i) = \text{src}(e_j)$: $\text{lab}(e_i) \neq \text{lab}(e_j)$.

Henceforth, directed graphs are assumed to be deterministically edge-labeled if not explicitly stated otherwise.

Paths   An *edge sequence* is a possibly infinite list of edges $\langle e_1, e_2, \ldots \rangle$. For convenience, the first element of a non-empty edge sequence ρ is referenced to by $\text{head}(\rho)$ and – given that the edge sequence is finite – the last element is referenced to by $\text{tail}(\rho)$. The notions of $\text{src}()$, $\text{dst}()$, and $\text{lab}()$ as defined for edges in directed graphs are component-wise extended to edge sequences resulting in a possibly infinite sequence of source nodes, destination nodes, and edge labels, respectively. The *length* of an edge sequence ρ is defined as the number of its elements. It is denoted by $|\rho|$. Two edge sequences ρ_1 and ρ_2 are equal (in the notation $\rho_1 = \rho_2$), if both are of the same length and, if they are non-empty, any two elements of ρ_1 and ρ_2 are equal, that is, $\forall e_i \in \rho_1, \forall e_j \in \rho_2, i = j : e_i = (u, \ell, v) = e_j$.

The concatenation of edge sequences $\rho_1, \ldots, \rho_n$ (denoted by $\rho_1 \cdot \ldots \cdot \rho_n$) means the joining of these edge sequences in the order from ρ_1 to ρ_n, thereby forming a new edge sequence $\rho = \rho_1 \cdot \ldots \cdot \rho_n$. An edge sequence ρ is termed a *path* if the destination node of each edge in ρ is the source node of its following edge in ρ, formally $\forall e_i, e_{i+1} \in \rho : \text{src}(e_{i+1}) = \text{dst}(e_i)$. Paths are *properly connected* in contrast to edge sequences that must not necessarily be properly connected.

A path α is a *path prefix* of a path ρ if there exists a path β such that their concatenation $\alpha \cdot \beta$ is path $\rho = \alpha \cdot \beta$. Analogously, a path β is a *path suffix* of a path ρ if there exists a path α such that their concatenation $\alpha \cdot \beta$ is path $\rho = \alpha \cdot \beta$. For example, consider path $\rho = \langle e_1, e_3 \rangle$ in Figure 3.4 (a) connecting node B to node B and this node to node C. The paths $\alpha_1 = \langle e_1 \rangle$ and $\alpha_2 = \langle e_1, e_3 \rangle$ are path prefixes of path ρ and the paths $\beta_1 = \langle e_3 \rangle$ and $\beta_2 = \langle e_1, e_3 \rangle$ are path suffixes of path ρ.

Root and Leaf Nodes   The root and leaf nodes of a directed graph are defined via the notions of *prefix-maximal* and *suffix-maximal* paths as follows. A non-empty path ρ is *prefix-maximal* if for any non-empty path

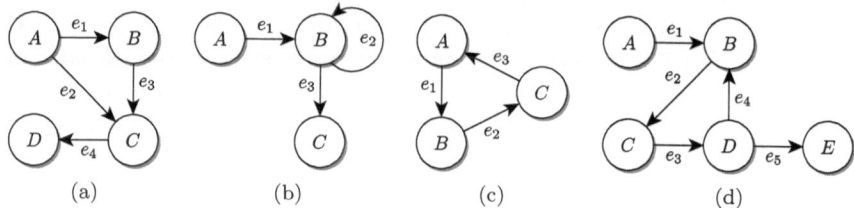

Figure 3.4: Illustration of Directed Graph Structures

prefix α of ρ there exists no non-empty path α' such that their concatenation $\alpha' \cdot \alpha$ is a path. In other words, for any non-empty path prefix α of a prefix-maximal path ρ, there exists no edge $e_i \in E$ with $\mathrm{dst}(e_i) = \mathrm{src}(\mathrm{head}(\alpha))$ such that $\mathrm{head}(\alpha)$ is a properly connected following edge of edge e_i. In a prefix-maximal path ρ, the node $\mathrm{src}(\mathrm{head}(\rho))$ has no incoming edges and is termed a *root node*. The set of all root nodes is for convenience referenced to by $N_{\mathrm{Root}} \subseteq N$. For example, the paths $\rho_1 = \langle e_3, e_4 \rangle$, $\rho_2 = \langle e_3 \rangle$, and $\rho_3 = \langle e_4 \rangle$ in Figure 3.4 (a) are not prefix-maximal since the edge e_3 is a subsequent edge of e_1 and the edge e_4 is a subsequent edge of e_2 and e_3. However, paths having a path prefix of $\langle e_1 \rangle$ or $\langle e_2 \rangle$ are prefix-maximal. As a second example, consider Figure 3.4 (b) in which only paths with the path prefix $\langle e_1 \rangle$ are prefix-maximal. For paths having the path prefix $\langle e_2 \rangle$, there exists a path α' being either $\langle e_1 \rangle$ or (repeatedly) $\langle e_2 \rangle$ itself such that the path is not prefix-maximal. Alike, paths having the path prefix $\langle e_3 \rangle$ are not prefix-maximal.

A non-empty path ρ is *suffix-maximal* if for any non-empty path suffix β of ρ there exists no non-empty path β' such that their concatenation $\beta \cdot \beta'$ is a path. In particular, for a path suffix β of a suffix-maximal path ρ there exists no edge $e_j \in E$ with $\mathrm{src}(e_j) = \mathrm{dst}(\mathrm{tail}(\beta))$ such that the edge e_j is a properly connected following edge of $\mathrm{tail}(\beta)$. The node $\mathrm{dst}(\mathrm{tail}(\rho))$ of a suffix-maximal path ρ has no leaving edges and is termed a *leaf node*. The set of all leaf nodes is referenced to by $N_{\mathrm{Leaf}} \subseteq N$. For example, in Figure 3.4 (a), all paths with the path suffix $\langle e_4 \rangle$ are suffix-maximal. In Figure 3.4 (b), only paths with the path suffix $\langle e_3 \rangle$ are suffix-maximal. The path $\rho_1 = \langle e_1, e_2 \rangle$ is not suffix-maximal and neither is a path $\rho_2 = \langle e_1, e_2, \ldots \rangle$ indefinitely repeating e_2. However, a path $\rho_3 = \langle e_1, e_2, \ldots, e_3 \rangle$ is suffix-maximal.

A path ρ is *maximal* if it is prefix-maximal and suffix-maximal. For example, the paths $\rho_1 = \langle e_1, e_3, e_4 \rangle$ and $\rho_2 = \langle e_2, e_4 \rangle$ in Figure 3.4 (a) are maximal as they are suffix-maximal and prefix-maximal. In Figure 3.4 (b), a path $\rho = \langle e_1, e_2, \ldots, e_3 \rangle$ is maximal.

Cyclic and Acyclic Directed Graphs   A maximal path $\rho = \alpha \cdot \sigma \cdot \beta$ is *cyclic* if the path $\rho' = \alpha \cdot \beta$ is maximal for some non-empty paths α and β and some non-empty path σ. Intuitively, this means that albeit not traversing the edges of σ, the node $\mathrm{dst}(\mathrm{tail}(\beta))$ is reached by a traversal of the path's edges starting from $\mathrm{src}(\mathrm{head}(\alpha))$, and this with traversing fewer edges. For example, in Figure 3.4 (b), the maximal path $\rho = \alpha \cdot \sigma \cdot \beta$ with $\alpha = \langle e_1 \rangle$, $\sigma = \langle e_2 \rangle$, and $\beta = \langle e_3 \rangle$ is cyclic since the path $\rho' = \alpha \cdot \beta$ is maximal. In Figure 3.4 (c), no path is maximal since none is suffix- and prefix-maximal. In Figure 3.4 (d), the maximal path $\rho = \alpha \cdot \sigma \cdot \beta$ with $\alpha = \langle e_1 \rangle$, $\sigma = \langle e_2, e_3, e_4 \rangle$, and $\beta = \langle e_2, e_3, e_5 \rangle$ is cyclic since the path $\rho' = \alpha \cdot \beta$ is maximal.

A directed graph is *acyclic* if it has maximal paths and for every path ρ there are only path prefixes α and path suffixes β extending ρ to a maximal path $\rho' = \alpha \cdot \rho \cdot \beta$ that is not cyclic.

It is henceforth assumed for directed acyclic graphs to have a single dedicated root node, that is, $|\mathrm{N}_{\mathrm{Root}}| = 1$, albeit the definition allows for multiple root nodes. As a consequence, directed acyclic graphs are assumed to be *strictly connected*: There is only one node without incoming edges, namely the single dedicated root node. Thereby, unconnected nodes in directed acyclic graphs are prohibited.

A directed acyclic graph is a (directed) *tree graph* if each node has exactly one incoming edge with the only exception being the single dedicated root node having none.

Based on these graph-structural definitions, tree-shaped voting structures are formally introduced next.

Tree-Shaped Voting Structure Definition

Tree-shaped voting structures as illustrated in Figure 3.5 on page 101 for the Tree Quorum Protocol, Majority Consensus Voting, and the optimized Grid Protocol are defined as follows:

Definition 3.1 (Tree-Shaped Voting Structure)   A tree-shaped voting structure is a tree graph associated with a vote, quorum, edge priority, and process mapping function $\mathrm{tsVS} = (\mathrm{N}, \mathrm{E}, s, q, o, m)$ where $\mathrm{N} \subset \mathcal{L}^*$ is the non-empty finite set of labeled nodes with $\mathcal{L}$ being a totally ordered non-empty set of labels and $\mathcal{L}^*$ being the set of all non-empty strings over labels in $\mathcal{L}$ that is also totally ordered,

$E \subseteq N \times \mathcal{L}^* \times N$ is the finite set of node-interconnecting labeled edges,

$s : N \to N$ is the vote function defining the vote of a node,

$q : N \to N_0 \times N_0$ is the quorum function defining the operation-specific minimal number of votes to collect among a node's child nodes in order to form a read or write quorum with the quorum function evaluating to $(0,0)$ for leaf nodes,

$o : E \to N \times N$ is the edge priority function that defines the operation-specific quorum probing ordering (with lower numbers representing higher priorities and the symbol ∞ denoting the lowest and default priority), and

$m : N_{\text{Leaf}} \to P$ is the process mapping function assigning leaf nodes to processes.

The former three functions are defined as for voting structures supporting two types of operations. The latter process mapping function restricts the process-representing nodes of a tree-shaped voting structure to its leaf nodes and maps the leaf nodes to processes. For convenience, the read operation-specific value of the quorum function for some node $u \in N$ is henceforth referenced to by $q_R(u)$ and the write operation-specific value is referenced to by $q_W(u)$. Furthermore, if understood from the context, the process mapping function assignment is not stated explicitly and edge labels are omitted.

Next, three examples of tree-shaped voting structures are presented to illustrate the definition.

Example: The Tree Quorum Protocol As a first example of a tree-shaped voting structure, consider the tree-shaped voting structure in Figure 3.5 (a) that specifies the Tree Quorum Protocol managing four processes. Except for edge labels, it is identical to the (tree graph) voting structure shown in Figure 3.2 (a) and it is constructed following the same construction rules. The set of nodes is $N = \{V_1, V_2, p_1, p_2, p_3, p_4\}$ of which the set of root nodes is $N_{\text{Root}} = \{V_1\} \subset N$ and the set of leaf nodes is $N_{\text{Leaf}} = \{p_1, p_2, p_3, p_4\} \subset N$. The set of edges is $E = \{(V_1, a, p_1), (V_1, b, V_2), (V_2, a, p_2), (V_2, b, p_3), (V_2, c, p_4)\}$. The vote function assigns each node a vote of 1 and is $s = \{(V_1, 1), (V_2, 1), (p_1, 1), (p_2, 1), (p_3, 1), (p_4, 1)\}$, or in a suggestive short notation $s(N) = 1 \equiv \forall n \in N : s(n) = 1$. The quorum function is $q = \{(V_1, (1,2)), (V_2, (2,2)), (p_1, (0,0)), (p_2, (0,0)), (p_3, (0,0)), (p_4, (0,0))\}$. The edge priority function is $o = \{((V_1, a, p_1), (1, \infty)), ((V_1, b, V_2), (2, \infty)),$

$((V_2, a, p_2), (\infty, \infty)), ((V_2, b, p_3), (\infty, \infty)), ((V_2, c, p_4), (\infty, \infty)) \}$. In order to match the quorum system expressed by the voting structure of Figure 3.2 (a), the process mapping function is set to $m = \{(p_1, p_1), (p_2, p_2),$ $(p_3, p_3), (p_4, p_4)\}$. In the underlying logical tree structure imposed on the set of processes by the Tree Quorum Protocol, the process p_1 is the root node and the processes p_2, p_3, and p_4 are its three child nodes.

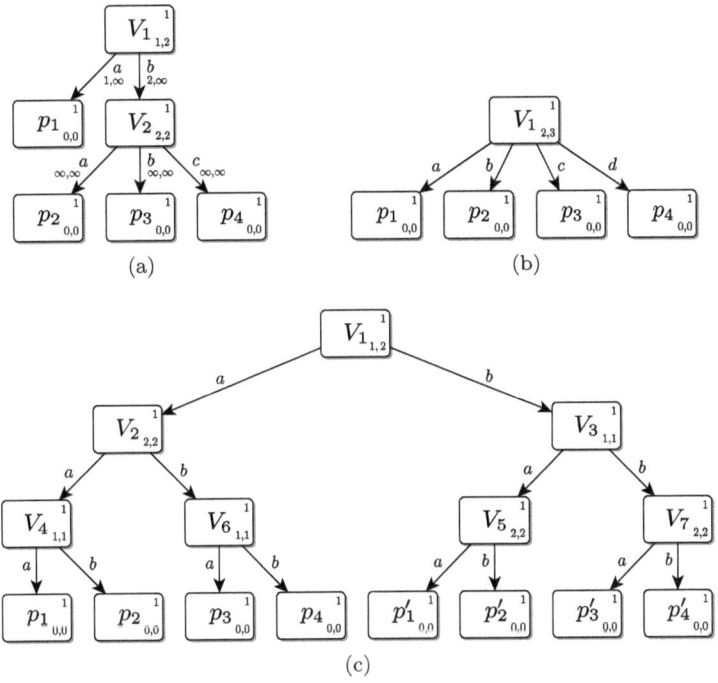

Figure 3.5: Tree Shaped Voting Structures with Four Processes each for the Tree Quorum Protocol (a), Majority Consensus Voting (b), and the Optimized Grid Protocol (c)

Example: Majority Consensus Voting   As a second example, consider the tree-shaped voting structure in Figure 3.5 (b) that specifies Majority Consensus Voting with four processes. Like for the former example, the Majority Consensus Voting tree-shaped voting structure is identical to the voting structure shown in Figure 3.2 (c) except for edge labels and it is constructed following the same construction rules. With the process mapping function set to $m = \{(p_1, p_1), (p_2, p_2), (p_3, p_3), (p_4, p_4)\}$, the quorum system expressed by this tree-shaped voting structure resembles that of the voting structure in Figure 3.2 (c). The edge priority function value is (∞, ∞) for each edge and is not shown in the figure as it is the default value.

Example: The Optimized Grid Protocol   The third example tree-shaped voting structure shown in Figure 3.5 (c) specifies the optimized Grid Protocol with four processes arranged in a logical rectangular 2×2 grid. Like for the Majority Consensus Voting example tree-shaped voting structure, the edge priority function evaluates to the default value (∞, ∞) for each edge and is therefore not shown in the figure. Unlike the previous two examples, the voting structure counterpart shown in Figure 3.2 (b) is a directed acyclic graph in which inner (virtual) nodes modeling the C-Cover and inner (virtual) nodes modeling the CC-Cover lead to the same (physical) leaf nodes. Since a tree-shaped voting structure cannot have nodes with multiple incoming edges, the C-Cover and the CC-Cover are modeled as separate subtrees of the root node as visibly exposed in Figure 3.5 (c): The C-Cover is modeled by the left subgraph of the root node and the CC-Cover is modeled by the right subgraph. Also unlike the previous two examples and as a result of tree-shaped voting structures being tree graphs, the mapping of leaf nodes to processes is not bijective since a process is referenced to by a leaf node in the C-Cover subgraph as well as by a leaf node in the CC-Cover subgraph. With the process mapping function set to $m = \{(p_1, p_1), (p_1', p_1),$ $(p_2, p_2), (p_2', p_2), (p_3, p_3), (p_3', p_3), (p_4, p_4) (p_4', p_4)\}$, the tree-shaped voting structure in Figure 3.5 (c) specifies the same quorum system as the voting structure in Figure 3.2 (b).

Interpretation of Tree-Shaped Voting Structures

The algorithm to derive quorums from a voting structure as presented in Section 3.1 can be applied to tree-shaped voting structures when (1) identifying leaf nodes with physical nodes and inner nodes with virtual nodes and (2) applying the process mapping function to some particular physical nodes in order to translate them into a quorum of processes, in case of a successful quorum building. For the sake of completeness, the algorithm to derive a quorum from a voting structure adapted to respect these specifics of tree-shaped voting structures is as follows.

Starting with the root node, each node queries as many of its child nodes for their votes as needed to satisfy its minimal vote requirement for the read (write) operation while obeying the query ordering specified via edge priorities. A queried non-leaf node casts its vote if the sum of votes casted by its queried child nodes satisfies this node's minimal operation-specific vote requirement. A queried leaf node casts its vote if its associated process has not failed and it has not casted its vote for a concurrent competitive operation. If a queried node does not cast its vote, then the querying node chooses an alternative and not yet queried child node to query for its vote, again respecting the query ordering specified via edge priorities. If there are no alternative nodes left to query and the querying node's minimal operation-specific vote requirement cannot be satisfied, then it does not cast its vote to its father node. Eventually, the root node either has received sufficiently many votes and grants permission to execute the read (write) operation or must refuse to do so. In the latter case, no quorum can be found and the operation is not available. In the former case, the read (write) operation is executed with a quorum of processes corresponding to those process mapping function-mapped leaf nodes that have casted their votes and for which their respective father nodes – if any – have also casted their votes.

Next, the universality of tree-shaped voting structures in expressing quorum systems is discussed by a transformation between tree-shaped voting structures and voting structures for which universality has been shown [Theel, 1993a,b].

3.2.1 Universality of Tree-Shaped Voting Structures

Any directed acyclic graph with a single root node can be transformed into a tree graph via unfolding in terms of the duplication of those subgraphs whose root nodes have more than one incoming edge. Consequently, any voting structure – as being a directed acyclic graph – can be transformed into a semantically equivalent tree-shaped voting structure. The reverse direction is realized via repeatedly replacing multiple leaf nodes being mapped to the same process by a single one that is mapped to this particular process and redirecting the corresponding edges to this leaf node. This simple transformation is not further elaborated on and only the transformation from voting structures to tree-shaped voting structures is shown in the following. The universality of voting structures in expressing quorum systems has been shown by Theel [1993a,b] and, by the transformations, it also applies to tree-shaped voting structures.

As an illustrating example, consider the voting structure in Figure 3.6 (a) which has also been shown in Figure 3.2 (b). It specifies the quorum system complying to the optimized Grid Protocol with four processes in which the processes p_1, p_2 and p_3, p_4 each form a column of the logical rectangular 2×2 grid. This voting structure's unfolded counterpart – which visibly exposes the C-Cover in the left subgraph of the root node and the CC-Cover in the right subgraph of the root node – is shown in Figure 3.6 (b) and has also already been shown in Figure 3.5 (c). Each leaf node label identifies the process the leaf node is mapped to. Multiple leaf nodes mapping to the same process are distinguished by prime-affixed node labels in Figure 3.6 (b). The

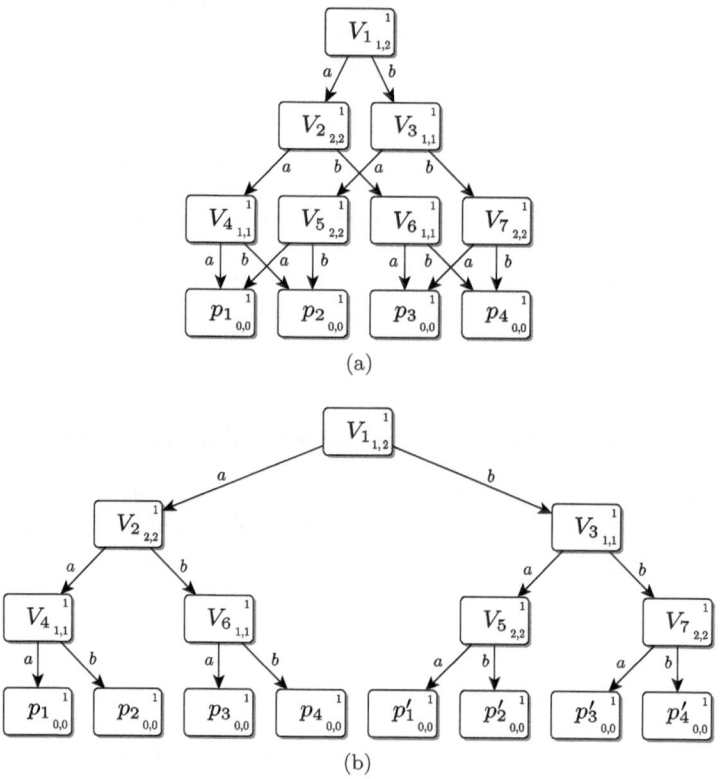

Figure 3.6: Voting Structure of Theel [1993a] (a) and Corresponding Tree-Shaped Voting Structure (b) for the Optimized Grid Protocol with Four Processes

subgraphs in Figure 3.6 (a) whose root nodes have more than one incoming edge, that is, the subgraphs consisting of the single (leaf) nodes p_1, p_2, p_3, and p_4, are duplicated by the following procedure for the duplication of a subgraph.

Recall that directed graphs and hence voting structures are assumed to be deterministically edge-labeled. Note that the universality of voting structures in expressing quorum systems is not affected by a deterministic edge labeling. In preparation to the transformation of a voting structure into a tree-shaped voting structure, the *one-time* duplication of a subgraph whose root node $u \in N$ has more than one incoming edge is done in five steps as follows.

STEP 1 (DUPLICATING THE SUBGRAPH ROOT NODE)
The subgraph's root node $u \in N$ is duplicated by joining a node u' with the set of nodes and assigning u' the quorum function value and vote function value as assigned to its original node u. If u' is a leaf node, then the process mapping function is adapted to map u' to the same process as the original node u.

STEP 2 (CONNECTING THE DUPLICATED SUBGRAPH ROOT NODE)
For an arbitrarily chosen edge $e \in E$ leading to the subgraph's root node u, a substitute edge e' having the destination node u' and the same source node, label, and edge priority as the edge e is joined with the set of edges. Then, the edge e is removed from the set of edges.

STEP 3 (DUPLICATING THE SUBGRAPH NODES)
For each node $v \in N$ in the subgraph of u that is reachable by a non-empty path from the subgraph root node, a duplicate node v' is joined with the set of nodes. The duplicate node v' is assigned the quorum function value and vote function value as assigned to its original node v. If v' is a leaf node, then the process mapping function is adapted to map v' to the same process as the original node v.

STEP 4 (CONNECTING THE DUPLICATED SUBGRAPH NODES)
For each edge $e \in E$ connecting two nodes in the subgraph of u, a duplicate edge e' whose source (destination) node is the duplicate node of the original edge's source (destination) node is joined with the set of edges. The duplicate edge e' is assigned the same label and edge priority as the original edge e.

STEP 5 (CONNECTING WITH NON-SUBGRAPH NODES)
For each edge $e \in E$ whose source node is not in the subgraph of u while its destination node is in the subgraph but not the subgraph root node

u, an edge e' with the same source node but with the destination node being the original edge's duplicated destination node is joined with the set of edges. The duplicate edge e' is assigned the same edge priority as the original edge e but it is uniquely labeled to preserve the deterministic edge labeling.

Note that the interconnection of duplicated subgraph nodes in Step 4 maintains the deterministic edge labeling. The unique edge label required in Step 5 is found by choosing a random element from $\mathcal{L}^*$ (the non-empty totally ordered set of all non-empty strings over labels in $\mathcal{L}$) reduced by the label set of this edge's adjacent edges, if any. The node duplication in Step 1 and Step 3 implicitly assumes a duplicated node to have a unique identity. This assumption can be realized in a deterministic manner by selecting the first element from $\mathcal{L}^*$ reduced by the set of nodes N. However, for convenience, a tree-shaped voting structure's nodes and edges are labeled more expressively here.

Based on the procedure for the one-time duplication of a subgraph, a voting structure is transformed into a tree-shaped voting structure as follows. Starting with the root node and in an ordering established by the prevails-relation of edges, the voting structure is traversed until either a node $u \in N$ with more than one incoming edge is reached or it is revealed that the voting structure is already a tree graph. In the former case, the subgraph starting with the root node u is duplicated as many times as u has more than one incoming edge. Thereafter, only one incoming edge to the node u is left and the traversal is repeated. Eventually, no node having more than one incoming edge is left and each node – with the sole exception of the root node – has exactly one incoming edge.

Next, two examples illustrate the steps to transform a voting structure into its tree-shaped voting structure counterpart.

Example: The Optimized Grid Protocol Reconsider the voting structure and its tree-shaped voting structure counterpart shown in Figure 3.6. The first voting structure traversal iteration finds via the path $\rho_1 = \langle a, a, a \rangle$ a leaf node p_1 that maps to process p_1. This node has two incoming edges, an edge a from its preceding node V_4 and an edge a from its other preceding node V_5 that is the path suffix of the path $\rho_2 = \langle b, a, a \rangle$. The subgraph starting with the root node p_1 – which is coincidentally the only node in the subgraph – is duplicated once as the subgraph root node p_1 has two incoming edges. In Step 1, the subgraph root node p_1 is duplicated to p'_1.

This duplicate subgraph root node is assigned the same quorum function value and vote function value as the original subgraph root node. Since the duplicated subgraph root node is a leaf node, the process mapping function is adapted to map it to the same process as the original node, namely to process p_1. In Step 2, the edge connecting the node V_5 to the original subgraph root node p_1 is substituted by an edge connecting V_5 to the duplicate subgraph root node p_1'. The default edge priority is assigned to this new edge as for the original edge. The Steps 3, 4, and 5 are not applicable to the subgraph starting with the root node p_1. In fact, the Steps 3 and 4 are not applicable to any to be duplicated subgraph in this example as each subgraph root node with more than one incoming edge is a leaf node (and thus has no child nodes to which Steps 3 and 4 can be applied) and Step 5 is not applicable to a subgraph root node. After having processed the entire voting structure, the tree-shaped voting structure as shown in Figure 3.6 (b) results.

Example: The Read One Write All Protocol As a more elaborated example, consider the voting structure in Figure 3.7 (a). It specifies the Read One Write All Protocol for two processes p_1 and p_2 in an intentionally complicated and obfuscated manner to illustrate the Steps 3, 4, and 5 of the subgraph duplication algorithm. This voting structure's transformed tree-shaped voting structure counterpart is illustrated in Figure 3.7 (c). Like in the above example, multiple leaf nodes mapping to the same process are distinguished by prime-affixed labels. Alike, the labels of duplicated inner nodes are prime-affixed to visually indicate duplicated inner nodes.

The first voting structure traversal leads to the inner node V_5 that has two incoming edges, one from V_2 via the path $\rho_1 = \langle a, a \rangle$ and one from V_3 via the path $\rho_2 = \langle b, a \rangle$. In Step 1, the subgraph root node V_5 is duplicated to V_5'. The duplicate subgraph root node is assigned the same quorum function value and vote function value as the original subgraph root node. The process mapping function needs not to be adapted since V_5 is not a leaf node. In Step 2, the edge connecting the node V_3 to the original subgraph root node V_5 is substituted by an edge connecting V_3 to the duplicate subgraph root node V_5'. The default edge priority is assigned to this new edge as for its original edge. In Step 3, the subgraph of V_5 consisting of the nodes V_6, V_7, p_1, and p_2 is duplicated. The duplicate nodes are labeled as their original nodes but affixed with a prime. Each node retains the quorum function and vote function value as its original node. The process mapping function is adapted to map the duplicate leaf nodes p_1' and p_2' to the processes p_1 and p_2,

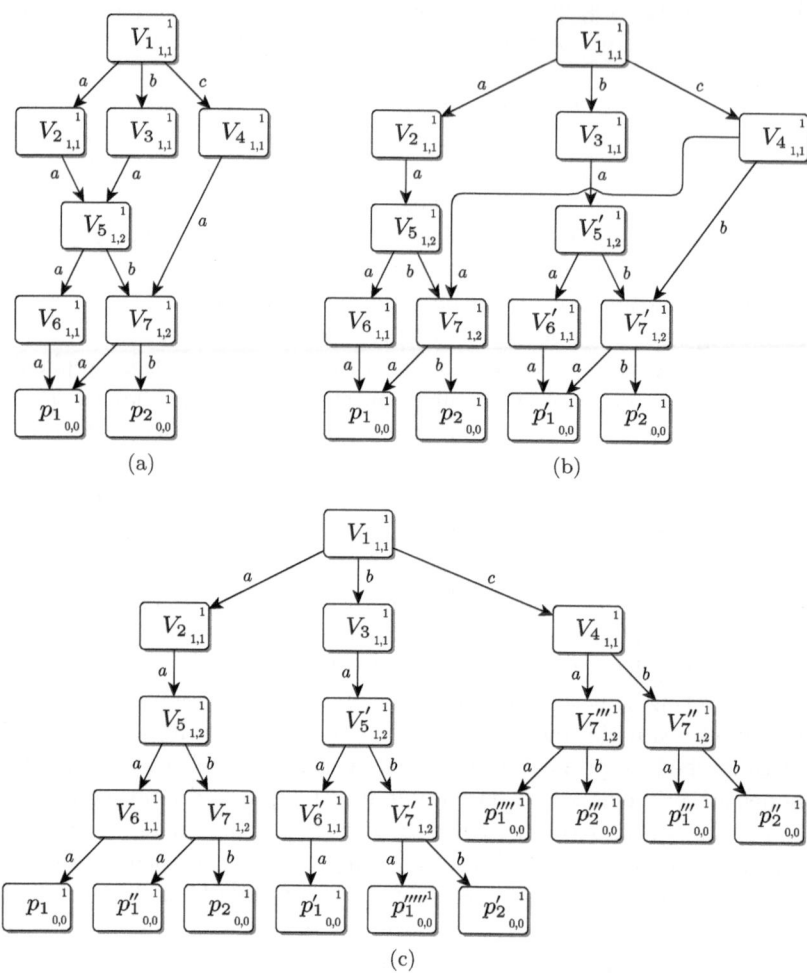

Figure 3.7: A Voting Structure for the Read One Write All Protocol with Two
Processes (a), the Voting Structure after the First Subgraph Duplication (b), and the Final Tree-Shaped Voting Structure (c)

respectively. In Step 4, the duplicated subgraph nodes are interconnected
by edges, each having the same label and edge priority as its original edge.
In Step 5, the edge connecting V_4 and V_7 is identified to have a source
node V_4 that is not in the subgraph while its destination node V_7 is in the

subgraph. For this edge, a new edge connecting V_4 to the duplicate node V_7' is created. This new edge is assigned the same edge priority as its original edge connecting V_4 and V_7 and is labeled b to preserve the deterministic edge labeling. The voting structure resulting from this first subgraph duplication is shown in Figure 3.7 (b). The final tree-shaped voting structure after having processed all nodes with more than one incoming edge is shown in Figure 3.7 (c).

Essentially, a tree-shaped voting structure can be seen as a voting structure transformed from a directed acyclic graph into a tree graph. Like a voting structure, a tree-shaped voting structure is also limited to represent the quorum system for a particular set of processes only. Next, *voting structure shapes* are introduced that are – conceptually speaking – construction directives for tree-shaped voting structures by the means of tree-shaped voting structure-composition steered by composition graphs, the so-called voting structure shapes. This way, tree-shaped voting structures for arbitrary numbers of processes can be constructed, allowing homogeneous dynamic data replication schemes to overcome the restriction of having a static upper bound on the number of processes manageable at run-time.

3.3 Specification of Tree-Shaped Voting Structures

A tree-shaped voting structure represents the quorum system complying to a specific static data replication scheme for a particular subset of the set of processes as determined by the process mapping function mapping leaf nodes to processes. However, by varying the leaf-node-to-process-mapping, a tree-shaped voting structure is capable of expressing the quorum system for all subsets of the set of processes having a particular common cardinality. For example, the tree-shaped voting structure in Figure 3.7 (c) specifies the quorum system for the two processes p_1 and p_2 according to the Read One Write All Protocol. By changing the process mapping function, for example, by mapping the leaf node p_1 and its duplicates to a process p_3 and mapping the leaf node p_2 and its duplicates to a process p_4, the tree-shaped voting structure specifies the quorum system for the two processes p_3 and p_4 instead of for the two processes p_1 and p_2. Hence, this tree-shaped voting structure can specify quorum systems complying to the Read One Write All Protocol for all subsets of the set of processes having a cardinality of two.

Regardless of the concrete subset of processes for which a particular tree-shaped voting structure is constructed, the scheme-specific quorum system construction rules are manifested in each tree-shaped voting structure complying to the same static data replication scheme. For example, the root node of a tree-shaped voting structure specifying the quorum system complying to the optimized Grid Protocol – as shown for four processes in Figure 3.6 (b) – always has two child nodes, one being the root node of the subgraph modeling the C-Cover and one being the root node of the subgraph modeling the CC-Cover. Both of these subgraph root nodes have a number of child nodes corresponding to the number of columns in the logical rectangular grid structure. Each of those child nodes has in turn a number of child (leaf) nodes corresponding to the number of processes in the respective column of the logical grid. Thus, graph-structural resemblances among tree-shaped voting structures complying to the same static data replication scheme but for different cardinality subsets of processes can be discerned. These resemblances are the graph-structural manifestation of the scheme-specific quorum system construction rules.

The underlying idea of voting structure shapes is to (1) identify the elementary graph building blocks of tree-shaped voting structures complying to a particular static data replication scheme and to (2) translate the graph-structural resemblances into composition rules for these graph building blocks. The following four examples considering the Tree Quorum Protocol, the optimized Grid Protocol, the Triangular Lattice Protocol, and Majority Consensus Voting illustrate the identification of elementary graph building blocks and their composition rules.

Example: The Tree Quorum Protocol   As a first example, consider the (Generalized) Tree Quorum Protocol that imposes a logical tree structure on the set of processes as shown in Figure 3.8 for nine processes. This logical tree structure is depicted in terms of a tree-shaped voting structure in Figure 3.9.

For the read operation, the root node p_1 of the logical tree structure is required or, in case it has failed, a simple majority of its child nodes p_2 and p_3 is required. In this example, either node is sufficient since the write operation requires both nodes and thereby guarantees the mutual exclusion of read and write operations. This semantics is resembled in the tree-shaped voting structure by the nodes p_1 and V_2 each having one vote (whereby each of them satisfies the root node's quorum function value for the read operation), the node p_1 having a higher incoming edge's priority for the read

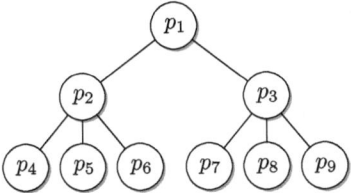

Figure 3.8: Logical Processes Layout of the Generalized Tree Quorum Protocol with Nine Processes

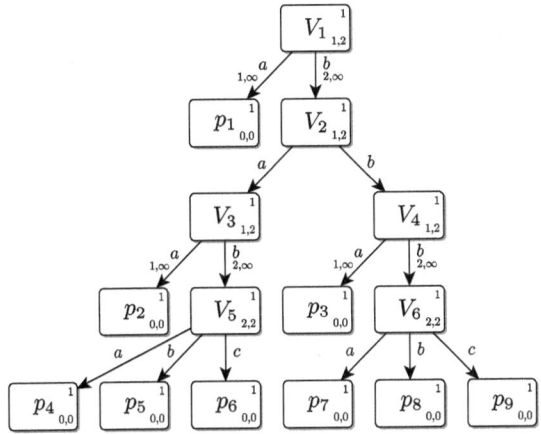

Figure 3.9: Corresponding Tree-Shaped Voting Structure to the Logical Processes Layout of the Generalized Tree Quorum Protocol with Nine Processes of Figure 3.8

operation, and V_2 requiring a simple majority of its child nodes V_3 and V_4.

The write operation requires the root node p_1 and a proper majority of its child nodes in the logical tree structure, that is, both nodes p_2 and p_3. This is reflected in the tree-shaped voting structure by the root node V_1 requiring the votes of both nodes p_1 and V_2 and the node V_2 requiring a proper majority being both of its child nodes V_3 and V_4 for the write operation.

The subgraph in the tree-shaped voting structure formed by the nodes V_1, p_1, and V_2 with their interconnecting edges (V_1, a, p_1) and (V_1, b, V_2) expresses the semantics of the logical tree structure's root node: A read (write) operation requires the logical tree structure's root node process represented by the subgraph's leaf node p_1 or (and) a majority of its child nodes represented by V_2 having a quorum function value resembling the simple (proper) majority of its child nodes.

The subgraphs formed by the nodes V_3, p_2, V_5 and V_4, p_3, V_6 with their respective interconnecting edges express the semantics of the logical tree structure's nodes p_2 and p_3, respectively. Note that this semantics is identical to that of the logical tree structure's root node.

Because leaf nodes have no child nodes, they are treated differently from inner nodes of the logical tree structure. If a leaf node is reached while traversing the logical tree structure for forming an operation-specific quorum, then the recursive traversal is aborted. Hence, leaf nodes in the logical tree structure directly translate to leaf nodes in the tree-shaped voting structure.

Subsuming these observations, there are two types of subgraphs in tree-shaped voting structures expressing quorum systems complying to the Tree Quorum Protocol, namely one resembling the semantics of the root node and another one resembling the semantics of a leaf node in the logical tree structure. Exploiting this observation, a logical tree structure can be transformed into its tree-shaped voting structure counterpart by substituting its nodes with the respective semantics-resembling subgraphs and assigning the subgraph interconnection nodes a quorum function value resembling the majority of its child subgraphs for both, the read and the write operation. Essentially, the construction of tree-shaped voting structures complying to the Tree Quorum Protocol is by (1) recursively attaching and properly interconnecting subgraphs resembling the semantics of the logical tree structure's root node until an abort condition in terms of the number of inner nodes in the logical tree structure is met and then (2) attaching subgraphs resembling the semantics of a logical tree structure's leaf node to each leaf subgraph of the tree-shaped voting structure, followed by (3) mapping leaf nodes to processes.

Example: The Optimized Grid Protocol   As a second example, consider the logical grid layout of the 2×2 optimized Grid Protocol in Figure 3.10 with four processes p_1, p_2, p_3, and p_4 – the former two and the latter two forming a column in the logical rectangular grid – and the corresponding tree-shaped voting structure in Figure 3.11. The root node's two child nodes V_2 and V_3 represent the C-Cover in the left subgraph and the CC-Cover in the right subgraph, respectively. The number of their respective child nodes matches the number of columns in the logical rectangular

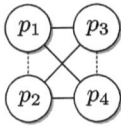

Figure 3.10: Logical Processes Layout of the Optimized 2×2 Grid Protocol with Four Processes

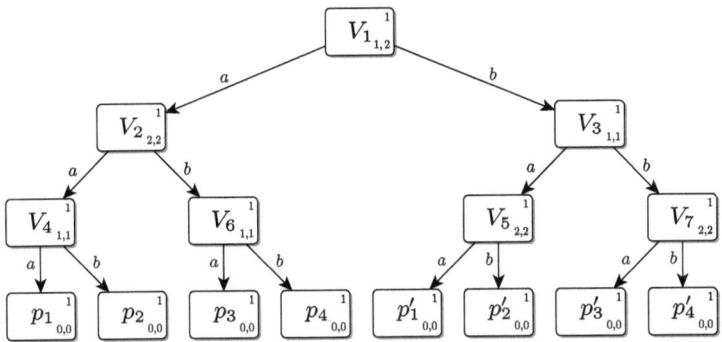

Figure 3.11: Corresponding Tree-Shaped Voting Structure to the Logical Processes Layout of the Optimized 2×2 Grid Protocol with Four Processes of Figure 3.10

grid. In this case, for the 2×2 Grid Protocol, there are two nodes V_4 and V_6 attached to V_2 and two nodes V_5 and V_7 are attached to V_3. In general, for a $k \times j$ logical rectangular grid with $(k-1) \cdot j \leq n \leq k \cdot j$ processes – where k is the number of columns and j is the number of rows – there are k child nodes representing the number of columns in the logical grid attached to both nodes V_2 and V_3. The number of rows j in the logical rectangular grid is equal to the highest number of leaf nodes attached to one of the column-representing nodes. In this example, the grid is fully populated by processes such that each one of the column-representing nodes V_4, V_6, V_5, and V_7 has two leaf child nodes as there are two fully populated rows of processes in the logical rectangular grid in Figure 3.10. Because of the twofoldedness stemming from the two subgraphs expressing the C-Cover and the CC-Cover, two leaf nodes are mapped to a single process, namely one leaf node in the C-Cover and one leaf node in the CC-Cover. Here, the nodes p_1 and p_1' are mapped to process p_1, the nodes p_2 and p_2' are mapped to process p_2, the nodes p_3 and p_3' are mapped to process p_3, and the nodes p_4 and p_4' are mapped to process p_4.

Example: The Triangular Lattice Protocol   As a third example, consider the logical processes layout of the 3×2 Triangular Lattice Protocol in Figure 3.12 with six processes p_1, p_2, p_3, p_4, p_5, and p_6 – the former two, the intermediate two, and the latter two each forming a column in the lattice – and the corresponding tree-shaped voting structure in Figure 3.13.   For convenience, edge labels are omitted and leaf nodes map to correspondingly labeled processes (with a prime-affixed leaf node label indicating a different node identity but the same process mapping as its non-primed relative).

The root node of a tree-shaped voting structure complying to the Triangular Lattice Protocol always has two child nodes, one representing vertical crossings (V-Cover) and the other one representing horizontal crossings (H-Cover). The root node has a quorum function value of 1 for the read operation and a value of 2 for the write operation, that is, either a H-Cover or a V-Cover is required for forming read quorums while both are required for forming write quorums. The root node's child node V_2 represents the V-Cover and V_3 the H-Cover. To both of the nodes V_2 and V_3, a number of nodes is attached that matches the number of processes in the topmost row and the leftmost column of the logical lattice structure, respectively. Recall that a H-Cover is a horizontal path from the leftmost column to the rightmost column of the lattice and a V-Cover is a vertical path from the topmost row to the bottommost row. In this example, the three nodes V_4, V_5, and V_6 according to the three columns of the lattice are child nodes of V_2 and the two nodes V_7 and V_8 according to the two rows of the lattice are child nodes of V_3. Each of these nodes V_4, V_5, V_6, V_7, and V_8 is the root node of a recurring subgraph pattern that represents traversing an edge in the logical lattice structure. For example, the nodes V_7, p_1', and V_{12} in conjunction with their interconnecting edges form such a subgraph in the horizontal crossing. This subgraph's semantics is such that the process p_1 – to which the leaf node p_1' is mapped – is included in a horizontal crossing as well as at least one further process that is adjacent to p_1 in the logical lattice, the

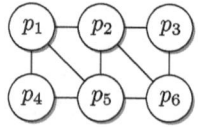

Figure 3.12: Logical Processes Layout of the 3×2 Triangular Lattice Protocol with Six Processes

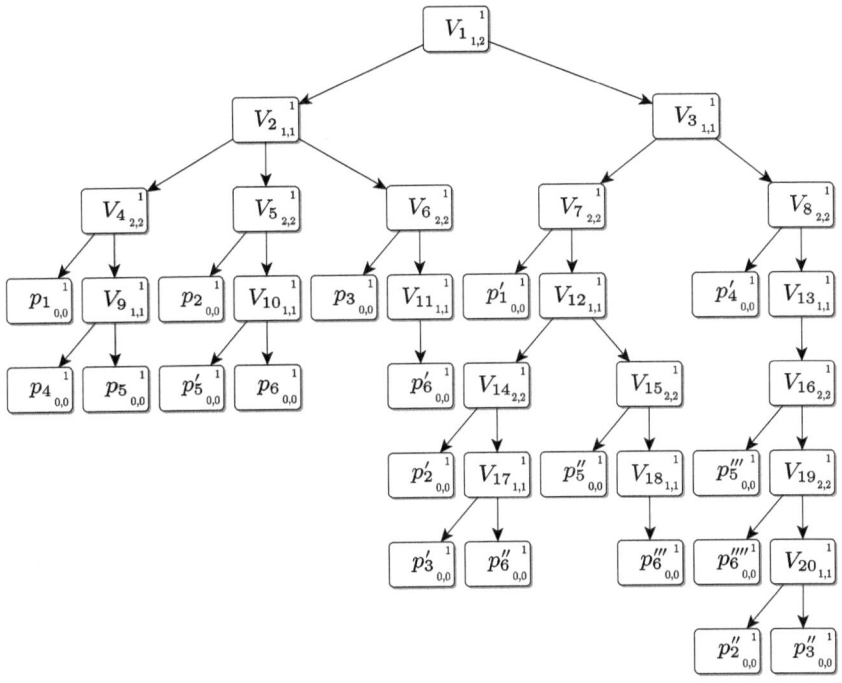

Figure 3.13: Corresponding Tree-Shaped Voting Structure to the Logical Processes Layout of the 3×2 Triangular Lattice Protocol with Six Processes of Figure 3.12

latter expressed by the presence of the node V_{12} representing the requirement for a further edge traversal in the logical lattice structure. A process is adjacent to another process if it is reachable by traversing exactly one edge in the logical lattice structure. Each of these three nodes has a vote function value of 1 and the subgraph root node V_7 requires the two votes from its two child nodes p_1' and V_{12}. A number of child subgraphs that matches the number of adjacent processes of p_1 in the logical lattice structure is attached to the node V_{12}. Since only one of them is required, the quorum function value of the node V_{12} is set to 1 for both operations. Here, only p_2 and p_5 are considered as being adjacent to p_1 while p_4 – albeit permitted by the horizontal crossing rules – is omitted since its right-adjacent process p_5 is the downwards diagonal-adjacent process of p_1 and thus directly reachable without the detour in terms of p_4. The subgraphs formed by the nodes V_{14},

p'_2, V_{17} and V_{15}, p''_5,V_{18} in conjunction with their interconnecting edges have the same semantics as the subgraph formed by the nodes V_7, p'_1, and V_{12}, just for different processes, namely for the processes p_2 and p_5, respectively. The subgraph consisting of the nodes V_{17}, p'_3, p''_6 may seem as an exception to this pattern of subgraphs since it consists of two (leaf) nodes that are mapped to processes. Instead, it is a necessary shortcut for and compression of the subgraph patterns for the processes p_3 and p_6 since leaf nodes in tree-shaped voting structures are required to be mapped to processes. If instead the according above identified subgraph patterns are attached to V_{17}, this requirement is violated. The same explanations apply to the left subgraph of the root node V_1 representing a vertical crossing.

Subsuming these observations, the types of subgraphs in tree-shaped voting structures expressing Triangular Lattice Protocol quorum systems are (1) the selection of a H-Cover or a V-Cover or both, (2) the selection of a path out of a set of paths within the H-Cover or V-Cover, and (3) the recurring subgraph pattern representing the traversal of the chosen path. Abstracting from the specifics of the Triangular Lattice Protocol, these three subgraph types are characteristic for tree-shaped voting structures that explicitly reflect all possible traversals of a structured static data replication scheme's underlying logical structure on which two path-based traversal methods are defined. If only one traversal method is defined as it is the case for the Triangular Grid Protocol [Cheng-Hong and Jer-Tsang, 1998; Kuo and Huang, 1997] (cf. Section 2.5.1), then the types of subgraphs reduce to (1) the selection of a path out of a set of paths and (2) the recurring subgraph pattern representing the traversal of the chosen path.

Essentially, such tree-shaped voting structures are the explicit plain enumeration of a quorum system represented in the syntax and semantics of tree-shaped voting structures, that is, in terms of a semantics-enriched tree graph composed of the subgraph patterns identified. Since each read or write quorum can be modeled as a path, every quorum system can be expressed in such a path-based manner. For example, the above Grid Protocol and Tree Quorum Protocol examples could have as well been modeled by tree-shaped voting structures that explicitly reflect the possible traversals of the underlying logical structures. Unfortunately, since such tree-shaped voting structures are closely tied to the underlying logical structures and the position-aware traversal rules defined thereon, an abstraction beyond the identified characteristic subgraph patterns is not feasible. In particular, a convenient abstraction from the number of processes as presented for the Grid Protocol and the Tree Quorum Protocol is not feasible. This is

attributed to the manyfold possibilities of constructing logical structures to
arrange processes in such as two-dimensional planar graphs [Bazzi, 2000;
Kuo and Huang, 1997; Naor and Wieder, 2005] or grid-based structures
[Cheng-Hong and Jer-Tsang, 1998; Kuo and Huang, 1997; Naor and Wieder,
2005; Wu and Belford, 1992] and the definition of according position-aware
traversal rules on these structures.

Example: Majority Consensus Voting As a final example, tree-shaped
voting structures expressing quorum systems complying to Majority Consensus Voting always consist of a root node and a number of its child (leaf)
nodes that equals the number of processes for which the tree-shaped voting
structure is instantiated. Specifically, a Majority Consensus Voting tree-

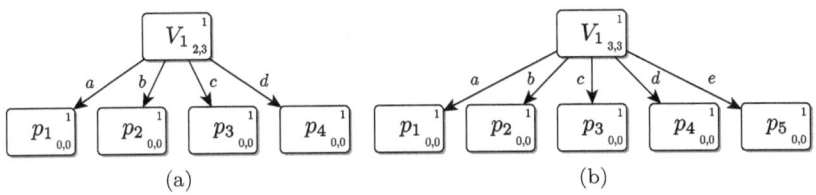

(a)   (b)

Figure 3.14: Majority Consensus Voting Tree-Shaped Voting Structures with
Four (a) and Five Processes (b)

shaped voting structure is constructible for any number of processes n by
attaching n leaf nodes – each having one vote and being mapped to a distinct process – to a single root node that has a vote function value of 1
and a quorum function value of $\lceil n/2 \rceil$ for the read operation and of $\lceil (n+1)/2 \rceil$
for the write operation. This tree-shaped voting structure construction rule
is a direct application of the Majority Consensus Voting quorum system
construction rules expressed in terms of tree-shaped voting structures. The
two tree-shaped voting structures in Figure 3.14 with four and five processes
illustrate this construction.

These examples illustrate the diversity of quorum system construction rules
and how they are manifested in tree-shaped voting structures in terms of
specific subgraph patterns. By having identified (1) the specific constituting
subgraph patterns of tree-shaped voting structures complying to a particular data replication scheme and (2) the scheme-specific pattern composition

rules, tree-shaped voting structures complying to this particular data replication scheme become constructible via graph composition guided by the pattern composition rules. In other words, the diverse quorum system construction rules – possibly accompanied by logical structures imposed on the set of processes – are transposed to and expressed in terms of graph patterns and according graph composition rules. Next, *voting structure shapes* as a means to express graph patterns and their graph composition rules in a uniform manner are presented.

3.3.1 Voting Structure Shapes

A specification formalism for tree-shaped voting structures must be capable of expressing the elementary graph building blocks and their composition rules of tree-shaped voting structures complying to different static data replication schemes. The *voting structure shape* formalism allows to specify both in a uniform and graph-based manner. Conceptually, a voting structure shape is a directed graph whose "nodes" are the identified elementary graph building blocks of a particular static data replication scheme expressed in terms of tree-shaped voting structures. The edges govern the traversal of the nodes and, in conjunction with a function specifying which particular nodes to duplicate and interconnect how many times, represent the graph building block composition rules. A universal algorithm interprets a voting structure shape and outputs a tree-shaped voting structure for a particular number of processes. Once having specified a voting structure shape for a data replication scheme, tree-shaped voting structures complying to this data replication scheme can be constructed in an automated manner, for arbitrary numbers of processes. Hence, homogeneous dynamic data replication schemes not having a static upper bound on the number of processes manageable at run-time can be realized.

The remainder of this section is structured as follows. First, voting structure shapes are informally introduced by an example. Then, after the formalization of voting structure shapes, their instantiation is discussed. Finally, some exemplary voting structure shapes are presented in detail.

Introductory Example

As an introductory example, consider the voting structure shape in Figure 3.15 complying to the original Tree Quorum Protocol and assume it is to be instantiated for 13 processes. The underlying logical tree structure has

the height $h = 3$ and the degree $d = 1$, that is, the logical tree structure has
three levels (counting from zero) and each (non-leaf) process has three child
processes as illustrated in Figure 2.8 (a) on page 62. The basic elements of a
voting structure shape are *frames* that encapsulate a variant of tree-shaped
voting structures and *frame edges* that interconnect the frames.

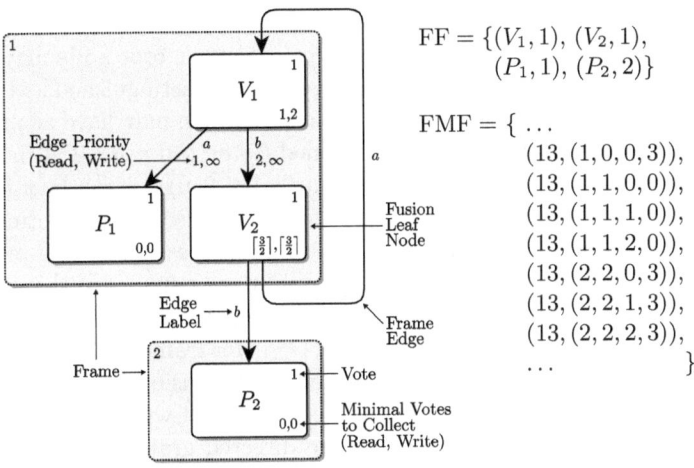

$$FF = \{(V_1, 1), (V_2, 1),$$
$$(P_1, 1), (P_2, 2)\}$$

$$FMF = \{ \dots$$
$$(13, (1, 0, 0, 3)),$$
$$(13, (1, 1, 0, 0)),$$
$$(13, (1, 1, 1, 0)),$$
$$(13, (1, 1, 2, 0)),$$
$$(13, (2, 2, 0, 3)),$$
$$(13, (2, 2, 1, 3)),$$
$$(13, (2, 2, 2, 3)),$$
$$\dots \qquad\qquad \}$$

Figure 3.15: Voting Structure Shape for the Original Tree Quorum Protocol,
its Frame Function (FF) Allocation, and the Frame Multiplicity
Function (FMF) for 13 Processes

Frames   A frame is the formally captured counterpart of the elementary
graph building blocks identified for a particular data replication scheme.
The nodes that constitute a frame are determined by the *frame function*
$FF : N \to N$ that maps nodes to not necessarily distinct natural numbers.
By mapping the nodes of disjoint subsets of the set of nodes to distinct
natural numbers and with the ordering relation $u \leq v \Leftrightarrow FF(u) \leq FF(v)$
for $u, v \in N$, a total order on equivalence classes, that is, on the frames, is
defined. As a suggestive shortcut, $FF^{-1}(i)$ gives the subset of nodes that are
associated to a *frame number* $i \in N$. Each (non-empty) disjoint subset of
the set of nodes given by $FF^{-1}(i)$ for an $i \in N$ represents in conjunction with
(1) the nodes' vote function and quorum function values and (2) the (non-
cyclic) node-interconnecting edges plus their edge priority function values

a variant of a tree-shaped voting structure that is termed a *frame*. In this example, the nodes V_1, V_2, and P_1 plus their interconnecting edges a and b constitute frame 1. The node P_2 is the single node of frame 2 that has no frame-internal edges. Note that while the nodes in this example are labeled to illustrate the frame function, node labels are henceforth omitted from voting structure shape figures to increase their readability as node labels are not crucial to illustrate the meaning of voting structure shapes. In contrast to a tree-shaped voting structure, a frame's root node may have a frame-external incoming edge that emerges from a distinguished leaf node of another and not necessarily distinct frame. A frame may have at most one such distinguished leaf node which is termed *fusion leaf node*. The fusion leaf node's quorum function must not necessarily be $(0,0)$ but can be a function of, for example, the number of processes for which the voting structure shape is to be instantiated or the number of its child nodes after having processed the voting structure shape. In this example voting structure shape that is to be instantiated for 13 processes, the quorum function value is $(0,0)$ for frame 2's fusion leaf node and it is $(\lceil 3/2 \rceil, \lceil 3/2 \rceil)$ for frame 1's fusion leaf node since three child nodes are to be attached to this fusion leaf node of which a majority is required for the read as well as for the write operation.

Treating frames as the "nodes" of the directed graph, the *frame multiplicity function*

$$\underset{(a)}{\text{FMF}} : \underset{}{\mathbb{N}} \to (\ \underset{(b)}{\mathbb{N}} \times \underset{(c)}{\mathbb{N}_0} \times \underset{(d)}{\mathbb{N}_0} \to \underset{(e)}{\mathbb{N}_0})$$

specifies – in relation to the number of processes for which the voting structure shape is to be instantiated [a] – the number of duplicates [e] for a frame as identified by its number [b] on a particular (frame-)level of the voting structure shape graph [c] and there in a specific (absolute) position [d]. Note that the duplication of a frame includes duplicating its child frames. The frame to be duplicated may itself be a duplicate of a frame as specified in the frame multiplicity function assignment.

For example, a frame multiplicity function mapping $n \mapsto (x,y,z) = a$ specifies the frame x (or a duplicate thereof) on level y and there in the absolute position z to be duplicated a times (which includes the duplication of its child frames) when the voting structure shape is to be instantiated for n processes.

Frame Edges Frame edges steer the traversal and processing of a voting structure shape, that is, the duplication of frames in order to transform the voting structure shape into a tree-shaped voting structure for a particular number of processes. More specifically, the edge prevails-relation determines the ordering in which frames are traversed. If the destination frame (and its subgraph) of a frame edge is to be duplicated, then the frame duplicates are attached to the frame edge's source node, that is, to the fusion leaf node of the frame it emerges from.

In order to give an idea of a voting structure shape's instantiation, the partial instantiation of the Tree Quorum Protocol voting structure shape for 13 processes as illustrated in Figure 3.15 is schematically shown in Figure 3.16 and is explained next.

Voting Structure Shape Instantiation Illustration The voting structure shape traversal starts with the root frame having the lowest frame number which is frame 1 in this example. It has an incoming (cyclic) frame edge and the frame multiplicity function is inspected for a frame 1 (or a duplicate thereof) on (frame-)level 0 of the graph and there in the absolute position 0 with respect to other frames on level 0. According to the found frame multiplicity function entry $(13, (1, 0, 0, 3))$, a total of three duplicates of frame 1 and its child frames – that is, frame 1 itself, frame 2, and their frame edges – have to be attached to the fusion leaf node of frame 1 as being the source node of the cyclic frame edge. The so far processed voting structure shape is schematically illustrated in Figure 3.16 (a).

Intuitively, cyclic frame edges that connect a frame's fusion leaf node to the same frame's root node expand the graph structure vertically while non-cyclic frame edges expand the graph structure horizontally. Cyclic frame edges model recursive graph structures. They are given precedence over non-cyclic frame edges if a frame's root node has cyclic as well as non-cyclic incoming frame edges.

After having processed the destination frame of a cyclic frame edge, the cyclic frame edge is removed and the subgraph of frames that is lead to by the next frame edge in the order established by the prevails-relation of edges as well as the frame edge itself are removed. Intuitively, the removed subgraph of frames represents the "recursion-abort" case. Therefore, it has to be removed while recursively descending until eventually the recursion is aborted. Then, the removed subgraph's duplicates are processed forming the leaf subgraphs of the resulting tree-shaped voting structure.

In this example, the cyclic frame edge connecting the fusion leaf node of frame 1 to its root node is removed and the frame edge connecting frame 1 to frame 2 as well as frame 2 itself are removed. The so far resulting voting structure shape is schematically illustrated in Figure 3.16 (b).

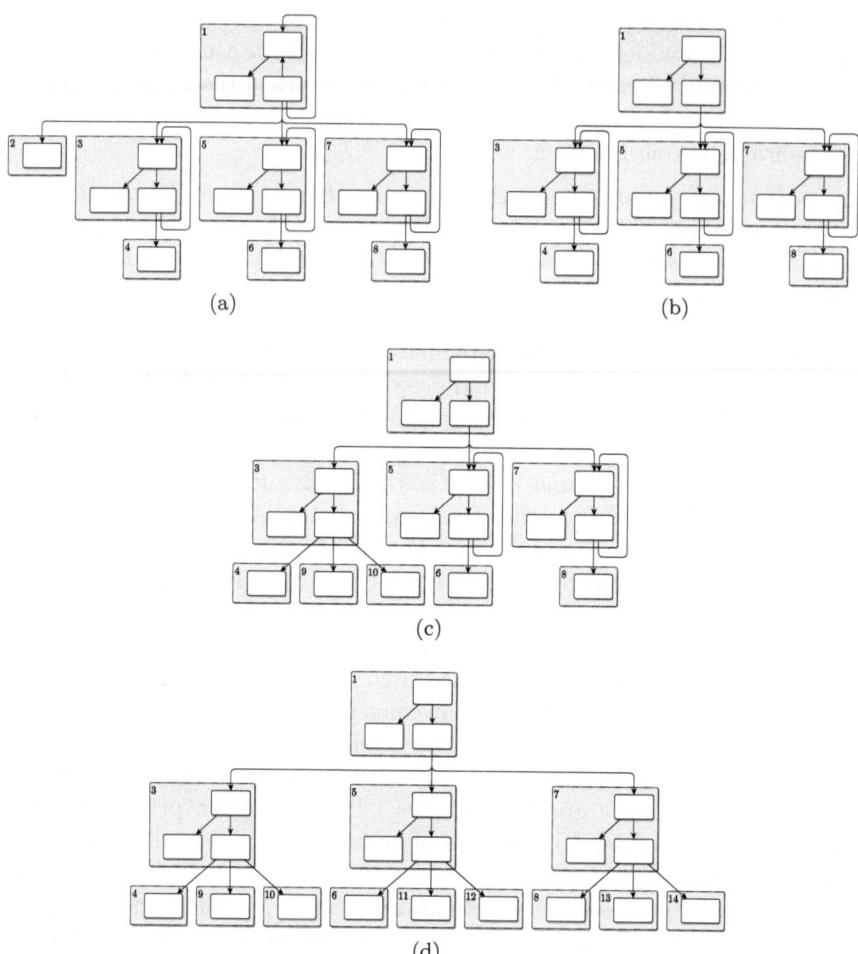

Figure 3.16: Schematic Instantiation Illustration of the Original Tree Quorum
Protocol Voting Structure Shape of Figure 3.15 after the Three
Times Duplication of Frame 1 (a), after the Removal of Frame 2
(b), after the Removal of Frame 3's Cyclic Frame Edge and the
Two Times Duplication of Frame 4 (c), and the Final Tree-Shaped
Voting Structure (d)

After having processed the root frame, the next frame to process is determined by the frame edge that prevails the other frame edges emerging from the root frame's fusion leaf node. Assuming the frame edge connecting frame 1 to frame 3 in Figure 3.16 (b) prevails the other frame edges leaving the fusion leaf node of frame 1, frame 3 is next to be processed. The root node of frame 3 has two incoming frame edges, a frame edge emerging from the fusion leaf node of frame 1 and a cyclic frame edge emerging from the fusion leaf node of frame 3. The cyclic frame edge is considered first as cyclic frame edges are given precedence over non-cyclic ones. The frame multiplicity function is inspected for a frame 1 (since frame 3 is a duplicate thereof) that is on (frame-)level 1 of the voting structure shape graph and there in the absolute position 0 with respect to other frames on the same level 1. According to the found frame multiplicity function entry $(13, (1, 1, 0, 0))$, this frame must not be duplicated, meaning that the "recursive descent" is aborted. The cyclic frame edge is removed and the "recursion-abort" case in terms of frame 4 – which is a duplicate of frame 2 – is processed next.

The root node of frame 4 has one incoming frame edge. The frame multiplicity function is inspected for a frame 2 (since frame 4 is a duplicate thereof) that is on (frame-)level 2 of the graph and there in the absolute position 0 with respect to other frames on the same level. According to the found frame multiplicity function entry $(13, (2, 2, 0, 3))$, a total of three duplicates of frame 4 have to be attached to the fusion leaf node of frame 3 as being the source node of the only incoming frame edge to frame 4. The so far resulting voting structure shape is schematically illustrated in Figure 3.16 (c).

Since frame 4 is a leaf frame having no child frames to process, a backtracking is started to find a frame that has a frame multiplicity function entry but has not been processed yet. The next to be processed frame is identified as being frame 5 – assuming the frame edge connecting frame 1 to frame 5 prevails the other frame edge connecting to frame 7 – as the frames 9 and 10 do not have a frame multiplicity function entry and frame 3 has been processed. After having processed the remaining unprocessed frames, the tree-shaped voting structure schematically illustrated in Figure 3.16 (d) results.

Frame Edge Priority Function   Not introduced in this example – as it does not apply to Tree Quorum Protocol tree-shaped voting structures – is the *frame edge priority function* that assigns operation-specific edge priorities to frame edges. Formally, the frame edge priority function

FEPF : $\mathbb{N} \to (\mathbb{N} \times \mathbb{N}_0 \times \mathbb{N}_0 \times \mathbb{N}_0 \to \mathbb{N} \times \mathbb{N})$
      (a)   (b) (c)   (d)   (e)   (f)   (g)

specifies the operation-specific edge priorities of frame edges [f][g] – in relation to the number of processes for which the voting structure shape is to be instantiated [a] – emerging from the fusion leaf node of a frame as identified by its number [b] on a particular (frame-)level [c], there in a specific (absolute) position [d], and among the edges leaving the same fusion leaf node in an order defined by the prevails-relation of edges [e]. Lower numbers represent higher edge priorities and the symbol ∞ denotes the lowest and default priority.

For example, a frame edge priority function mapping $n \mapsto (x, y, z, a) = (r, w)$ specifies the – with respect to the total ordering of edges – a^{th} edge emerging from the fusion leaf node of frame x (or a duplicate thereof) on level y and there in the absolute position z to have an edge priority function value of (r, w) when the voting structure shape is to be instantiated for n processes.

Process Mapping Function For structured data replication schemes, the quorum system construction rules rely on logical structures the processes are arranged in. If these structures are constructible for specific numbers of processes only, then the voting structure shape – as a representation of the data replication scheme's quorum system construction rules – specifies tree-shaped voting structures for those specific numbers of processes only. For example, a voting structure shape for the Grid Protocol only specifies tree-shaped voting structures for numbers of processes $n = k \cdot j$ with k being the number of columns and j being the number of rows in the logical rectangular grid. This problem is alleviated by (1) the voting structure shape specifying – for numbers of processes not supported by the underlying logical structure – tree-shaped voting structures for the next higher number of processes the logical structure is constructible for and (2) removing the additional processes (leaf nodes) from the resulting tree-shaped voting structure via post-processing it.

The choice of which specific process(es)-representing leaf nodes to remove – and thereby indirectly which processes to remove from the underlying logical structure imposed on the set of processes – depends on the particular quorum system construction rules and has a strong influence on the post-processed tree-shaped voting structure's quality measures. For example, in a tree-shaped voting structure complying to the Tree Quorum Protocol, removing the leaf node that is mapped to the root node of the logical tree structure degrades quality measures more drastically than removing a leaf node that is mapped to a process on lower levels of the logical tree structure.

In the context of voting structure shapes, the process mapping function $m : \mathbb{N} \rightarrow (\mathcal{L}^* \rightarrow P \cup \{\bot\})$ relates leaf nodes (in terms of node labels) to processes or to undefined otherwise, depending on the number of processes for which the voting structure shape is to be instantiated: Those leaf nodes in the instantiated voting structure shape that are not mapped to a process by the process mapping function are to be removed from the tree-shaped voting structure by the post-processing. Note that an instantiated voting structure shape is deterministically node and edge-labeled as to be described below. For convenience, $\mathrm{N_{Leaf}}$ is henceforth used in the context of the process mapping function to refer to the set of leaf nodes in an instantiated voting structure shape.

Next, voting structure shapes are formally introduced prior to the voting structure shape instantiation and the tree-shaped voting structure post-processing algorithms.

Voting Structure Shape Definition

Voting structure shapes are formally captured in the following definition.

Definition 3.2 (Voting Structure Shape)   A voting structure shape is a directed graph VSS = (N, E, s, q, o, m, FF, FMF, FEPF) where
   N $\subset \mathcal{L}^*$ is the non-empty finite set of labeled nodes with $\mathcal{L}$ being a totally ordered non-empty set of labels and $\mathcal{L}^*$ being the set of all non-empty strings over labels in $\mathcal{L}$ that is also totally ordered,
   E $\subseteq$ N $\times \mathcal{L}^* \times$ N is the finite set of labeled edges,
   $s : \mathrm{N} \rightarrow (\mathrm{N} \rightarrow \mathrm{N})$ is the vote function defining the vote of a node in relation to the number of processes for which the voting structure shape is to be instantiated,
   $q : \mathrm{N} \rightarrow (\mathrm{N} \rightarrow \mathrm{N_0} \times \mathrm{N_0})$ is the quorum function defining the operation-specific minimal number of votes to collect among a node's child nodes in relation to the number of processes for which the voting structure shape is to be instantiated,
   $o : \mathrm{E} \rightarrow \mathrm{N} \times \mathrm{N}$ is the edge priority function defining the operation-specific quorum probing ordering within a frame (with lower numbers representing higher priorities and the symbol ∞ denoting the lowest and default priority),

$m : \mathbb{N} \rightarrow (\mathbb{N}_{\text{Leaf}} \rightarrow P \cup \{\bot\})$ is the process mapping function relating leaf nodes to processes and defining leaf nodes to remove from the resulting tree-shaped voting structure, depending on the number of processes for which the voting structure shape is to be instantiated,

$FF : \mathbb{N} \rightarrow \mathbb{N}$ is the frame function that maps nodes to not necessarily distinct natural numbers, thereby partitioning the set of nodes and totally ordering these partitions,

$FMF : \mathbb{N} \rightarrow (\mathbb{N} \times \mathbb{N}_0 \times \mathbb{N}_0 \rightarrow \mathbb{N}_0)$ is the frame multiplicity function specifying – in relation to the number of processes for which the voting structure shape is to be instantiated – the number of duplicates for a frame as identified by its number on a particular (frame-)level of the graph and there in a specific (absolute) position, and

$FEPF : \mathbb{N} \rightarrow (\mathbb{N} \times \mathbb{N}_0 \times \mathbb{N}_0 \times \mathbb{N}_0 \rightarrow \mathbb{N} \times \mathbb{N})$ is the frame edge priority function specifying the operation-specific priority of frame edges – in relation to the number of processes for which the voting structure shape is to be instantiated – emerging from a frame's fusion leaf node on a particular (frame-)level, there in a specific (absolute) position, and among the frame edges leaving the same fusion leaf node in an order defined by the prevails-relation of edges (with lower numbers representing higher priorities and the symbol ∞ denoting the lowest and default priority).

Because voting structure shapes are directed graphs, they may not have an outstanding root node and thus no distinctive root frame from which to start processing as it is the case for the exemplary voting structure shape shown in Figure 3.15. Though, such a distinguished root frame from which on the voting structure shape can be processed is mandatory for its deterministic instantiation. For this purpose, the total ordering of natural numbers in the image of the frame function is utilized by defining the root node of a voting structure shape to be the root node of the frame that is mapped to the lowest natural number in the frame function's image, which is without loss of generality the root node of frame 1.

Next, the algorithm to instantiate a voting structure shape is presented, followed by the algorithm for post-processing the resulting tree-shaped voting structure.

Instantiating Voting Structure Shapes

Instantiating a voting structure shape for a number of processes $n \in \mathbb{N}$ requires the traversal of its frames while duplicating (some of) them according to the frame multiplicity function for n processes. In the following algorithm, the variables *frame number*, *frame edge*, and *frame level* are used to control the voting structure shape's traversal while the *duplicate frame mapping function* keeps track of a frame's duplicates:

Frame Number F_{no} – The currently processed frame number is designated by $F_{no} \in \mathbb{N}$. It is initialized to the root frame $F_{no} = 1$.

Frame Edge F_e – The frame edge $F_e \in E \cup \{\bot\}$ holds the edge that emerges from a frame's fusion leaf node and leads to the currently processed (and not necessarily distinct) frame's root node. It is initially undefined, that is, $F_e = \bot$.

Frame Level F_{level} – The frame level $F_{level} \in \mathbb{N}_0$ holds the level (with respect to frames) of the currently processed frame in the voting structure shape graph. It is used to inspect the frame multiplicity function and is initialized to $F_{level} = 0$, that is, to the root frame which is without loss of generality assumed to be on level 0 and there in the absolute position 0.

Duplicate Frame Mapping Function ϕ_{FF} – The duplicate frame mapping function $\phi_{FF} : \mathbb{N} \to \mathbb{N} \cup \{\bot\}$ keeps track of a frame's duplicates and is used to inspect the frame multiplicity function. It is initially undefined for all $i \in \mathbb{N}$, in short $\phi_{FF}(\mathbb{N}) = \bot$.

While traversing a voting structure shape, some encountered frames are not immediately processed because the frame edges leading to them are prevailed by other frame edges whose destination frames are processed first. Both are tracked by the two sets of *unprocessed frame edges* and *processed frame edges*:

Unprocessed Frame Edges F_{E^*} – The set of unprocessed frame edges $F_{E^*} \subseteq E$ is used to keep track of encountered but yet unprocessed frame edges while processing a voting structure shape. It is initialized to the empty set $F_{E^*} = \emptyset$.

Processed Frame Edges F_E – The set of processed frame edges $F_E \subseteq E$ holds the processed frame edges. It is also initialized to the empty set $F_E = \emptyset$.

The algorithm to instantiate a voting structure shape for a number of processes $n \in \mathbb{N}$ using the above defined variables and auxiliary function comprises three steps. The first step is to traverse the voting structure shape starting from its root frame in order to identify the next to be processed frame. The second step is to process the found frame by duplicating the subgraph starting with this frame a number of times according to its frame multiplicity function assignment. The third step handles the special case of cyclic frame edges that connect the currently processed frame's fusion leaf

node to this frame's root node. These steps are repeated until no frames to
process are left and the voting structure shape is transformed into a tree-
shaped voting structure for $n' \geq n$ processes which is then post-processed
to remove the $n' - n$ processes.

STEP 1 (NEXT FRAME TO PROCESS IDENTIFICATION)

The current frame as identified by its frame number F_{no} is traversed to
its fusion leaf node. From this node's emerging frame edges – if any – a
frame edge $e \in E$ that (1) is not yet processed ($e \notin F_E$) and (2) prevails
its other possibly existing adjacent frame edges is selected. This edge e
is set as frame edge $F_e := e$, joined with the set of processed frame edges
$F_E := F_E \cup \{e\}$, and removed from the set of unprocessed frame edges by
$F_{E^*} := F_{E^*} \setminus \{e\}$ if $e \in F_{E^*}$. The other not yet processed adjacent frame
edges of e, if any, are joined with the set of unprocessed frame edges F_{E^*}
to keep track of encountered and left to be processed frame edges.

The frame edge F_e is followed to its destination frame for which the
frame number F_{no} and the frame level F_{level} are updated to reflect this
subsequent frame. The frame multiplicity function is inspected for an
entry matching the frame number F_{no} or $\phi_{FF}(F_{no})$ on frame level F_{level}
and there in the frame's absolute position.

If no entry with a multiplicity value greater than zero is found in
the frame multiplicity function, the frame is not to be processed and
↑Step 1 is repeated for the updated frame number F_{no}.

Otherwise, this frame has to be processed by executing ↑Step 2.

This procedure is repeated until a leaf frame is reached whose fusion leaf
node has no leaving frame edges. Then, the voting structure shape is
traversed backwards until either a yet unprocessed frame edge in the set
of unprocessed frame edges F_{E^*} is found or no such frame edges are left to
be processed. In the latter case, the voting structure shape instantiation
has finished. In the former case, ↑Step 1 is repeated after having set F_{no}
to the frame number of the found frame edge's source frame.

STEP 2 (SUBGRAPH DUPLICATION)

The following three duplication and interconnection steps are repeated
a number of times as given by the frame multiplicity function value of
the current frame F_{no} or $\phi_{FF}(F_{no})$ if the frame edge F_e leading to its
root node is a cyclic frame edge and one time less otherwise (because
the subgraph starting with the current frame accounts for the number of
duplicates as determined by the frame multiplicity function value).

STEP 2.1 (NODE DUPLICATION)
   Grouped by frame affiliation, each node $u \in FF^{-1}(F_{no})$ of the current
   frame F_{no} as well as each node in this frame's successive frames that is
   not already duplicated by Step 2 (to not duplicate already duplicated
   nodes) is processed by (1) joining the node's uniquely labeled duplicate
   node u' with the set of nodes $N := N \cup \{u'\}$, (2) assigning the duplicate
   node the original node's vote function and quorum function values by
   $s(u') := s(u)$ and $q(u') := q(u)$, and (3) setting the duplicate node's
   frame affiliation to a unique frame number $FF(u') := F'_{no}$. Then,
   the set of duplicate nodes (that constitutes a frame) is marked as a
   duplicate frame by $\phi_{FF}(F'_{no}) := F''_{no}$ where F''_{no} is the frame number
   of the frame holding the set of original nodes if F''_{no} is not mapped by
   ϕ_{FF}. Otherwise, F'_{no} is marked as a duplicate frame of F''_{no}'s original
   frame $\phi_{FF}(F''_{no})$.

STEP 2.2 (EDGE DUPLICATION)
   Each edge $e \in E$ frame-internally connecting the nodes in frame
   $FF^{-1}(F_{no})$ as well as each frame-internal edge in its successive frames
   that is not already duplicated by Step 2 is processed by (1) joining
   its duplicate edge $e' = (\phi_N(src(e)), lab(e), \phi_N(dst(e)))$ with the set of
   edges $E := E \cup \{e'\}$ where ϕ_N gives a node's by Step 2.1 duplicated
   node, and (2) assigning the duplicate edge e' the edge priority function
   value of the original edge by $o(e') := o(e)$.
   The frame edges that are not already duplicated by Step 2 are processed alike but with maintaining the frame edge priority function by
   setting an edge's priority value to that of its original frame edge in case
   no different value is defined for it by the frame edge priority function.

STEP 2.3 (SUBGRAPH INTERCONNECTION)
   Finally, the duplicated subgraph is attached to the fusion leaf node
   $src(F_e)$ by a frame edge $e' = (src(F_e), lab(e'), dst(\phi_N(dst(F_e))))$ that
   is prevailed by its possibly existing adjacent frame edges (ϕ_N gives the
   node's by Step 2.1 duplicated node). The frame edge e' is joined with
   the set of edges $E := E \cup \{e'\}$ and the set of unprocessed frame edges
   $F_{E^\star} := F_{E^\star} \cup \{e'\}$. It is assigned the default priority if no frame edge
   priority function value is explicitly defined.

After having performed Step 2, ↑Step 3 is executed if the frame edge F_e
connecting to the currently processed frame F_{no} is a cyclic frame edge.
Otherwise, ↑Step 1 is executed to find the next to be processed frame.

STEP 3 (CYCLIC EDGE PROCESSING)

The currently processed frame F_{no} is traversed to its fusion leaf node. Then, the next frame edge with respect to the prevails-relation of edges (which is not duplicated by Step 2) as well as the subgraph starting with the root node to which this frame edge leads to is removed. This subgraph represents the "recursion-abort" case illustrated in the above instantiation example. Specifically, the removal includes (1) unmapping the subgraph frames' duplicate frame mapping function assignments (2) removing the subgraph's nodes and edges, and (3) removing the frame edge leading to the subgraph's root node from the set of edges and the set of unprocessed frame edges. Finally, the frame edge referenced to by F_e is removed from the set of edges and the set of processed frame edges. Then, ↑Step 1 is executed.

Note that a unique frame number F'_{no} as required in Step 2.1 is found by maintaining a frame number counter that is initialized with the number of frames in the initial voting structure shape plus one and that is monotonically increased after having assigned a set of nodes a frame number. A unique duplicate node label as required in Step 2.1 is deterministically found by selecting the first element of $\mathcal{L}^*$ (the non-empty totally ordered set of all non-empty strings over labels in $\mathcal{L}$) reduced by the set of nodes N. The unique frame edge label required in Step 2.3 for the new frame edge e' is found by choosing the next element from $\mathcal{L}^*$ such that the possibly existing adjacent frame edges of e' prevail this new frame edge.

For structured data replication schemes, the underlying logical structures may not be regularly constructible for all numbers of processes. In such cases, tree-shaped voting structures are generated for the next higher number of processes the logical structures are constructible for and the additional processes in terms of process-mapped leaf nodes are removed from the resulting tree-shaped voting structures via *post-processing*.

Post-Processing Tree-Shaped Voting Structures

Voting structure shapes that capture the quorum system construction rules of structured data replication schemes may be restricted to generate tree-shaped voting structures for particular numbers of processes only, namely to numbers of processes for which the underlying logical structures the processes are arranged in are regularly constructible. For example, a Grid Protocol voting structure shape is only able to yield tree-shaped voting structures for numbers of processes $n = k \cdot j$ with k being the number of columns and j being the number of rows in the logical rectangular grid. In order to allow the generation of tree-shaped voting structures for all numbers of processes from such a voting structure shape, it is instantiated for the next higher number of processes the logical structure is regularly constructible for. Then, the additionally introduced leaf nodes are removed from the resulting tree-shaped voting structure by post-processing it. Specifically, those leaf nodes that are not mapped to a process by the process mapping function are removed from the tree-shaped voting structure.

When removing leaf nodes, the quorum function values of a removed leaf node's preceding father node must be adapted. This adaptation must maintain the original ratio of the father node's quorum function values and its child leaf nodes' accumulated votes as close as possible in order to preserve the semantics of the original tree-shaped voting structure. For a to be removed leaf node $u \in N_{\text{Leaf}}$, let $s_{\bar{u}}$ be the sum of u's adjacent nodes' vote function values, that is, the accumulated votes of those nodes that are child nodes of u's father node $v \in N$ but not the node u itself. To maintain the quorum function and vote function value ratios of u's father node v and its child nodes after the removal of u, the quorum function values of v are multiplied by the ratio of u's adjacent nodes' accumulated votes (excluding u) and the accumulated votes of all of v's child nodes (including u). More specifically, the new write quorum function value of u's father node v calculates to

$$q_W(v) = \begin{cases} \lfloor q_W(v) \cdot s_{\bar{u}}/(s_{\bar{u}} + s(u)) \rfloor & \text{if } 2 \cdot \lfloor q_W(v) \cdot s_{\bar{u}}/(s_{\bar{u}} + s(u)) \rfloor > s_{\bar{u}} \\ \lceil q_W(v) \cdot s_{\bar{u}}/(s_{\bar{u}} + s(u)) \rceil & \text{otherwise,} \end{cases}$$

and – based on the new write quorum function value – the new read quorum function value of v calculates to

$$q_R(v) = \begin{cases} \lfloor q_R(v) \cdot s_{\bar{u}}/(s_{\bar{u}} + s(u)) \rfloor & \text{if } q_W(v) + \lfloor q_R(v) \cdot s_{\bar{u}}/(s_{\bar{u}} + s(u)) \rfloor > s_{\bar{u}} \\ \lceil q_R(v) \cdot s_{\bar{u}}/(s_{\bar{u}} + s(u)) \rceil & \text{otherwise.} \end{cases}$$

The algorithm to post-process a tree-shaped voting structure as being a transformed voting structure shape follows the conceptual ideas of Theel and Strauß [1998] for deriving the current voting structure for a particular number of processes from the master voting structure (cf. Section 3.1). It works in two steps as follows.

STEP 1 (QUORUM ADJUSTMENT AND LEAF NODE DELETION)
   For each leaf node $u \in N_{Leaf}$ that is not mapped to a process by the
   process mapping function and as long as there are process-unmapped
   leaf nodes left, the following actions are performed. The read and write
   quorum function values of u's preceding father node $v \in N$ are adapted
   as described above. The connecting edge emerging from u's preceding
   father node v is removed from the set of edges by $E := E \setminus \{e : e \in
   E \wedge dst(e) = u\}$. Then, the node u is removed from the set of nodes by
   $N := N \setminus \{u\}$.
   Note that, resulting from the leaf node removal, there might be nodes
   that have become (new) leaf nodes and that are not mapped to processes.
   These new leaf nodes must also be removed because leaf nodes in tree-
   shaped voting structures have to be mapped to processes. Therefore, this
   step is repeated as long as there are process-unmapped leaf nodes left.

STEP 2 (GRAPH COMPACTION)
   The preceding graph modifications may have resulted in inner nodes having only a single child leaf node. These inner nodes can be safely replaced
   by their single child leaf nodes. For each inner node $v \in N$ having only a
   single child leaf node $u \in N_{Leaf}$, the node v gets assigned u's quorum function value and process mapping function value by $q(v) := q(u) = (0,0)$
   and $m(v) := m(u)$. The edge connecting v to u is removed from the set
   of edges by $E := E \setminus \{e : e \in E \wedge dst(e) = u\}$. Then, the node u is removed
   from the set of nodes by $N := N \setminus \{u\}$. This step is repeated until no
   inner nodes having only a single child leaf node are left to process.

Post-Processing Example   As an example of the post-processing, consider the Grid Protocol tree-shaped voting structure for four processes
shown in Figure 3.17, the process set $P = \{p_1, p_2, p_3\}$ with three processes,
and assume the process mapping function to be $m = \{(p_a, \bot), (p'_a, \bot),
(p_b, p_1), (p'_b, p_1), (p_c, p_2), (p'_c, p_2), (p_d, p_3) (p'_d, p_3)\}$ specifying the leaf nodes
labeled p_a and p'_a to be removed.

   Figure 3.18 (a) shows the tree-shaped voting structure after having performed Step 1 in which these leaf nodes as well as the edges connecting to
them are removed. After the graph compaction by Step 2, the final post-
processed tree-shaped voting structure as shown in Figure 3.18 (b) with the
process mapping function $m = \{(V_4, p_1), (V_5, p_1), (p_c, p_2), (p'_c, p_2), (p_d, p_3)
(p'_d, p_3)\}$ results.

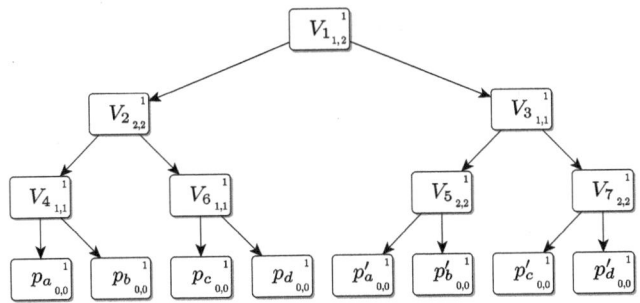

Figure 3.17: Grid Protocol Tree-Shaped Voting Structure with Leaf Nodes for Four Processes

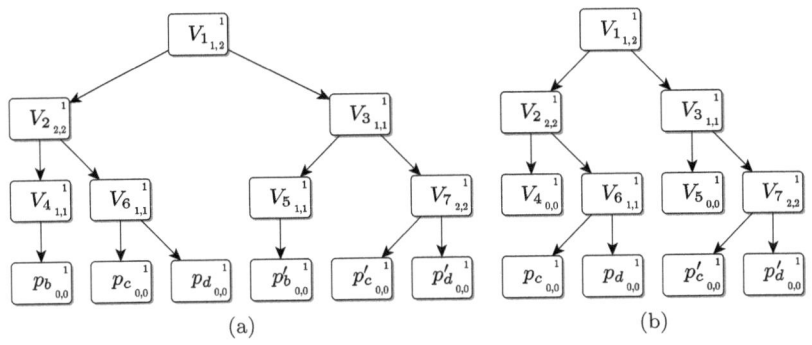

Figure 3.18: The Grid Protocol Tree-Shaped Voting Structure of Figure 3.17 after Step 1 of the Post-Processing (a) and the Resulting Tree-Shaped Voting Structure with Leaf Nodes for Three Processes (b)

In the next section, exemplary voting structure shapes for the structured Grid Protocol, the structured Tree Quorum Protocol, and for the unstructured Majority Consensus Voting, Weighted Voting, and the Read One Write All Protocol are presented.

3.3.2 Voting Structure Shape Examples

The challenge of lifting tree-shaped voting structures from reflecting a quorum system complying to a particular data replication scheme for a specific number of processes to reflect the quorum systems for arbitrary numbers of processes lies in (1) finding suitable frames and (2) finding an adequate frame multiplicity function. Next, voting structure shapes for some prominent data replication schemes, namely for the Grid Protocol, the Tree Quorum Protocol, Majority Consensus Voting, Weighted Voting, and the Read One Write All Protocol are presented.

The Grid Protocol   As a first example, consider the Grid Protocol voting structure shapes favoring rows over columns and favoring columns over rows, each with seven frames, as illustrated in Figure 3.19 (a) and Figure 3.19 (b). For the Grid Protocol favoring rows over columns, the number of columns in the logical rectangular $k \times j$ grid imposed on the set of processes that has a cardinality of n is $k = \lfloor \sqrt{n} \rfloor$ and the number of rows is $j = \lceil \sqrt{n} \rceil$ if $\lfloor \sqrt{n} \rfloor \cdot \lceil \sqrt{n} \rceil \geq n$, and $k = j = \lceil \sqrt{n} \rceil$ otherwise. For the Grid Protocol fa-

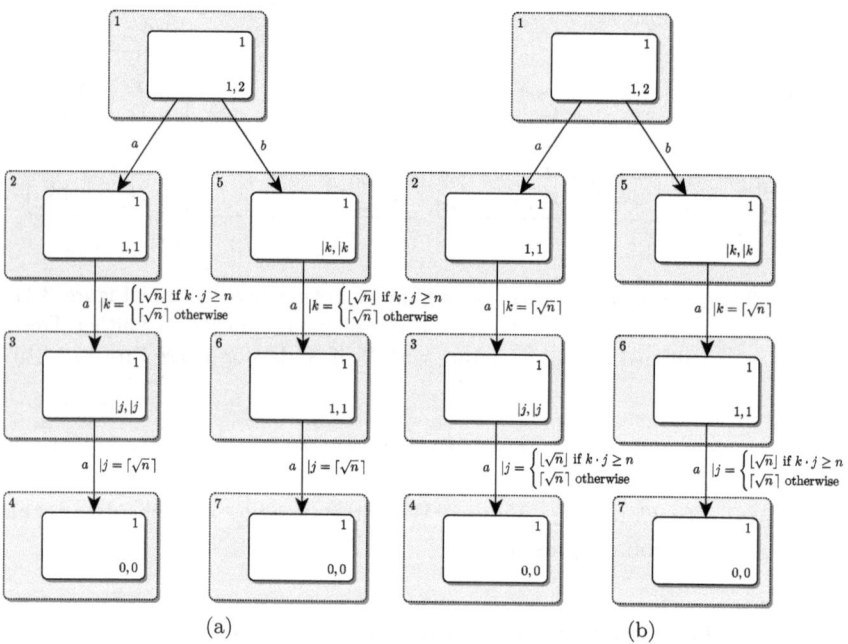

Figure 3.19: Voting Structure Shapes for the Grid Protocol Favoring Rows over Columns (a) and the Grid Protocol Favoring Columns over Rows (b)

voring columns over rows, the number of columns in the logical rectangular grid imposed on the set of processes that has a cardinality of n is $k = \lceil \sqrt{n} \rceil$ and the number of rows is $j = \lfloor \sqrt{n} \rfloor$ if $\lceil \sqrt{n} \rceil \cdot \lfloor \sqrt{n} \rfloor \geq n$, and $k = j = \lceil \sqrt{n} \rceil$ otherwise. Note that by this means the voting structure shape is instantiated for a number of processes that calculates to $n' = k \cdot j \geq n$ and hence – if necessary – the resulting tree-shaped voting structure must be post-processed to remove $2 \cdot (n' - n)$ process-unmapped leaf nodes, namely $(n' - n)$ process-unmapped leaf nodes in the C-Cover and $(n' - n)$ process-unmapped leaf nodes in the CC-Cover.

The process mapping function may assign leaf nodes to processes in a round-robin manner on the set of processes, that is, it assigns from left to right n leaf nodes to processes, it is undefined for the next $n' - n$ leaf nodes, it assigns n leaf nodes to processes as above, and it is undefined for the remaining $n' - n$ leaf nodes.

The frame multiplicity function for both Grid Protocol voting structure shapes and for all numbers of processes $n \in \mathbb{N}$ is

$n \mapsto (3, 2, 0) = k,$

$n \mapsto (6, 2, k) = k,$

$n \mapsto (4, 3, (i \cdot j)) = j$ for $0 \leq i \leq k$, and

$n \mapsto (7, 3, (i \cdot j) + (k \cdot j)) = j$ for $0 \leq i \leq k,$

with k and j initialized for a specific n as described above. Visually, the number of times a particular frame (or a duplicate thereof) is to be duplicated (including the duplication of its child frames) is indicated by the frame edge annotation, for example, for frame 4 in Figure 3.19 (a), by $\lfloor j = \lceil \sqrt{n} \rceil$ meaning that the subgraph starting with the frame edge's destination frame 4 is duplicated $\lceil \sqrt{n} \rceil$ times. The frame edge priority function for both voting structure shapes defaults to $\mathbb{N} \mapsto (\mathbb{N}, \mathbb{N}_0, \mathbb{N}_0, \mathbb{N}_0) - (\infty, \infty)$. The vote function values of all nodes in the voting structure shapes are constantly 1 over all $n \in \mathbb{N}$. The fusion leaf nodes of the voting structure shapes' root frames 1 have a constant quorum function value of 1 for the read operation and a constant value of 2 for the write operation. The fusion leaf nodes of the frames 2 and 6 both have a constant quorum function value of 1 for both, the read and the write operation. The fusion leaf nodes of the frames 3 and 5 have a quorum function assignment of j and k, respectively, for both, the read and the write operation. Finally, the leaf nodes of the voting structure shapes' leaf frames have a constant quorum function value of $(0, 0)$.

Tree Quorum Protocol   As a second example, the original Tree Quorum Protocol voting structure shape is illustrated in Figure 3.20. It consists of two frames 1 and 2 and of two frame edges, one frame edge b that connects the fusion leaf node of frame 1 to the root node of frame 2 and one cyclic frame edge a connecting the fusion leaf node of frame 1 to its root node. Recall that the number of processes n in a logical tree structure of the original Tree Quorum Protocol is given by $n = \sum_{i=0}^{h}(2 \cdot d + 1)^i$ which is dependent on the logical tree structure's height h and degree d (cf. Section 2.5.1). For a particular degree d, for example, for $d = 1$ resulting in a ternary logical tree structure, the actual number of processes n' is determined by the height h and is restricted to numbers of processes matching $\sum_{i=0}^{h} 3^i$. To enable the generation of tree-shaped voting structures for arbitrary numbers of processes, the original Tree Quorum Protocol voting structure shape is instantiated for the next higher number of processes $n' \geq n$ and then post-processed. For a given designated number of processes n and a particular fixed degree d, the logical tree structure's height calculates to $h = \lceil \ln(2 \cdot d \cdot n + 1) - \ln(2 \cdot d + 1) / \ln(2 \cdot d + 1) \rceil$ resulting in $n' = (2 \cdot d + 1)^{h+1} - 1 / 2 \cdot d$ processes in the tree-shaped voting structure which is then post-processed to remove the $n' - n$ processes.

As for the Grid Protocol voting structure shapes, the process mapping function may assign leaf nodes to processes in a round-robin manner on the set of processes and specify a number $n' - n$ of process-unmapped leaf nodes that are to be removed by post-processing. For example, the process

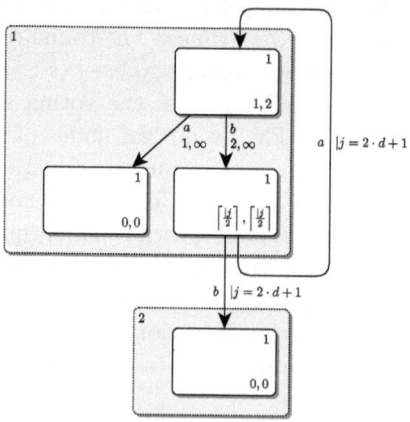

Figure 3.20: Voting Structure Shape for the Original Tree Quorum Protocol

mapping function may assign leaf nodes to processes such that the underlying logical tree structure is level-wise populated by processes from top to
bottom. If a level cannot be fully populated with processes, the remaining
processes are evenly balanced among the corresponding leaf nodes for this
level and the remaining $n' - n$ process-unmapped leaf nodes are removed
by the post-processing.

The frame multiplicity function for the original Tree Quorum Protocol
voting structure shape for a particular degree d with $j = 2 \cdot d + 1$ and height
h calculated as described above is

$n \mapsto (1, 0, 0) = j,$

$n \mapsto (1, 1, i) = j \quad \text{for } 0 \leq i < j^1,$

$n \mapsto (1, 2, i) = j \quad \text{for } 0 \leq i < j^2,$

$$\vdots$$

$n \mapsto (1, h - 1, i) = j \quad \text{for } 0 \leq i < j^{h-1}, \text{ and}$

$n \mapsto (2, h, (i \cdot j)) = j \quad \text{for } 0 \leq i \leq j^{h-1}.$

The frame edge priority function defaults to $\mathbb{N} \mapsto (\mathbb{N}, \mathbb{N}_0, \mathbb{N}_0, \mathbb{N}_0) = (\infty, \infty)$.
The vote function values of all nodes in the voting structure shape are con-
stantly 1 over all $n \in \mathbb{N}$. The fusion leaf node of the voting structure shape's
root frame 1 has a quorum function value of $\lceil j/2 \rceil$ for the read as well as
for the write operation. The single node of the leaf frame 2 has a constant
quorum function value of $(0, 0)$.

In contrast to the original Tree Quorum Protocol, the Generalized Tree
Quorum Protocol allows a logical tree structure to be incomplete, meaning
a node in the logical tree structure must not have exactly $2 \cdot d + 1$ child
nodes but may have any number of child nodes exceeding one. Incomplete
logical tree structures can be expressed by the frame multiplicity function
if they are regularly constructible, meaning that the recurrent subgraph
patterns can be captured in an according quorum system construction rule.
For example, the rule stating that nodes on even levels of the logical tree
structure have $d > 1$ child nodes while nodes on odd levels of the structure
have $d' > 1$ child nodes describes a logical tree structure that is expressible in terms of a frame multiplicity function. Otherwise, the logical tree
structure is specifically crafted for a particular number of nodes (processes)
and therefore is neither intended nor suited for a generalization in terms of
voting structure shapes.

Majority Consensus Voting, Weighted Voting, and the Read One Write All Protocol   The voting structure shapes for Majority Consensus Voting, Weighted Voting, and the Read One Write All Protocol are shown in Figure 3.21. The three voting structure shapes each have two frames 1 and 2 and one frame edge a that interconnects the two frames.

The frame multiplicity function for each of the three voting structure shapes is $n \mapsto (2,1,0) = n$ over all $n \in \mathbb{N}$, meaning that frame 2 is attached n times to its preceding frame 1 resulting in a tree-shaped voting structure for precisely n processes. The only difference among the three is the fusion leaf nodes of the respective frames 1 having different quorum function values and, for the Weighted Voting voting structure shape, the duplicates of frame 2's single node having potentially different vote function values. For the Weighted Voting voting structure shape, the vote function assignment may follow some distribution function assigning the duplicates of frame 2's node (non-)uniform votes such that frame 1's fusion leaf node quorum function is $\mu_R = \lceil 1/2 \cdot \sum \{s(u) : u \in \mathbb{N} \setminus \mathrm{N_{Root}}\} \rceil$ for the read and $\mu_W = \lceil 1/2 \cdot \sum \{s(u) : u \in \mathbb{N}\} \rceil$ for the write operation.

For the three voting structure shapes, the process mapping function may assign leaf nodes to processes in a round-robin manner on the set of processes with the assignment for Weighted Voting sensibly taking the vote assignment into account since leaf nodes being equipped with more votes should be mapped to processes having high process availabilities. The frame edge priority function defaults to $\mathbb{N} \mapsto (\mathbb{N}, \mathbb{N}_0, \mathbb{N}_0, \mathbb{N}_0) = (\infty, \infty)$ for the three voting structure shapes but may consider the vote assignment in case of

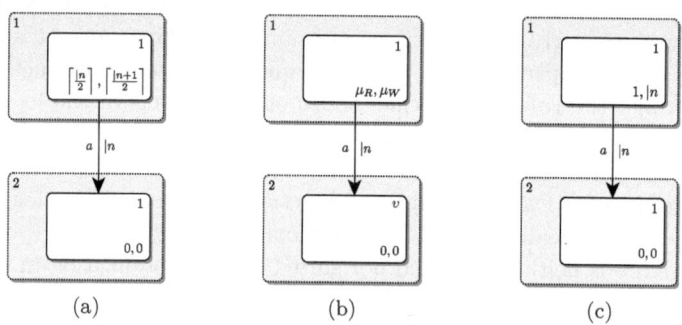

(a)   (b)   (c)

Figure 3.21: Voting Structure Shapes for Majority Consensus Voting (a), Weighted Voting (b), and the Read One Write All Protocol (c)

Weighted Voting such that leaf nodes equipped with a higher number of votes are prioritized during quorum building. For example, if leaf nodes are assigned votes in a decreasing manner from left to right with the leftmost leaf node having the most votes, the frame edge priority function may respect this vote assignment and be specified as $n \mapsto (1, 0, 0, k - 1) = (k, k)$ for $1 \leq k \leq n$.

All three voting structure shapes reflect the quorum system construction rules of unstructured data replication schemes not imposing a logical structure on the set of processes. Therefore, the number of processes $n \in \mathbb{N}$ for which the respective voting structure shape is instantiated always equals the number of process-mapped leaf nodes in the resulting tree-shaped voting structure. Hence, the resulting tree-shaped voting structures do not need to be post-processed.

Path-Based Quorum System Construction Rules Unfortunately, quorum system construction rules that are expressed in a path-based manner withstand an abstraction beyond the two subgraph patterns as identified for the Triangular Lattice Protocol on page 114ff. These subgraph patterns are characteristic and universal for all quorum system construction rules expressed in a path-based manner. As of sharing these subgraph patterns, their only difference lies in having different frame multiplicity function specifications, each closely tied to the locality-guided traversal rules defined on the respective underlying logical structures the processes are arranged in. This locality-sensitive traversal has to be expressed in terms of specific sequences of frames whose composition is guided by the frame multiplicity function. Hence, the frame multiplicity function specification for quorum system construction rules expressed in a path-based manner is much more complex (due to the explicit path-modeling) than its specification for quorum system construction rules not expressing locality-sensitive traversal rules such as, for example, the Tree Quorum Protocol or the Grid Protocol. While the logical structure and its traversal rules for, say, the Grid Protocol, are embodied in the specific frames and their interconnection, this must be explicitly modeled and manifested in the frame multiplicity functions for quorum system construction rules expressed in a path-based manner *per number of processes* for which a voting structure shape is to be instantiated. Due to the necessary locality-awareness of the frame multiplicity function, the process mapping function and the frame edge priority function specifications have to be specifically tailored to the concrete frame multiplicity function assignment and also have to be locality-aware. For example, for tree-shaped voting structures complying to the Grid Protocol or the Tree Quorum Protocol quorum system construction rules, a leaf-node-to-process-mapping may be performed in a round-robin manner on the set of processes as described above. For quorum system construction rules expressed in a path-based manner, the process mapping function must consider and respect the specific tree-shaped voting structure manifestation of paths in the underlying logical structure for the mapping.

From an implementation perspective, for a particular number of processes $n \in \mathbb{N}$ for which a voting structure shape modeling quorum system construction rules expressed in a path-based manner is to be instantiated, the frame multiplicity function must (1) construct an internal representation of the logical structure and (2) explicitly enumerate all its paths (for example, via an exhaustive breadth-first search) during which the concrete frame multiplicity function, frame edge priority function, and process mapping function allocation for the n processes is constructed. Thus, the frame multiplicity function for quorum system construction rules expressed in a path-based manner is best described by an algorithm that specifies the appropriate function allocations per number of processes for which to generate tree-shaped voting structures. This can be realized, for example, as described in [Storm, 2006; Storm and Theel, 2006] for Voting Structure Generators with the algorithms not generating tree-shaped voting structures but instead concrete function allocations.

Nonetheless, the various quorum system construction rules are uniformly expressible in terms of voting structure shapes and its resulting tree-shaped voting structures. Therefore – amongst other reasons – they qualify as quorum system representation means in the system model for the analytical evaluation of data replication schemes that is to be presented in Chapter 4.

So far, a voting structure shape is a specification of the quorum systems complying to a particular data replication scheme but for arbitrary numbers of processes, that is, it is a specification formalism for unbounded homogeneous dynamic data replication schemes. While on itself not sufficient to realize heterogeneous dynamic data replication schemes, different voting structure shapes may be employed for distinct numbers of processes whereby heterogeneous dynamic data replication schemes are realized. The next section introduces a data replication scheme specification formalism that allows to uniformly specify unstructured and structured static as well as bounded or unbounded homogeneous and heterogeneous dynamic data replication schemes.

3.4 Uniform Specification of Data Replication Schemes

A data replication scheme specification assigns quorum systems to specific numbers of processes. In this sense, a voting structure shape is a data replication scheme specification as it assigns quorum systems in the form of tree-shaped voting structures to all natural numbers of processes. While each tree-shaped voting structure specifies the quorum system for a specific number of processes, all of them comply to the same quorum system construction rules of a particular data replication scheme that is reflected in the voting structure shape. Therefore, a data replication scheme specification in terms of a voting structure shape cannot specify heterogeneous dynamic data replication schemes but only homogeneous dynamic data replication schemes.

A *uniform* data replication scheme specification formalism must be able to specify (unbounded) homogeneous and heterogeneous dynamic as well as static data replication schemes. Supporting heterogeneous dynamic data replication schemes requires the ability to assign distinct voting structure shapes to different numbers of processes. Then, homogeneous dynamic data replication schemes are covered by assigning the same single voting structure shape to all natural numbers of processes. Static data replication schemes are supported by assigning a single voting structure shape to a particular fixed number of processes. Effectively, a static data replication scheme can be seen as a dynamic data replication scheme with restricted dynamics, that is, one in which the dynamics is "disabled".

Note that for the pure purpose of specification, tree-shaped voting structures and voting structure shapes can be considered equivalent in the sense that the former is a result of processing the latter for a particular number of processes. From an implementation perspective, however, specifying a voting structure shape avoids the problem of having to store and to a priori create tree-shaped voting structures for a potentially unbounded number of processes. Nevertheless, considering tree-shaped voting structures in a data replication scheme specification can be desirable, for example, if an adequate voting structure shape does not yet exist or if an application-specific tree-shaped voting structure should be used that is neither intended nor suited for generalization in terms of a voting structure shape.

A static data replication scheme is specified by a tuple (D_{tsVS}, k) where D_{tsVS} is a tree-shaped voting structure representing the quorum system for

$k \in \mathbb{N}$ processes. Equivalently, a static data replication scheme can be specified by a tuple (D_{VSS}, k) where D_{VSS} is a voting structure shape that is instantiated for a number of processes $k \in \mathbb{N}$ resulting in a tree-shaped voting structure that represents the quorum system for k processes.

A dynamic data replication scheme is specified by a set of tuples $\mathfrak{D} = \{(D_{tsVS_1}, k_1), \ldots, (D_{tsVS_m}, k_m)\}$, $|\mathfrak{D}| > 1$, where each element specifies a static data replication scheme for a distinct number of processes such that $\forall (D_{tsVS_i}, k_i), (D_{tsVS_j}, k_j) \in \mathfrak{D}, i \neq j : k_i \neq k_j$ but not necessarily $\bigcup_{i=1}^{m} k_i = \mathbb{N}$. A homogeneous dynamic data replication scheme is specified if the tree-shaped voting structures of all tuples in $\mathfrak{D}$ are constructed using the same quorum system construction rules. Otherwise, a heterogeneous dynamic data replication scheme is specified. Equivalently, a dynamic data replication scheme can be specified by a set of tuples $\mathfrak{D} = \{(D_{VSS_1}, K_1), \ldots, (D_{VSS_m}, K_m)\}$ with $|\mathfrak{D}| \geq 1$ and $K_i \subseteq \mathbb{N}$ for $1 \leq i \leq m$ such that $\forall (D_{VSS_i}, K_i), (D_{VSS_j}, K_j) \in \mathfrak{D}, i \neq j : K_i \cap K_j = \emptyset$ but not necessarily $\bigcup_{i=1}^{m} K_i = \mathbb{N}$. If all tuples in $\mathfrak{D}$ use the same voting structure shape, then a homogeneous dynamic data replication scheme is specified. Otherwise, a heterogeneous dynamic data replication scheme is specified.

Uniformly, a data replication scheme is specified by a non-empty set of tuples $\mathfrak{D} = \{(D_1, K_1), \ldots, (D_m, K_m)\}$ with each tuple (D_i, K_i), $1 \leq i \leq m$, consisting of (1) either a voting structure shape D_i and a set of process numbers $K_i \subseteq \mathbb{N}$ or (2) a tree-shaped voting structure D_i and a single number of processes $K_i \subset \mathbb{N}$, $|K_i| = 1$, such that $\forall (D_i, K_i), (D_j, K_j) \in \mathfrak{D}$, $i \neq j : K_i \cap K_j = \emptyset$ but not necessarily $\bigcup_{i=1}^{m} K_i = \mathbb{N}$.

A data replication scheme specification is interpreted as follows. Whenever a new quorum system for a number of processes $j \in \mathbb{N}$ has to be installed, then the tuple (D_i, K_i), $1 \leq i \leq m$, with $j \in K_i$ is searched. If no such tuple can be found, then no quorum system is explicitly specified to be used for stage j of the dynamics. In this case, the reconfiguration is aborted and the currently used quorum system remains in use, that is, the dynamics is "disabled" for this stage of the dynamics. Otherwise, D_i of the tuple found is used as the quorum system for stage j of the dynamics if it is a tree-shaped voting structure. If D_i is a voting structure shape, then it is used to generate the tree-shaped voting structure for stage j of the dynamics. Note that the initial quorum system is determined alike with a mandatory existing tuple for the initial number of processes $j \in \mathbb{N}$.

The following five examples illustrate the data replication scheme specification formalism.

Examples The five examples to illustrate the data replication scheme specification formalism are depicted in Figure 3.22 (a) – (e). The left columns in the figures represent the numbers of processes ranging from 1 to infinity and the right columns relate them to their corresponding voting structure shape or tree-shaped voting structure. Numbers of processes that are not related to either are indicated by $\perp$.

A voting structure shape represents the quorum systems complying to a particular data replication scheme for arbitrary numbers of processes. Hence, an unbounded homogeneous dynamic data replication scheme $\mathfrak{D}_{hom}$ is specified by a single tuple stating one particular voting structure shape to be used for all natural numbers of processes. For example, the unbounded homogeneous dynamic Grid Protocol data replication scheme favoring columns over rows is specified by $\mathfrak{D}_{homGPcols} = \{(VSS_{GPcols}, \mathbb{N})\}$ as illustrated in Figure 3.22 (a).

A heterogeneous dynamic data replication scheme is specified by a number of tuples with each tuple relating a voting structure shape to specific numbers of processes for which it is used to generate tree-shaped voting structures. For example, the heterogeneous dynamic data replication scheme that uses Majority Consensus Voting for one, two, and three processes and the Grid Protocol favoring columns over rows for all numbers of processes greater than three, that is, $\mathfrak{D}_{het} = \{(VSS_{MCV}, \{1, 2, 3\}), (VSS_{GPcols}, \mathbb{N} \setminus \{1, 2, 3\})\}$, is depicted in Figure 3.22 (b).

An example of a homogeneous dynamic data replication scheme that has a static upper bound of four processes and uses the Grid Protocol favoring rows over columns for numbers of processes ranging from one to four, that is, $\mathfrak{D}_{\lceil homGProws \rceil} = \{(VSS_{GProws}, \{1, \ldots, 4\})\}$, is shown in Figure 3.22 (c).

Static data replication schemes are covered by the specification formalism via explicitly specifying one single voting structure shape (or tree-shaped voting structure) for a particular number of processes. For example, the static Grid Protocol with four processes $\mathfrak{D}_{static} = \{(VSS_{GPcols}, \{4\})\}$ is illustrated in Figure 3.22 (d). For a 2×2 grid with four processes, the Grid Protocol favoring rows over columns is equivalent to the Grid Protocol favoring columns over rows such that it could have been equivalently specified as $\mathfrak{D}_{static} = \{(VSS_{GProws}, \{4\})\}$.

Disabling the dynamics in terms of not allowing the transition to quorum systems for specific numbers of processes allows, for example, to "lower-

Number of Processes	Data Replication Scheme
∞	Grid Protocol$_{cols}$
:	Grid Protocol$_{cols}$
5	Grid Protocol$_{cols}$
4	Grid Protocol$_{cols}$
3	Grid Protocol$_{cols}$
2	Grid Protocol$_{cols}$
1	Grid Protocol$_{cols}$

(a)

Number of Processes	Data Replication Scheme
∞	Grid Protocol$_{cols}$
:	Grid Protocol$_{cols}$
5	Grid Protocol$_{cols}$
4	Grid Protocol$_{cols}$
3	Majority Consensus Voting
2	Majority Consensus Voting
1	Majority Consensus Voting

(b)

Number of Processes	Data Replication Scheme
∞	$\perp$
:	$\perp$
5	$\perp$
4	Grid Protocol$_{rows}$
3	Grid Protocol$_{rows}$
2	Grid Protocol$_{rows}$
1	Grid Protocol$_{rows}$

(c)

Number of Processes	Data Replication Scheme
∞	$\perp$
:	$\perp$
5	$\perp$
4	Grid Protocol$_{cols}$
3	$\perp$
2	$\perp$
1	$\perp$

(d)

Number of Processes	Data Replication Scheme
∞	Majority Consensus Voting
:	Majority Consensus Voting
5	Majority Consensus Voting
4	Majority Consensus Voting
3	$\perp$
2	$\perp$
1	$\perp$

(e)

Figure 3.22: Examples of a Homogeneous Dynamic (a), a Heterogeneous Dynamic (b), an Upper-Bounded Homogeneous Dynamic (c), a Static (d), and a Lower-Bounded Homogeneous Dynamic (e) Data Replication Scheme

bound" a dynamic data replication scheme as has been proposed by Jajodia and Mutchler [1988] for Dynamic Voting. As shown in Figure 3.22 (e), the "lower-bounded" homogeneous dynamic data replication scheme $\mathfrak{D}_{\lfloor \text{homMCV} \rfloor}$ $= \{(\text{VSS}_{\text{MCV}}, \mathbb{N} \setminus \{1, 2, 3\})\}$ specifies to use Majority Consensus Voting for numbers of processes exceeding three and thereby imposes a lower bound on the number of processes.

Next, the specification formalism is refined to not only allow a different static data replication scheme to be used per stage of the dynamics but to also allow different static data replication schemes within a stage of the dynamics, depending on the concrete subset of the set of processes forming the new epoch.

Intra-Stage Dynamics   The data replication scheme specification formalism introduced above allows to specify different quorum systems in terms of tree-shaped voting structures to be used over the various stages of the dynamics and is, in this sense, an *inter-stage* specification formalism. Recall that a tree-shaped voting structure specifies the quorum system for all subsets of the set of processes having a common cardinality by varying the leaf-node-to-process-mapping (cf. Section 3.3). Hence, for a particular number of processes, a tree-shaped voting structure specifies the quorum system in a *process-set independent* manner.

In the same line of argumentation as there is no single data replication scheme superior for all numbers of processes, there must not necessarily be a superior data replication scheme for each distinct number of processes in a given application scenario, in particular when considering the vast number of possible network topologies. Thus, even for a single number of processes, the best-option static data replication scheme to use for a given application scenario is not predetermined but instead may depend on the concrete actual network topology and the specific non-failed processes, as opposed to just their number. This fact gives rise to the need for *intra-stage* heterogeneous dynamic data replication schemes that allow different static data replication schemes to be used within a particular stage of the dynamics, depending on the very nature of the subset of the set of processes forming the new epoch. Hence, a tree-shaped voting structure specifies the *process-set dependent* quorum system for a particular subset of the set of processes.

Note that intra-stage heterogeneous dynamic data replication schemes cover inter-stage ones by specifying a particular static data replication scheme to be used for all subsets of the set of processes in a certain stage of the dynamics and specifying potentially different schemes for different stages of the dynamics. Inter-stage homogeneous dynamic data replication schemes are realized simply by specifying a particular data replication scheme to be used for all subsets of the set of processes in each stage of the dynamics.

The specification formalism is extended to support intra-stage dynamics as follows. Instead of relating numbers of processes to specific voting structure shapes or to specific (distinct) tree-shaped voting structures, the non-empty set of tuples specifying a data replication scheme must relate numbers of processes to data replication scheme specifications for particular stages of the dynamics, that is, $\hat{\mathfrak{D}} = \{(\mathfrak{D}_1, K_1), \ldots, (\mathfrak{D}_m, K_m)\}$ with $|\hat{\mathfrak{D}}| \geq 1$, $K_i \subseteq \mathbb{N}$ for $1 \leq i \leq m$, and $\forall (\mathfrak{D}_i, K_i), (\mathfrak{D}_j, K_j) \in \hat{\mathfrak{D}}, i \neq j : K_i \cap K_j = \emptyset$ but not necessarily $\bigcup_{i=1}^{m} K_i = \mathbb{N}$. Each tuple $(\mathfrak{D}_i, K_i) \in \hat{\mathfrak{D}}$ is a data replication scheme specification for numbers of processes and specific subsets of the set of processes having a cardinality as determined by (some of) the elements of K_i, formally $\mathfrak{D}_i = \{(D_{i_1}, K_{i_1}, P_{i_1}), \ldots, (D_{i_{m'}}, K_{i_{m'}}, P_{i_{m'}})\}$ with $|\mathfrak{D}_i| \geq 1$, $K_{i_j} \subseteq K_i$, $P_{i_j} \subseteq P$, and D_{i_j} referring either to a voting structure shape or to a tree-shaped voting structure, the latter if $|K_{i_j}| = 1$. For determinism and consistency, the following conditions must be met by each $(\mathfrak{D}_i, K_i) \in \hat{\mathfrak{D}}$:

(1) For each number of processes the data replication scheme specification $\mathfrak{D}_i$ is responsible and thus has at least one triple for, exactly one of them must have an empty process set, formally $\forall k \in \bigcup_{j=1}^{m'} K_{i_j}$ $\exists! (D_{i_l}, K_{i_l}, P_{i_l}) \in \mathfrak{D}_i : k \in K_{i_l} \wedge P_{i_l} = \emptyset$. This triple determines the quorum system for k processes if no other triple having a non-empty process set is defined for k processes.

(2) If a triple in $\mathfrak{D}_i$ has a non-empty process set, then the process set cardinality matches the single number of processes for which the triple is destined to be used, formally
$$\forall (D_{i_l}, K_{i_l}, P_{i_l}) \in \mathfrak{D}_i, P_{i_l} \neq \emptyset : |K_{i_l}| = 1 \wedge |P_{i_l}| = k \in K_{i_l}.$$

(3) Triples in $\mathfrak{D}_i$ specified to be used for the same single number of processes and having a non-empty process set must not have the same process set, formally $\forall (D_{i_j}, K_{i_j}, P_{i_j}), (D_{i_l}, K_{i_l}, P_{i_l}) \in \mathfrak{D}_i, |K_{i_j}| = 1 = |K_{i_l}|, K_{i_j} = K_{i_l} : P_{i_j} \neq P_{i_l}$.

The identification of a tree-shaped voting structure or a voting structure shape to create the tree-shaped voting structure for the new epoch constituted with the processes $P_{e+} \subseteq P$ is as follows: First, the tuple $(\mathfrak{D}_i, K_i) \in \hat{\mathfrak{D}}$ for the number of processes $|P_{e+}| = k \in K_i$ participating in the new epoch is searched. If none is found, the currently used quorum system remains in use and the dynamics is "disabled" for this stage k of the dynamics. Otherwise, the triple $(D_{i_j}, K_{i_j}, P_{i_j})$ with $k \in K_{i_j}$ and $P_{i_j} = P_{e+}$ is identified in $\mathfrak{D}_i$. If none is found, then the always existing triple with $k \in K_{i_j}$ and $P_{i_j} = \emptyset$ is identified in $\mathfrak{D}_i$. Finally, if D_{i_j} refers to a voting structure shape, then it is interpreted to yield the according tree-shaped voting structure. Otherwise, the tree-shaped voting structure referred to by D_{i_j} is installed as the new epoch's quorum system.

Note that if different process subsets having the same cardinality are related to (different) tree-shaped voting structures, their process mapping functions must be specified such that the intended quorum systems (in the form of tree-shaped voting structures) result. If necessary, multiple tree-shaped voting structures (or voting structure shapes) being identical except for their process mapping functions have to be provided and to be referenced to accordingly.

Also note that the set of processes P may be explicitly referenced to by some $P_{i_j} \subseteq P$. The set of processes is a priori initialized in the sense that it is defined at design-time and so is any $P_{i_j} \neq \emptyset$. As a result, processes joining the system at run-time cannot be respected in the specification. This fact, however, is no real problem since intra-stage dynamics is as such a means for manual fine-tuning to suit a data replication scheme to a particular application scenario and thus not intended for general application. Nevertheless, the data replication scheme specification – in terms of an implementation's data structure – can be adapted at run-time to respect varying process sets due to processes joining or deliberately departing from the system. Analogously to the realization of the concept of epochs (cf. Section 2.5.2), a specification can be seen as the data of a replicated data object and can therefore be consistently managed using the same means, namely by using quorum systems.

The next section spotlights some aspects of voting structure shapes that are not covered here and are left for future work.

3.5 Future Work

Enhanced Modeling Power of Voting Structure Shapes   The expressive power of voting structure shapes in their current form is limited as, for example, cyclic frame edges are only allowed to interconnect a frame's fusion leaf node to the same frame's root node. Alike, a hierarchical layering of voting structure shapes with the higher-leveled ones' leaf nodes actually representing lower-leveled voting structure shapes is not directly supported. Such a layering allows to specify more elaborated data replication schemes in terms of blends of possibly multiple data replication schemes' quorum system construction rules. Supporting more sophisticated data replication scheme specifications requires a more advanced and flexible concept of frames and modifications to the frame multiplicity function and the voting structure shape instantiation algorithm.

Voting Structure Shape Equivalence Voting structure shapes – as well as tree-shaped voting structures – are graphs that have a specific interpretation semantics. Therefore, the notion of equivalence has two dimensions, one being the *graph structure-equivalence* and the other one being the *quorum system-equivalence.* Two tree-shaped voting structures are quorum system-equivalent if they express identical – or with respect to process identities isomorphic – read and write quorum sets. Two voting structure shapes are quorum system-equivalent if their resulting tree-shaped voting structures are quorum system-equivalent for every number of processes. Two voting structure shapes (tree-shaped voting structures) are graph structure-equivalent if they have the same number of nodes and edges and are identical or isomorphic with respect to their node and edge labels.

The two dimensions of graph structure-equivalence and quorum system-equivalence are not necessarily interdependent in the sense that the former implies the latter and vice versa. For example, the Grid Protocol voting structure shapes in Figure 3.19 (a) and Figure 3.19 (b) are graph structure-equivalent but not quorum system-equivalent for all numbers of processes. The former favors rows over columns while the latter favors columns over rows in the logical rectangular grids imposed on processes such that they are only quorum system-equivalent for grid structures having an identical number of rows and columns. A simple example of quorum system-equivalence but not graph structure-equivalence is illustrated by the two tree-shaped voting structures in Figure 3.23. Both express the quorum sets $\mathcal{Q}_W = \mathcal{Q}_R = \{\{p_1, p_2\}, \{p_1, p_3\}, \{p_2, p_3\}\}$ but they are not graph structure-equivalent because of the tree-shaped voting structure in Figure 3.23 (b) having one node and edge less. The according quorum system-equivalent but not graph structure-equivalent voting structure shapes are depicted in Figure 3.24 (a) and 3.24 (b).

Unlike the notion of quorum system-equivalence, the notion of graph structure-equivalence – being a strict structural measure not taking the

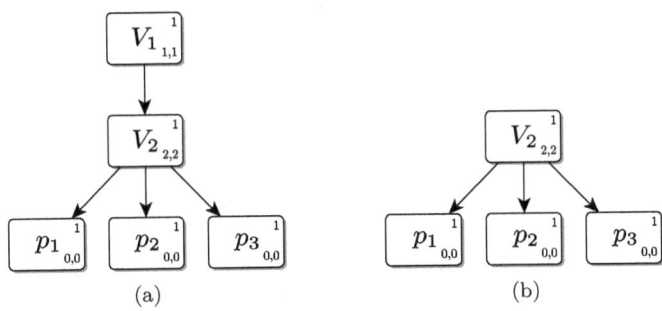

Figure 3.23: Two Quorum System-Equivalent but not Graph Structure-Equivalent Tree-Shaped Voting Structures (a) and (b)

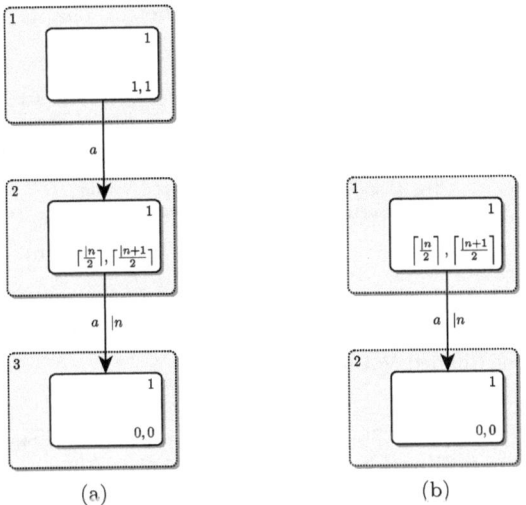

Figure 3.24: Two Quorum System-Equivalent but not Graph Structure-Equivalent Voting Structure Shapes (a) and (b)

semantics into account – is as such of limited expressiveness. However, by the prior application of semantics-guided graph transformation rules to the voting structure shapes (tree-shaped voting structures), its expressiveness can be improved. For example, the node V_1 and its connecting edge to the node V_2 in the tree-shaped voting structure of Figure 3.23 (a) are semantically not required and can therefore be removed without altering the specified quorum system. The same is true for the voting structure shape's frame 1 and its interconnecting frame edge in Figure 3.24 (a). After having removed these semantically superfluous elements, the two tree-shaped voting structures and the two voting structure shapes are graph structure-equivalent. This simple example may motivate the search for more sophisticated semantics-guided graph transformations in order to render the notion of graph structure-equivalence more expressive.

Automatic Voting Structure Shape Derivation A voting structure shape captures the inherent quorum system construction rules of a particular data replication scheme and represents the quorum systems complying to this scheme for arbitrary numbers of processes. As illustrated in Figure 3.25 (a), tree-shaped voting structures for arbitrary numbers of processes n can be derived from a voting structure shape. The reverse di-

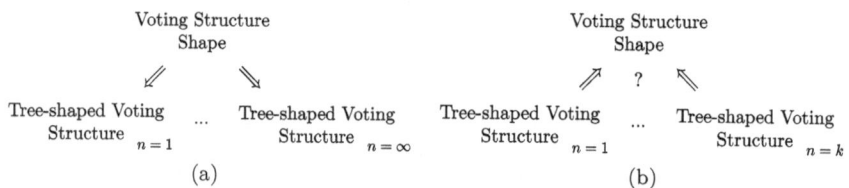

Figure 3.25: Derivation of Tree-Shaped Voting Structures from a Voting Structure Shape (a) and Distillation of a Voting Structure Shape from Tree-Shaped Voting Structures (b)

rection, that is, deriving a voting structure shape from a set of tree-shaped voting structures, is illustrated in Figure 3.25 (b). The essence of a set of tree-shaped voting structures – each being the manifestation of the quorum system construction rules of the same data replication scheme but for distinct numbers of processes – is distilled and incorporated into the resulting voting structure shape. This voting structure shape then allows to generate tree-shaped voting structures for numbers of processes beyond the cardinality k of the input set of tree-shaped voting structures from which it was distilled. Effectively, such a mechanism allows to transpose any static data replication scheme into its (homogeneous) dynamic counterpart in an automatic manner. Apparently, there is a tight coupling with the above sketched notion of voting structure shape- and tree-shaped voting structure-equivalence and semantics-guided graph transformation alongside with semantic and graph-structural abstraction of tree-shaped voting structures, the latter suggesting the application of graph shape analysis techniques.

Deriving Quality Measures from Voting Structure Shapes   Currently, (heterogeneous) dynamic data replication schemes can be evaluated by (1) deriving tree-shaped voting structures from the voting structure shapes referenced in the data replication scheme's specification followed by (2) the analysis on the resulting set of tree-shaped voting structures with respect to the quality measures of interest. The results may then be attributed to the (particular blend of) voting structure shapes. Since a voting structure shape captures the essence of a particular data replication scheme, it predetermines certain quality measures of its derived tree-shaped voting structures that are attributed to the therein embodied specific quorum system construction rules of the particular data replication scheme. For example, the write operation availability of the Tree Quorum Protocol is upper-bounded by the process availability of the logical tree structure's root node process. This upper bound is inherently anchored in the quorum system construction rules and thus also reflected by the particular frames and their composition rules as expressed in a Tree Quorum Protocol voting structure shape. Hence, there are bounds on quality measures inherently defined by a voting structure shape using particular frames in specific ways. Alike, other quality measures may be deducible from the characteristics of the individual frames of a voting structure shape.

A method that allows to directly deduce quality measures – or bounds on them – from a voting structure shape avoids the currently necessary indirection of generating and analyzing the resulting tree-shaped voting structures. One possible method is to determine data replication scheme-specific quality measure formulas that are independent of a particular number of processes and to associate voting structure shapes with these formulas. Then, the quality characteristics of a voting structure shape (or a particular blend of voting structure shapes) can be rapidly evaluated, simply by calculating the formula for the quality measure of interest. For many prominent static data replication schemes, formulas for operation availability and operation costs can be found, for example, in [Koch, 1994]. Unfortunately, for dynamic data replication schemes and in particular for heterogeneous ones, no such closed formulas are known yet. The system model for the analytical evaluation of data replication schemes to be presented in the next chapter may serve as a foundation for the development and validation of such formulas.

3.6 Summary

The concept of (intersecting) quorum sets and quorum systems is a well-established means to realize coordination and agreement among processes in distributed systems as required to implement data replication schemes guaranteeing sequential consistency. The varying needs a data replication scheme has to face during the system's lifetime, such as, for example, fluctuating usage patterns [Theel, 1993c] and changing system characteristics because of component failures and recoveries, has given rise to the development of unifying quorum system specification formalisms and universal data replication scheme frameworks [Ahamad, Ammar et al., 1990, 1991; Theel, 1993a,b; Theel and Strauß, 1998]. They introduce a flexibility and improve on maintainability in terms of enabling an easy quorum system reconfiguration, simply by adopting the specification rather than the implementation. Hence, only the particular data replication scheme specification is specifically tailored towards the application scenario. However, common to these approaches is the restriction to either static or homogeneous dynamic data replication schemes, the latter with having an at design-time determined upper bound on the number of processes manageable at run-time.

In this chapter, a data replication scheme specification formalism employing voting structure shapes has been presented by which dynamic data replication schemes are (1) dispensed from their restriction to homogeneity and are (2) relieved from the a priori defined static upper bound on the number of processes manageable at run-time. The latter enables and fosters the application of quorum-based data replication schemes to more dynamic environments in which processes join and leave the system deliberately at run-time. Such systems cannot be adequately addressed by traditional bounded dynamic data replication schemes. In addition to the flexibility in the number of processes, a second dimension of flexibility is introduced by allowing dynamic data replication schemes to be heterogeneous. Thereby, new possibilities to balance quality measures such as operation availability and operation costs are unveiled that allow to match an application's needs more closely than possible using traditional homogeneous (and bounded) dynamic data replication schemes.

Having chosen a particular, potentially heterogeneous dynamic data replication scheme for a specific application scenario, the chosen data replication scheme must be carefully evaluated as it has a strong impact on the quality-of-service and the performance of the system. The next chapter introduces a novel analytical quality measure evaluation method that is based on tree-shaped voting structures and voting structure shapes introduced in this chapter. This foundation enables the analytical evaluation of heterogeneous dynamic data replication schemes, including homogeneous dynamic and static data replication schemes, the latter as a special case.

4 Analytical Evaluation of Heterogeneous Dynamic Data Replication Schemes

The choice of a data replication scheme – and thus a particular quality measure trade-off – needs to be carefully drawn and evaluated as it is crucial to the resulting quality of the distributed system. Evaluation methods based on simulation are no good candidates because of their massive time complexity or, if run in an acceptable amount of time, their approximate nature of results. Contrarily, methods based on stochastic analysis are fast and accurate but demand for a carefully chosen higher level of abstraction in the system model: An analytical model which is as detailed as a simulation model is in general not tractable due to exponential time and space requirements. On the other hand, a higher abstraction bears the risk of oversimplification. Therefore, the analytical system model must be as precise as necessary and as abstract as possible for it to provide meaningful results and to be tractable at all.

While static data replication schemes can be modeled by and are easily analyzed via calculating combinatorial formulas (given some simplifying assumptions such as perfect channels), modeling and analyzing dynamic data replication schemes is a difficult task. It needs a careful modeling of the system as the dynamics greatly increases the complexity of the system model such that it is no longer easily analytically solvable – if solvable at all. There have been some approaches to analytically evaluate dynamic data replication schemes [Chen and Wang, 1996a,b,c; Chen, Wang et al., 2004a; Dugan and Ciardo, 1989; Jajodia and Mutchler, 1990; Pâris, 1986a; Wang, Chen et al., 2000], but all these approaches are restricted to *unstructured homogeneous* dynamic data replication schemes in terms of homogeneous dynamic variants of the unstructured static Majority Consensus Voting [Thomas, 1979]. Therefore, their application is limited to this very specific subclass of data replication schemes. Besides being limited to a specific subclass of data replication schemes, each of these approaches is specifically tailored to evaluate a particular data replication scheme and, therefore, is inapplicable to the evaluation of other schemes. Moreover, these approaches only consider the write operation. Also, they are concerned with (write) operation availability – or closely related measures such as (write) operation reliability – as the only quality measure of interest. They neglect the read operation and other quality measures such as message complexity – a measure of operation costs in terms of the number of processes in a quorum and thus the number of messages needed to effectuate a quorum. Hence, they neglect a distinguishing aspect of different data replication schemes in terms of their individual quality measure trade-off.

In this chapter, a *comprehensive* approach to the analytical evaluation of quorum-based data replication schemes in terms of a compositional system model framework is presented. In contrast to previous approaches, it allows to evaluate unstructured and structured homogeneous and moreover heterogeneous dynamic data replication schemes. It also applies for static data replication schemes as a simple special case. The system model is capable of reflecting different data replication schemes – which is realized simply by exchanging the quorum systems specification – without requiring modifications to the general system model. Finally, the system model allows other quality measures besides operation availability and its related measure operation reliability to be evaluated for the read operation as well as for the write operation.

This chapter is structured as follows. First, a synopsis on petri nets and their various extensions up to *Generalized Stochastic Petri Nets* [Marsan, Conte et al., 1984; Marsan, Balbo et al., 1995] and finally *Stochastic Reward Nets* [Ciardo, Blakemore et al., 1993; Ciardo, Muppala et al., 1992] is given in Section 4.1 to assist the understanding of the discussion on related work and the system model. Readers familiar with the matter may skip this section. Subsequently, related work and commonly made assumptions to simplify system models are discussed in Section 4.2. Then, the modular system model is presented in Section 4.3. A detailed overview of the aspects discussed is given in the section's introduction. After the presentation of the system model, its instrumentation to evaluate different quality measures is outlined in Section 4.4. An example evaluation is presented in the next chapter. Finally, future work is sketched in Section 4.5 prior to the conclusion of this chapter in Section 4.6.

4.1 Introduction to Petri Nets

In this section, a brief synopsis on petri nets is given that introduces the notions used for petri nets to assist the understanding of the means and concepts presented in the remainder of this chapter. For a more thorough introduction confer, for example, to the books by Peterson [1981] and Marsan, Balbo et al. [1995] or to the survey papers by Peterson [1977] and Murata [1989].

A *petri net structure* [Peterson, 1977] is composed of a set of places S, a set of transitions T, an input function I, and an output function O. The input and output functions relate places and transitions: The input function associates *input places* to a transition while the output function associates a transition to *output places*. The corresponding graphical structure, termed *petri net graph* [Peterson, 1977], is a bipartite directed multigraph. This means that the graph's nodes belong to two different classes, namely places and transitions. A directed edge (termed *arc*) is only allowed to connect nodes belonging to different classes. Originally, arcs were restricted to have a *cardinality* of one, that is, for a place and a transition, at most one arc connects the place (transition) to the transition (place). However, the modeling power of petri nets allowing multiple-cardinality arcs is the same as for petri nets allowing only single-cardinality arcs but offers better modeling convenience [Murata, 1989]. Therefore, multiple arcs connecting a place (transition) to a transition (place) are allowed as defined by an arc's cardinality. A petri net structure is formally defined as follows.

Definition 4.1 (Petri Net Structure)   A petri net structure is a quadruple (S, T, I, O) where
$S = \{s_1, \ldots, s_n\}$ is the set of places,
$T = \{t_1, \ldots, t_m\}$ is the set of transitions with $S \cap T = \emptyset$,
$I : S \times T \; \rangle \; \mathbb{N}_0$ is the input function defining a transition's incoming arcs from its input places and their cardinality, and
$O : T \times S \to \mathbb{N}_0$ is the output function defining a transition's outgoing arcs to their output places and their cardinality.

For a transition $t \in T$,
$^\bullet t = \{s : I(s, t) > 0\}$ is the set of its input places and
$t^\bullet = \{s : O(t, s) > 0\}$ is the set of its output places.
Analogously, for a place $s \in S$,
$^\bullet s = \{t : O(t, s) > 0\}$ is the set of its input transitions and
$s^\bullet = \{t : I(s, t) > 0\}$ is the set of its output transitions.

The notion of a state is introduced to petri net structures by assigning so-called *token* to the places via an assignment function called *marking* $M : S \to \mathbb{N}_0$.

Definition 4.2 (Petri Net)   A petri net structure with an initial marking $M_0 \in \mathbb{N}_0^{|S|}$ is termed a *marked petri net* (in short *petri net*) and is defined by the 5-tuple (S,T,I,O,M_0) where (S, T, I, O) forms a petri net structure.

The distribution of token among places – the so-called *current marking* – represents the current state of a petri net. Graphically, the number of token that reside on a place are represented by the same number of filled black circles on that place. For example, one token resides on place s_1 in Figure 4.1 (a) while no token is assigned to place s_2. For a given marking M, $M(s)$ gives the number of token on place $s \in S$ in this marking M. For example, $M(s) = k$ denotes that k token are on place s in marking M. A marking can also be represented as a $|S|$-vector $(M(s_1), \ldots, M(s_n))^\mathsf{T}$.

The current state of a petri net is changed to a subsequent state by *firing* an enabled transition. A transition t is *enabled* in a state M, denoted by $M[t\rangle$, if the number of token on each of its input places in ${}^\bullet t$ is greater than or equal to the cardinality of the arc connecting them. An enabled transition t in a state M may fire whereupon (1) from each place in its input set ${}^\bullet t$ as many token as defined by their connecting arc's cardinality are removed and (2) on each place in its output set $t^\bullet$ as many token as defined by their connecting arc's cardinality are deposited, thereby resulting in a subsequent state $M' = M + O(t) - I(t)$, in a more compact form: $M[t\rangle M'$. The notion $O(t)$ is a suggestive shortcut for $(O(t, s_1), \ldots, O(t, s_n))^\mathsf{T}$ and $I(t)$ is a shortcut for $(I(s_1, t), \ldots, I(s_n, t))^\mathsf{T}$. Note that the subsequent state reached by firing a transition only depends on the current state.

If more than one transition is enabled in a marking, then the choice of which transition to fire is non-deterministic. The firing of one of the multiple enabled transitions results in a subsequent marking in which formerly enabled transitions may no longer be enabled and formerly not enabled transitions may become enabled. If no transition is enabled in a marking, then the *execution* of the petri net in terms of firing transitions stops. The sequential firing $M[t_1, \ldots, t_n\rangle M'$ of the transitions $t_1, \ldots, t_n$ reaching the marking M' from a marking M is termed a *firing sequence*. A marking M' that results from firing the single transition t_1 is said to be *immediately reachable* from the marking M in which t_1 is enabled. A marking M' is *reachable* from a marking M if it is either immediately reachable or there

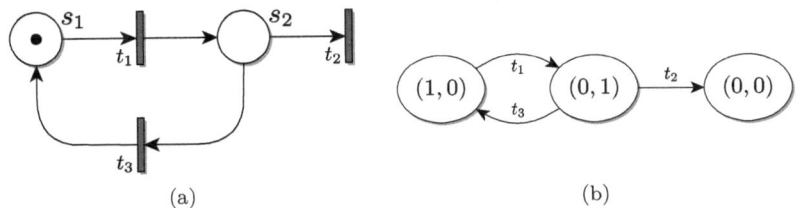

Figure 4.1: Example Petri Net (a) and its Reachability Graph (b)

exists a firing sequence transitioning from the marking M to the marking M' in which the intermediate markings are immediately reachable.

Recall that the current state of a petri net is represented by its current marking. The state space is the set of all possible markings $\mathbb{N}_0^{|S|}$. The *reachability set* is the – possibly infinite – set of states to which the petri net can potentially evolve from the initial marking by firing transitions. Thus, a system model's behavior does not only depend on the petri net graph but also on the initial marking: Changing the initial marking can completely change the system model behavior. The *reachability graph* is the graph representation of the reachability set in terms of a directed graph. From an infinite reachability graph, a finite one can be obtained by applying abstraction techniques [Peterson, 1981]. For a method on how to construct reachability sets and reachability graphs refer to, for example, Peterson [1981] or Marsan, Balbo et al. [1995].

As a simple example of reachability sets and reachability graphs, consider the petri net in Figure 4.1 (a) with the place set $S = \{s_1, s_2\}$ and the transition set $T = \{t_1, t_2, t_3\}$. The transition t_2 is a sink transition which consumes token when fired while not producing any. The initial marking is $M_0 = (1,0)^\mathsf{T}$. The transitions' incoming arcs and their cardinalities are $I(s_1, t_1) = 1$, $I(s_2, t_2) = 1$, $I(s_2, t_3) = 1$, and zero otherwise. The transitions' outgoing arcs and their cardinalities are $O(t_1, s_2) = 1$, $O(t_3, s_1) = 1$, and zero otherwise. The state space is $\{(1,0), (0,1), (0,0), (1,1)\}$. The reachability set is $\{(1,0), (0,1), (0,0)\}$. The reachability graph is depicted in Figure 4.1 (b) in which the initial state is marked by the label $(1,0)$ conforming to the initial marking $M_0 = (1,0)^\mathsf{T}$. The state labeled $(0,0)$ is an end state of the petri net. Whenever this state is reached, the only token in the petri net is consumed by the sink transition t_2. Thereafter, no transition is enabled and the execution of the petri net stops.

A number of extensions to petri nets have been proposed to increase modeling power and modeling convenience. A selection of them is informally introduced in the following.

Inhibitor Arcs The concept of *inhibitor arcs* [Cumani, 1985; Dugan, Bobbio et al., 1985; Dugan, Trivedi et al., 1984; Peterson, 1981] allows to test places for a zero marking or a marking less than the cardinality of the inhibitor arc. A transition that is connected by inhibitor arcs to so-called *inhibition places* is enabled only if each of its inhibition places has a number of token that is strictly less than the cardinality of their connecting inhibitor arc. An inhibitor arc is graphically represented as a hollow rhombic-head arc originating from a transition and leading to the inhibition place.

As a simple example, consider the petri net in Figure 4.2 (a). The place s_1 has four token and is connected via the two transitions t_1 and t_2 to the place s_2. If enabled, the transitions consume one token from place s_1 and deposit one token on place s_2. While transition t_1 is enabled as long as there is a token on place s_1, transition t_2 is only enabled if in addition place s_2 has zero token as tested for by the inhibitor arc. Hence, once either transition t_1 or transition t_2 has fired, transition t_2 does not become enabled anymore.

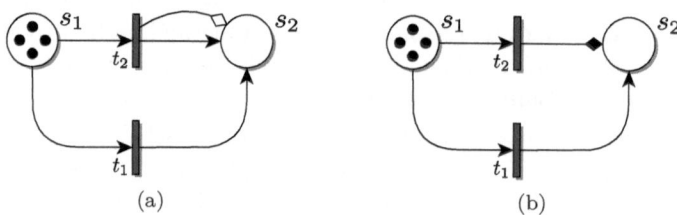

(a)   (b)

Figure 4.2: Example of an Inhibitor Arc (a) and a Combined Inhibitor and Regular Arc (b)

For a more concise graphical representation of an inhibitor arc connecting a transition to a place and an ordinary arc emerging from the same transition and leading to the same place, both are combined into one arc which is depicted as an inhibitor arc with a solid black filled rhombic head as illustrated in Figure 4.2 (b).

Inhibitor arcs give petri nets the same computational power as Turing Machines and are, therefore, a significant extension to the modeling power of petri nets [Peterson, 1981]. Unfortunately, increasing modeling power decreases decision power in terms of the set of properties that may be analyzed. Thus, many decision problems become undecidable in general when using inhibitor arcs. Examples are *liveness*, that is, from each marking there is a firing sequence that eventually enables any transition, and *boundedness*, that is, the number of token on any place in the petri net does not exceed an upper bound.

Transition Priorities *Transition priorities* [Cumani, 1985; Dugan, Bobbio et al., 1985] can be employed to sequentialize the otherwise non-deterministic firing behavior of petri nets by prioritizing the transitions in the firing order intended. Firing higher-prioritized transitions is given precedence over firing lower-prioritized transitions. The lowest transition priority is 0 and the symbol ∞ identifies the highest transition priority. The same priority can be assigned to multiple transitions, thereby introducing a partial order and forming a *priority set* in which the firing behavior is non-deterministic. Priority sets having higher priority are considered prior to lower-prioritized priority sets for firing one of their enabled transitions. The priority of a transition is represented by a superscript on the transition label. For example, if the transition t_2 should be prioritized over the transition t_1 in Figure 4.2 (b), the two transitions become, for example, t_2^1 and t_1^0. In absence of an explicitly defined priority, the lowest priority 0 is assumed as default and henceforth omitted from figures and transition labels.

Note that transition priorities can be expressed by inhibitor arcs. Therefore, transition priorities also give petri nets the same computational power as Turing Machines.

Stochastic Petri Nets and Generalized Stochastic Petri Nets The original petri net formalism has no explicit notion of time. In order to use petri nets for the quantitative analysis of performance and reliability measures, an explicit notion of time has been introduced. It led to *Deterministic Petri Nets* in which transitions are associated with time variables that are deterministic and to *Stochastic Petri Nets* [Molloy, 1982] in which the time variables associated to transitions are exponentially distributed random variables.

The petri net in Figure 4.3 (a) is a stochastic petri net with two *timed transitions* T_1 and T_2 that are graphically represented by hollow bars having uppercase transition labels T_1 and T_2. A stochastic petri net is a high-level

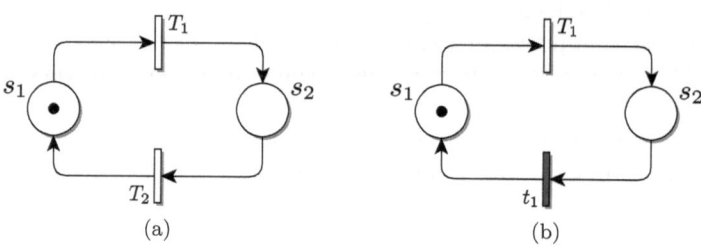

Figure 4.3: Example of a Stochastic Petri Net (a) and a Generalized Stochastic Petri Net (b)

representation of the underlying stochastic process in terms of its reachability graph, given that the stochastic petri net is k-bounded, that is, the number of token on any of its places does not exceed an upper bound $k \in \mathbb{N}$ [Molloy, 1982]. Then, the reachability graph is isomorphic to a *continuous-time Markov chain* [Molloy, 1982]. Analysis methods for qualitative properties like boundedness or liveness of ordinary petri nets are applicable unaltered to such stochastic petri nets since the state space of the underlying stochastic process and the reachability set of the stochastic petri net are isomorphic.

However, stochastic petri nets are inappropriate if in addition to the evolution over time purely logical aspects that cannot be reasonably associated with time are to be expressed in the system model since every transition has to be associated with stochastic firing times. *Generalized Stochastic Petri Nets* [Marsan, Conte et al., 1984; Marsan, Balbo et al., 1995] relieve this restriction by introducing – in addition to timed transitions that are associated with stochastic firing delays – a second type of transition that fires in zero time, the *immediate transition*. Markings in which immediate transitions are enabled are said to be in the *logics domain* while markings in which timed transitions are enabled are in the *time domain*. Figure 4.3 (b) depicts a generalized stochastic petri net with a timed transition labeled T_1 and an immediate transition labeled t_1. A generalized stochastic petri net can be automatically transformed into a continuous-time Markov chain if the reachability set is finite and no *vanishing loop* exists meaning that not always only immediate transitions are enabled [Ciardo, 1989; Ciardo, Blakemore et al., 1993]. In case of a finite reachability set, the extensions raising petri nets to the power of Turing Machines improve modeling convenience but do not extend the class of systems that may be represented beyond that of finite state machines [Ciardo, Blakemore et al., 1993; Peterson, 1981].

Generalized stochastic petri nets by the definition of Marsan, Balbo et al. [1995] support inhibitor arcs and transition priorities. To further increase modeling convenience, variable marking-dependent arc cardinalities and transition enabling functions have been introduced and are explained next.

Variable Marking-Dependent Arc Cardinalities The cardinality of an arc is defined as a constant natural number. If, for example, all token of a place should be moved to another place without knowing beforehand how many token reside on the source place, this cannot be modeled in a compact way and auxiliary constructions are required. A more convenient way is to use *variable marking-dependent arc cardinalities* [Meyer, Movaghar et al., 1985] that allow to specify the cardinalities of a transition's input and output arcs as functions of the net's current marking. Note that allowing variable marking-dependent arc cardinalities only affects modeling convenience since semantically equivalent constructs can be built using inhibitor arcs.

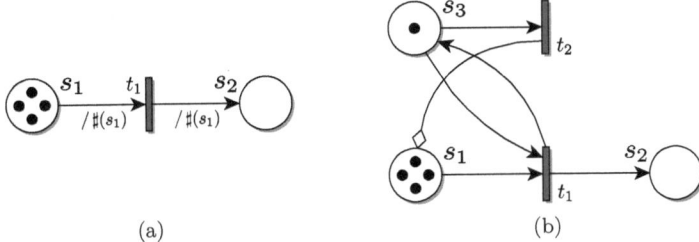

(a)   (b)

Figure 4.4: Example of the Semantical Equivalence of using Variable Marking-Dependent Arc Cardinalities (a) and Inhibitor Arcs (b) by Moving All Token from Place s_1 to Place s_2

For example, an excerpt from a petri net by which all token are moved from place s_1 to place s_2 is shown in Figure 4.4. In Figure 4.4 (a), this is realized via marking-dependent arc cardinalities. The transition's input arc from s_1 to t_1 and the transition's output arc from t_1 to s_2 are both attributed with $/\,\sharp(s_1)$ which is a function of the net's current marking and evaluates the arc cardinality to $M(s_1)$, the number of token on place s_1. In Figure 4.4 (b), moving all token from place s_1 to place s_2 is realized by an auxiliary construction using an inhibitor arc.

Henceforth, more elaborated arc cardinality functions are represented in figures by the symbol $/\,\text{\Lightning}$ for an outgoing and by $/\,\Psi$ for an incoming arc cardinality function that are implemented separately. For example, the arc cardinality functions for the above example are

function $/\Psi(t_1 \leftarrow s_1)$:
    return $\sharp(s_1)$

and

function $/\textrm{\ddh}(t_1 \rightarrow s_2)$:
    return $\sharp(s_1)$.

The shortcut $/\sharp$ attributed to a transition's incoming arc refers to the marking of the place the arc emerges from.

Transition Enabling Functions (Guards)   A transition enabling function [Dugan, Bobbio et al., 1985; Meyer, Movaghar et al., 1985], in short called a *guard*, is a boolean function of the petri net's current marking. A transition's guard must evaluate to true for the transition to become enabled in the current marking, in addition to the enabling condition on the number of token on the transition's input places and the conditions possibly expressed by inhibitor arcs and transition priorities. Guards represent a convenient modeling shortcut compared to the modeling of enabling condition logics via inhibitor arcs and transition priorities.

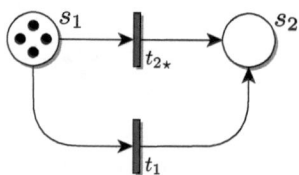

Figure 4.5: Example of a Transition Enabling Function (Guard)

For example, consider the petri net in Figure 4.5 that models the same behavior as the petri nets in Figure 4.2 used to illustrate inhibitor arcs. Instead of an inhibitor arc testing the place s_2 for zero token, the transition t_2 is attached a guard which is graphically represented by the transition label being suffixed with a star. In accordance to the inhibitor arcs of Figure 4.2, the guard expression is

$$\textrm{true} \leftarrow [\sharp(s_2) = 0] \qquad\qquad\qquad\qquad\qquad \textrm{(Guard } t_2)$$

such that the guarded transition $t_{2\star}$ can only become enabled if place s_2 has zero token (and place s_1 has at least one token as required by its incoming arc from its input place s_1).

Stochastic Reward Nets   *Stochastic Reward Nets* [Ciardo, Blakemore et al., 1993; Ciardo, Muppala et al., 1992] are an extension to generalized stochastic petri nets and additionally support, amongst other features, variable marking-dependent arc cardinalities, guards, and rewards. *Rewards* are numerical values associated with certain conditions on the petri net expressed in terms of a marking. The employment of rewards can reduce the size of the petri net because many aspects of a system model that had to be explicitly modeled by introducing dedicated places and transitions if generalized stochastic petri nets were used instead, can be expressed by arithmetic and boolean expressions on the markings of the petri net. These expressions translate to reward rates being attached to each state of the underlying stochastic process, which is a *Markov reward model*. For example, to compute the reliability of a system, those states (markings of the petri net) in which the system is functioning are assigned a reward of 1 while the other states get a reward of 0. The expected value of the reward rate function at a given time instant then gives the availability of the system at that time. Thus, system dependability quality measures can be computed as reward-based measures.

By the features provided, stochastic reward nets permit a much more concise system model description than possible with generalized stochastic petri nets. Let aside reward-based measures (as some are not expressible by generalized stochastic petri net-means [Ciardo, Muppala et al., 1989]), a stochastic reward net can be transformed into a continuous-time Markov chain like for generalized stochastic petri nets.

Next, related work to the analytical evaluation of quorum-based data replication schemes is discussed in preparation to present the system model in Section 4.3.

4.2 Related Work

Generally, models for dependability measure evaluation can be categorized into (1) combinatorial models and (2) state space-based models.

The former category comprises, for example, the well-known fault trees with repeated events and reliability block diagrams. Calculating combinatorial formulas to evaluate the operation availability of static data replication schemes also belongs to this category. For example, the operation availability provided by the unstructured static Majority Consensus Voting is given by the formula $\sum_{k=\text{maj}(n)}^{n} \binom{n}{k} \cdot a^k \cdot (1-a)^{n-k}$ where a is the uniform process availability, n is the number of processes, and $\text{maj}(n) = \lceil n/2 \rceil$ for calculating the read operation availability and $\text{maj}(n) = \lceil (n+1)/2 \rceil$ for calculating the write operation availability [Koch, 1994], provided that processes fail independently and are fully interconnected by perfect channels.

The latter category of state space-based models includes, for example, continuous-time Markov chains and stochastic petri net-based models such as generalized stochastic petri nets and stochastic reward nets. State space-based models have a greater modeling power than combinatorial models as they are able to, for example, capture the evolution of a system over time and to reflect dependencies with respect to failure and repair facilities, both of which combinatorial models are not capable of. A system employing a – in a broader sense – dynamic data replication scheme to manage a replicated data object evolves over time, for example, by the number of processes varying due to failures and recoveries or by switching among quorum systems. Hence, initial approaches to the analytical evaluation of dynamic data replication schemes have used state space-based models in terms of continuous-time Markov chains to model the system behavior.

Continuous-Time Markov Chain-Based System Models   Conceptually, continuous-time Markov chain-based approaches to model a system explicitly enumerate the state space of the system and define a state predicate against which each state is tested. The predicate evaluates to true if the quality measure of interest is satisfied, for example, if the read or write operation is available, and to false otherwise.

The model by Pâris [1986a] to evaluate *Voting with a Variable Number of Witnesses* may serve as a first example of this type of system modeling. It assumes that processes are fully interconnected and that channels (respectively, their underlying communication links) are perfect while processes may fail by crashing. A process is assigned a vote and it manages a local copy of the replica plus its metadata. A *witness* [Pâris, 1986b] is a process not managing a local copy of the replica: It is assigned a vote, it manages replica metadata like non-witness processes do, and it may cast its vote to perform operations just like non-witness processes. Processes can be transformed into witnesses and witnesses can be equipped with a copy of the replica data. At least one non-witness process must be present in every quorum. Otherwise, a read operation cannot be served since witness processes do not have a local copy of the replica data to read from. Alike, a value written by a write operation only to witness processes cannot be read afterwards. On the other hand, a witness process needs no process-local storage space to maintain the replica data and it is updated cheaply upon write operations as only metadata instead of the usually much larger replica data must be updated.

As a second example, Jajodia and Mutchler [1990] have modeled *Dynamic (Linear) Voting* by a continuous-time Markov chain. They also assume a fully interconnected network topology but allow channels to crash-fail while processes are perfect or vice versa.

In both models, process (channel) failures and recoveries are assumed to be stochastically independent with identical failure and recovery rates. Hence, processes (channels) are identical with respect to their availability and, as unstructured data replication schemes are used, processes are considered equivalent as each is equally suited for being in a particular read or write quorum. Three commonly made assumptions to simplify a system model and to considerably reduce its complexity are (1) *instantaneous operations*, (2) *frequent operations*, and (3) *perfect channels*. While the former two are assumed for both system models, the latter is assumed for the model by Pâris [1986a] whereas either perfect channels or perfect processes are assumed for the model by Jajodia and Mutchler [1990].

Instantaneous Operations Assumption   Assuming *instantaneous operations* requires operations to take effect immediately on the time instant they are performed, thereby neglecting and alleviating the need to incorporate delays due to message propagation or processing time into a system model. More importantly, the handling of failures while an operation is being executed, for example, by integrating a (non-blocking) commit protocol [Skeen, 1981] into the system model, must not be considered. The instantaneous operations assumption can be justified by the very high speed of modern hardware and network infrastructure leaving only a very small window of vulnerability – and thus probability of occurrence – to such events.

Nevertheless, this simplifying assumption results in an overestimation of the quality measures provided by a system in favor of a tractable system model. For example, Liu, Chen et al. [2003] have proposed a system model that uses the unstructured static Majority Consensus Voting to study the impact of network and processing time delays on the performance of the system. In this system model, neither processes nor channels are allowed to fail for it to be tractable.

The instantaneous operations assumption greatly simplifies system models since failures and recoveries as well as problems arising therefrom must not be considered while performing operations.

Frequent Operations Assumption   The second assumption of frequent operations is concerned with the dynamics in terms of quorum system reconfiguration in response to detected failures. Failure detection and quorum system reconfiguration are usually closely tied to operation execution: Process failures are assumed to be detected while forming a quorum for executing an operation and, if a process has been detected as failed, a quorum system reconfiguration attempt is initiated. Assuming *frequent operations* means assuming that in between two failure or recovery events always at least one operation execution is triggered. To guarantee this assumption, an operation execution is triggered upon the failure or recovery event. Hence, the quorum system can potentially be adapted upon every failure and recovery event, thereby alleviating the need to model sequences of failure and recovery events in the system model after each of which a quorum system reconfiguration has to be attempted. Joint failure or recovery events are implicitly prohibited by assuming frequent operations. The dynamics is employed in an optimal fashion when assuming frequent operations – which is the reason for the resulting operation availabilities representing upper bounds. The frequent operations assumption is justified by the assumption that operations are usually far more frequent than failure and recovery events. Otherwise, the replicated data object may be used too infrequently to justify the employment of data replication techniques for providing high operation availability in the first place.

An (un)available operation remains (un)available at least until the next failure or recovery event. When assuming frequent operations and evaluating operation availability only, therefore, no further intermittent operation executions in between two failure or recovery events have to be performed. Only exactly one operation execution is triggered in between two process failure or recovery events, namely upon the failure or recovery event. As a consequence, replica actuality is negligible as a process' replica remains either current or outdated after the failure- or recovery-induced operation execution until the next operation execution is triggered by the next process failure or recovery event. Alike, a failed process is assumed to be detected, even if it is not (unsuccessfully) probed while forming a quorum: As the failure event of a process triggers an operation execution, the actually failed process must not be probed and thereby detected during quorum building in order to know that some process has failed. When concerned with operation availability only, these consequences of assuming frequent operations allow for a simpler system model. For the evaluation of other quality measures considering, for example, replica actuality, further intermittent operations in between two process failure or recovery events may have to be triggered.

Perfect Channels Assumption Assuming perfect channels and thus neglecting network partitioning due to channel failures seems contradictory to using quorum systems as they are actually designed to tolerate network partitioning without sacrificing consistency. Nonetheless, in order to give generally comparable quality measure results, this assumption may be well justified considering the vast number of possible network topologies. However, channel failures cannot be disregarded when evaluating a data replication scheme for a concrete application scenario. Doing so results in overestimated quality measures as the following example will illustrate.

In the setting of frequent operations and perfect channels interconnecting every two processes, the optimal data replication scheme with respect to operation availability and message complexity is the 2-out-of-3 quorum system: Out of a set of $n \geq 3$ processes, three arbitrarily chosen processes form the quorum system of the current epoch. Note that this quorum system resembles the quorum system of the unstructured static Majority Consensus Voting with three processes. The 2-out-of-3 quorum system tolerates the failure of exactly one process as the two remaining non-failed processes form a write quorum which is necessary for the quorum system reconfiguration in terms of an epoch change operation. Upon a process failure – and as long as there are at least three non-failed processes in the system – the epoch change operation switches to a subsequent 2-out-of-3 quorum system in which the failed process is replaced by an arbitrarily chosen non-failed process. Otherwise, if only two non-failed processes are left in the system, the epoch change operation switches to a Majority Consensus Voting quorum system with these two remaining non-failed processes. Upon the recovery of a failed process, this process is reintegrated into the quorum system, resulting in a 2-out-of-3 quorum system. Otherwise, in case of a further process failure, the write operation and the epoch change operation become unavailable as no two processes forming a write quorum are non-failed. The read operation remains available with the single non-failed process. Upon the failure of this last process, the read operation also becomes unavailable. Eventually, the read operation as well as the write operation become available again as failed processes recover from their failure. With an available write operation, the epoch change operation can switch to a 2-out-of-3 quorum system upon the recovery of a further process. Note that only processes considered in the current quorum system may perform operations while processes not considered therein are assumed to be "passive" until they become "active" upon being considered in a successive current quorum system.

Hence, as long as at least two processes are non-failed, the write operation is available while the read operation is available as long as at least one process has not failed, regardless of the total number $n \geq 3$ of processes in the system. At most three processes are required for a write quorum and at most two processes are required for a read quorum.

Petri Net-Based System Models A major drawback of using continuous-time Markov chain-based modeling approaches for quality measure evaluation is the need to explicitly enumerate the states of the system to be modeled. For complex systems, the state space rapidly grows very large. Apart from the state space explosion problem, it is a very difficult and challenging task to (1) identify the (minimal) relevant state space-constituting aspects and to (2) manually craft appropriate continuous-time Markov chains for such systems. Therefore, stochastic petri net-based modeling approaches in terms of generalized stochastic petri nets and stochastic reward nets have become popular: They allow to model a system in a concise fashion and the underlying stochastic process to be generated automatically from the petri net system model. Stochastic petri net-based system models can be seen as a high-level interface to the specification of stochastic processes as the reachability graph of a (k-bounded) stochastic petri net is isomorphic to a continuous-time Markov chain [Molloy, 1982]. Hence, various stochastic petri net-based approaches to the evaluation of a data replication scheme's dependability quality measures have been proposed [Chen and Wang, 1996a,b,c; Chen, Wang et al., 1999, 2000, 2004a,b; Dugan and Ciardo, 1989; Wang, Chen et al., 2000].

The System Model by Dugan and Ciardo   Dugan and Ciardo [1989]
have modeled the unstructured static Majority Consensus Voting enhanced
with the concept of witnesses [Pâris, 1986b] but without the ability to transform processes into witnesses and vice versa. Only write operations are
considered in this model. As frequent operations triggering an operation
execution upon the failure or recovery of a process are not assumed, write
operations are triggered periodically by a so-called *write operation driver*
which is modeled by a timed transition. A write operation is assumed
to take effect immediately if performed successfully, that is, instantaneous
(write) operations are assumed. Processes (witnesses) may fail by crashing.
They are assumed to be fully interconnected by perfect channels. Furthermore, it is assumed that the local replica copy (metadata) of a process
(witness) becomes outdated upon crashing. Processes (witnesses) have indistinguishable identities and their crash-failure and subsequent recovery is
assumed to be stochastically independent with identical failure and recovery
rates, respectively. Upon the recovery of a witness, its metadata remains
outdated until it is updated by a future write operation whereas a recovering non-witness process actively tries to update its local replica copy by
initiating a write operation. Whenever the write operation is not available,
a reconstruction phase is initiated. Then, an administrator is assumed to
reset all processes and witnesses – including the crash-failed ones for whose
recovery is being waited – to a common and consistent (initial) state.

Based on the manual reconstruction phase, the global knowledge about
process and witness states, and exploiting perfect channels, Dugan and Ciardo [1989] have proposed a "dynamic" variant of Majority Consensus Voting
with witnesses. In this variant, write operations are performed on a majority of *non-failed* processes instead of on a majority of all processes in the
system. Hence, write operations can be performed until the last non-witness
process fails whereupon the manual reconstruction phase is initiated.

The Original System Model by Chen and Wang   The system models by Chen and Wang [1996a,c]; Chen, Wang et al. [1999, 2000, 2004a,b];
Wang, Chen et al. [2000] are based on the original system model introduced by Chen and Wang [1996b]. This model implements Dynamic Linear
Voting which is due to Jajodia and Mutchler [1990]. The system model
only considers write operations that are immediately effective, that is, instantaneous (write) operations are assumed. Processes as well as channels
may fail by crashing. They are implemented in dedicated petri net-subnets,
thereby allowing (1) processes and channels to have individual independent

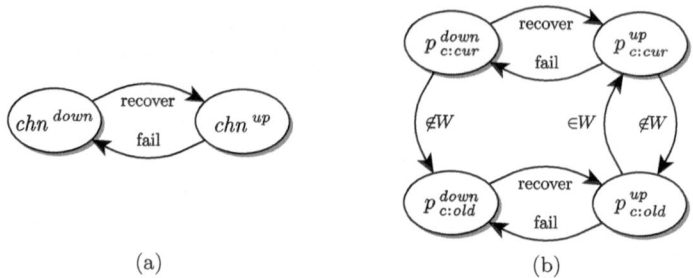

(a)   (b)

Figure 4.6: States and State Transitions of Channels (a) and Processes (b) in
the Original Petri Net System Model due to Chen and Wang [1996b]

failure and recovery rates and (2) the processes to have a unique identity
which, however, is not exploited beyond allowing for individual failure and
recovery rates.

A petri net-subnet modeling a channel that interconnects two processes
consists of two state places representing the channel's state of either being
functional or failed. These two state places are connected via two timed
transitions modeling the channel's failure and recovery, respectively. For
a simpler presentation, the behavior of a channel as illustrated in Figure 4.6 (a) is shown in terms of a state transition diagram rather than in
terms of a petri net. The state chn^{up} represents a channel's state of being
functional and chn^{down} represents the channel's state of being failed.

A process subnet comprises four state places, namely being functional
with a current replica copy, being functional with an outdated replica copy,
being failed with a current replica copy, and being failed having an outdated replica copy. In favor of a simpler presentation, the states and state
transitions of a process instead of its petri net implementation are illus-
trated in Figure 4.6 (b) with $p^{up}_{c:cur}$, $p^{up}_{c:old}$, $p^{down}_{c:cur}$, and $p^{down}_{c:old}$ having the
respective meaning. The meaning and causes of the state transitions are
further explained in Section 4.3.1 where this process model is discussed in
more detail.

Write operations are either triggered by failure and recovery events of
channels or processes – whereby frequent (write) operations are ensured –
or by a write operation driver. In the latter case, frequent (write) operations
are realized via performing so-called *null updates* in addition to regular write
operations. A null update is a write operation that updates the processes'

metadata but does not alter their replica copy. The absence or presence of a network partitioning – which hinders successfully performing write operations – is judged by a boolean expression on the channel states in terms of an enabling condition to the attempt to perform a write operation. If the expression evaluates to true, then an arbitrarily drawn majority of the set of processes is connected and the write operation execution is initiated. Otherwise, the write operation execution is not initiated as no majority partition exists. Consequently, the write operation is not available.

A process' replica copy becomes outdated whenever the process has not participated in the most recent write operation, thus generally making no (explicit) assumption about the status of a process' replica copy when the process has failed. However, a failed process is assumed to perform a reintegration protocol in terms of a write operation upon its recovery. While this write operation, the replica copy either becomes current or is classified as outdated if the write operation is unavailable and cannot be performed. Since in this model, an available write operation is performed not just with the set of processes forming a write quorum but with *all non-failed* processes (in the majority partition), a recovered process' replica copy can become updated even if the process is not part of the actual write quorum (but in the majority partition). Hence, while no explicit assumption about the status of a failed process' replica copy is made, it is (implicitly) assumed that upon the process' recovery, its replica copy is either updated to the current value or marked as outdated.

The System Model by Chen and Wang – Repair Dependencies   A slightly modified variant of the original system model described above has been employed by Chen and Wang [1996a,c] to study the effect of repair dependencies on write operation availability. In contrast to the original system model – in which processes and channels each have individual and independent repair facilities – processes and channels share a single repair facility. The repair service works either in a linear order, in a FIFO order, or in a best-effort manner repairing those failed components first that are more likely to have a positive effect on write operation availability. For example, the repairing of a channel by which partitions are rejoined is given precedence over repairing some randomly chosen process. In favor of a more tractable system model, only write operations that are triggered by crash-failure and recovery events of channels and processes are considered, that is, frequent (write) operations are assumed.

The System Model by Chen, Wang, and Chu – Dynamics Reconfiguration Interval   Finding the optimal reconfiguration interval for Dynamic Linear Voting with regular write operations and null updates – based on the original system model by Chen and Wang [1996b] – is the concern of Wang, Chen et al. [2000] and Chen, Wang et al. [2004a]. More specifically, a reconfiguration attempt is triggered by detected failures during the course of performing a write operation or a null update operation. The objective is to find a (reasonable) frequency of performing write operations and null update operations such that a reconfiguration attempt is performed upon every failure or recovery event, that is, the frequency satisfies the frequent operations assumption.

The System Model by Chen, Wang, and Chu – Deadline Constraints   A variant of the original system model by Chen and Wang [1996b] without support for dynamics has been employed by Chen, Wang et al. [1999, 2000] to study whether quorum-based data replication schemes in terms of the unstructured static Majority Consensus Voting are capable of meeting write operation deadline constraints. Each state of the system is classified either as a "bad" or as a "good" system state: A bad system state is a state in which the write operation is not available due to too many failed processes or channels whereas a good system state is one in which the write operation is available. For each initial bad system state, the time required to arrive in a good system state is calculated. Note that a good system state is always eventually reached as processes and channels recover from their failure. From the individual state time distributions, the overall time distribution is derived which testifies whether a write operation deadline constraint can be met or not.

The same system model and the same means have been used by Chen, Wang et al. [2004b] to evaluate a slightly different measure of interest, namely the (average) wait time as perceived by an individual process of the system. More specifically, given the system is in a bad (initial) state upon a coordinator's write operation attempt, the time until the write operation becomes available is measured.

Both of these measures are closely related to operation reliability and thereby to operation availability (cf. Section 2.4). In a sense, they describe the inverse of reliability in terms of how long (on average) the write operation is not succeeding until eventually a system state is reached in which it becomes available.

Exponentially Distributed State Sojourn Times   A handicap of all
continuous-time Markov chain-based approaches – including those ones
based on stochastic petri net models – is the underlying assumption of exponentially distributed sojourn times, meaning that failure and recovery events
are assumed to be Poisson distributed. While technical equipment like computers and network hardware may be believed to follow exponential lifetime
distributions, repair times do not as they may depend on human interaction,
for example, by an administrator. Nevertheless, lifetime as well as repair
times are commonly assumed to be exponentially distributed as this assumption allows to analytically solve a system model using tool packages such as
the Stochastic Petri Net Package (SPNP) by Ciardo, Muppala et al. [1989].

A related aspect is that the system components' physical aging is not
taken into consideration due to the exponential distribution's property of
being memoryless. The lifetime of a process or channel is always sampled
from the same (individual) exponential distribution function and each sample reading is statistically equivalent to the initial sample reading. Physical
aging can be considered and implemented, for example, by adopting the
distribution function parameter(s) after a component's failure and prior to
a new life cycle of the component by decreasing, for example, the mean.
However, while the system model to be presented is not constrained in
this respect, tool support to alter distribution function characteristics at
analysis run-time is currently lacking. Hence, assuming exponentially distributed firing times poses no general limitation *per se* on a stochastic petri
net-based system model since the model by itself in terms of the petri net
is independent of the stochastic process underlying it.

Summary of Related Work

Abstractly speaking, all discussed approaches [Chen and Wang, 1996a,b,c;
Chen, Wang et al., 1999, 2000, 2004a,b; Dugan and Ciardo, 1989; Jajodia
and Mutchler, 1990; Pâris, 1986a; Wang, Chen et al., 2000] have in common that they judge by the mere number of non-failed processes (channels)
whether the write operation is available or not. Therefore, they are restricted to the unstructured static Majority Consensus Voting or one of its
homogeneous dynamic variants – even excluding the unstructured Weighted
Voting [Gifford, 1979] with non-uniform vote assignments, let alone structured homogeneous or heterogeneous dynamic data replication schemes.
Hence, (1) only an unstructured majority voting data replication scheme
must be modeled that is (2) used homogeneously for every stage of the

dynamics. Moreover, (3) since structured data replication schemes imposing a logical structure on the set of processes are not supported, individual process identities can be neglected (except for modeling individual failure and recovery rates) as every process is equally suited for being in a specific quorum. These facts help to keep the system models small and tractable but also limit their applicability to only a subset of a specific subclass of data replication schemes, namely to a subset of unstructured static and unstructured homogeneous dynamic data replication schemes being Majority Consensus Voting and its dynamic counterparts. Besides, the system models consider the write operation only and are concerned with no quality measures other than operation availability and its related measures such as the (inverse) operation reliability. For example, message complexity or the probability of a particular process participating in quorums cannot be easily evaluated with these system models. Furthermore, the system model of each approach discussed is specifically tailored towards a particular data replication scheme, thereby rendering the respective system model unsuited for the evaluation of other schemes.

In contrast, the system model to be presented in the following section allows the evaluation of unstructured and structured homogeneous as well as of heterogeneous dynamic data replication schemes. Static data replication schemes are supported as a simple special case. It is a compositional system model in the sense that different data replication schemes can easily be evaluated simply by instantiating the system model with a different quorum systems specification. The system model allows quality measures to be evaluated for the read as well as for the write operation. Besides operation availability, other quality measures such as, for example, the (average) message complexity or a process' participation in quorums can be evaluated.

4.3 System Model

The system model to be presented in this section consists of several template petri net-subnets that are instantiated and composed to form the system model for a specific evaluation scenario, that is, for a configuration of processes and channels and the data replication scheme used to manage the replicated data object. More specifically, these subnets are:

THE PROCESS SUBNET TEMPLATE. The process subnet template models the status and behavior of an individual process and is instantiated n

times for a system comprising n processes. Process subnet templates are explained in detail in Section 4.3.1.

THE EPOCH LIST SUBNET. The system model employs the concept of epochs [Rabinovich and Lazowska, 1992b] as introduced in Section 2.5.2 to realize the consistent switching among quorum systems in dynamic data replication schemes. The epoch list holds the processes that form the current epoch. It is introduced in Section 4.3.2.

THE PROCESS LIST SUBNET. The set of currently non-failed processes that may participate in an operation-specific quorum building is hold in the process list which is introduced in Section 4.3.3.

THE QUORUM SYSTEM REPRESENTATION SUBNETS. Quorum systems are represented in the system model by petri net counterparts of tree-shaped voting structures as introduced in Section 3.2. How tree-shaped voting structures are transformed and embedded into the system model is explained in Section 4.3.4.

THE POST-OPERATION SUBNET. After having performed an operation, the replica status of processes may have to be updated. For example, after having performed a write operation, the replicas of those processes that have participated in the write quorum must be updated while the other processes' replicas must be marked as outdated. This is the purpose of the post-operation subnet which is introduced in Section 4.3.5.

THE OPERATION DRIVER SUBNET. When assuming frequent operations, failure and recovery events trigger operation executions. An operation driver subnet is responsible for triggering operations if frequent operations are not assumed. They are discussed in Section 4.3.8 – until which frequent operations are assumed for a more concise introduction of the above system model subnets.

THE CHANNEL SUBNET TEMPLATE. A channel subnet models the status and behavior of a channel that interconnects two processes. A concrete network topology is modeled by multiple channel subnets. The channel subnet template is discussed in Section 4.3.10 – until which channels are assumed to be perfect and to fully interconnect the processes, again for a more concise presentation of the fundamental system model subnets.

After the post-operation subnet has been introduced in Section 4.3.5, a simple example of a composed system model is given in Section 4.3.6 to summarize and illustrate the interplay for operation execution and the dependencies among the subnets presented so far. Then, optimizations in place count and analysis time of the system model are presented in Section 4.3.7. Prior to the modeling of network topologies in Section 4.3.10, the modeling of dependent process failures is discussed in Section 4.3.9. The motivation for the process subnet template, the quorum system representation subnets, the process list subnet, and the epoch list subnet is as follows.

Process Subnet Template Motivation   The ability to not only support (homogeneous dynamic variants of) the unstructured static Majority Consensus Voting but also structured (dynamic) data replication schemes requires the processes to have unique identities. Structured data replication schemes arrange processes in a logical structure and use structural properties to define quorum systems such that *specific* processes form a quorum rather than a number of processes as it is the case for unstructured data replication schemes. This requirement is realized by instantiating a *process subnet template* n times for an evaluation scenario comprising n processes. An individual process identity is reflected in the system model by an individual number of token on one of a process subnet's state places. Besides, having individual process subnets allows the processes to have non-uniform individual process availabilities in terms of individual failure and recovery rates.

Quorum System Representation and Process List Subnet Motivation   To support dynamic data replication schemes, a quorum system representation for each combination of non-failed processes must be encoded in the system model (cf. Chapter 3). An explicit encoding, that is, explicitly encoding the plain enumeration of all quorums, is not viable as it leads to a system model that scales exponentially in the number of processes and therefore becomes intractable: Up to $2^n - 1$ quorum system representation subnets are required to be encoded in the system model for a system comprising n processes, each modeling the quorum system for a particular combination of non-failed processes. Consider, for example, a system using Dynamic Voting with three processes p_1, p_2, and p_3 resulting in a set of seven quorum systems, each complying to the unstructured Majority Consensus Voting for a different set of processes. More specifically, this set consists of one quorum system for no process being failed, namely
$$\mathcal{Q}_R = \mathcal{Q}_W = \{\{p_1, p_2\}, \{p_1, p_3\}, \{p_2, p_3\}\},$$
three quorum systems for one process being failed, namely
$$\mathcal{Q}_W = \{\{p_1, p_2\}\} \text{ and } \mathcal{Q}_R = \{\{p_1\}, \{p_2\}\} \text{ for process } p_3,$$
$$\mathcal{Q}_W = \{\{p_1, p_3\}\} \text{ and } \mathcal{Q}_R = \{\{p_1\}, \{p_3\}\} \text{ for process } p_2, \text{ and}$$
$$\mathcal{Q}_W = \{\{p_2, p_3\}\} \text{ and } \mathcal{Q}_R = \{\{p_2\}, \{p_3\}\} \text{ for process } p_1, \text{ and}$$

three quorum systems for two processes being failed, namely
$\mathcal{Q}_R = \mathcal{Q}_W = \{\{p_1\}\}$ for process p_2 and p_3,
$\mathcal{Q}_R = \mathcal{Q}_W = \{\{p_2\}\}$ for process p_1 and p_3, and
$\mathcal{Q}_R = \mathcal{Q}_W = \{\{p_3\}\}$ for process p_1 and p_2.
As explicitly encoding quorum systems renders the system model size intractable due to an exponential scaling in the number of processes, an implicit quorum systems representation from which operation-specific quorums are derived is mandatory. Naturally, such an implicit quorum system encoding must be flexible enough to encode unstructured as well as structured data replication schemes. For this purpose, tree-shaped voting structures as introduced in Section 3.1 are adopted to petri nets to represent quorum systems in the system model. Conceptually and until thoroughly introduced in Section 4.3.4, the petri net counterpart of a tree-shaped voting structure can be seen as a tree-shaped voting structure whose nodes are substituted by places, whose edges are substituted by transitions, and whose traversal logics is encoded by guards, transition priorities, and variable marking-dependent arc cardinalities. A quorum building outcome is designated by process identity token counts put on its leaf places. A particular leaf place is populated by a process identity token count only if (1) the process it refers to is chosen to participate in the quorum and (2) this process has not failed such that its process subnet place(s) representing its state of being non-failed are not empty.

Recall that a tree-shaped voting structure represents the quorum system complying to a specific static data replication scheme for a particular subset of the set of processes. This subset is referenced to by its leaf nodes that are mapped to specific processes via the process mapping function. Hence, its petri net counterpart also models the quorum system for exactly one particular subset of the set of processes that is referenced to by the potential leaf place markings in terms of process identity token counts deposited thereon. Thus, while the adoption of tree-shaped voting structures to petri nets allows the modeling of unstructured as well as of structured static data replication schemes for a particular subset of processes in a uniform manner, still up to $2^n - 1$ quorum system representations are required to be encoded in the system model for realizing dynamic data replication schemes.

Recall that, by varying the leaf-node-to-process-mapping, a single tree-shaped voting structure is capable of expressing the quorum system for all subsets of the set of processes having a particular common cardinality (cf. Section 3.3). Hence, in order to avoid the exponential scaling of the system model in the number of processes, varying the leaf-node-to-process-mapping is realized for its petri net counterpart as follows. Instead of a tree-shaped voting structure petri net counterpart's leaf places referencing particular process subnet places representing a process' state of being non-failed, the process subnets are decoupled from the tree-shaped voting structure petri net counterparts by the places of the *process list*. The individual tree-shaped voting structure petri net counterpart's leaf places do not reference specific process subnet places but instead specific process list places such that the tree-shaped voting structure petri net counterparts and the process sub-nets are both related to the process list places but not directly to each other. Prior to a quorum building attempt, the process list places are pop-ulated with process identity token counts by the process list subnet. Hence, a tree-shaped voting structure counterpart models the quorum system for a particular number of process list places with the process identities de-termined by the process list places' marking. By this indirection, only n as opposed to $2^n - 1$ tree-shaped voting structure petri net counterparts must be encoded in the system model: Each models the quorum system for all subsets of the set of processes having a particular common cardinality, thereby avoiding the exponential scaling of the system model size in the number of processes and allowing for a linear one. Heterogeneous dynamic data replication schemes are realized by using different tree-shaped voting structure petri net counterparts for different numbers of processes, that is, for different numbers of process list places.

Epoch List Subnet Motivation   Realizing dynamic data replication schemes requires a means to consistently switch among quorum systems. For this purpose, the concept of epochs [Rabinovich and Lazowska, 1992b] as presented in Section 2.5.2 is implemented in the system model. Recall that, at any time, a subset of the set of processes forms the current epoch meaning that (1) those processes contained in this subset know the current quorum system and that (2) operations are only allowed to be performed using quorums derived from the current quorum system. Which specific pro-cesses participate in the current epoch is kept track of by the places of the *epoch list*. The epoch list marking determines the population of the process list places which in turn determines those processes that may participate in an operation-specific quorum building.

Subnet Cooperation for Operation Execution   The interplay and de-pendencies among the process subnets, the process list subnet, the quorum system representation subnets, the post-operation subnet, and the epoch

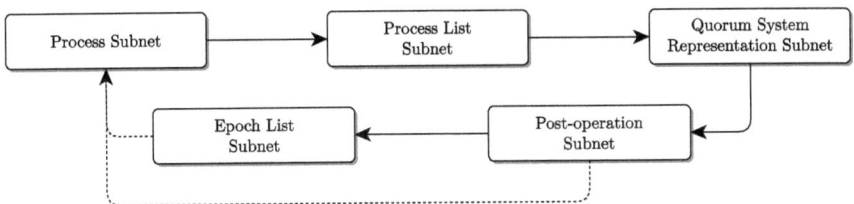

Figure 4.7: Schematic Control Flow of an Operation Execution

list subnet are conceptually illustrated in Section 4.3.6 by an example of a simple composed system model, following the introduction of these fundamental system model subnets. To assist the understanding of the following sections, the schematic control flow of executing operations is shown in Figure 4.7. The failure or recovery of a process activates the process list subnet (as frequent operations are assumed until Section 4.3.8). The process list subnet activates one of the quorum system representation subnets that models the quorum system for the current epoch. Thereafter, the post-operation subnet is activated to update the replica status of processes if necessary and given that the operation has been successfully performed. Finally, the epoch list subnet is activated to perform an epoch change operation, provided that it can be successfully performed. Then, or if the epoch change operation cannot be performed, the operation execution is finished and the eventual failure or recovery of a process triggers another operation execution (visually represented in the figure by dashed lines).

The remainder of this section on the system model is structured as follows. First, the question of how to model processes is addressed in Section 4.3.1. Subsequently, the epoch list management subnet and the process list management subnet are presented in Sections 4.3.2 and 4.3.3, both of which are a prerequisite to the support of (heterogeneous) dynamic data replication schemes. The modeling of quorum system representations is described in Section 4.3.4. Managing the processes' replica status update and triggering the quorum system reconfiguration is discussed in Section 4.3.5 on the post-operation subnet. Then, the interplay of the so far presented system model subnets is illustrated by an example in Section 4.3.6. Subsequently, optimizations to the quorum systems representation in the system model with respect to place count and analysis time are presented in Section 4.3.7. Thereafter, the frequent operations assumption – so far made for the purpose of a simpler presentation – is revisited and relaxed in Section 4.3.8, followed by a discussion on how to model dependent failures in the system model in Section 4.3.9. The modeling of network topologies and channel failures is discussed in Section 4.3.10 until which only processes are assumed to be subject to failures while channels are perfect and fully interconnect the processes – again for a more concise introduction of the general system model.

4.3.1 Process Subnets

A process subnet models the status and behavior of a single individual process in the system. The quality measures to be evaluated and the system model-simplifying assumptions made result in different process state and behavior models. These models are the four-states process model, the optimistic and pessimistic three-states process models, and the two-states process model. Following their presentation, the effect of performing operations on state transition semantics is discussed. Finally, the process subnet templates for three process state models are presented.

Process State Models

The state of an individual process is defined by (1) it either being functional or failed, (2) the local data it manages in terms of a local copy of the replicated data object and its associated metadata such as its version number, and (3) its local copy of the quorum system.

Recall that write operations update the replicas of all processes participating in the write quorum and set their version numbers to a new global maximum. Hence, there is a direct correspondence between a replica's version number and its actual data value such that the version number value can be regarded as a representative of the replica's actual data value. In an extreme example, the replica data value may actually be the replica version number value. For the purpose of evaluating quality measures, the actual replica data is of little interest and can be safely abstracted in the system model by its version number, thereby reducing the state space-constituting variables of a process by one.

Despite abstracting the replica data value, the state space size of only a single process grows unbounded even when only considering the replica version number: Performing write operations increases the version number strictly monotonic, thereby resulting in an unbounded number of states per process – and thereby in the system model – with the per-process states being (possibly) equivalent except for the version number. Hence, in order to model processes with finitely many states, the version number is abstracted by a boolean variable indicating the actuality of a process' replica: If it is true, then the replica is current and, otherwise, it is outdated. As a consequence, during the course of a write operation execution, the replicas of those processes participating in the write quorum must be marked as current while all other processes' replicas must be marked as outdated. This is implicitly also the case when using version numbers, namely by setting the replica version numbers of those processes participating in the write quorum to a new global maximum whereby the replicas of those processes not in the write quorum become outdated because of them having a less than maximal version number. The global maximal version number is always unambiguously identified due to the strict intersection property of quorum systems: In every quorum, at least one process has participated in the most recent write operation and thus has a current replica with the global maximal version number.

In general, a process cannot decide by itself and based only on its local information whether its replica is current or not. It needs to assemble a read or write quorum and then to compare its replica version number with those of the other processes in the quorum in order to learn about the actuality of its replica. Hence, a process can consistently establish a "global view" on the system concerning the actuality of the replicas via assembling a quorum. This ability to compile a "global view" can be exploited for alleviating the individual processes in the system model to store a copy of the (current) quorum system. As elaborated on in Section 2.5.2, a process is only allowed to perform an operation with knowing and using a quorum drawn from the current quorum system. If it has an outdated quorum system, then a newer one has meanwhile been installed about which it learns prior to executing an operation.

Seen from a more abstract perspective, if the system model is constructed such that it only allows processes that know the current quorum system to initiate an operation execution, then the individual process (sub)models are relieved from storing a local copy of the quorum system.

The ability to compile a "global view" on the system is explicitly exploited by abstracting the quorum system as well as the replica data plus its version number and cumulates in the following process state models.

The Four-States Process Model   The state space of an individual process complying to the four-states process model as used by Chen and Wang [1996b] comprises four states, namely being functional (in short called *up*) with a current replica ($p_{c:cur}^{up}$), being up with an outdated replica ($p_{c:old}^{up}$), being failed (in short called *down*) with a current replica ($p_{c:cur}^{down}$), and being down having an outdated replica ($p_{c:old}^{down}$) as depicted in Figure 4.8. The state of a process changes due to the execution of operations or due to its failure and eventual recovery. The state transition from $p_{c:cur}^{up}$ to $p_{c:old}^{up}$ is due to the process not participating in the write quorum of the write operation currently being performed. The transition from $p_{c:old}^{up}$ to $p_{c:cur}^{up}$ is a result of the process participating in the write quorum of the write operation currently being performed, given it was in the state of being up and having an outdated replica. Otherwise, it remains in the state $p_{c:cur}^{up}$. Note that this transition may also be caused by the process participating in a read operation's quorum which, however, is not considered by Chen and Wang [1996b]. The transitions from $p_{c:cur}^{up}$ to $p_{c:cur}^{down}$ and from $p_{c:old}^{up}$ to $p_{c:old}^{down}$ are caused by the process failing and the transitions from $p_{c:cur}^{down}$ to $p_{c:cur}^{up}$ and from $p_{c:old}^{down}$ to $p_{c:old}^{up}$ are caused by the process recovering from its failure. While the process is failed with an outdated replica, it cannot participate in a write operation by which its replica would become current which is why there is no transition from $p_{c:old}^{down}$ to $p_{c:cur}^{down}$. However, other processes may perform a write operation while the process is failed with having a current replica whereby its state changes from $p_{c:cur}^{down}$ to $p_{c:old}^{down}$. The system model by Chen and Wang [1996b] as well as the system models based thereon [Chen and Wang, 1996a,c; Chen, Wang et al., 1999, 2000, 2004a,b; Wang, Chen et al., 2000] employ this four-states process model, also without the read operation-caused state transition.

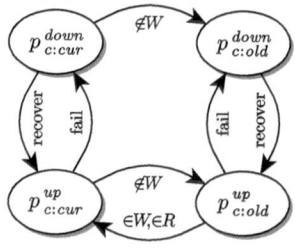

Figure 4.8: Process States and State Transitions According to the Four-States Process Model due to Chen and Wang [1996b] plus the Read Operation-Caused State Transition

The Pessimistic Three-States Process Model In the process model
due to Dugan and Ciardo [1989], the replica status of a failing process is
neglected with the failing process unconditionally transitioning from $p_{c:cur}^{up}$
or $p_{c:old}^{up}$ to p^{down}, resulting in the pessimistic three-states process model as
depicted in Figure 4.9. A process' state of being failed is effectively identified
with its state being $p_{c:old}^{down}$ since, upon recovery, the process is assumed to
have an outdated replica and thus transitions to the state $p_{c:old}^{up}$. Then, the
process is obliged to execute an operation for updating its replica, resulting
in a transition to $p_{c:cur}^{up}$, given that a quorum can be successfully formed
and the operation is successfully executed. Otherwise, it remains in the
state $p_{c:old}^{up}$.

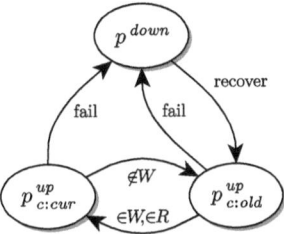

Figure 4.9: Process States and State Transitions According to the Pessimistic
Three-States Process Model that Neglects the Replica Status of
Failed Processes due to Dugan and Ciardo [1989] plus the Read
Operation-Caused State Transition

The pessimistic assumption of failed processes unconditionally having an
outdated replica can result in system states in which no process is marked
as having a current replica. Such a system state is about to be reached
whenever a recovering process cannot update its replica due to no quorum
being available as a result of too many processes having failed such that
the recovering process is stuck in the state $p_{c:old}^{up}$, regardless of the real
actuality of its replica. The remaining non-failed processes – possibly having
current replicas – will eventually fail and are, upon their recovery, also stuck
in the state $p_{c:old}^{up}$, also regardless of the real actuality of their replicas.
Meanwhile, other processes may have recovered but due to all previously
recovered processes being in the state $p_{c:old}^{up}$, they were unable to form a
quorum containing at least one process being in the state $p_{c:cur}^{up}$. Eventually,
all processes that are non-failed are in the state $p_{c:old}^{up}$.

A read operation is not allowed to be performed with a quorum solely
consisting of processes being in the state $p_{c:old}^{up}$, although at least one of

them must have an actually current replica because it has participated in the most recent write operation due to the strict quorum system intersection property. Since the replica version number is abstracted, there is no means to learn the real actuality of replicas on this level of abstraction. Note that, in an actual implementation, the real actuality of replicas can be learned by comparing replica version numbers.

Since Dugan and Ciardo [1989] only consider the write operation, this problem might seem negligible as by performing a write operation, a quorum of processes is updated such that their replicas become current. However, also the write operation requires at least one process being in the state $p_{c:cur}^{up}$ to be included in the write quorum in order to be able to learn about and then to increase the global maximal replica version number. This is required for (1) guiding successive read operations from which process in the read quorum to return the replica value and for (2) enabling subsequent write operations to determine and then set the new global maximal replica version number. As the replica version number is abstracted, those processes being in the state $p_{c:old}^{up}$ and having actually current replicas cannot be identified on this level of abstraction.

As a result, once such a system state in which recovering processes cannot update their replicas is reached, the write operation as well as the read operation must remain indefinitely unavailable.

In order to circumvent this problem, a (manual) reconstruction phase in which all processes – including the failed ones for whose recovery is being waited – are reset to their initial state $p_{c:cur}^{up}$ was integrated into the system model. The reconstruction is triggered whenever a recovering process cannot execute an operation for updating its replica due to no quorum being available as a consequence of too many failed processes.

Such a reconstruction phase is not necessary when employing the four-states process model as it is always known which processes have current replicas and, eventually, sufficiently many processes will have recovered such that a quorum containing at least one process having a current replica can be formed.

The Optimistic Three-States Process Model The optimistic three-states process model depicted in Figure 4.10 avoids the need for a (manual) reconstruction phase. The replica status of a failing process is neglected with the failing process unconditionally transitioning from $p_{c:cur}^{up}$ or $p_{c:old}^{up}$ to p^{down}. Upon recovery, the process transitions from p^{down} to $p_{c:cur}^{up}$. This unconditional recovery state transition to a state of being up and having a current replica seems to be invalid as write operations may have been performed while the process was failed. As a result, its replica must have become outdated and the process has to perform a successful replica update prior to transitioning to $p_{c:cur}^{up}$ or else it has to transition to $p_{c:old}^{up}$. Yet, while the recovery state transition from p^{down} to $p_{c:cur}^{up}$ is certainly too optimistic in unconditionally assuming the replicas of recovering processes to be current, it is valid and justified as follows.

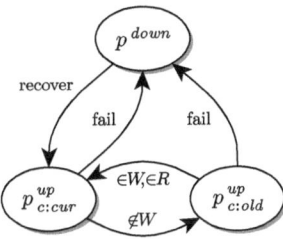

Figure 4.10: Process States and State Transitions According to the Optimistic Three-States Process Model Neglecting the Replica Status of Failed Processes

Recall the fact that due to the strict quorum system intersection property, at least one process in every successfully formed read or write quorum has a current replica because it has participated in the most recent write operation. Consequently, it is impossible to successfully form a read or write quorum comprising only processes having outdated replicas. Hence, a process can consistently establish a "global view" on the system concerning the replicas' actuality via forming a read quorum or, equivalently, a write quorum. For the purpose of this process model, it is only relevant that there is at least one process having a current replica in every successfully formed quorum rather than the question of which specific processes have current replicas or how to identify them. The identification can be accomplished in an actual implementation by comparing replica version numbers. Thus, the global maximal replica version number can always be identified by successfully forming a quorum such that a write operation coordinator can set the new global maximal replica version number and a read operation coordinator can read from a process having a current replica.

In system states in which a read or write quorum can be successfully formed, a recovering process is always able to update its replica from at least one of the processes in the quorum if necessary. A replica update is necessary if the recovering process has an actually outdated replica. Otherwise, no write operation has been performed while the process was failed such that the recovering process already has a current replica. Note that the recovering process itself may be required for the read or write quorum to be successfully formed. Because of the strict quorum system intersection property, there is definitely at least one process having a current replica in the successfully formed read or write quorum which is either the recovering process itself or some other process from which the recovering process can then update its replica.

In system states in which – due to too many processes having failed – no write quorum but a read quorum can be successfully formed, a recovering process is also able to update its replica if necessary. Again, the read quorum may require the recovering process to participate for being successfully formed.

Due to further process failures, system states may be reached in which neither a read nor a write quorum can be successfully formed such that the read operation and the write operation are unavailable. In those system states, the replica status of non-failed processes remains unaltered as no operation to change them can be performed. Eventually, (1) some failed process recovers such that a quorum can be successfully formed, (2) some failed process recovers but no quorum can be formed, or (3) some non-failed process fails, including the case that all processes have finally failed. In the first case, there is due to the strict quorum system intersection property at least one process in the quorum – either a non-failed or the recovered process – that has a current replica from which the recovering process can update its replica if necessary. In the second case, the non-failed processes plus the recovering process are not sufficient to form a quorum such that the recovering process is unable to update its replica albeit it may be necessary. Regardless of the real actuality of its replica, the recovering process transitions to $p_{c:cur}^{up}$. As discussed above, at least one process having an actually current replica is included in every successfully formed quorum and processes having actually current replicas can be identified such that operations can be performed consistently, even if some processes are too optimistically considered as having a current replica. By further process recoveries, the first case is resembled. By further process failures, the third case is resembled. The aftermath of the third case eventually resembles the second case or the first case when sufficiently many processes already have recovered and in conjunction with a currently recovering process form a quorum.

In summary, whenever a quorum can be successfully formed, there is at least one process having a current replica included in this quorum – which can always be identified in an actual implementation by comparing replica version numbers – such that read operations can return the most recently written value and write operations can set the replica version numbers of the participating processes to a new global maximum. The recovery state transition from p^{down} to $p^{up}_{c:cur}$ certainly is too optimistic in unconditionally assuming the replicas of recovering processes to be current but this assumption does not sacrifice sequential consistency.

The Two-States Process Model Revisiting the fact of a process is always able to compile a "global view" on the system concerning replica actuality – given that it can successfully form a quorum – the optimistic three-states process model is consequently adapted to consist of only two states, namely either being up or being down, with explicitly disregarding the replica status altogether. Hence, the need to track individual replica states in addition to the process states itself is avoided. As a result, the overall processes state space size for a system comprising n processes consists of only 2^n states as opposed to 3^n or even 4^n states. The resulting two-states process model is shown in Figure 4.11.

Figure 4.11: Process States and State Transitions According to the Two-States Process Model Neglecting the Replica Status Altogether

Unfortunately, if the quality measure of interest requires to *exactly* track individual replica states, then the two-states process model and also the three-states process models are inapplicable, the latter because of their assumptions regarding a failed, respectively, recovering process' replica status. Such a measure is, for example, the steady state probability that a *specific* process has a current replica. For suchlike measures, the four-states process model must be employed, accepting a processes state space size of 4^n for a system comprising n processes. Alike, the two-states process model and the three-states process models are inapplicable to the evaluation of, for example, probabilistic quorum systems [Malkhi, Reiter et al., 2001] that do not have the strict quorum system intersection property which is exploited for these process models. Fortunately, important quorum system quality measures like, for example, operation availability and message complexity can be evaluated using the two-states or the (optimistic) three-states process model.

Next, operation execution-induced process state transitions and their relation to the instantaneous operations assumption are discussed.

Operation Execution State Transition Semantics

The execution of an operation may affect the state of multiple processes in the system. While obvious for the write operation, performing a read operation may also require to update the state of several processes in the system.

Operation Execution-Induced Process State Transition Semantics
Performing a write operation alters the state of several processes in the system, namely the state of those processes participating in the write quorum to have a current replica and the state of those processes not participating in the write quorum to have an outdated replica. Alike, when assuming that during the course of a read operation execution those processes in the read quorum that have an outdated replica update their replicas from other processes having a current one, then the read operation also alters the state of possibly several processes, namely the state of those processes participating in the read quorum that have an outdated replica to have a current one. This is a reasonable assumption an actual data replication framework implementation will opt for as those processes participating in a read quorum and having an outdated replica will be revealed while performing the read operation. This gratuitous knowledge can be exploited to increase the number of processes having a current replica at low additional costs. Otherwise, if the state of those processes in the read quorum having an outdated replica is not updated (for whatever reason), the state of the read operation coordinator process may change if it has an outdated replica and reads from another process' current replica whereby it sensibly updates its own local replica.

In summary, performing operations affects the state of potentially more than one process. Thus, it follows non-interleaving semantics as opposed to interleaving semantics which restricts state transitions to alter the state of a single process only (cf. Section 2.1.1). Likewise, if several processes may jointly fail or be jointly recovered, then the state of potentially several processes is affected, thereby also following non-interleaving semantics.

The Instantaneous Operation Assumption's Relation to State Transition Semantics Depending on the level of abstraction and fine-grain atomicity, non-interleaving semantics can be implemented by interleaving semantics [Abadi and Lamport, 1995]. Employing interleaving semantics, an operation execution requires multiple state transition steps to be completed during which, for example, a process participating in the quorum chosen for performing this operation may fail. Thus, the handling of failures while an operation is being executed must be explicitly considered, for example, by incorporating a (non-blocking) commit protocol [Skeen, 1981] into the system model. However, doing so would increase the system model complexity beyond tractability which is why the integration of a commit protocol is traded-off for an overestimation of the evaluated operation availabilities. This decision can be justified by the very high speed of modern hardware and network infrastructure that leaves only a very low probability to processes failing while an operation is being executed. In particular, since a quorum usually does not comprise all processes, the probability of those processes failing that participate in the operation quorum is even lower.

A means to avoid the integration of a commit protocol into the system model is to specify a safety property that requires the execution of an operation to be a sequence of state transitions during which no process participating in the operation quorum may fail. This requirement effectively resembles non-interleaving semantics for operation executions but it allows processes that are not participating in a quorum to fail (or to recover) while the operation is being executed. Employing non-interleaving semantics, this can be modeled by multiple state transitions with each, in addition to changing the replica status of (some of) those processes participating in the quorum, changing the state of a different combination of processes not participating in the operation quorum to be failed or to be recovered. However, such joint state transitions comprising operation execution, process failures, and process recoveries are in fact not necessary as for each run with joint transitions there is an equivalent run without joint transitions modeling the exact same behavior. Hence, it is more convenient to assume non-interleaving semantics for the system model with two types of exclusive state transitions affecting a process' state, namely (joint) process failure and recovery transitions and operation execution transitions. Specifically, the successive global state of the system either results from a transition that changes process states from failed to functional and vice versa or from an operation execution transition that changes process states from having an outdated replica to have a current replica and vice versa, but not from both of them simultaneously. This is the reason to not have state transitions changing both, the replica status and the process state itself in the four-states process model as depicted in Figure 4.8. Note that this is also the case for the three-states process models shown in Figures 4.9 and 4.10 since the actual status of a replica is not changed but assumptions on a failed, respectively, recovering process' replica status are made. The two-states process model neglects the replica status altogether.

In summary, traded-off for a slight overestimation of the evaluated operation availabilities, a commit protocol must not be incorporated into the system model since the handling of failures during an operation execution is not considered. This abstraction resembles the instantaneous operations assumption which neglects delays due to message propagation or processing time. In fact, when assuming the components' life- and repair times to be exponentially distributed (cf. Section 4.2), components cannot fail or recover while an operation is being performed instantaneously because of the exponential distribution's property of different samples drawn having different sample values.

Next, the petri net incarnations of the above presented two-states process model, optimistic three-states process model, and four-states process model are introduced.

Process Subnet Templates

The modeling of structured data replication schemes requires the processes to have unique identities. Consequently, for an evaluation scenario comprising n processes, n subnets with each subnet modeling the status and behavior of an individual and unique process are required to be incorporated into the system model. Besides, having unique individual process subnets allows the processes to have non-uniform individual process availabilities in terms of individual failure and recovery rates. The multiple process subnets only differ in their respective identity and possibly individual failure and recovery rates. Therefore, each process subnet is an instance of a *process subnet template* that models the general status and behavior of a process. Each instance has specific failure and recovery rates and a specific process identity. This identity is determined by the number of token assigned to one of its state places. The process subnet templates for the two-states process model, the optimistic three-states process model, and finally the four-states process model are introduced in the remainder of this section.

Henceforth, the numeric constant PROCESSMODEL $\in \{2, 3, 4\}$ reflects the chosen process model by its number of states being the value of this constant.

The Two-States Process Subnet Template   The two-states process subnet template for a process p_i that is either functional (in short called *up*) or failed (in short called *down*) is shown in Figure 4.12. The process p_i is up if its state place $p_i{}^{up}$ has i token and it is down if this place has zero token. A failure of the process p_i is modeled by the timed transition T_{fail_i} which draws i token from the place $p_i{}^{up}$ (graphically represented by the arc cardinality $/ i$). The recovery of the process p_i is modeled by the timed transition $T_{recover_i}$ which puts i token back on the place $p_i{}^{up}$, given that it has zero token meaning that the process p_i is actually failed (graphically represented by the combined regular and inhibitor arc with the regular arc's cardinality $/ i$ and the inhibitor arc's cardinality $/ 1$). Upon the failure or recovery of the process p_i, a token is put on the system model-global place $ctrl_{op}$, thereby triggering the execution of an operation by activating successive subnets that are explained later.

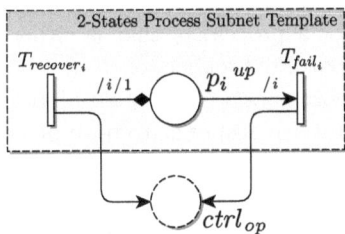

Figure 4.12: Two-States Process Subnet Template

Recall that for the sake of a simpler presentation, frequent operations and perfect channels are assumed until the end of Section 4.3.8 and Section 4.3.10, respectively. Under these assumptions, operation executions are triggered by the failure or recovery of processes. Thereby, it is ensured that in between two failure or recovery events at least one operation execution is triggered, namely upon the failure or recovery event of a process (cf. Section 4.2). No further (intermittent) operation executions are triggered in between two failure or recovery events since an (un)available operation remains (un)available at least until the next failure or recovery event. Therefore, quality measures other than operation availability such as, for example, the probability of particular processes being probed or a process' participation in (successfully built) operation-specific quorums cannot be directly evaluated. However, such quality measures other than operation availability may possibly be derived from the time distribution, that is, the relative time spent in each stage of the dynamics, as illustrated in the example evaluation of Chapter 5. Also, because of only one operation being triggered in between two process failure or recovery events, replica actuality has no meaning. A process' replica remains either current or outdated after the failure- or recovery-induced operation execution until the next operation execution is triggered by the next process failure or recovery event. Therefore, the two-states process model lacking replica states is appropriate when assuming frequent operations and when operation availability is the primary quality measure to be evaluated.

The evaluation of quality measures besides operation availability such as the processes' replica actuality requires a process model with replica states and intermittent operations to be triggered in between two process failure or recovery events via operation drivers (cf. Section 4.3.8).

The Three-States Process Subnet Template   The three-states process subnet template for a process p_i that is either (1) up with a current replica, (2) up with an outdated replica, or (3) down is shown in Figure 4.13. The former two states correspond to the state place $p_i{}^{up}_{c:cur}$ or $p_i{}^{up}_{c:old}$ having i token and the latter state corresponds to both places having zero token. A failure of the process p_i is modeled by the guarded timed transition $T_{fail_{i,\star}}$ which draws all token from the places $p_i{}^{up}_{c:cur}$ and $p_i{}^{up}_{c:old}$, provided that at least one of them has a non-zero token count (that is, the process p_i has

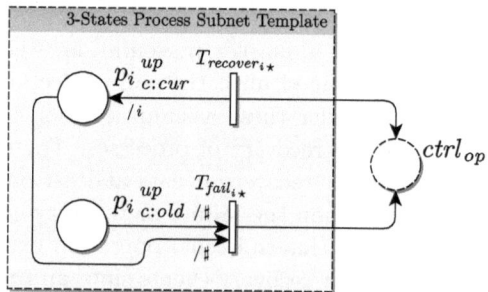

Figure 4.13: Three-States Process Subnet Template

not already failed) as expressed by its guard

$$\text{true} \leftarrow [\sharp(p_i\,^{up}_{c:cur}) + \sharp(p_i\,^{up}_{c:old}) = i]. \qquad \text{(Guard } T_{fail_i})$$

The process p_i recovers by the guarded timed transition $T_{recover_{i\star}}$ firing whereby i token are deposited on the place $p_i\,^{up}_{c:cur}$, given that the places $p_i\,^{up}_{c:old}$ and $p_i\,^{up}_{c:cur}$ both have zero token (that is, the process p_i is actually failed) as expressed by its guard

$$\text{true} \leftarrow [\sharp(p_i\,^{up}_{c:cur}) + \sharp(p_i\,^{up}_{c:old}) = 0]. \qquad \text{(Guard } T_{recover_i})$$

Like for the two-states process subnet template, a token is put on the system model-global place $ctrl_{op}$ upon the failure or recovery of the process p_i whereby the execution of an operation is triggered.

Note that, as a result of an operation execution, the i token from $p_i\,^{up}_{c:old}$ ($p_i\,^{up}_{c:cur}$) may have to be shifted to $p_i\,^{up}_{c:cur}$ ($p_i\,^{up}_{c:old}$) in order to reflect the new replica status of the process p_i. The update of a process' replica status as a result of an operation execution is done by the post-operation subnet that is to be introduced in Section 4.3.5.

The Four-States Process Subnet Template The four-states process subnet template for a process p_i that is either up with a current replica, up with an outdated replica, or down with either a current or an outdated replica is shown in Figure 4.14. The respective state corresponds to one of its state places $p_i\,^{up}_{c:cur}$, $p_i\,^{up}_{c:old}$, $p_i\,^{down}_{c:cur}$, or $p_i\,^{down}_{c:old}$ having i token and the other places having zero token. A failure of the process p_i is modeled by the timed transition T_{fail_i} which, provided that the places $p_i\,^{down}_{c:cur}$ and $p_i\,^{down}_{c:old}$ are clear

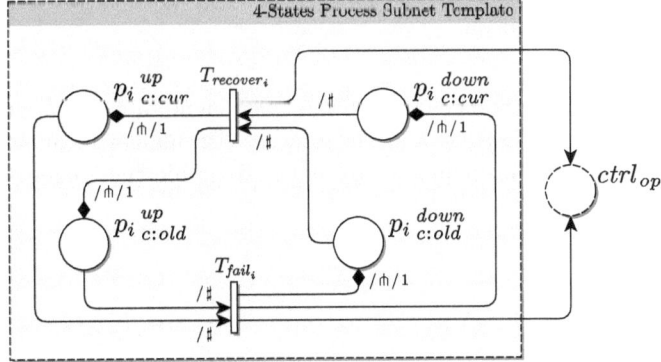

Figure 4.14: Four-States Process Subnet Template

of token, consumes all token from the places $p_i \,_{c:cur}^{up}$ and $p_i \,_{c:old}^{up}$ and then emits i token either to the place $p_i \,_{c:cur}^{down}$ or to the place $p_i \,_{c:old}^{down}$, depending on which one of the places $p_i \,_{c:cur}^{up}$ or $p_i \,_{c:old}^{up}$ has had i token upon transition enabling. The latter is expressed by the two arc cardinality functions

 function / $\text{⋔}(T_{fail_i} \rightarrow p_i \,_{c:cur}^{down})$:
  return $\sharp(p_i \,_{c:cur}^{up}) > 0 \;?\; i : 0$

and

 function / $\text{⋔}(T_{fail_i} \rightarrow p_i \,_{c:old}^{down})$:
  return $\sharp(p_i \,_{c:old}^{up}) > 0 \;?\; i : 0.$

The recovery of the process p_i is modeled by the timed transition $T_{recover_i}$ which, provided that the places $p_i \,_{c:cur}^{up}$ and $p_i \,_{c:old}^{up}$ are clear of token, clears the places $p_i \,_{c:cur}^{down}$ and $p_i \,_{c:old}^{down}$ of token and emits either i token to the place $p_i \,_{c:cur}^{up}$ or $p_i \,_{c:old}^{up}$, depending on the place $p_i \,_{c:cur}^{down}$ or the place $p_i \,_{c:old}^{down}$ having had a non-zero token count upon transition enabling. The latter is expressed by the two arc cardinality functions

 function / $\text{⋔}(T_{recover_i} \rightarrow p_i \,_{c:cur}^{up})$:
  return $\sharp(p_i \,_{c:cur}^{down}) > 0 \;?\; i : 0$

and

 function / $\text{⋔}(T_{recover_i} \rightarrow p_i \,_{c:old}^{up})$:
  return $\sharp(p_i \,_{c:old}^{down}) > 0 \;?\; i : 0.$

Analogously to the former two process subnet templates, a token is put on the system model-global place $ctrl_{op}$ upon the failure or recovery of the process p_i whereby the execution of an operation is triggered. Like for the three-states process subnet template, the post-operation subnet that is to be introduced in Section 4.3.5 maintains the process' replica status in response to an operation execution.

Next, the *epoch list* and the epoch list management subnet are introduced. Thereafter, the *process list* and the process list management subnet are presented. Both are prerequisites to realize dynamic (heterogeneous) data replication schemes.

4.3.2 The Epoch List and its Management Subnet

The epoch list holds the processes that are in the current epoch in terms of their process identity token counts. The epoch list subnet serves the purpose of filtering the set of processes by their participation in the current epoch.

Epoch List   The epoch list consists of n system model-global places $el_1, \ldots, el_n$ for a system comprising n processes. Each epoch list place having non-zero token represents a process by this list place's token count matching the identity token count of the process. The epoch list places' token distribution is ordered by process identities in ascending order padded with zeros such that if el_i has $k > 0$ token and el_j has $l > 0$ token for $i < j$, then $\sharp(p_k{}^{up}) < \sharp(p_l{}^{up})$ and the possibly remaining epoch list places have zero token. If a process model with replica states is employed, then the replica status must be considered such that $\sharp(p_k{}^{up}_{c:cur}) + \sharp(p_k{}^{up}_{c:old}) < \sharp(p_l{}^{up}_{c:cur}) + \sharp(p_l{}^{up}_{c:old})$ holds if el_i has $k > 0$ token and el_j has $l > 0$ token for $i < j$.

A dedicated system model-global place *stage* contains the number of non-empty epoch list places and reflects the number of processes in the current epoch. The marking of this place is considered by the quorum building subnets – to be described in Section 4.3.4 – in order to determine which specific tree-shaped voting structure petri net represents the quorum system of the current epoch from which operation-specific quorums are derived. Note that this state space size-increasing place *stage* is not necessarily required as the information of how many processes participate in the current epoch can as well be computed by the quorum building subnets themselves, namely by counting the non-empty epoch list places. However, it is included for the sake of a clearer presentation.

Initially, the place *stage* is assigned n token and the epoch list places contain the process identity token counts of all n processes in ascending order, that is, all processes participate in the current epoch and none is initially failed. For the evaluation of static data replication schemes – because of the absence of dynamics in terms of epoch change operations – the epoch list places as well as the place *stage* retain their initial token assignment indefinitely.

Epoch List Subnet   The epoch list places are populated with process identity token counts in ascending order by the epoch list subnet as conceptually illustrated in Figure 4.15. It consists of $n + 1$ transitions, namely

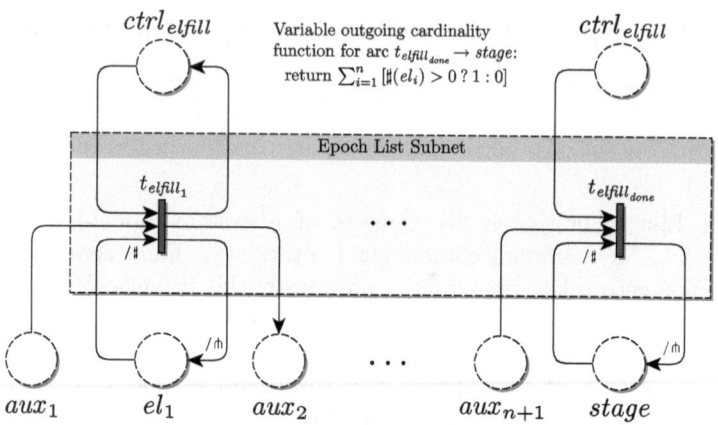

Figure 4.15: Conceptual Illustration of the Epoch List Subnet

of the transitions $t_{elfill_1}, \ldots, t_{elfill_n}$ and $t_{elfill_{done}}$. The epoch list subnet is triggered by depositing one token on the system model-global control place $ctrl_{elfill}$ and also one token on the system model-global helper place aux_1. Concerning the epoch list subnet, the system model-global helper places $aux_1, \ldots, aux_{n+1}$ serve the purpose of sequentializing the n transitions that fill the epoch list places: A transition t_{elfill_i} is only enabled if its helper place aux_i and additionally the control place $ctrl_{elfill}$ each have one token. Sequentializing the n transitions is necessary to implement the ordering on the epoch list places' token counts. Note that the sequentialization could have been as well implemented by using transition priorities. However, some of the multiple purpose auxiliary places are required anyway and as they have a zero marking in the time domain (and therefore do not increase the state space size), the auxiliary places are employed to sequentialize the n transitions.

When fired, a transition t_{elfill_i} draws the one token from its helper place aux_i, one token from the control place $ctrl_{elfill}$, and all token from the epoch list place el_i. It outputs one token to its subsequent transition's helper place aux_{i+1}, puts one token back on the control place $ctrl_{elfill}$, and deposits either zero token or a number of token corresponding to a process' identity token count on the epoch list place el_i. The variable arc cardinality of the outgoing arc $t_{elfill_i} \to el_i$ that connects the transition t_{elfill_i} to the epoch list place el_i is determined by the following function that is suitable for the two-states process model:

```
1  function / ⬩(t_{elfill_i} → el_i):
2    if i = 1:
3      loop := prev := 0
4    else:
5      loop := prev := ♯(el_{i-1})
6      if prev = 0: return 0
7    while loop < n:
8      loop := loop + 1
9      if (♯(p_loop^{up}) > 0) ∧ (♯(p_loop^{up}) ≠ prev):
10        return ♯(p_loop^{up})
11    return 0
```

This function returns the next higher process identity token count of a non-failed process relative to the previous epoch list place marking $\sharp(el_{i-1})$ or zero token in case no non-failed process is found. The rationale for considering the previous epoch list place marking is that all non-failed processes having a lower (or equal) identity token count than the previous epoch list place have already been assigned to an epoch list place since the places are populated with process identity token counts in ascending order. Hence, only those processes having a higher identity token count are left to be assigned to an epoch list place. More specifically, for the first transition t_{elfill_1}, there is no previous epoch list place marking to consider (line 2 evaluates to true) and the loop starts with process p_1 by setting prev := 0 and loop := 0 (line 3), the latter being incremented to 1 in line 8. For transitions t_{elfill_i} with $i > 1$, the previous epoch list place marking is considered (line 4ff.) by assigning the variables loop and prev the previous epoch list place marking $\sharp(el_{i-1})$ such that the loop in line 7ff. starts with the process having the identity token count $\sharp(el_{i-1}) + 1$ (as the variable loop is incremented by one in line 8). However, if the previous epoch list place marking is zero (line 6), then no non-failed processes are left to be assigned to epoch list places and thus zero is returned, avoiding an unnecessary looping over process subnet places. The loop over the process subnet places (lines 7–10) returns the process identity token count of a process p_{loop}^{up} by line 10 if the process has not failed ($\sharp(p_{loop}^{up}) > 0$) and its identity token count does not equal prev ($\sharp(p_{loop}^{up}) \neq$ prev), that is, it has a higher identity token count than the one put on the previous epoch list place. Otherwise, zero is returned by line 11 if no such process is found.

If the three-states process model or the four-states process model is employed, then a process' state of being up and its replica status must be considered since two places represent a process' state of being up, one with a current replica and one with an outdated replica. This requirement is manifested in the following function excerpt by which the lines 9 and 10 in the above function are replaced such that a non-failed process' status of having a current or an outdated replica is explicitly distinguished for these process models:

if $(\sharp(p_{loop}{}^{up}_{c:cur}) > 0) \wedge (\sharp(p_{loop}{}^{up}_{c:cur}) \neq \text{prev})$:
    return $\sharp(p_{loop}{}^{up}_{c:cur})$
if $(\sharp(p_{loop}{}^{up}_{c:old}) > 0) \wedge (\sharp(p_{loop}{}^{up}_{c:old}) \neq \text{prev})$:
    return $\sharp(p_{loop}{}^{up}_{c:old})$

After the transitions $t_{elfill_1}, \ldots, t_{elfill_n}$ have fired, the transition $t_{elfill_{done}}$ of the epoch list subnet conceptually shown in Figure 4.15 finally fires. It empties its helper place aux_{n+1}, the control place $ctrl_{elfill}$, and the place *stage*. It emits via its variable-cardinality outgoing arc a number of token to the place *stage* that is determined by the function

function $/ \pitchfork (t_{elfill_{done}} \to stage)$:
    return $\sum_{i=1}^{n} [\sharp(el_i) > 0\,?\,1:0]$

which accumulates the number of epoch list places having non-zero token. Then, the epoch change operation is completed, the epoch list places are populated with the non-failed processes' identity token counts in ascending order padded with zeros, and the place *stage* contains the number of processes in the new current epoch.

Notes on the Epoch Change Operation   Recall that performing an epoch change operation requires the participation of a subset of the set of processes forming a write quorum in the current epoch's quorum system as well as a subset of the set of processes forming a write quorum in the new epoch's quorum system (cf. Section 2.5.2). Also recall that the state transition semantics does not allow processes (and channels) to fail or to recover while an operation is being executed (cf. Section 4.3.1). Therefore, an epoch change operation can be consistently performed if a write quorum of the current epoch's quorum system is available. Due to the absence of failures during the epoch change operation, a write quorum of the new epoch's quorum system can always be formed, given that the new epoch's quorum system does reflect the new system state. Specifically, the new epoch's quorum system may contain failed processes in its read and write quorums but at least one write quorum – which is then used for the epoch change operation – must contain non-failed processes only.

By exploiting global knowledge and in favor of a simpler system model as well as a simpler presentation, not only those processes in the union of an epoch change operation's two write quorums form the new epoch but all non-failed processes. Supported by the above argumentation, this simplification alleviates the need to form a write quorum of the new epoch's quorum system in addition to a write quorum of the current epoch's quorum system to perform an epoch change operation. Alike, a process' state of having a current or an outdated quorum system must not be tracked. Hence, updating the quorum system of processes that have not participated in the epoch change operation's two write quorums must not be considered. Note that tracking a process' quorum system actuality can indeed be realized analogously to the tracking of a process' replica actuality. As a result of this simplification, the epoch change operation is more expensive in terms of writing the new quorum system to more processes than necessary compared to writing the new quorum system to the union of an epoch change operation's two write quorums. However, correctness is not sacrificed since the new quorum system is written to at least the processes being in the union of the two epoch change operation's write quorums. Therefore, a more expensive epoch change operation is accepted here in favor of a simpler system model and also a simpler presentation.

By this simplification, the number of processes knowing the new quorum system may be overestimated since the number of non-failed processes may be higher than the number of (unique) processes in an epoch change operation's two write quorums. However, the failure or recovery of processes is usually assumed to be infrequent compared to regular read and write operations. Therefore, when writing the new quorum system to the union of an epoch change operation's two write quorums, potentially all non-failed processes not yet knowing the new quorum system may learn about it until the next epoch change operation, depending on the quorum probing strategy selecting quorums of processes for performing operations. When assuming frequent operations, an operation is triggered by the failure or recovery of a process and no further operations are triggered until the next process failure or recovery event. Hence, writing the new quorum system only to the union of an epoch change operation's two write quorums may underestimate the number of processes knowing the new quorum system while writing it to all non-failed processes may be an overestimation. As potentially all non-failed processes learn about (or already know) the new quorum system in between two process failure or recovery events, slightly overestimating the number of processes knowing the new quorum system is accepted here. When not assuming frequent operations, an operation driver triggers operation executions (cf. Section 4.3.8). The frequency of executing ordinary operations compared to the frequency of quorum system reconfigurations determines the degree of overestimation in the number of processes knowing the new quorum system. If many operations with different quorums are performed, then the number of processes not knowing the new quorum system converges to zero for sufficiently many operations performed until which their number is overestimated. Otherwise, if only few operations are performed, the number of processes knowing the new quorum system may be overestimated, depending on the quorums chosen for performing operations.

A related aspect is that the token count of the place *stage* cannot be used to select the tree-shaped voting structure petri net that models the quorum system for the (new) current epoch if writing the new quorum system only to the union of an epoch change operation's two write quorums. Then, this place's token count does not necessarily reflect the (total) number of processes in the new epoch. Assembling this information prior to a quorum building, namely by counting the non-empty epoch list places, does not solve the problem. However, counting the number of non-failed processes when performing an epoch change operation instead of counting the epoch list places having a non-zero token count solves this problem. This is identical to counting the number of epoch list places having a non-zero token count when writing the new quorum system to all non-failed processes.

Recall that during an epoch change operation, the replicas of those processes in the union of the epoch change operation's two write quorums are updated (cf. Section 2.5.2). Since all non-failed processes form the new epoch here, the replica status of all non-failed processes is updated and not just the replica status of processes being in the union of the two write quorums. As a consequence, the replica status of processes cannot be precisely tracked, resulting in an overestimation of the processes' replica actuality when evaluating a dynamic data replication scheme. Hence, quality measures such as a process' participation in write quorums or the probability of a process having a current replica cannot be precisely evaluated with the above discussed system model simplification applied. However, the (slight) overestimation of replica actuality is accepted here and traded-off for a simpler system model as this imprecision is only an issue when using a process model with replica states. For the two-states process model lacking replica states, replica actuality has no meaning.

Next, the idea of the *process list* and its management by the process list subnet are introduced, realizing the decoupling of the n process subnets from the quorum system representation subnets.

4.3.3 The Process List and its Management Subnet

The *process list* consists of n system model-global places $pl_1, \ldots, pl_n$ for a system comprising n processes. It serves the two purposes of (1) determining the non-failed processes that may participate in an operation-specific quorum building and (2) decoupling the process subnets from the quorum system representation subnets (in the form of tree-shaped voting structures adopted to petri nets). Next, the need for the process list is motivated, followed by the presentation of the process list subnet that populates the process list places.

Motivation for the Process List   At any time instant, a subset of the set of processes represented by the epoch list places' marking reflecting their process identity token counts constitutes the current epoch. Operations may only be performed using quorums that are derived from the current epoch's quorum system. Quorum systems are encoded in the system model by adopting tree-shaped voting structures (cf. Section 3.1) to petri nets. Until the construction of tree-shaped voting structure petri net counterparts is introduced in detail in the next Section 4.3.4, they can – for the purpose of this section – be seen as tree-shaped voting structures whose nodes are substituted by places, whose edges are substituted by transitions, and whose traversal logics is encoded by guards, transition priorities, and variable marking-dependent arc cardinalities. A quorum building outcome is designated by process identity token counts put on their leaf places. A particular leaf place is populated with a process identity token count only if (1) the process it refers to – in terms of a particular process subnet's place(s) – is chosen to participate in the quorum and (2) this process has not failed such that the process subnet place(s) representing its state of being non-failed are not empty.

A tree-shaped voting structure – and hence its petri net counterpart – models the quorum system complying to a specific static data replication scheme for a particular subset of the set of processes. For a tree-shaped voting structure, this subset is determined by its leaf nodes being mapped to specific processes via the process mapping function. For its petri net counterpart, this subset of processes is determined by the potential markings of its leaf places in terms of process identity token counts deposited thereon. As a result of a tree-shaped voting structure's petri net counterpart modeling the quorum system for exactly one particular subset of the set of processes only, up to $2^n - 1$ must be integrated into the system model to realize dynamic data replication schemes: Each tree-shaped voting structure petri net models the quorum system for a particular combination of processes that constitutes an epoch.

Recall that, by varying the leaf-node-to-process-mapping, a single tree-shaped voting structure is capable of expressing the quorum system for all subsets of the set of processes having a particular common cardinality (cf. Section 3.3). Hence, in order to avoid the exponential scaling of the system model size with increasing numbers of processes, varying the leaf-node-to-process-mapping is realized for its petri net counterpart as follows. Instead of a tree-shaped voting structure petri net's leaf places referencing particular process subnet places representing a process' state of being non-failed, the process subnets are decoupled from the tree-shaped voting structure petri net counterparts by the process list's places. The individual tree-shaped voting structure petri net's leaf places do not reference specific process subnet places but specific process list places such that the tree-shaped voting structure petri nets and the process subnets are both related to the places of the process list but not directly to each other. Prior to a quorum building attempt, the process list places are populated with process identity token counts of processes that (1) have not failed and that (2) may participate in an operation-specific quorum building as determined by the epoch list. By the decoupling, a tree-shaped voting structure petri net models the quorum system for a particular number $1 \leq k \leq n$ of process list places with the specific process identities determined by the process list places' marking. All subsets of the set of processes having a cardinality of k are reflected simply by assigning the respective (different) process identity token counts to the process list places $pl_1, \ldots, pl_k$. A single tree-shaped voting structure petri net models the quorum system for all those subsets of cardinality k as it is independent of which actual processes are represented by the process list places' marking. As a result, only n as opposed to up to $2^n - 1$ tree-shaped voting structure petri nets are required to model dynamic data replication schemes, thereby avoiding the exponential scaling of the system model size in the number of processes. Next, the process list subnet managing the process list places is introduced.

Process List Subnet The process list is populated by the process list subnet as conceptually illustrated in Figure 4.16. It consists of the single immediate transition t_{plfill} that is connected via n variable-cardinality outgoing arcs to the n process list places $pl_1, \ldots, pl_n$, via two fixed-cardinality outgoing arcs to the system model-global places $ctrl_{qbuild}$ and aux_1, and via a fixed-cardinality incoming arc to the control place $ctrl_{op}$.

This subnet is activated by placing a token on the system model-global place $ctrl_{op}$ which – for now because of the frequent operations assumption – is due to one of the timed transitions T_{fail_i} or $T_{recover_i}$ of a process subnet modeling the process p_i having fired. When fired, the transition t_{plfill} draws one token from the control place $ctrl_{op}$ and deposits one token on the system model-global helper place aux_1 as well as one token on the control place $ctrl_{qbuild}$. By the latter, the actual quorum building using the tree-shaped voting structure petri net for the current epoch – which is determined with the help of the *stage* place marking – is triggered.

The number of token put on a process list place pl_i via the variable-cardinality outgoing arc $t_{plfill} \rightarrow pl_i$ is dependent on (1) the token count of a specific process subnet place representing this process' state of being non-failed as well as on (2) the number of token on the corresponding epoch list place el_i. If the two-states process model is employed, then the token count of the place $p_{\sharp(el_i)}{}^{up}$ that corresponds to the process subnet modeling the process $p_{\sharp(el_i)}$ is considered. For the three- or the four-states process model, the token count of one of the places $p_{\sharp(el_i)}{}^{up}_{c:cur}$ and $p_{\sharp(el_i)}{}^{up}_{c:old}$ is considered. Only if the epoch list place el_i as well as (one of) the according process subnet place(s) have a non-zero token count, the cardinality function returns

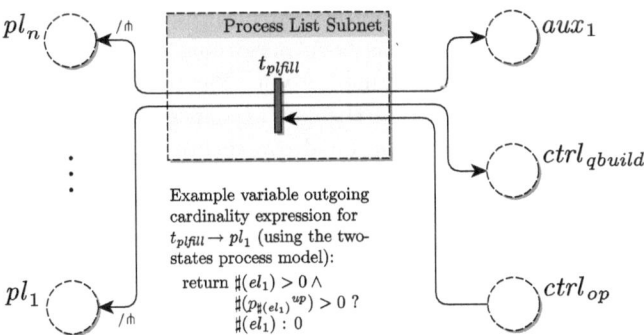

Figure 4.16: Conceptual Illustration of the Process List Subnet

the epoch list place's token count. Otherwise, zero is returned as either the process has failed or it may not participate in an operation-specific quorum building. Consequently, for the two-states process model, the cardinality of the arc $t_{plfill} \rightarrow pl_i$ connecting the transition t_{plfill} to the process list place pl_i is determined by the function

function $/ \text{m}(t_{plfill} \rightarrow pl_i)$:
   return $(\sharp(el_i) > 0) \wedge (\sharp(p_{\sharp(el_i)}{}^{up}) > 0) ? \sharp(el_i) : 0.$

If the three- or four-states process model is used, this function must consider the process subnet places $p_{\sharp(el_i)}{}^{up}_{c:cur}$ and $p_{\sharp(el_i)}{}^{up}_{c:old}$ instead of the place $p_{\sharp(el_i)}{}^{up}$ and becomes

function $/ \text{m}(t_{plfill} \rightarrow pl_i)$:
   return $((\sharp(el_i) > 0) \wedge ((\sharp(p_{\sharp(el_i)}{}^{up}_{c:cur}) > 0) \vee$
   $(\sharp(p_{\sharp(el_i)}{}^{up}_{c:old}) > 0))) ? \sharp(el_i) : 0.$

Note that the process list inherits the ordering in token counts from the epoch list. Hence, the petri net counterpart of a tree-shaped voting structure's leaf node p_i always refers – via the process list place pl_i – to a process with a lower identity token count than the petri net counterpart of a leaf node p_j for $i < j$. For a specific association of leaf node places to processes, intra-stage dynamics with an according specific tree-shaped voting structure petri net may be employed (cf. Sections 3.4 and 4.3.4).

Emptying the Process List Places   The process list places are assumed to be empty upon activation of the process list subnet. This is why there are no n variable-cardinality incoming arcs to the transition t_{plfill} emptying those places by each incoming arc's cardinality resembling the token count of one of the process list places. Instead, the process list places are emptied by the post-operation subnet – that is to be described in Section 4.3.5 – after the quorum building attempt has been performed, regardless of whether a quorum has been successfully formed or not. The reason to unconditionally clear the process list places is that they are accounted for the state space size if not being emptied after having tried to execute an operation since they have a non-constant marking in the time domain. Besides, the information represented by the process list places' marking is potentially outdated when initiating subsequent operations as processes (or channels) may have failed in the meantime.

Support for Static Data Replication Schemes   When evaluating a static data replication scheme, the epoch list places as well as the place *stage* keep their initial token assignment because of the absence of dynamics in terms of epoch change operations. Recall that the epoch list places are initialized with the process identity token counts in ascending order and that the place *stage* is initialized with n token. For a static data replication scheme, the token count of a process list place equals the token count (of one) of a process subnet's place(s) representing this process' state of being non-failed with the process subnet having the same index as the process list place. Assuming the two-states process model is employed, the function determining the cardinality of an outgoing arc $t_{plfill} \rightarrow pl_i$ is in this case simplified to

function / ⋔ $(t_{plfill} \rightarrow pl_i)$:
    return $(\sharp(p_i{}^{up}) > 0) \,?\, \sharp(p_i{}^{up}) : 0$

since $\sharp(p_i{}^{up})$ equals $\sharp(el_i)$ if process p_i has not failed. Otherwise, if p_i has failed, the condition $\sharp(p_i{}^{up}) > 0$ results in returning 0 for the arc cardinality anyway. Analogously, if using the three- or the four-states process model, the expression becomes

function / ⋔ $(t_{plfill} \rightarrow pl_i)$:
    if $\sharp(p_i{}^{up}_{c:cur}) > 0$: **return** $\sharp(p_i{}^{up}_{c:cur})$
    return $(\sharp(p_i{}^{up}_{c:old}) > 0) \,?\, \sharp(p_i{}^{up}_{c:old}) : 0.$

The next section elaborates on the encoding of quorum systems in the system model. Specifically, tree-shaped voting structures as introduced in Section 3.2 are transformed into their petri net counterparts and embedded into the system model.

4.3.4 Tree-Shaped Voting Structure Subnets

Quorum systems are to be represented in the system model by the petri net counterparts of tree-shaped voting structures as introduced in Section 3.2. The 2×2 optimized Grid Protocol tree-shaped voting structure with four processes as depicted in Figure 4.17 serves as an illustrative running example while the forthcoming explanation of the transformation. The first transformation step is to graph-wise transform a tree-shaped voting structure into a petri net graph. Following this syntactic graph-structural transformation, the semantics of the tree-shaped voting structure is transposed to and expressed in terms of petri net means. The vote function and quorum function assignment is modeled by the token flow in the petri net, that is, by

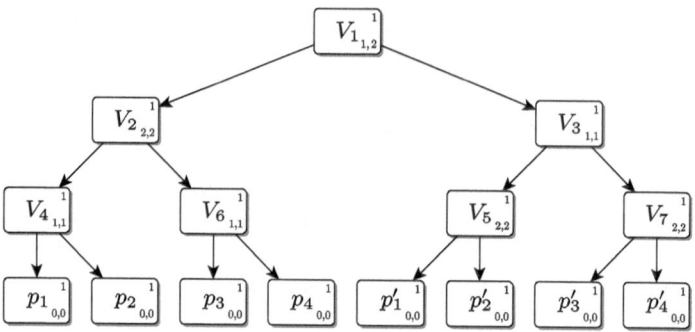

Figure 4.17: Tree-Shaped Voting Structure of the Optimized 2×2 Grid Protocol

the (operation-specific) cardinalities of incoming and outgoing arcs to and from the transitions. Thereafter, the traversal ordering of the tree-shaped voting structure, for example, with respect to the edge priority function, is transposed to its counterpart via assigning priorities and guards to the transitions. Finally, the tree-shaped voting structure's petri net counterpart is embedded into the system model in order to communicate the outcome of a quorum building to subsequent subnets. Specifically, a tree-shaped voting structure is transformed into its petri net counterpart and embedded into the system model by the following five steps:

STEP 1 (GRAPH-STRUCTURAL TRANSFORMATION)

The tree-shaped voting structure directed tree graph is transformed into a bipartite directed petri net tree graph with place nodes and immediate transition nodes. Specifically, the tree-shaped voting structure's nodes are substituted by place nodes and its edges are substituted by immediate transition nodes. Each immediate transition node is connected to the source and destination (place) nodes of the edge it replaces by an incoming and an outgoing transition arc.

In order to avoid confusion of tree-shaped voting structure leaf nodes with its petri net counterpart leaf place nodes, leaf place node labels are henceforth prefixed with the letter l. For example, the process-representing leaf node in the tree-shaped voting structure of Figure 4.17 that is labeled p_1 becomes lp_1 in its petri net counterpart.

STEP 2 (VOTE LOGICS APPLICATION)

Incoming transition arcs are assigned a static cardinality that resembles the number of votes of the replaced edge's destination node in the original tree-shaped voting structure. Outgoing transition arcs are assigned variable and marking-dependent arc cardinalities depending on (1) whether a read quorum or a write quorum is attempted to be formed and (2) whether the outgoing arc connects to a leaf place or to an inner place. Outgoing transition arcs connecting to leaf places are a special case since their cardinality reflects a specific process' state of being failed or not as determined by the corresponding process list place's token count.

STEP 3 (TRANSITION FIRING SEQUENTIALIZATION)
Priorities and guards are assigned to transitions, resulting in a (partial) order established on the possible transition firing sequences. This ordering reflects the tree-shaped voting structure's edge priority order within the levels of the petri net graph and also imposes an ordering over the levels of the petri net graph. The latter is necessary to coordinate the non-deterministic firing behavior of petri nets for the purpose of correctly reflecting the quorum construction rules as expressed in the original tree-shaped voting structure.

STEP 4 (QUORUM BUILDING CONTROLLING)
The outcome of a quorum building needs to be propagated to subsequent subnets for them to take according measures. For this purpose, guarded success and failure transitions are introduced to act upon a successful or failed quorum building. These transitions plus an initialization and a retry transition control the quorum building.

STEP 5 (SYSTEM MODEL EMBEDDING)
Finally, the petri net counterpart of a tree-shaped voting structure is embedded into the system model, that is, the initialize, success, and failure transitions are connected to system model-global places.

Next, these steps to transform a tree-shaped voting structure into its petri net counterpart are described in detail, sparing an explanation of the simple first graph-structural transformation step.

Step 2: Tree-Shaped Voting Structure Vote Logics Application

The vote logics expressed in a tree-shaped voting structure in terms of the quorum function and vote function assignments are modeled by (operation-specific) cardinalities of incoming and outgoing arcs to and from transitions. After the first graph-structural transformation step, each transition in the tree-shaped voting structure petri net has exactly one incoming arc and exactly one outgoing arc. The incoming arc cardinality is static and resembles the number of votes of the by Step 1 replaced edge's destination node in the original tree-shaped voting structure. For example, the transition $t_{V_1-V_2}$ in Figure 4.18 has an incoming arc cardinality of 1, that is, it draws one token from place V_1 when fired. The outgoing arc cardinality – with the exception of arcs connecting to leaf places – is dependent on whether a read quorum or a write quorum is to be formed.

The outgoing arc cardinality of arcs connecting to non-leaf places corresponds to the operation-specific minimal number of votes to collect among child nodes of the by Step 1 replaced edge's source node in the original tree-shaped voting structure. This is graphically represented by variable outgoing arc cardinalities $/\Uparrow = r, w$ with r being the cardinality for read operations and w being the cardinality for write operations, respectively. For example, the transition $t_{V_1-V_2}$ in Figure 4.18 has an outgoing arc cardinality of 2 for both operations, that is, it puts two token on place V_2 when fired, in this case regardless of whether a read or a write quorum is to be formed. Note that for Grid Protocol tree-shaped voting structure petri nets, the operation-specific outgoing arc cardinalities for arcs not connecting to leaf places are coincidentally identical.

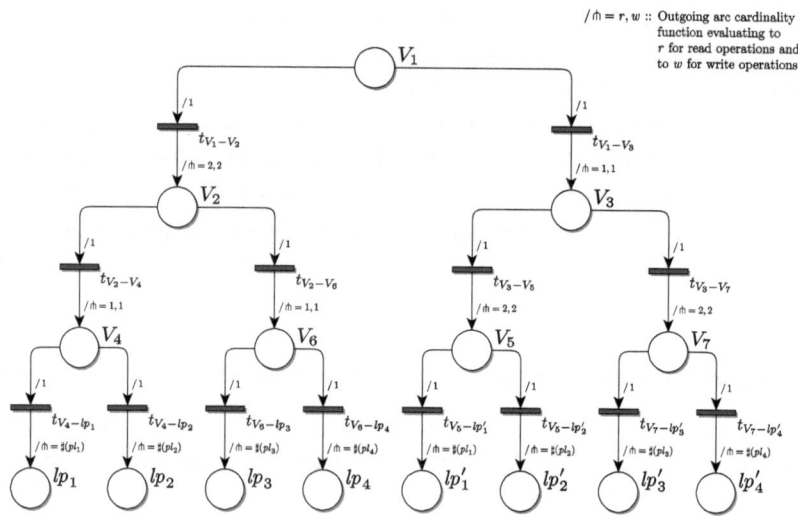

Figure 4.18: Tree-Shaped Voting Structure Petri Net Counterpart of the Optimized 2×2 Grid Protocol after the Application of Step 2

The cardinality of outgoing arcs connecting to leaf places is dependent on the process list places' marking. For a leaf node p_i in the original tree-shaped voting structure, the cardinality of the outgoing arc connecting to the corresponding leaf place lp_i in the tree-shaped voting structure petri net evaluates to the token count of the process list place pl_i. For example, for the leaf node p_4 (p_4') in the tree-shaped voting structure shown in Figure 4.17, the cardinality of the outgoing arc of the transition $t_{V_6-lp_4}$ $(t_{V_7-lp_4'})$ connecting to the leaf place lp_4 (lp_4') in Figure 4.18 evaluates to the number of token on the process list place pl_4 as indicated by $/ \pitchfork = \sharp(pl_4)$ in the figure.

The cardinalities of outgoing arcs connecting to non-leaf places are dependent on the operation-specific quorum to be formed such that read quorums as well as write quorums can be derived from a single tree-shaped voting structure petri net. For this reason, tree-shaped voting structure petri nets are initially unmarked such that depositing an operation-specific number of token on the root place yields an according operation-specific quorum – if it is possible to be formed. For example, according to the operation-specific quorum function value of the tree-shaped voting structure's root node in Figure 4.17, one token is to be deposited on the root place V_1 in Figure 4.18 for forming a read quorum and two token are to be deposited thereon for forming a write quorum.

The next transformation step is to impose a (partial) order on transition firing such that the quorum construction rules expressed in the original tree-shaped voting structure are correctly reflected by its petri net counterpart.

Step 3: Transition Firing Sequentialization

The choice of which transition out of a set of concurrently enabled transitions to fire is non-deterministic. This non-determinism may permit a firing sequence in the so far transformed tree-shaped voting structure petri net that results in an invalid quorum according to the quorum construction rules expressed in the original tree-shaped voting structure. As a consequence, the quorum system intersection property may be violated. For example, while forming a write quorum, only those transitions in the left subgraph of the root place V_1 in Figure 4.18 which belong to the C-Cover may fire. Thereby, the two token initially put on the root place V_1 are consumed, preventing a CC-Cover (right subgraph of the root place V_1) from being formed. More specifically, the following firing sequence is possible in the tree-shaped voting structure petri net in Figure 4.18: Initially, two token are put on the root place V_1 indicating that a write quorum is to be formed. Then, the transition $t_{V_1-V_2}$ is enabled and fires, thereby drawing one token from V_1 and depositing two token on place V_2. Due to the non-determinism, the transition $t_{V_1-V_2}$ is not hindered from firing a second time as it is still enabled after having fired once since one token is left on the root place V_1. As it is enabled, the transition $t_{V_1-V_2}$ fires a second time. Note that even this firing sequence on its own already prevents the CC-Cover from being built. Nonetheless, assume the transition $t_{V_2-V_4}$ then fires, resulting in one token on place V_4 and leaving three token on place V_2. Then, the transition $t_{V_2-V_6}$ fires three times. Finally, the firing of $t_{V_4-lp_1}$ leads to $\sharp(pl_1)$ token on the leaf place lp_1 and three times firing the transition $t_{V_6-lp_3}$ results in $3 \cdot \sharp(pl_3)$ token on the leaf place lp_3. This firing sequence results in an invalid write quorum according to the Grid Protocol write quorum construction rules since no CC-Cover (right subgraph of the root place V_1) is formed. Alike, this write quorum violates the quorum system intersection property which, if using this quorum for performing a write operation, may result in the violation of sequential consistency. Furthermore, the token count on the leaf place lp_3 may not correspond to a valid process identity token count or it may reference a different process than the token count of the process list place pl_3.

Vertical and Horizontal Transition Firing Order   As the above example firing sequence has shown, the possible firing sequences in a tree-shaped voting structure petri net must be ordered such that the resulting operation-specific quorums comply to the quorum system construction rules expressed in the original tree-shaped voting structure. Specifically, (1) the firing sequences must be sequentialized in a vertical order on the levels of the tree-shaped voting structure petri net and (2) the operation-specific quorum construction logics expressed in the original tree-shaped voting structure via votes and votes to collect among child nodes must be respected within each level.

The vertical order on the firing sequences is established by assigning higher priorities to transitions on lower levels of the petri net graph (that is, less distant transitions as perceived from the root place) such that all potentially enabled transitions on a level k fire prior to transitions on level $k+1$ becoming enabled and potentially firing. For example, the transitions $t_{V_1-V_2}$ and $t_{V_1-V_3}$ on level one in Figure 4.19 are assigned a higher priority, namely 6, than the transitions $t_{V_2-V_4}$, $t_{V_2-V_6}$, $t_{V_3-V_5}$, and $t_{V_3-V_7}$ on level two which have a priority of 5. Compared to these transitions on level two, the transitions on level three connecting to leaf places have a lower priority of 4. Note that tree-shaped voting structure petri nets are mutually exclusive enabled and that they are also not enabled concurrently to other subnets of the system model. Therefore, the different tree-shaped voting structure petri nets may share a range of common transition priorities. This range starts with a priority of 4 since the lower transition priorities are used in the next Step 4 on quorum building controlling and result propagation.

If edges in the original tree-shaped voting structure that emerge from the same node have assigned distinct edge priorities, then a (partial or total) horizontal ordering among the corresponding transitions in the petri net counterpart must be introduced. This ordering is realized by assigning appropriate intra-level priorities to those transitions while maintaining the vertical ordering over the levels of the tree-shaped voting structure petri net. For example, if the C-Cover should be prioritized over the CC-Cover when forming read quorums, the transition $t_{V_1-V_2}$ in Figure 4.19 is assigned a higher priority than the transition $t_{V_1-V_3}$, namely 7. For forming write quorums, this priority assignment must have no effect since both, a C-Cover and a CC-Cover are required anyway. Therefore, the transition $t_{V_1-V_2}$ must be hindered from firing twice which it does as it has a higher priority than

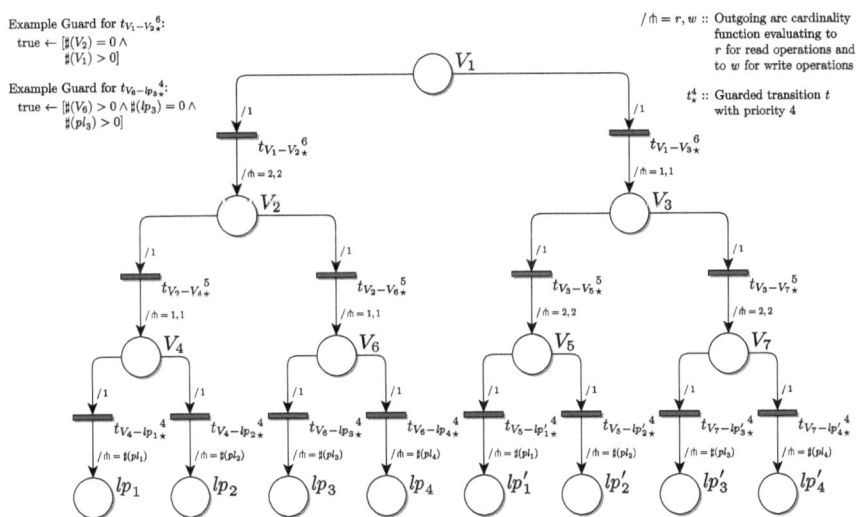

Figure 4.19: Tree-Shaped Voting Structure Petri Net Counterpart of the Optimized 2×2 Grid Protocol after the Application of Step 3

the transition $t_{V_1-V_3}$ and the place V_1 has two token when a write quorum is to be formed. This is realized via assigning guards to transitions as explained next.

Maintaining the Quorum Construction Logics Apart from the vertical (and horizontal) ordering of firing sequences, a tree-shaped voting structure petri net must follow the quorum construction logics expressed in the original tree-shaped voting structure. For example, in the tree-shaped voting structure shown in Figure 4.17, the nodes V_2 and V_3 are required to grant their respective vote to the root node V_1 in order to form a valid write quorum. This requirement is met in the tree-shaped voting structure petri net in Figure 4.19 by the means of a guard attached to the transitions $t_{V_1-V_2}{}^6$ and $t_{V_1-V_3}{}^6$ that enforces them to fire exactly once. The transition $t_{V_1-V_2}{}^6$ is guarded by the expression

$$\text{true} \leftarrow [\sharp(V_2) = 0 \wedge \sharp(V_1) > 0] \qquad\qquad (\text{Guard } t_{V_1-V_2}{}^6)$$

stating that it is enabled if and only if the place V_2 has zero token and the place V_1 has at least one token. The latter condition just serves for the purpose of a more verbose presentation as a transition whose input place has less than the required number of token cannot become enabled anyway. Note that instead of assigning guards to transitions, the same effect could have been achieved by using inhibitor arcs but at the cost of a much more cluttered graphical representation which is why guards are used here. In accordance with the guard attached to the transition $t_{V_1-V_2}{}^6$, the transition $t_{V_1-V_3}{}^6$ is attached a guard such that it becomes enabled if and only if the place V_3 has zero token and the place V_1 has at least one token, in guard notation

$$\text{true} \leftarrow [\sharp(V_3) = 0 \wedge \sharp(V_1) > 0]. \qquad\qquad (\text{Guard } t_{V_1-V_3}{}^6)$$

Analogously, every transition in a tree-shaped voting structure petri net connecting two non-leaf places is attached a guard that evaluates to true only if its outgoing arc's destination place has zero token and its incoming arc's source place has at least a number of token as required by the incoming arc's cardinality.

Finally, a guard is attached to every transition connecting to a leaf place such that it is enabled only if (1) its input place has at least a number of token that resembles the number of votes of the replaced edge's destination leaf node in the original tree-shaped voting structure, (2) its output leaf place has zero token, and (3) its corresponding process list place has a non-zero token count. The first condition again serves for the purpose of a more verbose presentation. The second condition ensures that a process identity token count (which is always greater than zero) as determined by the transition's outgoing arc cardinality is put on the leaf place at most once. The third condition ensures that the actual process represented by the according process list place's token count has not failed. If it has failed, the transition must not fire since firing the transition consumes token from its input place and outputs zero token to its output leaf place, thereby possibly resulting in invalid quorums formed. Hence, a transition connecting to a leaf place fires at most once. For example, the guarded transition $t_{V_6 - lp_3\star}^{4}$ in Figure 4.19 is enabled if and only if (1) the place V_6 has at least one token, (2) the leaf place lp_3 has zero token, and (3) the process list place pl_3 has a non-zero token count, in guard notation

$$\text{true} \leftarrow [\sharp(V_6) > 0 \wedge \sharp(lp_3) = 0 \wedge \sharp(pl_3) > 0]. \qquad\qquad (\text{Guard } t_{V_6 - lp_3}^{4})$$

The condition on the place V_6 again just serves for the purpose of a more verbose presentation since the transition $t_{V_6 - lp_3\star}^{4}$ cannot become enabled if its input place V_6 has less than the required number of token.

The next step is to propagate the quorum building outcome and, depending on the process model chosen, the operation-specific quorum's process identity token counts to subsequent subnets.

Step 4: Quorum Building Controlling and Result Propagation

Eventually, all potentially enabled transitions in the tree-shaped voting structure petri net have fired. Then, either an operation-specific quorum consisting of the processes referenced to by the leaf places having non-zero token counts has been successfully formed or the quorum building has failed because some probed processes are failed. In the latter case and provided that a quorum can still be successfully formed despite the failure of some processes, the quorum building is retried by depositing the operation-specific number of token on the tree-shaped voting structure petri net's root place.

These three cases are acted upon by three guarded transitions that are specific to a tree-shaped voting structure petri net, namely the *success transition* $t_{success\star}^{3}$, the *retry transition* $t_{retry\star}^{2}$, and the *failure transition* $t_{failure\star}^{1}$. A fourth tree-shaped voting structure petri net-specific guarded transition, the *initialize transition* $t_{init\star}$, triggers the quorum building if the tree-shaped voting structure petri net models the quorum system for the current epoch. A tree-shaped voting structure petri net constitutes in conjunction with its specific success, retry, failure, and initialize transitions a *tree-shaped voting structure subnet* as conceptually illustrated in

Figure 4.20. As indicated in the figure, the subnet-local initialize, success, and failure transitions interact with and depend on system model-global places and transitions. These are explained next as they are required for the understanding of the tree-shaped voting structure subnet-local transitions which are discussed thereafter.

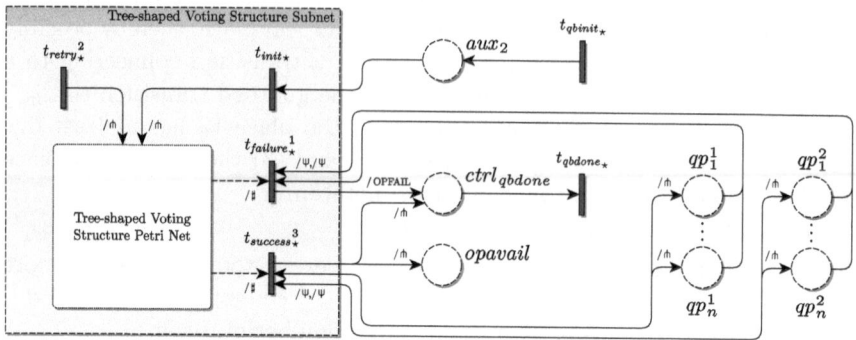

Figure 4.20: Conceptual Illustration of a Tree-Shaped Voting Structure Subnet and, partly, its Relation to System Model-Global Places and Transitions

System Model Context Among other system model-global places, a tree-shaped voting structure subnet interacts with the places aux_2, $ctrl_{qbdone}$, and $opavail$. The auxiliary place aux_2 serves the purpose of an enabling input place to the tree-shaped voting structure subnet-local initialize transition(s). It is populated with one token by the system model-global quorum building initialize transition $t_{qbinit_\star}$ that is to be described in Step 5 on the system model embedding. This transition as well as the tree-shaped voting structure subnet-local transitions depend via guards on the marking of the system model-global place $ctrl_{qbuild}$ (not shown in the figure) that is assigned one token by the process list subnet in order to trigger a quorum building (cf. Section 4.3.3). Also not shown in the figure is the system model-global place *stage* that is populated with token by the epoch list subnet (cf. Section 4.3.2). A tree-shaped voting structure subnet-local transition $t_{init_\star}$ is dependent on this place's marking as it only becomes enabled if the tree-shaped voting structure petri net models the quorum system for the current stage of the dynamics (cf. Section 4.3.2). Populating the system model-global place $ctrl_{qbdone}$ with token marks the end of a quorum building and enables the subsequent transition $t_{qbdone_\star}$ that is described in Step 5. The marking of the system model-global place *opavail* designates the operations that are available. Specifically, its marking is (1) one of the numeric constants OPREAD=1 or OPWRITE=2 if the read or the write operation is available, (2) the sum of both if both operations are available, or (3) zero token in case no operation is available.

Recall that frequent operations and perfect channels fully interconnecting the processes are assumed until Section 4.3.8 and Section 4.3.10, respectively. Under these assumptions, exactly one operation execution is triggered in between two process failure or recovery events, namely upon the failure or recovery event of a process. Therefore, quality measures other than operation availability cannot be directly evaluated and replica actuality has no meaning such that the two-states process model is appropriate in this setting as argued in Section 4.3.1 on the two-states process subnet template.

A further implication of assuming frequent operations is that read and write operations must be performed *concertedly* upon a failure or recovery event since no further operation executions are triggered until the next failure or recovery event. Otherwise, only the write operation can be evaluated when using a dynamic data replication scheme since the quorum system reconfiguration in terms of the epoch change operation relies on write quorums. In the context of tree-shaped voting structure subnets, the system model-global auxiliary place aux_{n+1} (not shown in the figure) keeps track of which operation quorum is currently being built in order to allow probing read and write quorums concertedly. The place aux_{n+1} is managed by the system model-global transition $t_{qbdone_\star}$ that is to be described in Step 5 on the system model embedding. If this place has zero token, then a write quorum is to be formed whereas a read quorum is to be formed if it has one token.

The newly introduced system model-global *quorum places* $qp_1^1, \ldots, qp_n^1$ and $qp_1^2, \ldots, qp_n^2$ hold the process identity token counts of processes participating in a (successfully built) quorum for the first and the second operation as indicated by their superscripts 1 and 2. Depending on the quality measures of interest and on the chosen process model, a single set of system model-global quorum places may not be sufficient. For example, if the quality measure has an interest in a process' participation in (successfully built) operation-specific quorums and both operations are to be performed concertedly, then the quorum places' marking for both operations must be preserved until the next operation execution. Thereby, they have a potentially non-constant marking in the time domain (and thus account for the state space size of the system model) such that their marking can be evaluated by the means to be described in Section 4.4.

Alike, a single set of quorum places is not sufficient if a process model with replica states is chosen and quality measures of a *dynamic* data replication scheme for the read operation (or for both operations) are to be evaluated. To evaluate read operation quality measures of a dynamic data replication scheme, a means to probe read quorums *and* write quorums is mandatory since the dynamics management by the concept of epochs is based on write quorums. As a process model with replica states is chosen, successfully built quorums of both operations may have to be considered for updating the replica status of processes by the post-operation subnet (that is to be introduced in Section 4.3.5) since the union of the epoch change operation's two write quorums must not necessarily include all processes of every read quorum. However, because of the simplified epoch change operation (cf. Section 4.3.2), the latter reason does not apply here as the replica status of all non-failed processes is updated.

Nonetheless, depending on the combination of quality measures and process models, two operation-specific sets of quorum places are required to be incorporated into the system model as illustrated in Figure 4.20. They are managed by the tree-shaped voting structure subnet-local success and failure transitions. Note that in case of using the two-states process model and evaluating operation availability only, the quorum places can be omitted from the system model altogether as the information of which processes participate in a quorum is not of interest and there is no need to update a process' replica status in the two-states process model.

A new system model-global place *OPS* is introduced whose marking determines which operations to perform. Specifically, its marking is either one of the numeric constants OPREAD=1 or OPWRITE=2 by which read and write operations are distinguished, or the sum of both. In the latter case, a read quorum as well as a write quorum is to be formed while in the former cases either a read quorum or a write quorum is to be formed. Note that in the setting of frequent operations and concertedly performing read and write operations, the place *OPS* is statically assigned a constant marking of OPREAD+OPWRITE=3 token. When not assuming frequent operations, an operation driver subnet populates the place *OPS* (cf. Section 4.3.8).

Next, the relation of a tree-shaped voting structure petri net to its specific
success, retry, failure, and initialize transitions as well as the subnet's interaction with system model-global places and transitions is explained in the
order of the subnet-local transitions (potentially) becoming enabled.

The Tree-Shaped Voting Structure Subnet Initialize Transition
A subnet-specific initialize transition $t_{init\star}$ initiates a quorum building if
(1) its preset place aux_2 has one token, (2) the place $ctrl_{qbuild}$ has one
token, and (3) the place *stage* has a token count matching the number of
processes for which the tree-shaped voting structure petri net models the
quorum system, the latter two expressed by a guard. For example, the guard
suitable for the 2×2 Grid Protocol tree-shaped voting structure petri net
in Figure 4.19 evaluates to true only if the place $ctrl_{qbuild}$ has one token and
the place *stage* has a token count of four, in guard notation

$$\text{true} \leftarrow [\sharp(stage) = 4 \wedge \sharp(ctrl_{qbuild}) = 1]. \hspace{2cm} (\text{Guard } t_{init})$$

When fired, the transition consumes the one token from place aux_2 and
emits an operation-specific number of token to the root place of its related
tree-shaped voting structure petri net. This number of token resembles the
operation-specific minimal number of votes to collect among the child nodes
of the original tree-shaped voting structure's root node. For example, if a
read quorum should be formed with the tree-shaped voting structure petri
net in Figure 4.19, then one token is put on the root place V_1 whereas for
forming a write quorum, two token are placed on V_1. Specifically, depending
on the quorum building for the first or the second operation to be performed,
a potentially different number of token must be placed on the tree-shaped
voting structure petri net's root place – referenced to by *tsvspgroot* – as
specified in the following outgoing arc cardinality function:

function / $\mathrm{\hbar}(t_{init} \rightarrow tsvspgroot)$:
   if $\sharp(OPS) >$ OPWRITE:
      return $(\sharp(aux_{n+1}) = 0)$? tsvsOPWRITE : tsvsOPREAD
      return $(\sharp(OPS) =$ OPWRITE$)$? tsvsOPWRITE : tsvsOPREAD

The numeric constants tsvsOPWRITE and tsvsOPREAD refer to the tree-
shaped voting structure petri net-specific number of token to be put on
its root place for forming a write quorum or a read quorum, respectively.
If both quorums are to be formed ($\sharp(OPS) >$ OPWRITE), then either
tsvsOPREAD or tsvsOPWRITE token are put on the tree-shaped voting
structure petri net's root place, depending on whether the first operation
quorum building has been performed or not. In the above cardinality func-

tion, the write operation marks the first operation (for which $\sharp(aux_{n+1})$ is zero) and the read operation is the second operation. Otherwise, in case a single operation-specific quorum is to be formed, the arc cardinality function evaluates to either tsvsOPREAD or tsvsOPWRITE, depending on the token count of the place *OPS*.

If an intra-stage heterogeneous dynamic data replication scheme is used (cf. Section 3.4), then not only the marking of the place *stage* but also the state of specific processes being (non-)failed has an influence on the tree-shaped voting structure subnet selection. Recall that in an intra-stage heterogeneous dynamic data replication scheme, different tree-shaped voting structures can be used within a stage of the dynamics, depending on the *concrete* subset of the set of processes. Hence, the state of specific processes must be considered by the initialize transition guards to activate the according tree-shaped voting structure subnet. Alike, the further tree-shaped voting structure subnet-specific transitions must be adapted accordingly. As these modifications are rather simple, they are omitted henceforth for the sake of a more stringent presentation.

The firing of the $t_{init_\star}$ transition enables transitions internal to the tree-shaped voting structure petri net which in turn enable successive internal transitions until eventually all potentially enabled transitions have fired. Then, one of the three tree-shaped voting structure subnet-local transitions $t_{success_\star}^3$, $t_{retry_\star}^2$, or $t_{failure_\star}^1$ becomes enabled.

The Tree-Shaped Voting Structure Subnet Success Transition
A subnet-local success transition becomes enabled if (1) the place $ctrl_{qbuild}$ has one token, (2) the place *stage* has a token count matching the number of processes for which the tree-shaped voting structure petri net models the quorum system, and (3) the tree-shaped voting structure petri net marking meets a certain operation-specific condition indicating a successful quorum building. For the decision on a positive (or negative) quorum building outcome, not the mere number of token-populated places is decisive but which specific ones of them do have a non-zero token count.

The condition on the tree-shaped voting structure petri net marking stating a successful quorum building is deduced from traversing the original tree-shaped voting structure as follows: The initial condition expression is given by the root node's petri net counterpart place to have zero token, a necessary (but generally not sufficient) condition for a successfully built quorum. For example, for the 2×2 Grid Protocol tree-shaped voting structure petri net in Figure 4.19 on page 213, this initial expression is

true $\leftarrow [\sharp(V_1) = 0]$.

Then, this expression on the root node (place) is substituted by an operation-specific expression on its child nodes' petri net counterpart place markings that reflect a successful quorum building. Those markings are determined by the root node's operation-specific quorum function value in terms of a disjunction of each combination of its child nodes' petri net counterpart places that satisfy the quorum function value requirement if having zero token. For example, the above expression for the 2×2 Grid Protocol tree-shaped voting structure petri net in Figure 4.19 becomes

true $\leftarrow [\sharp(V_2) = 0 \vee \sharp(V_3) = 0]$

for the read operation and

true $\leftarrow [\sharp(V_2) = 0 \wedge \sharp(V_3) = 0]$

for the write operation. Alike, every term in this expression is itself treated like the root node (place) expression and is substituted by an according expression on its child nodes' petri net counterpart places until finally a node's set of child nodes solely consists of leaf nodes. This node's petri net counterpart place is a representative of the leaf places it is connected to via immediate transitions: If this place has a non-zero token count, then some processes have failed such that they cannot be accounted for participating in a quorum. More specifically, the processes whose identity token counts resemble the identity token counts of those process list places that correspond to the empty leaf places have failed. Otherwise, the (possibly) formed quorum includes those processes having an identity token count as represented by the leaf places having a non-zero token count. The resulting final success marking condition for the tree-shaped voting structure petri net in Figure 4.19 is

true $\leftarrow [(\sharp(V_4) = 0 \wedge \sharp(V_6) = 0) \vee (\sharp(V_5) = 0 \vee \sharp(V_7) = 0)]$

for the read operation and

true $\leftarrow [(\sharp(V_4) = 0 \wedge \sharp(V_6) = 0) \wedge (\sharp(V_5) = 0 \vee \sharp(V_7) = 0)]$

for the write operation.

Like in two expressions above, a success marking condition may contain (sub)expressions being the conjunction of several places to have zero token. Rather than explicitly stating combinations of places to have zero token, such expressions can be simplified if a node's child nodes have a uniform vote assignment by stating a threshold on the child nodes' petri net counterpart places that may have non-zero token up to which a quorum can be successfully formed. For example, the above conditions become

true $\leftarrow [(\sharp(V_4) + \sharp(V_6) < 1) \vee (\sharp(V_5) + \sharp(V_7) < 3)]$

for the read operation and

true $\leftarrow [(\sharp(V_4) + \sharp(V_6) < 1) \wedge (\sharp(V_5) + \sharp(V_7) < 3)]$

for the write operation. As another example, consider a tree-shaped voting structure's node V_1 requiring the votes of two of its four child nodes V_2, V_3, V_4, and V_5 with each of them having one vote. Instead of the explicit condition on V_1's child node petri net counterpart places to have zero token which is

$$
\begin{aligned}
\text{true} \leftarrow \ & [(\sharp(V_2) = 0 \wedge \sharp(V_3) = 0) \vee \\
& (\sharp(V_2) = 0 \wedge \sharp(V_4) = 0) \vee \\
& (\sharp(V_2) = 0 \wedge \sharp(V_5) = 0) \vee \\
& (\sharp(V_3) = 0 \wedge \sharp(V_4) = 0) \vee \\
& (\sharp(V_3) = 0 \wedge \sharp(V_5) = 0) \vee \\
& (\sharp(V_4) = 0 \wedge \sharp(V_5) = 0)],
\end{aligned}
$$

this expression can be simplified to

true $\leftarrow [\sharp(V_2) + \sharp(V_3) + \sharp(V_4) + \sharp(V_5) < 3]$.

This optimization is also applicable to non-uniform vote assignments of a node's child nodes with accordingly set thresholds on the child nodes' petri net counterpart places that may have non-zero token counts. Alike, further optimizations exploiting data replication scheme specifics may be applied to the success condition on the markings of a tree-shaped voting structure petri net.

Recall that if (1) the success marking condition is satisfied, (2) the place $ctrl_{qbuild}$ has one token, and (3) the token count of the place $stage$ matches the number of processes for which this tree-shaped voting structure petri net models the quorum system, then the success transition $t_{success_*}^3$ is enabled and fires. First, it deposits either OPREAD=1 or OPWRITE=2 token on both of the system model-global places $opavail$ and $ctrl_{qbdone}$, depending on whether a read quorum or a write quorum has been successfully built. Specifically, if a single operation quorum was to be formed, then a number of token that matches the marking of the place OPS is deposited on the places $ctrl_{qbdone}$ and $opavail$. Otherwise, a number of token that is dependent on the marking of the place aux_{n+1} and, thereby, on which operation quorum building has been performed, is deposited on the places $ctrl_{qbdone}$ and $opavail$ as determined by the following outgoing arc cardinality expression for both arcs $t_{success} \rightarrow ctrl_{qbdone}$ and $t_{success} \rightarrow opavail$:

if $\sharp(OPS) >$ OPWRITE:
    return $(\sharp(aux_{n+1}) = 0)\,?$ OPWRITE : OPREAD
return $\sharp(OPS)$.

If a process model with replica states is used, the information of which processes are contained the quorum is needed to update the replica status of processes via the post-operation subnet (cf. Section 4.3.5). Alike, if, for example, a process' participation in (successfully built) quorums is of interest, the tree-shaped voting structure petri net's leaf place markings must be copied to the system model-global quorum places $qp_1^1, \ldots, qp_n^1$ and $qp_1^2, \ldots, qp_n^2$. This shifting of token is realized by variable-cardinality input and output arcs from and to the quorum places as illustrated in Figure 4.20 on page 216. It is dependent on whether a single operation quorum or quorums for both operations are to be formed, and, in the latter case, also dependent on which operation quorum building has been performed. The variable-cardinality input arcs clear the operation-specific quorum places, for example, for the quorum places qp_3^1 and qp_3^2, by the two cardinality functions

function $/\Psi(t_{success} \leftarrow qp_3^1)$:
    if $(\sharp(aux_{n+1}) = 0)$: **return** $\sharp(qp_3^1)$
    return 0

and

function $/\Psi(t_{success} \leftarrow qp_3^2)$:
    return $\sharp(qp_3^2)$.

While the quorum places for the second operation quorum building can be emptied unconditionally, the quorum places for the first operation quorum building may only be emptied if it has been performed. The variable-cardinality output arcs to the operation-specific quorum places transfer the leaf place markings. For example, for the 2×2 Grid Protocol tree-shaped voting structure petri net in Figure 4.19 on page 213, the cardinality functions for the outgoing arcs connecting to the quorum places qp_3^1 and qp_3^2 are

function $/\,\text{\th}(t_{success} \rightarrow qp_3^1)$:
    if $(\sharp(aux_{n+1}) = 0)$: **return** $(\sharp(lp_3) = 0)\,?\ \sharp(lp_3') : \sharp(lp_3)$
    return 0

and

function $/\,\text{\th}(t_{success} \rightarrow qp_3^2)$:
    if $(\sharp(aux_{n+1}) = 1)$: **return** $(\sharp(lp_3) = 0)\,?\ \sharp(lp_3') : \sharp(lp_3)$
    return 0.

Depending on which operation quorum building has been performed, the place qp_3^1 or the place qp_3^2 is assigned the token count of one of the leaf places lp_3 and lp_3' – as both represent the same process p_3 – or zero token by the zero token count of the leaf place lp_3' if process p_3 is not contained in the quorum.

Finally, the success transition empties all (internal) places of the tree-shaped voting structure petri net as indicated by the dash-shaped incoming arc in Figure 4.20.

If the success marking condition is not satisfied, then the lower-prioritized retry transition may become enabled.

The Tree-Shaped Voting Structure Subnet Retry Transition

A subnet-local retry transition $t_{retry_\star}^2$ becomes enabled whenever retrying a failed quorum building is worthwhile. For example, consider the tree-shaped voting structure petri net in Figure 4.19 on page 213 and assume the processes p_3 and p_4 to have failed. Initially, one token is assigned to the root place V_1, indicating that a read quorum is to be formed. This token is subsequently consumed by the transition $t_{V_1-V_2\star}^6$ which deposits two token on its output place V_2. Then, the transitions $t_{V_2-V_4\star}^5$ and $t_{V_2-V_6\star}^5$ fire, thereby consuming the two token on place V_2 and depositing one token on each of the places V_4 and V_6. Subsequently, either $t_{V_4-lp_1\star}^4$ or $t_{V_4-lp_2\star}^4$ may fire, thereby consuming the one token from V_4 and emitting $\natural(pl_1)$ or $\natural(pl_2)$ token to the leaf place lp_1 or lp_2, respectively. As of the processes p_3 and p_4 being failed and the process list places pl_3 and pl_4 both having zero token, neither the transition $t_{V_6-lp_3\star}^4$ nor the transition $t_{V_6-lp_4\star}^4$ becomes enabled such that one token remains on place V_6. In this case, no read quorum in terms of a C-Cover can be formed and, therefore, the success transition is disabled. However, the non-failed processes p_1 and p_2 can successfully form a read quorum in terms of a CC-Cover such that the retry transition should fire. Hence, if the success transition is disabled, then the lower-prioritized retry transition $t_{retry_\star}^2$ fires if its guard evaluates to true which is the case if (1) the place $ctrl_{qbuild}$ has one token, (2) the token count of the place *stage* matches the number of processes for which the tree-shaped voting structure petri net models the quorum system, and (3) the tree-shaped voting structure petri net's root place has zero token.

When fired, the tree-shaped voting structure petri net marking is altered with respect to the root place on which an operation-specific number of token is placed that corresponds to the respective quorum function value of the original tree-shaped voting structure's root node. Specifically, either tsvsOPREAD or tsvsOPWRITE token are deposited on the root place if a single operation quorum is to be formed. Otherwise, in case both operation quorums are to be formed, the number of token depends on which quorum building is currently performed. These cases are expressed by the outgoing arc cardinality function

function $/\text{m}(t_{retry} \rightarrow tsvspgroot)$:
  if $\sharp(OPS) > \text{OPWRITE}$:
    return $(\sharp(aux_{n+1}) = 0)$? tsvsOPWRITE : tsvsOPREAD
    return $(\sharp(OPS) = \text{OPWRITE})$? tsvsOPWRITE : tsvsOPREAD.

By this means, the quorum building is retried until either the success transition fires or the token have piled up to the root place such that the retry transition is disabled. Then, definitely no quorum can be successfully formed because of too many failed processes and the subnet-local failure transition becomes enabled.

Note that instead of repeatedly retrying the quorum building until either the success transition fires or the failure transition must finally fire, the retry transition may be equipped with a more sophisticated guard that expresses an operation-specific condition on the possible tree-shaped voting structure petri net markings for which a quorum building retry is worthwhile. This condition can be derived analogously to the success marking condition. Depending on the structure of the tree-shaped voting structure petri net and the modeled quorum system, analysis time may be reduced.

The Tree-Shaped Voting Structure Subnet Failure Transition
Whenever no operation-specific quorum can be successfully formed, the subnet-local failure transition $t_{failure_{\star}^1}$ finally becomes enabled as it has a lower priority than the success and retry transitions. Specifically, it becomes enabled if (1) the place $ctrl_{qbuild}$ has one token and (2) the token count of the place $stage$ matches the number of processes for which the tree-shaped voting structure petri net models the quorum system. When fired, it (1) empties all (internal) places of the tree-shaped voting structure petri net (indicated by the dash-shaped incoming arc in Figure 4.20), it (2) empties the quorum places like the success transition (if applicable), and finally (3) outputs OPFAIL=4 token to the control place $ctrl_{qbdone}$. The latter enables the transition $t_{qbdone_{\star}}$ that is explained in Step 5 on the system model embedding.

Depending on the structure and the quorum system modeled by the tree-shaped voting structure petri net, a priority reordering of its specific success, failure, and retry transitions can be beneficial to analysis time. This is the case, for example, if failure condition markings are expressible in a more concise manner than success and retry condition markings. Then, the failure transition – whose guard states the fatal conditions for which a quorum cannot be formed – may have the highest priority, followed by the success transition while the retry transition has the lowest priority among the three transitions.

Next, tree-shaped voting structure petri net examples of Weighted Voting, Majority Consensus Voting, and the Tree Quorum Protocol are presented, followed by the discussion of Step 5 on the system model embedding.

Examples of Tree-Shaped Voting Structure Petri Nets The Weighted Voting tree-shaped voting structure with four processes in which process p_1 is assigned two votes while the other processes have one vote each and its corresponding petri net counterpart are shown in Figure 4.21. The successful quorum building condition is

$$\text{true} \leftarrow [\sharp(V_1) = 0]$$

for both operations. A retry transition is not necessary and can therefore be omitted. The value of the numeric constants tsvsOPREAD and tsvsOPWRITE as used by the initialize transition is 3 for both of them.

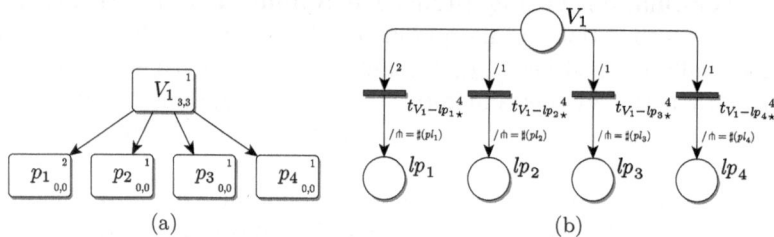

(a)   (b)

Figure 4.21: Tree-Shaped Voting Structure of Weighted Voting with Four Processes Having a Vote Assignment of $p_1 = 2$, $p_2 = p_3 = p_4 = 1$ (a) and its Petri Net Counterpart (b)

The Majority Consensus Voting tree-shaped voting structure with four processes and its corresponding petri net counterpart are depicted in Fig-

ure 4.22. The successful quorum building condition for both operations is
true ← [♯(V_1) = 0].

A retry transition is not necessary and is therefore omitted. The numeric constants as used by the initialize transition are tsvsOPREAD=2
and tsvsOPWRITE=3.

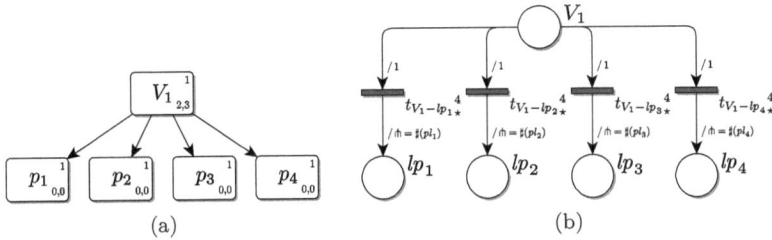

(a)   (b)

Figure 4.22: Tree-Shaped Voting Structure of Majority Consensus Voting with
Four Processes (a) and its Petri Net Counterpart (b)

Finally, the Tree Quorum Protocol tree-shaped voting structure with four
processes alongside with its corresponding petri net counterpart are shown
in Figure 4.23. The successful quorum building condition for both operations is

true ← [♯(lp_1) > 0 ∧ ♯(V_2) = 0].

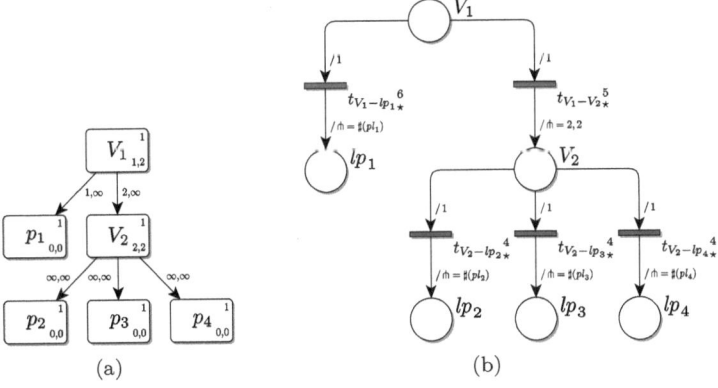

(a)   (b)

Figure 4.23: Tree-Shaped Voting Structure of the Tree Quorum Protocol with
Four Processes (a) and its Petri Net Counterpart (b)

Like for the preceding two examples, a retry transition is not necessary and is omitted. The two numeric constants as used by the initialize transition are tsvsOPREAD=1 and tsvsOPWRITE=2.

The final step is to embed the tree-shaped voting structure subnet into the system model as explained next.

Step 5: System Model Embedding

The modeling of a dynamic data replication scheme requires up to n tree-shaped voting structure subnets in the system model for a system comprising n processes, each modeling the quorum system for a particular stage of the dynamics. For a static data replication scheme – due to the absence of dynamics – a single one is sufficient. The embedding of n tree-shaped voting structure subnets is schematically illustrated in Figure 4.24. The tree-shaped voting structure subnets are controlled by the system model-global guarded transitions $t_{qbinit_\star}$ and $t_{qbdone_\star}$. The former transition is enabled by the process list subnet (cf. Section 4.3.3). It triggers a quorum building by activating the initialize transition $t_{init_\star}$ of the tree-shaped vot-

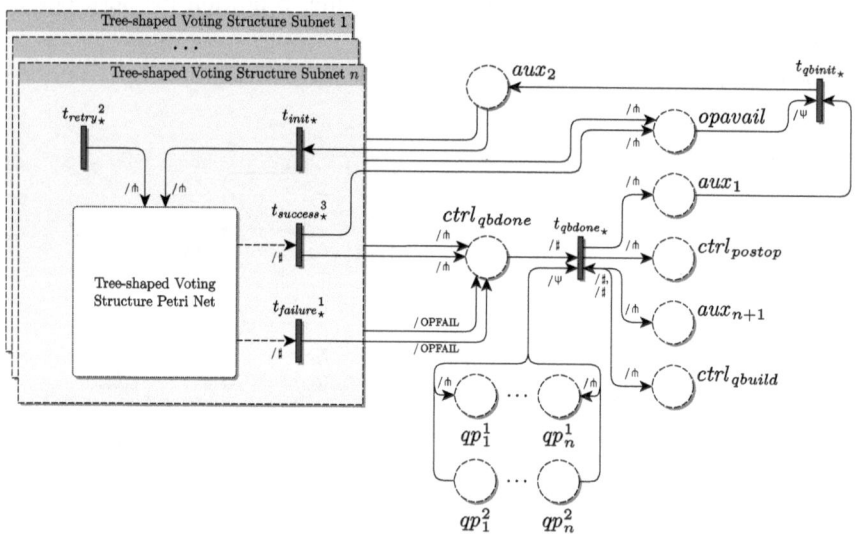

Figure 4.24: Conceptual Illustration of Embedding n Tree-Shaped Voting Structure Subnets into the System Model

ing structure subnet that models the quorum system for the current stage of the dynamics via populating its input place aux_2 with one token. The latter transition $t_{qbdone_\star}$ is enabled after the quorum building has finished by one of the tree-shaped voting structure subnet transitions $t_{success_\star^3}$ or $t_{failure_\star^1}$ firing. If the quorum building has been successful, the transition $t_{success_\star^3}$ deposits either OPREAD=1 or OPWRITE=2 token on both of the system model-global places $opavail$ and $ctrl_{qbdone}$. Otherwise, only $ctrl_{qbdone}$ is assigned OPFAIL=4 token by the transition $t_{failure_\star^1}$. The transition $t_{qbdone_\star}$ is responsible for (1) triggering a second operation quorum building to concertedly form read and write operation quorums and for (2) activating the post-operation subnet that is described in the next Section 4.3.5. The two transitions $t_{qbinit_\star}$ and $t_{qbdone_\star}$ are explained in the remainder of this section.

The System Model-Global Quorum Building Initialize Transition

A quorum building is triggered by depositing one token on each of the system model-global places aux_1 and $ctrl_{qbuild}$. Thereby, the system model-global guarded transition $t_{qbinit_\star}$ becomes enabled as its guard

$$\text{true} \leftarrow [\sharp(ctrl_{qbuild}) = 1] \qquad\qquad \text{(Guard } t_{qbinit})$$

evaluates to true and its input place aux_1 has one token. Note that if a read quorum and a write quorum are to be formed (concertedly), the first quorum building is triggered by the process list subnet (cf. Section 4.3.3) while the second quorum building is triggered by the transition $t_{qbdone_\star}$ described below. The system model-global place aux_{n+1} keeps track of which operation quorum is currently being built. Initially, it has a token count of zero indicating that the first operation quorum is to be formed. After the first operation quorum building attempt, the transition $t_{qbdone_\star}$ deposits one token on it.

When fired, the transition $t_{qbinit_\star}$ empties the place aux_1 and emits one token to the auxiliary place aux_2. If both operation quorums are to be formed concertedly, then the transition $t_{qbinit_\star}$ clears the place $opavail$ on the first operation quorum building. Otherwise, it draws a number of token from the place $opavail$ depending on which operation quorum is to be built and on this operation's availability as given by the token count of the place $opavail$, expressed by the incoming arc cardinality function

function $/ ^\Psi (t_{qbinit} \leftarrow opavail)$:
   if $(\sharp(OPS) > \text{OPWRITE}) \wedge (\sharp(aux_{n+1}) = 0)$: **return** $\sharp(opavail)$
   if $(\sharp(OPS) = \text{OPWRITE}) \wedge (\sharp(opavail) \geq \text{OPWRITE})$:
      return OPWRITE

if $(\sharp(OPS) = \text{OPREAD}) \wedge ((\sharp(opavail) = \text{OPREAD}) \vee$
$(\sharp(opavail) = \text{OPREAD+OPWRITE}))$: **return** OPREAD
return 0.

The System Model-Global Quorum Building Done Transition

The transition $t_{qbdone_\star}$ marks the end of a quorum building. It becomes enabled if the control places $ctrl_{qbuild}$ and $ctrl_{qbdone}$ both have a non-zero token count, in guard notation

$$\text{true} \leftarrow [(\sharp(ctrl_{qbuild}) = 1) \wedge (\sharp(ctrl_{qbdone}) > 0)]. \qquad \text{(Guard } t_{qbdone})$$

When fired, both places are emptied by the transition.

If quorums for both operations are to be formed concertedly, the transition $t_{qbdone_\star}$ must trigger the quorum building for the second operation after the first one has finished. The place aux_{n+1} is used to keep track of which operation quorum building has been performed. If it holds zero token, the first operation quorum building has been performed. Otherwise, it holds one token and the second operation quorum building has been performed. In this case, the post-operation subnet (cf. Section 4.3.5) has to be triggered and, depending on the process model chosen and at least one successful quorum building, either zero or one token are deposited on the place aux_{n+1}, indicating whether the replica status of processes must be updated or not. This behavior is reflected by the outgoing arc cardinality function

```
1  function / ⋔ (t_qbdone → aux_{n+1}):
2    if (♯(OPS) > OPWRITE) ∧ (♯(aux_{n+1}) = 0): return 1
3    if ( (PROCESSMODEL > 2) ∧ (♯(OPS) ≤ OPWRITE) ):
4      return (♯(ctrl_qbdone) ≠ OPFAIL) ? 0 : 1
5    if ( (PROCESSMODEL > 2) ∧ (♯(OPS) > OPWRITE) ):
6      return (∑_{i=1}^{n} qp_i^1 + qp_i^2) > 0 ? 0 : 1
7    return 1.
```

Note that the return statement's summation over the quorum places in line 6 is necessary since the marking of the place $ctrl_{qbdone}$ testifies the quorum building outcome for the last but not for both operations. By the sum of the quorum places' token counts, it is tested if (at least) one of the quorum place sets holds a successfully built quorum. Alternatively, a dedicated place providing this information could have been introduced instead of testing the sum of the quorum places' marking for a non-zero token count.

The cardinality of the outgoing arc to the place $ctrl_{qbuild}$ evaluates to 0 if either only one operation quorum is to be formed or both operation quorum building attempts have been performed. Otherwise, the second quorum building attempt is triggered by the cardinality function evaluating to 1:

function $/ \hbar(t_{qbdone} \rightarrow ctrl_{qbuild})$:
  if $(\sharp(OPS) \leq \text{OPWRITE})$: **return** 0
  return $(\sharp(aux_{n+1}) = 1)?0:1$.

The cardinality of the outgoing arc to the place aux_1 evaluates to 1 if two quorum building attempts are to be performed of which one has been attempted such that the transition $t_{qbinit_\star}$ can become enabled again. Otherwise, depending on the process model chosen and a successful quorum building, the subsequent post-operation subnet to be introduced in the next section is instructed to either update the replica status of processes or not.

1 **function** $/ \hbar(t_{qbdone} \rightarrow aux_1)$:
2   **if** $(\sharp(OPS) > \text{OPWRITE}) \wedge (\sharp(aux_{n+1}) = 0)$: **return** 1
3   **if** $(\text{(PROCESSMODEL} > 2) \wedge (\sharp(OPS) \leq \text{OPWRITE}))$:
4   **return** $(\sharp(ctrl_{qbdone}) \neq \text{OPFAIL})?1:0$
5   **if** $(\text{(PROCESSMODEL} > 2) \wedge (\sharp(OPS) > \text{OPWRITE}))$:
6   **return** $(\sum_{i=1}^{n} qp_i^1 + qp_i^2) > 0?1:0$
7   **return** 0

The same explanation as above applies to the return statement's summation over the quorum places in line 6.

If either both operation quorum buildings have been performed or only one operation quorum was to be and has been formed, then finally the post-operation subnet is triggered as expressed by the outgoing arc cardinality function

function $/ \hbar(t_{qbdone} \rightarrow ctrl_{postop})$:
  if $(\sharp(OPS) \leq \text{OPWRITE})$: **return** 1
  return $(\sharp(aux_{n+1}) = 1)?1:0$.

Note that if two operation quorums are to be formed, the two-states process model lacking replica states is used, frequent operations are assumed, and only operation availability is to be evaluated, the above cardinality functions can be simplified to activate the post-operation subnet if the first operation is the write operation and a write quorum has been successfully formed. In this case, the successfully formed write quorum accounts for read operation availability as it can be used to perform a read operation. A read quorum building must only be tried if the write quorum building has failed such that read operation availability must be explicitly tested.

When assuming frequent operations such that operations are triggered upon process failure and recovery events, an epoch change operation must be attempted whenever an operation execution is triggered – since always either a process has failed or recovered from its failure. When not assuming frequent operations, an epoch change operation attempt is performed upon detected process failures as determined by the token count of the new system model-global place $ctrl_{recfg}$ that is to be introduced in Section 4.3.8 on the relaxation of the frequent operations assumption.

In either case, if a process model with replica states is used, the subsequent post-operation subnet must update the replica status of processes that are in the union of the epoch change operation's two write quorums (cf. Section 2.5.2). Hence, if a write quorum of the current epoch's quorum system has been built, a write quorum of the new epoch's quorum system must be formed. For this purpose, the epoch list and the process list places as well as the place *stage* must be updated to reflect the processes in the new epoch. Thereafter, a write quorum building using the tree-shaped voting structure subnet for the new epoch must be triggered. Furthermore, the subnet-local success transition must be adapted to – if necessary – shift the process identity token counts of the new epoch's write quorum to the according quorum places that already hold the write quorum formed in the current epoch such that the identity token count of a process participating in both write quorums is assigned only once to a quorum place.

However, as discussed in Section 4.3.2, in favor of a simpler presentation and as updating the replica status of processes is not required for the two-states process model lacking replica states, the replica status of all non-failed processes is updated and not only the replica status of processes in the union of the epoch change operation's two write quorums. In order to enable the replica status update of all processes by the subsequent post-operation subnet, the process identity token counts of all non-failed processes are assigned to quorum places – provided that a write quorum of the current epoch's quorum system has been successfully built – as follows. First, the quorum places are emptied (since the replica status of all non-failed processes is updated anyway) after both quorum buildings have been performed or, if only the write operation quorum building is to be performed, after it has been performed. This is realized by n incoming arcs to the transition t_{qbdone} whose arc cardinalities evaluate to the respective token counts of the quorum places $qp_1^1, \ldots, qp_n^1$ and $qp_1^2, \ldots, qp_n^2$ as expressed by the following template cardinality function with $j \in \{1, 2\}$ and $1 \leq i \leq n$:

function $/^{\Psi}(t_{qbdone} \leftarrow qp_i^j)$:
   if ((PROCESSMODEL > 2) $\wedge$ ($\sharp(ctrl_{recfg}) > 0$) $\wedge$
     ($\sharp(opavail) \geq$ OPWRITE)):
     if (($\sharp(aux_{n+1}) = 1$) $\wedge$ ($\sharp(OPS) >$ OPWRITE)): **return** $\sharp(qp_i^j)$

if (($\sharp(aux_{n+1}) = 0$) $\wedge$ ($\sharp(OPS) = $ OPWRITE)): **return** $\sharp(qp_i^j)$
return 0.

Then, n outgoing arcs populate the quorum places $qp_1^1, \ldots, qp_n^1$ with process identity token counts of all non-failed processes as expressed by the following template cardinality function with $1 \leq i \leq n$:

function $/ \, \text{th}(t_{qbdone} \rightarrow qp_i^1)$:
  if ((PROCESSMODEL > 2) $\wedge$ ($\sharp(ctrl_{recfg}) > 0$) $\wedge$
    ($\sharp(opavail) \geq $ OPWRITE)):
    if (($\sharp(aux_{n+1}) = 1$) $\wedge$ ($\sharp(OPS) > $ OPWRITE)):
      return ($\sharp(p_i{}_{c:cur}^{up}) + \sharp(p_i{}_{c:old}^{up}) = i$) ? i : 0
    if (($\sharp(aux_{n+1}) = 0$) $\wedge$ ($\sharp(OPS) = $ OPWRITE)):
      return ($\sharp(p_i{}_{c:cur}^{up}) + \sharp(p_i{}_{c:old}^{up}) = i$) ? i : 0
  return 0.

Note that the replica status update of processes in a successfully formed read quorum is not affected when only a read quorum building was to be performed or both operation quorum buildings were to be performed but a write quorum cannot be built.

In case of assuming frequent operations, the condition on the place $ctrl_{recfg}$ can be omitted from the cardinality functions and the place itself can be omitted from the system model altogether.

Summary of Tree-Shaped Voting Structure Subnets

In summary, the transformation of tree-shaped voting structures into their petri net counterparts consisting of five steps being (1) the graph-structural transformation, (2) the application of the tree-shaped voting structure's vote logics to its petri net counterpart, (3) the transition firing sequentialization, (4) the quorum building controlling involving the quorum building outcome propagation, and (5) the system model embedding is deterministically applicable and can therefore be automatized. In fact, tree-shaped voting structures can be derived from a given data replication scheme specification (cf. Section 3.4), then be transformed into their petri net counterpart subnets, and finally be integrated into the system model automatically. In conjunction with an appropriate number of process subnet template instances, an accordingly instantiated process list management subnet, epoch list management subnet, and post-operation subnet, a composed system model can be instantiated in an automatic manner.

The next section presents the *post-operation subnet* which is responsible for updating the replica status of processes in response to a successful quorum building (if a process model with replica states is chosen) and for possibly triggering an epoch change operation after having cleared the process list places and – if applicable – the quorum places.

4.3.5 Post-Operation Subnet

The post-operation subnet as conceptually shown in Figure 4.25 serves the purposes of (1) updating a process' replica status if a process model with replica states is used, (2) emptying the process list places, (3) clearing the system model-global quorum places, provided that the quality measure of interest does not include, for example, a process' participation in quorums, and finally (4) triggering an epoch change operation in case a dynamic data replication scheme is used and the operation is necessary and at all possible. The post-operation subnet is activated by populating the place $ctrl_{postop}$ and either the place aux_1 or aux_{n+1} with one token. The place aux_1 has one token if the process model chosen has replica states and a quorum has been successfully built such that the replica status of processes must be updated. The place aux_{n+1} has one token if no quorum has been successfully built or if the two-states process model lacking replica states is chosen.

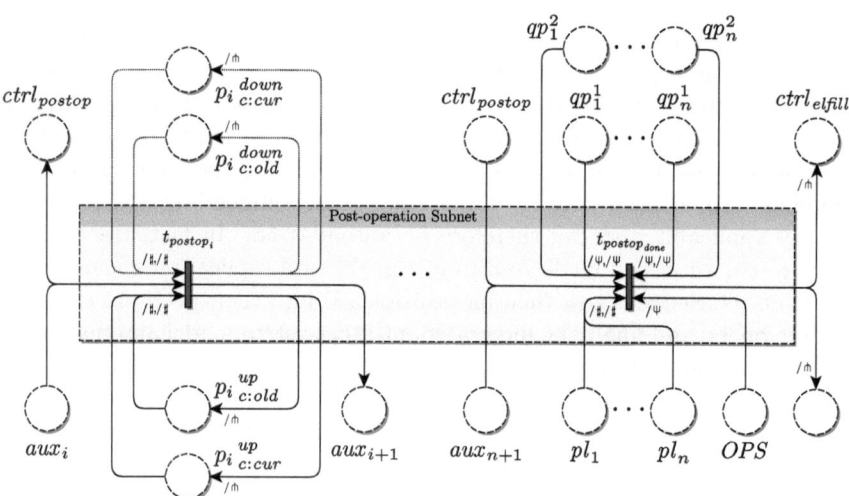

Figure 4.25: Schematic Illustration of the Post-Operation Subnet

Process Replica Status Update for the Three- and Four-States Process Models In case the place aux_1 has one token as a quorum has been successfully built, the first transition t_{postop_1} out of a sequence of transitions $t_{postop_1}, \ldots, t_{postop_n}$ becomes enabled for managing the replica status of the n processes. A transition t_{postop_i} consumes one token from the control place $ctrl_{postop}$ that is immediately put back thereon and draws one token from its helper place aux_i which is put on its successive helper place aux_{i+1} whereby its successive transition $t_{postop_{i+1}}$ subsequently becomes enabled. If the four-states process model is used, then the places $p_i \, _{c:cur}^{down}$ and $p_i \, _{c:old}^{down}$ are emptied in addition to the places $p_i \, _{c:cur}^{up}$ and $p_i \, _{c:old}^{up}$ that are cleared in case the three-states process model is chosen. For the three-states process model, there are no process subnet places besides $p_i \, _{c:cur}^{up}$ and $p_i \, _{c:old}^{up}$ such that the places $p_i \, _{c:old}^{down}$ and $p_i \, _{c:cur}^{down}$ in Figure 4.25 can be considered absent for it to comply to the three-states process model. This is visually indicated by the arcs emerging from and heading to these places having a dotted line shape.

The cardinality function for each outgoing arc $1 \le i \le n$ connecting a transition t_{postop_i} to a process subnet place $p_i \, _{c:cur}^{up}$ is

```
1  function / ⋔(t_postop_i → p_i c:cur^up):
2    if (♯(p_i c:cur^up) + ♯(p_i c:old^up) = 0): return 0
3    if ( (♯(OPS) = OPREAD) ∧ (♯(p_i c:cur^up) = i) ): return i
4    loop := 1
5    while loop ≤ n:
6      if ((♯(qp_loop^1) > i) ∨ (♯(qp_loop^2) > i)): return 0
7      if ((♯(qp_loop^1) = i) ∨ (♯(qp_loop^2) = i)): return i
8      loop := loop + 1
9    return 0.
```

First it is checked that the process has not failed. Otherwise, 0 is returned by line 2 since the process cannot be in the state $p_i \, _{c:cur}^{up}$ (nor in the state $p_i \, _{c:old}^{up}$). In case only a read operation has been performed and the process has a current replica, it stays in the state $p_i \, _{c:cur}^{up}$ by returning the process identity token count i (line 3). Performing a read operation does never outdate but only update a process' replica. If both cases do not apply, then the function iterates over the system model-global quorum places $qp_1^1, \ldots, qp_n^1$ and $qp_1^2, \ldots, qp_n^2$ (lines 5–8) and returns the process identity token count i if this token count is found on one of the quorum places (line 7). Otherwise, the process is not included in a quorum and its replica must not be updated such that 0 is returned by line 9. The fact of the process list and the quorum places' token counts being ordered in an ascending manner is exploited by returning 0 in case a quorum place's token count is greater than the process identity token count i (line 6) since this token count cannot be found on any subsequent quorum places.

Note that the quorum places' token counts are only ordered if the ordering of the process list places – due to the ordering of the epoch list places – is reflected by a tree-shaped voting structure petri net's leaf places. This is the case if the cardinality of every outgoing arc connecting to a leaf place lp_i evaluates to the token count of the process list place pl_i (cf. Section 4.3.4). Otherwise, this optimization cannot be applied to the cardinality functions of the outgoing arcs to process subnet places and all quorum places have to be inspected.

The cardinality function for each outgoing arc $1 \leq i \leq n$ connecting a transition t_{postop_i} to a process subnet place $p_i \, {}^{up}_{c:old}$ is

1 **function** / ⋔ $(t_{postop_i} \rightarrow p_i \, {}^{up}_{c:old})$:
2   **if** $(\sharp(p_i \, {}^{up}_{c:cur}) + \sharp(p_i \, {}^{up}_{c:old}) = 0)$: **return** 0
3   **if** ($(\sharp(OPS) = \text{OPREAD}) \wedge (\sharp(p_i \, {}^{up}_{c:cur}) = i)$): **return** 0
4   loop := 1
5   **while** loop $\leq n$:
6   **if** $((\sharp(qp^1_{loop}) > i) \vee (\sharp(qp^2_{loop}) > i))$: **return** i
7   **if** $((\sharp(qp^1_{loop}) = i) \vee (\sharp(qp^2_{loop}) = i))$: **return** 0
8   loop := loop + 1
9   **return** i.

Like in the former cardinality function for an outgoing arc leading to a process subnet place $p_i \, {}^{up}_{c:cur}$, it is first tested if the process has failed. In this case, 0 is returned by line 2. In case only a read operation has been performed and the process has a current replica, it remains in the state $p_i \, {}^{up}_{c:cur}$ by returning 0 (line 3). Otherwise, the quorum places are inspected (lines 5–8). If the process is included in a quorum (line 7), 0 is returned as the process is updated to have a current replica and thus cannot be in the state $p_i \, {}^{up}_{c:old}$. Exploiting the process list and the quorum places' ascending order in token counts, the loop (and the function) is prematurely aborted by returning i (line 6) if the process identity token count on the currently inspected quorum place exceeds i token. In this case, the process is not included in a quorum such that its replica is marked as outdated. The same is true if the iteration over the quorum places terminates (line 9) which is why the process identity token count i is then returned as well, thereby marking the process' replica as outdated.

In case the four-states process model is used and a write operation has been performed, a failed process' current replica must be marked as outdated since the process cannot have participated in the write quorum (cf.

Section 4.3.1). Otherwise, if no write operation has been performed and the process is failed with either a current or an outdated replica, it remains in the respective state. The corresponding outgoing arc cardinality function for each arc $1 \leq i \leq n$ connecting a transition t_{postop_i} to a process subnet place $p_i{}^{down}_{c:old}$ is

function / ⋔ $(t_{postop_i} \rightarrow p_i{}^{down}_{c:old})$:
  if $(\sharp(p_i{}^{up}_{c:cur}) + \sharp(p_i{}^{up}_{c:old}) = i)$: **return** 0
  if $(\sharp(p_i{}^{down}_{c:old}) = i)$: **return** i
  if ($(\sharp(opavail)$ & OPWRITE $> 0) \wedge (\sharp(OPS) \geq$ OPWRITE$)$):
    return i
  return 0

and the corresponding outgoing arc cardinality function connecting a transition t_{postop_i} to a process subnet place $p_i{}^{down}_{c:cur}$ is

function / ⋔ $(t_{postop_i} \rightarrow p_i{}^{down}_{c:cur})$:
  if $(\sharp(p_i{}^{up}_{c:cur}) + \sharp(p_i{}^{up}_{c:old}) = i)$: **return** 0
  if ($(\sharp(opavail)$ & OPWRITE $> 0) \wedge (\sharp(OPS) \geq$ OPWRITE$)$):
    return 0
  if $(\sharp(p_i{}^{down}_{c:cur}) = i)$: **return** i
  return 0.

Clearing Control Places and Triggering Dynamics Reconfiguration
The last transition $t_{postop_{done}}$ of the post-operation subnet as illustrated in Figure 4.25 becomes enabled (1) after the transitions $t_{postop_1}, \ldots, t_{postop_n}$ have fired, (2) if the two-states process model is used, or (3) if the single or both quorum buildings have failed. In the latter two cases, this transition instead of the transition t_{postop_1} is enabled by the transition t_{qbdone} as described in the previous section on tree-shaped voting structure subnets. When fired, the transition $t_{postop_{done}}$ consumes the single token of the control place $ctrl_{postop}$, the single token of the helper place uux_{n+1}, and all token of the n process list places, the latter via incoming arcs having marking-dependent cardinalities. If the quality measure to be evaluated has no interest in, for example, a process' participation in quorums, the system model-global quorum places are emptied via incoming arcs having marking-dependent arc cardinalities. Otherwise, the quorum places having an index exceeding the token count of the place *stage* are emptied if no epoch change operation is to be performed. When not assuming frequent operations, the place *OPS* is emptied since it is populated with token by an operation driver subnet (cf. Section 4.3.8).

Finally, if a dynamic data replication scheme is used and an epoch change operation must and indeed can be performed, a token is deposited on each of the places $ctrl_{elfill}$ and aux_1 via two variable-cardinality output arcs. Otherwise, the arc cardinalities evaluate to zero. Recall that when assuming frequent operations, an epoch change operation must be attempted whenever an operation execution is triggered by the failure or recovery of a process. If not assuming frequent operations, an epoch change operation attempt is performed upon detected process failures as determined by the token count of the system model-global place $ctrl_{recfg}$ that is to be introduced in Section 4.3.8 or also upon the recovery of a process. If the places $opavail$ and OPS both have at least OPWRITE token, then a write quorum has been successfully formed and, with this write quorum, an epoch change operation can be performed as argued in Section 4.3.2. Hence, when not assuming frequent operations, the expression determining the cardinality of both outgoing arcs from the transition $t_{postop_{done}}$ to the places $ctrl_{elfill}$ and aux_1 is

if (($\sharp(ctrl_{recfg}) > 0$) $\wedge$ ($\sharp(opavail) \geq$ OPWRITE) $\wedge$
   ($\sharp(OPS) \geq$ OPWRITE)): **return** 1
return 0.

Otherwise, in case of assuming frequent operations, the condition on the place $ctrl_{recfg}$ can be omitted from the expression.

If a static data replication scheme is used, then these outgoing arcs and the epoch list subnet need not to be incorporated into the system model at all because of the absence of dynamics and thus the need for quorum system reconfiguration.

Support for Dynamics Limitation It can be worthwhile to exclude particular stages from the dynamics in order to, for example, impose a lower bound on the dynamics for the benefit of a higher overall operation availability as mentioned in Section 3.4. Such a dynamics limit must be respected by the cardinality functions of the outgoing arcs to the places $ctrl_{elfill}$ and aux_1 emerging from the transition $t_{postop_{done}}$. For this purpose, an evaluation scenario-specific constant set of numbers DL $\subset \{1, \ldots, n\}$ specifying those stages of the dynamics to skip is stated and an epoch change operation is only performed if (1) a write quorum has been successfully formed and (2) the number of processes in the new epoch is not contained in the dynamics limit set DL. When not assuming frequent operations, the expression determining the cardinality of each of the outgoing arcs $t_{postop_{done}} \to ctrl_{elfill}$ and $t_{postop_{done}} \to aux_1$ becomes

if (($\sharp(opavail) \geq$ OPWRITE) $\wedge$ ($\sharp(ctrl_{recfg}) > 0$) $\wedge$
  ($\sharp(OPS) \geq$ OPWRITE) $\wedge$
  (($\sum_{i=1}^{n} [\sharp(p_i^{\,up}) > 0\,?\,1:0]) \notin$ DL)): **return** 1
return 0

if the two-states process model is used and

if (($\sharp(opavail) \geq$ OPWRITE) $\wedge$ ($\sharp(ctrl_{recfg}) > 0$) $\wedge$
  ($\sharp(OPS) \geq$ OPWRITE) $\wedge$
  (($\sum_{i=1}^{n} [\sharp(p_i{}_{c:cur}^{\,up}) + \sharp(p_i{}_{c:old}^{\,up}) > 0\,?\,1:0]) \notin$ DL)): **return** 1
return 0

for a process model with replica states. When assuming frequent operations, the cardinality functions may not include the condition on the place $ctrl_{recfg}$.

With the post-operation subnet, the fundamental system model-constituting subnets have been introduced. The next section illustrates the schematic control flow in a composed system model with four processes and using the two-states process model.

4.3.6 Schematic Control Flow in a System Model

The conceptual schematic control flow of an operation execution in a composed system model with four processes is shown in Figure 4.26. The frames in this figure do neither verbatim nor fully reflect the subnets introduced. Instead, they are an aggregation of system model-global and subnet-local places and transitions that are logically grouped by function in favor of a simpler illustration of the global control flow while executing an operation. A directed dashed edge connecting two frames means a marking change of (some of) the edge's destination frame places because of the firing of transitions in its source frame. Dotted directed edges express a dependency of the source frame's transitions – and thus the resulting marking in the source frame – on the destination frame places' marking.

The processes frame holds the $n = 4$ process subnets instantiated from the process subnet template for the two-states process model (cf. Section 4.3.1). Since frequent operations are assumed until Section 4.3.8, the process list frame (cf. Section 4.3.3) is activated by a token being deposited on the control place $ctrl_{op}$ upon the failure or recovery of a process. The process list frame's marking is dependent on the processes frame as well as on the epoch list frame (cf. Section 4.3.2) by the transition t_{plfill} querying the marking of specific processes frame places and of the places $el_1, \ldots, el_n$. The quorum building frame (cf. Section 4.3.4) is activated after the process list frame by

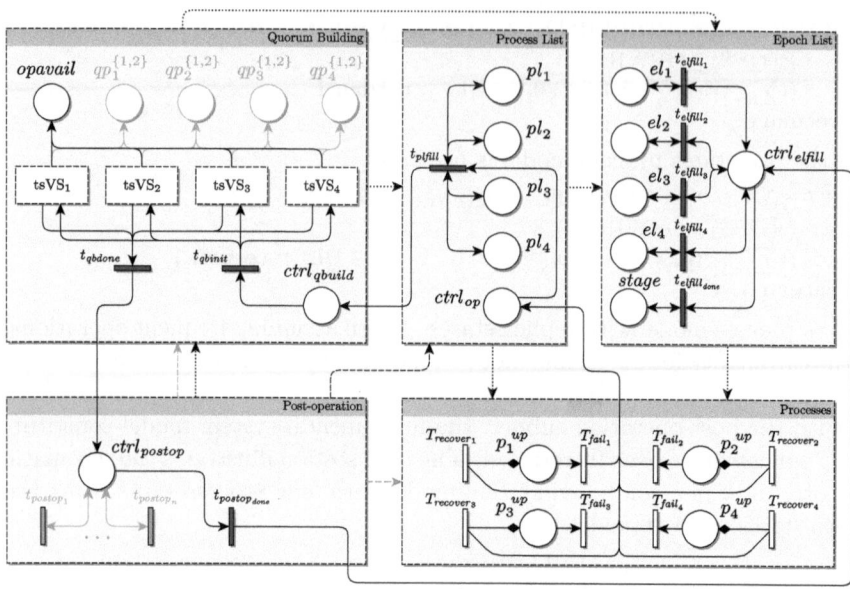

Figure 4.26: Conceptual Schematic Control Flow in a Composed System Model
with Four Processes and using the Two-States Process Model

the latter depositing a token on the place $ctrl_{qbuild}$. This frame is concerned
with forming quorums and is therefore dependent on the process list frame
marking (because of its function as an indirection of the process subnets) and
on the place *stage* of the epoch list frame for selecting the appropriate tree-
shaped voting structure subnet. As the two-states process model lacking
replica states is chosen in this example and assuming a quality measure to
be evaluated that has no interest in, for example, a process' participation in
quorums, the quorum places $qp_1^1, \ldots, qp_n^1$ and $qp_1^2, \ldots, qp_n^2$ are grayed. The
subsequent post-operation frame (cf. Section 4.3.5) is triggered by placing
a token on the place $ctrl_{postop}$. Only if the three- or the four-states process
model is used, the post-operation frame potentially alters the marking of the
processes frame in terms of the replica status of processes and the marking
of the quorum building frame in terms of the quorum places. Since the
two-states process model is used here, the transitions $t_{postop_1}, \ldots, t_{postop_n}$
as well as the dashed inter-frame edges connecting the post-operation frame
to the processes frame and the quorum building frame are grayed. The
post-operation frame always changes the marking of the process list frame

by clearing the process list places. Finally, if the quorum building frame in terms of the place *opavail* has a marking indicating a successful write quorum building, the epoch list frame is activated by a token deposited on the place $ctrl_{elfill}$. In this case, the processes frame marking influences the resulting marking of the epoch list frame's places $el_1, \ldots, el_n$ and the place *stage*.

Besides the local optimizations presented in the respective contexts so far, further optimizations of the quorum system representation subnets are high-lighted next.

4.3.7 Optimizations in Place Count and Analysis Time

The following three examples illustrate how to further optimize tree-shaped voting structure subnets (cf. Section 4.3.4) in order to reduce the place count of the overall system model and to improve analysis time. Apart from opti-mizations specific to quorum system representations, a global optimization in terms of specifically tailoring the system model to the evaluation scenario can be applied. For example, if the two-states process model is used, then references to processes' replica states in arc cardinality functions can be removed, the post-operation subnet can be simplified as it must not update the replica status of processes, and, if operation availability is the only qual-ity measure of interest, the two sets of quorum places and their management can be omitted from the system model. However, as these optimizations are evaluation scenario-specific, they are not further discussed here.

Sharing of Tree-Shaped Voting Structure Petri Net Leaf Places

A place count reduction of the system model is achieved by introducing n system model-global leaf places $lp_1, \ldots, lp_n$ that are shared among the tree-shaped voting structure petri nets in the system model for n processes. If a tree-shaped voting structure petri net models the quorum system for a number of processes k, $1 \leq k \leq n$, and it has exactly k leaf places, then all its transitions connecting to (local) leaf places are rerouted to connect to the globally shared leaf places $lp_1, \ldots, lp_k$ instead such that the local leaf places can be removed from the system model. For convenience, the system model-global leaf places are labeled like their local counterparts and, therefore, no (further) modifications to the system model described so far are required. Examples to which this optimization is applicable are the Weighted Voting,

Majority Consensus Voting, and Tree Quorum Protocol tree-shaped voting structure petri nets in Figure 4.21 (b), 4.22 (b), and 4.23 (b), respectively.

In case a tree-shaped voting structure petri net has more than k local leaf places, then up to n transitions connecting to local leaf places are rerouted to connect to the globally shared leaf places (and the according local leaf places are removed from the system model) while other possibly existing transitions connecting to (local) leaf places remain connected to the local leaf places. For example, the 2×2 Grid Protocol tree-shaped voting structure petri net with four processes shown in Figure 4.19 on page 213 has eight leaf places. When assuming a system comprising $n = 4$ processes, the transitions connecting to the local leaf places $lp_1, \ldots, lp_4$ are rerouted to connect to the $n = 4$ system model-global leaf places after which the local leaf places are removed while the transitions connecting to the leaf places $lp'_1, \ldots, lp'_4$ remain connected to these local leaf places.

Note that the tree-shaped voting structure petri nets are enabled mutually exclusive such that at any time, at most one has potentially enabled transitions. Therefore, introducing globally shared leaf places has no side-effects but the reduction of the overall place count in the system model.

Sequentializing Tree-Shaped Voting Structure Petri Net Transitions

Consider the Majority Consensus Voting tree-shaped voting structure petri net with five processes as shown in Figure 4.27. Initially, the root place V_1 has an operation-specific number of token and those transitions whose guards evaluate to true are concurrently enabled. Because of the non-deterministic selection of one of those concurrently enabled transitions, every possible transition firing must be considered in terms of a subsequent state of the current (initial) state while constructing the reachability (tree) graph: The initial state – represented by the operation-specific initial marking of the root place V_1 – is connected to a number of subsequent states that resembles the number of concurrently enabled transitions in the initial state. If no transition is enabled and the root place still has a non-zero token count, then the reachability graph construction is completed and the tree-shaped voting structure subnet-local failure transition fires since definitely no quorum can be successfully formed. Otherwise, one out of the enabled transitions is non-deterministically chosen and fired, resulting in a subsequent state as defined by the marking modification due to the fired transition's input and output functions. Again, because of the non-determinism,

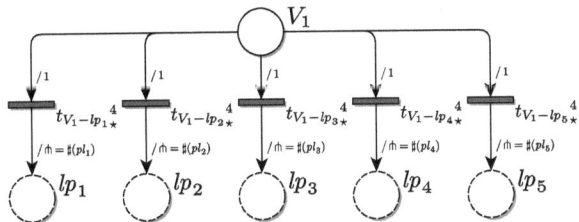

Figure 4.27: Majority Consensus Voting Tree-Shaped Voting Structure Petri
Net with Five Processes and using System Model-Global Leaf
Places

any other enabled transition is equally suited for being chosen instead of
the selected one such that every possible transition firing outcome must be
considered in the reachability graph. The respective subsequent states may
have itself a number of subsequent states resembling the number of the then
concurrently enabled transitions out of which one is non-deterministically
chosen and transitioned to, until a number of state transitions has been
performed that equals the operation-specific initial number of token put
on the root place V_1. Then, the root place has zero token and a quorum
has been successfully formed such that the subnet-local success transition
becomes enabled and fires. Otherwise, the subnet-local failure transition
has meanwhile fired and the quorum building has failed since no transitions
are enabled.

For example, if no process is failed, the reachability graph of the Majority
Consensus Voting tree-shaped voting structure petri net with five processes
as shown in Figure 4.27 has 86 nodes, regardless of whether a read quorum or
a write quorum is to be formed as both require three processes to participate
in the quorum. In general, for no process being failed, a Majority Consensus
Voting tree-shaped voting structure petri net reachability graph has $1 +
\sum_{i=0}^{q-1} f(i)$ nodes where q is the operation-specific number of token put on
the root place (that is, the operation-specific quorum function value of the
corresponding original tree-shaped voting structure's root node),

$$f(i) = \begin{cases} k & \text{if } i = 0 \\ f(i-1) \cdot (f(0) - i) & \text{otherwise} \end{cases}$$

is the function calculating the number of nodes on level $i + 1$ of the reachability tree graph, and k is the number of the tree-shaped voting structure
petri net's leaf places representing non-failed processes.

As a second example, a Majority Consensus Voting tree-shaped voting structure petri net with four processes has a reachability graph consisting of 41 nodes for the write operation and of 17 nodes for the read operation, again for no process being failed.

The reachability graph's node count of a Majority Consensus Voting tree-shaped voting structure petri net can be reduced to a number of nodes that is at most the operation-specific number of token put on the root place plus one for the initial state, namely via sequentializing transition firing by assigning distinct priorities to the transitions. For example, assume the transitions of the Majority Consensus Voting tree-shaped voting structure petri net in Figure 4.27 to have assigned priorities such that a transition $t_{V_1-lp_i}$ has a higher transition priority than a transition $t_{V_1-lp_j}$ for $i < j$. While constructing the reachability graph, the selection of which transition to fire becomes deterministic since at any time, only exactly one transition is enabled: If, for example, the transition $t_{V_1-lp_1}$ is enabled, then no other transitions are (concurrently) enabled because of them having a lower priority. There is no choice other than to fire this single enabled transition, resulting in a subsequent state as defined by the marking modification due to the transition's input and output functions. If $t_{V_1-lp_1}$ is not enabled, then the above is true for one of the transitions $t_{V_1-lp_2}, \ldots, t_{V_1-lp_5}$ in this order. If none of these transitions is enabled, then the subnet-local failure transition is enabled and fires since no quorum can be successfully formed. Otherwise, the respective next lower-prioritized transitions fire sequentially until either the root place has zero token or no transition is enabled. In the former case, a quorum is successfully formed. In the latter case, the quorum building has failed and the subnet-local failure transition becomes enabled and fires.

Transition sequentialization implies that an ordering is imposed on the set of read and write quorums. This contrasts the definition of Majority Consensus Voting that considers processes to be equally suited for being in a specific quorum (cf. Section 2.5.1). However, trading-off the explicit non-ordering for reduced reachability graph node counts and an improved reachability graph construction time is worthwhile if it can be tolerated that the participation of processes in quorums is not non-deterministically distributed. This is the case if, for example, the quality measure of interest is operation availability. As a counterexample, if the load of processes is to be evaluated, this optimization may not be applied.

Albeit being applied to Majority Consensus Voting in this example, this optimization lends itself to application whenever a non-deterministic choice among several concurrently enabled transitions has to be made while constructing the reachability graph.

Besides such a tree-shaped voting structure subnet-local optimization, an optimization of the (Majority Consensus Voting) tree-shaped voting structure subnets from a global perspective results in a place count reduction of the overall composed system model as the next optimization example illustrates.

Conjoining Tree-Shaped Voting Structure Petri Nets

For a homogeneous dynamic data replication scheme employing Majority Consensus Voting, n tree-shaped voting structure subnets must be incorporated into the system model with each of them modeling the quorum system for a particular stage of the dynamics. From a graph-structural point of view, two Majority Consensus Voting tree-shaped voting structure petri nets modeling the quorum systems for a number of processes i and j with $i < j$ differ only in the latter having $j - i$ additional (local) leaf places and connecting transitions. Thus, instead of integrating n distinct tree-shaped voting structure subnets into the system model, a single one that models the quorum system for n processes is incorporated into the system model. This single tree-shaped voting structure subnet expresses the quorum systems for all n stages of the dynamics if modified as follows: Its initialize transition emits a number of token to the root place that is dependent on the current stage of the dynamics and on whether a read quorum or a write quorum is to be formed. Its transition guards become dependent on the current stage of the dynamics such that only those transitions $t_{V_1 - lp_1}, \ldots, t_{V_1 - lp_i}$, $1 \leq i \leq n$, can potentially become enabled that have a leaf place index i lower than or equal to the current stage of the dynamics as determined by the token count of the place $stage$. This single Majority Consensus Voting tree-shaped voting structure subnet for numbers of processes up to and including n processes is illustrated in Figure 4.28. For example, the guard of the transition $t_{V_1 - lp_3}^{n+1}$ is

$$\text{true} \leftarrow [\sharp(V_1) > 0 \land \sharp(lp_3) = 0 \land$$
$$\sharp(pl_3) > 0 \land \sharp(stage) \geq 3]. \qquad \text{(Guard } t_{V_1 - lp_3}^{n+1})$$

As for the previous Majority Consensus Voting tree-shaped voting structure subnets, the successful quorum building marking condition for both operations is

$$\text{true} \leftarrow [\sharp(V_1) = 0].$$

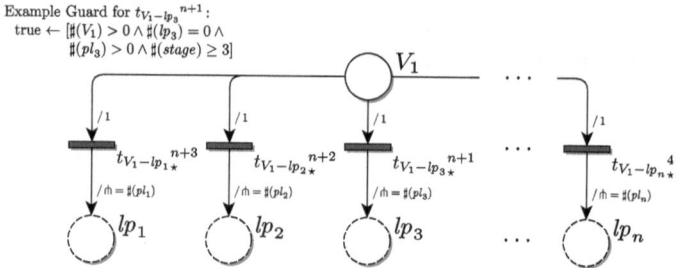

Figure 4.28: Conceptual Illustration of a Majority Consensus Voting Tree-Shaped Voting Structure Petri Net for Numbers of Processes up to and including n Processes with Distinctive Prioritized Transitions and using System Model-Global Leaf Places

If a process model with replica states is chosen, the subnet-local success transition must be adapted to populate a number of operation-specific system model-global quorum places matching the token count of the place *stage*. A retry transition is not needed and can therefore be omitted. The subnet-local failure transition needs not to be adapted but may omit its guard's dependency on the place *stage* since this tree-shaped voting structure petri net models the quorum system for all stages of the dynamics.

This optimization is also applicable to heterogeneous dynamic data replication schemes that employ Majority Consensus Voting for particular stages of the dynamics as follows. First, the Majority Consensus Voting tree-shaped voting structure subnet that models the quorum system for the highest number of processes among the Majority Consensus Voting tree-shaped voting structure subnets is incorporated into the system model. Then, its petri net transition guards are adapted to be dependent on the particular stages of the dynamics for which Majority Consensus Voting is designated to be used. Alike, its initialize transition is adapted to only deposit an operation-specific number of token on the tree-shaped voting structure petri net's root place if the current stage of the dynamics matches one of those stages for which Majority Consensus Voting is to be used. Also, the success transition must be adapted as indicated above, if applicable, and the failure transition may only become enabled for particular *stage* place markings matching those stages of the dynamics in which Majority Consensus Voting is to be used.

Analogously to the previous optimization, this optimization is not restricted to Majority Consensus Voting and may be applied to other quorum system construction schemes. In the next section, the frequent operations assumption is recapitulated and relaxed.

4.3.8 Relaxing the Frequent Operations Assumption

The frequent operations assumption has a significant impact on the quality measures derived from the system model as it allows the dynamics to be employed in an optimal manner. Therefore, the evaluated operation availabilities represent upper bounds when assuming frequent operations (and perfect channels that fully interconnect the processes).

Implications of the Frequent Operations Assumption   As argued in Section 4.2, in this setting, the quorum system of Majority Consensus Voting with three arbitrarily chosen processes out of a set of $n \geq 3$ processes is optimal with respect to operation availability and message complexity. This quorum system must (and can) tolerate only exactly one (arbitrary) process failure. Upon this failure, the quorum system is adapted such that the failed process is replaced by an arbitrarily chosen non-failed process – as long as there are non-failed processes to choose from. Otherwise, no quorum system reconfiguration can be performed. The frequent operations assumption states that at least one operation is triggered in between two failure or recovery events. Note that this implicitly excludes joint process failures. Hence, those tree-shaped voting structure subnets representing quorum systems that are able to tolerate at least one (arbitrary) process failure can be reduced to their success transition only, omitting the initialize, retry, and failure transitions and the tree-shaped voting structure petri net itself altogether. Then, instead of the initialize transition, the respective success transition must consume the token from the place aux_2 and it inherits the initialize transition guard's marking condition on the place *stage*. The success transition unconditionally places an operation-specific number of token on the place *opavail* (and on $ctrl_{qbdone}$). Unfortunately, this optimization is only applicable to the two-states process model but not to the three- and four-states process models. In these models, the replica status of processes may have to be updated, depending on their participation in quorums.

A further aspect of the frequent operations assumption is the certainty that an epoch change operation must be attempted whenever an operation execution is triggered since always either a process has failed or recovered from its failure. Upon recovery, a process is assumed to trigger an operation execution such that it is potentially reintegrated into the quorum system by the successive epoch change operation. As the failure event of a process triggers an operation execution, the actual failed process must not even be probed and thereby detected while the quorum building in order to know that some process has failed which qualifies for an epoch change operation to be attempted. Hence, an epoch change operation attempt on every operation execution event is justified.

Lastly, the frequent operations assumption has an impact on the exploitation of redundancy in space encoded in a quorum system by it (usually) having several quorums per operation to choose from for performing an operation. For example, the read operation availability of the dynamic variant of the original Grid Protocol strictly favoring columns over rows does not exceed its write operation availability. Recall that the original Grid Protocol restricts read quorums to C-Covers only. Upon every failure or recovery event, an epoch change operation is attempted which requires a write quorum consisting of a C-Cover and a CC-Cover. Hence, if the write operation is available in between two failure or recovery events, the read operation is also available. For some logical grid layouts such as for the two, three, and five processes grid constructions illustrated in Figure 4.29 (a), (b), and (d) in each of which (at least) one of the columns consists of a single process, the failure of the single process renders the C-Cover(s) unavailable while a CC-Cover remains available. In these cases, no epoch change operation can be performed and the write as well as the read operation are unavailable. Otherwise, if a C-Cover is available, a write quorum can be formed and be used to perform an epoch change operation (that is due to be executed since a process has failed). Hence, the read operation availability of the dynamic original Grid Protocol favoring columns over rows with read quorums restricted to C-Covers resembles its write operation availability.

When not assuming frequent operations, then multiple processes may fail (sequentially) prior to an epoch change operation attempt such that no

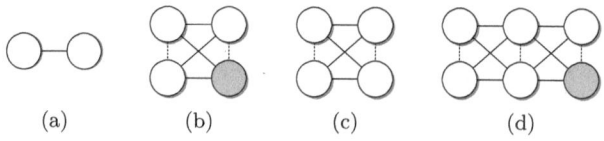

(a)   (b)   (c)   (d)

Figure 4.29: Logical Process Layouts of the Grid Protocol Favoring Columns over Rows for Two, Three, Four, and Five Processes. Shaded Grid Positions are not Populated by Processes.

CC-Cover may be available (and the epoch change operation cannot be performed). However, a C-Cover may be available, enabling the exploitation of redundancy in space to perform read operations while the write operation is unavailable. For example, in the 2×2 logical grid layout illustrated in Figure 4.29 (c), one process in each column may fail, thereby rendering the two CC-Covers but not the C-Covers unavailable.

Triggering Operations   With the frequent operations assumption, a process failure (and recovery) event triggers an operation execution. Without this assumption, operation executions must be triggered independently of process failures, demanding for an *operation driver* in the system model. An operation driver subnet is depicted in Figure 4.30. It consists of a single timed transition $T_{operation}$ that emits a token to the system model-global control place $ctrl_{op}$ upon being fired, thereby triggering an operation execution. The variable-cardinality outgoing arc to the system model-global place OPS determines the operation(s) to execute. It evaluates to OPREAD=1 for performing a read operation, to OPWRITE=2 for performing a write operation, or to the sum of both for performing both operations concertedly. The place OPS is emptied after the operation execution by the post-operation subnet since it is populated with token upon the next operation execution. The firing rate of the transition $T_{operation}$ determines the frequency of executing operations.

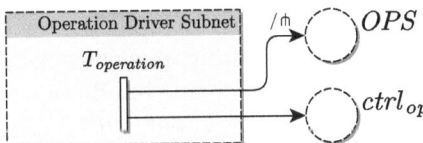

Figure 4.30: Operation Driver Subnet

Multiple instances of the operation driver subnet may be present in the system model, each triggering operations with a different frequency. For example, two instances are required to trigger read and write operations with different frequencies. Alike, multiple instances with different frequencies that trigger the same operation can be used to model operation workloads that cannot be reflected by a single operation driver subnet since, for example, the distribution function cannot be parameterized accordingly. Note that due to the exponential distribution's property of different samples drawn having different sample values, the probability of operation driver

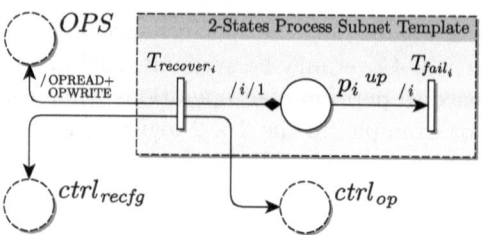

Figure 4.31: Two-States Process Subnet Template to be used when not Assuming Frequent Operations

subnet transitions firing at the same time instant is zero. If, for example, deterministic petri nets allowing for deterministic firing frequencies are used instead, the concurrent firing of operation driver transitions – each depositing a token on the control place $ctrl_{op}$ – must be prohibited by inhibitor arcs or guards, given the transition firing policy allows such a concurrency.

To disable the process failure-induced triggering of operations, the process subnet templates (cf. Section 4.3.1) must not deposit a token on the place $ctrl_{op}$ upon process failures. This is realized by removing the transition arc originating from the transition T_{fail_i} and leading to the place $ctrl_{op}$ in the process subnet templates, as exemplary illustrated for the two-states process subnet template in Figure 4.31. By this means, operations are either triggered by an operation driver or upon a process' recovery by the process subnet transition $T_{recover_i}$ firing, modeling the process' attempt to reintegrate itself into the quorum system. In addition to the token put on the place $ctrl_{op}$, the recovery transition puts OPREAD+OPWRITE token on the place OPS and signals that an epoch change operation attempt is to be performed by depositing a token on the new system model-global place $ctrl_{recfg}$ that is introduced below. The reason to also try to perform a read operation – in addition to a write operation as a prerequisite to the epoch change operation – is that the possibly not available read operation may become available by the process' recovery. In order to reflect the actual availability of operations by the token count of the place $opavail$, both operation quorum buildings must be performed. If only quality measures with respect to the write operation are to be evaluated, depositing OPWRITE token on the place OPS is sufficient.

Note that in favor of a simpler system model, an epoch change operation is always attempted upon a process' recovery, even if the process already participates in the current quorum system and, therefore, a quorum system reconfiguration for this process is not necessary. However, there may be other recovered processes not participating in the current quorum system because of an unavailable epoch change operation at the time of their recovery. Those processes may be integrated by this process' recovery and its (successful) epoch change operation execution as it considers all non-failed processes (cf. Section 4.3.2). This simplification alleviates the need to explicitly model a recovered process' efforts to reintegrate itself into the quorum system if the epoch change operation was not available upon its recovery. As a consequence, quality measures such as a process' participation in (successfully built) quorums are slightly overestimated. Also, the epoch list subnet is activated more often than strictly necessary. However, recovered processes are integrated into the current quorum system as soon as possible.

Combining Operation Drivers with the Frequent Operations Assumption   The evaluation of quality measures besides operation availability such as the processes' replica actuality under the frequent operations assumption requires operations to be triggered upon and likely in between process failure or recovery events. The latter can be realized by incorporating operation drivers into the system model. For the former requirement, the transition arc connecting T_{fail_i} to $ctrl_{op}$ in the process subnet templates must not be removed. Instead, transition arcs connecting T_{fail_i} to the places OPS and $ctrl_{recfg}$ must be introduced as described above for the recovery transition. Then, operations are triggered by process failure and recovery events as well as by operation drivers. Hence, an operation being triggered does not always imply that a process has failed or recovered. Alike, an epoch change operation must not be attempted upon every operation execution but only when it is triggered by a process failure or recovery. However, if a process has failed, then an operation is triggered by the process' failure transition firing. Unfortunately, the latter is not the case when not assuming frequent operations. Relaxing the frequent operations assumption requires a means to detect process failures whereupon an epoch change operation is attempted. It inheres two facets being (1) process failure detection timeliness and (2) process failure detection coverage.

Process Failure Detection Timeliness   A process failure may be detected, for example, by a system monitoring service that triggers an epoch change operation upon having detected a process failure or by revealing failed processes during quorum building whereupon an epoch change operation is initiated. In contrast to the frequent operations assumption that allows for an instant reaction to process failure events, process failure detection by a monitoring service or by quorum building does not necessarily do so. The timeliness of failure detection is determined by the monitoring service's process polling frequency or by the operation execution frequency and hence quorum building frequency. A process failure may remain undetected for a period of time during which further processes may fail, thereby potentially resulting in the inability to perform any operations until some (specific) processes recover. Therefore, the respective frequencies mark a trade-off that is determinant for the resulting quality measures of the system: If the interval is too long, then too many processes may have meanwhile failed for being able to successfully adapt the quorum system. In case of using a (homogeneous) dynamic data replication scheme, a too long interval effectively disables the dynamics and results in a behavior that resembles its static counterpart. Conversely, if the interval is sufficiently short such that in between two process failure or recovery events always at least one operation is triggered and – if possible – the quorum system is adapted, then the dynamics is exploited in an optimal manner. The latter resembles the frequent operations assumption.

When not assuming frequent operations, a process failure does not trigger operation executions but operation drivers (and process recoveries) do. As a consequence, the operation driver firing frequency determines the actuality of operation availability as given by the token count of the place *opavail*: A process failure that occurs in between the triggering of two operation executions may render operations unavailable that were previously available. Therefore, in order to precisely reflect the actual availability of operations by the token count of the place *opavail*, a process failure must also trigger an operation execution to determine the operations that are available. Depending on the outcome, the token count of the place *opavail* is updated. This operation execution must not have an influence on the accounting of other quality measures besides operation availability (in terms of the token count on the place *opavail*) as it is a special operation execution to determine the (un)availability of operations. Alike, it must not modify the epoch list marking or the replica status of processes. However, since the period of time in between the triggering of two operation executions is usually assumed to be short, only a small inaccuracy results from not updating the token count of the place *opavail* upon a process's failure. For the sake of a simpler presentation, this inaccuracy is accepted here.

Process Failure Detection Coverage   The frequent operations assumption as well as the system monitoring service approach provide a complete process failure detection in the sense that if a process has failed, then its failure is detected. The monitoring service approach may not be timely but it uncovers all failed processes since all processes are probed periodically. Note that, for a single monitoring service-providing process, this is only true if perfect channels are assumed such that network partitioning cannot happen. Otherwise, one monitoring service-providing process per network partition is required. In contrast to the frequent operations assumption and the monitoring service approach, process failure detection by quorum building is in general not complete as it does not necessarily reveal all failed processes during an operation execution. A quorum may not require all processes to participate such that – albeit the quorum is successfully formed – a failed process may not be probed and thereby detected as having failed.

The incomplete process failure detection via quorum building can be circumvented by unconditionally performing an epoch change operation whenever an operation execution is triggered by an operation driver, given that a write quorum has been successfully formed. Recall that the epoch list subnet considers all non-failed processes and populates the place *stage* with their number and the places $el_1, \ldots, el_n$ with their process identity token counts (cf. Section 4.3.2). Thus, every process failure is "detected" and – if possible – also acted upon by the process' exclusion from the set of processes forming the new epoch. Depending on operation driver firing frequencies, this approach yields more realistic quality measure results than the frequent operations assumption as it leaves a probability for process failures to occur that are not instantly reacted upon. However, unconditionally performing epoch change operations requires to always form a write quorum and, if it is successfully formed, to activate the epoch list subnet, even when not required as no process has failed.

A better approach is to perform process failure detection by the process list subnet and to attempt an epoch change operation only if a process failure is detected. A new system model-global place pl_{count} is introduced and the place $ctrl_{recfg}$ is instrumented for this purpose. The former place pl_{count} holds the number of process list places having a non-zero token count. It is emptied and then populated with token by the process list subnet such that it accounts for the state space size of the system model as it may have a non-constant marking in the time domain. The latter place $ctrl_{recfg}$ serves as a trigger for an epoch change operation attempt if its token count is not zero. It is assigned one token by the process list subnet if (1) this place is empty (as a process' recovery may put a token thereon) and (2) the number of token on the place pl_{count} – due to the population of the process list places by the process list subnet for the last operation execution – differs from the current number of process list places having a non-zero token count. If the place $ctrl_{recfg}$ has one token, either a process has recovered or a process has failed. In both cases, an epoch change operation attempt has to be performed. The post-operation subnet clears the place $ctrl_{recfg}$ and initiates an epoch change operation attempt if, in addition to its other guard conditions, this place was not empty. Since the epoch change operation relies on write quorums, the place OPS is ensured to have at least OPWRITE token by the process list subnet if $ctrl_{recfg}$ has one token. After a successful epoch change operation, the token count of the place pl_{count} is set to the number of token on the place $stage$. Note that by clearing and populating the place pl_{count} on every process list subnet activation, a detected failed process causes an epoch change operation attempt only once. If the epoch change operation is not available, then some (specific) processes must recover first and prior to attempting an epoch change operation again – by which this process, if still failed, is excluded from the quorum system. This approach effectively resembles the former approach of always performing an epoch change operation attempt – presuming a write quorum can be formed – in the sense that it has the same process failure detection completeness. Nonetheless, by exploiting global knowledge, it does not require to always activate the epoch list subnet.

The alternative to both previous approaches is to facilitate process failure detection by quorum building and to only attempt an epoch change operation in case a failed process is detected while building a quorum. This approach also requires the system model-global control place $ctrl_{recfg}$ to be incorporated into the system model and the post-operation subnet to clear this place. In contrast to the previous approach, the place $ctrl_{recfg}$ is populated with a token by a tree-shaped voting structure subnet when having detected a failed process (and this place is empty). For this purpose, the tree-shaped voting structure subnets must be enhanced with a more sophisticated process failure detection means and must be adapted to potentially emit a token to the place $ctrl_{recfg}$ in case of a detected process failure. For example, consider the Majority Consensus Voting tree-shaped voting structure petri net in Figure 4.32 (a) and assume the process list place pl_4 to be empty, meaning that the process $p_{\sharp(el_4)}$ has failed. The guard of the transition $t_{V_1-lp_{4\star}}^{\;4}$ evaluates to false but with the remaining three non-empty process list places, a read quorum as well as a write quorum can be suc-

Example Guard for $t_{V_1-lp_{4\star}}{}^4$:

$$\text{true} \leftarrow [\sharp(V_1) > 0 \wedge \sharp(lp_4) = 0 \wedge \\ \sharp(pl_4) > 0]$$

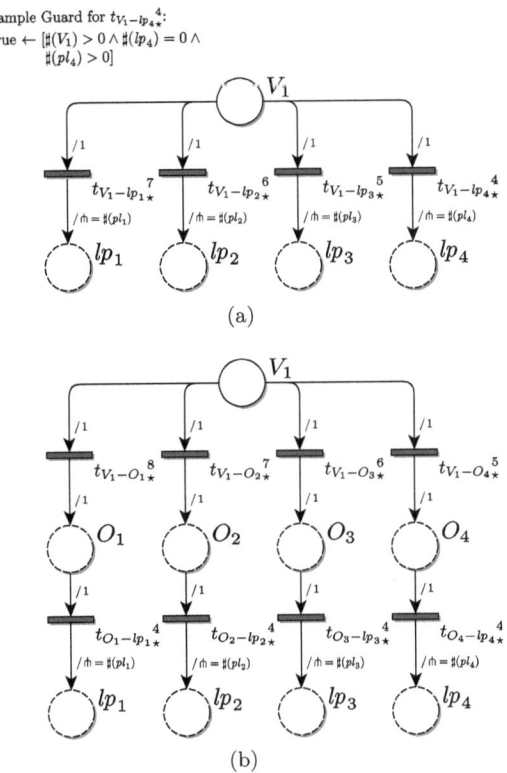

(a)

(b)

Figure 4.32: Majority Consensus Voting Tree-Shaped Voting Structure Petri Net (a) and Majority Consensus Voting Tree-Shaped Voting Structure Petri Net Extended for Process Failure Detection (b), both using System Model-Global Leaf Places and Distinctive Prioritized Transitions

cessfully formed. Note that, because of the distinctive transition priorities optimization, the transition $t_{V_1-lp_4}{}^4{}_\star$ is not even considered for becoming enabled. But also without the optimization, the transition is not considered for becoming enabled as its guard evaluates to false. The failure of the process $p_{\sharp(el_4)}$ remains undetected in terms of no action being performed because of this process' failure since a quorum is available such that the subnet-local success transition becomes enabled and fires. As a subnet-local retry transition that, when fired, indicates at least one detected process failure is not necessary for Majority Consensus Voting tree-shaped voting structure subnets, only the subnet-local failure transition firing indicates process failures. Hence, only if an additional second (and third) process fails, this process' failure is detected while forming a write (read) quorum because the root place then has a non-zero token count which qualifies for the subnet-local failure transition to be fired.

In order to detect and act upon process failures during quorum building without them being precluded by not enabled transitions (but still potentially by the distinctive transition priorities optimization), a set of n system model-global *trap places* $O_1, \ldots, O_n$ is introduced. Each tree-shaped voting structure petri net employs a number of trap places $O_1, \ldots, O_k$, $1 \leq k \leq n$, that matches the number of its leaf places in a manner illustrated in Figure 4.32 (b) for $k = 4$. Note that, analogously to sharing system model-global leaf places (cf. Section 4.3.7), further local trap places are required if a tree-shaped voting structure petri net has more than n leaf places as it is the case, for example, for the 2×2 Grid Protocol tree-shaped voting structure petri net shown in Figure 4.19 on page 213. Specifically, the trap places precede the leaf places in a tree-shaped voting structure petri net such that a transition formerly connecting to a leaf place then connects to a trap place. The transition keeps its incoming arc cardinality and emits one token to the trap place when fired. A new transition connecting the trap place to the leaf place consumes one token when fired and outputs a number of token to the leaf place as determined by the cardinality of the transition's outgoing arc formerly connecting to this leaf place. A trap place is populated with one token if the guard of the transition connecting to it evaluates to true. This is the case if the trap place has zero token. It keeps its token count – and thereby represents a detected failed process – if the guard of its subsequent transition connecting to a leaf place evaluates to false. Otherwise, the trap place's token is consumed by the transition connecting to the leaf place. The tree-shaped voting structure subnet-local success and failure transitions must be adapted to (1) output a token to the place $ctrl_{recfg}$ if it is empty and (at least) one of the trap places has a non-zero token count and to (2) clear the system model-global (and local) trap places. The information of which particular processes have failed – that can be deduced from the trap places having a non-zero token count – is not needed subsequently since the epoch change operation considers all non-failed processes (cf. Section 4.3.2) which is why the trap places are emptied by the success and failure transitions. Since the epoch change operation relies on write quorums, the place *OPS* must have at least OPWRITE token when a process failure is detected. Thus, either always at least a write quorum building must be performed or, if a dynamic data replication scheme should be evaluated with respect to the read operation only, the tree-shaped voting structure subnets and their embedding in the system model must be adapted to allow a write quorum building after a read quorum building.

This approach has the least complete process failure detection compared to the former two approaches since failed processes are not necessarily detected during an operation's quorum building. After a sequence of undetected process failures, a further process failure may render operations unavailable. Hence, employing quorum building for process failure detection does generally not result in the evaluated operation availabilities matching their upper bounds. However, it gives more realistic evaluation results.

The next section describes how dependent failures can be expressed in the system model.

4.3.9 Modeling Failure and Recovery Dependencies

In real-world distributed systems, the failure of one of its components may affect other components such that they also fail or – albeit not being actually failed – become incapable of contributing to the system's progress. An example of the former type of (directed) dependent failure is the outage of a power supply causing all components attached to it to crash-fail. The failure of a network routing device by which the network becomes partitioned such that no inter-partition communication but only intra-partition communication among processes is possible serves as an example of the latter type of dependent failure. In general, failures are not independent of each other but (some of them) are correlated (see, for example, [Amir and Wool, 1996; Warns, Storm et al., 2008]). Respecting dependent failures when designing quorum systems for application scenarios in which such failures potentially occur is beneficial to the operation availability provided by the system [Storm and Warns, 2008]. Therefore, the so far implicitly assumed structural failure model – that assumes processes to fail independently – must be refined to allow joint and dependent process failures. For this purpose, the presented system model must be adapted in order to be able to exhibit the behavior expressed in an explicitly given structural failure model.

A *directed dependent* failure means that the failure of a process $p_i \in P$ results in the processes in its *failure dependency set* $F_{p_i} \subseteq P \setminus \{p_i\}$ failing jointly with the process p_i. However, the failure of a process $p_j \in F_{p_i}$ must not necessarily imply the joint failure with the process p_i, depending on whether p_i is in p_j's failure dependency set or not. If it is, the failures of p_i and p_j are *undirected dependent*, that is, directed dependent in both directions: If one of them fails, then it fails jointly with (at least) the other process. If p_i is not included in any process' failure dependency set, then its failure is *independent* of the failure of other processes. If this is true for every process, the so far implicitly assumed structural failure model is resembled.

A directed dependent failure is modeled when using the two-states process model by introducing $|F_{p_i}|$ incoming variable-cardinality arcs from each process subnet place $p_j {}^{up}$ with $p_j \in F_{p_i}$ to p_i's process subnet failure transition T_{fail_i}. Each arc's cardinality evaluates to the process identity token count of the respective process p_j or to zero if the process is already failed.

If the three-states process model is chosen, then $2 \cdot |F_{p_i}|$ incoming arcs to p_i's failure transition T_{fail_i} must be introduced as a process' state of being non-failed is represented by two places, depending on the process' replica status. Specifically, the arcs emerge from the process subnet places $p_j {}^{up}_{c:cur}$ and $p_j {}^{up}_{c:old}$ for each $p_j \in F_{p_i}$. Their cardinalities evaluate to the token count of the respective process subnet places or to zero if process p_j is already failed. Note that the failure of a process p_j is represented by the two places $p_j {}^{up}_{c:cur}$ and $p_j {}^{up}_{c:old}$ having zero token instead of a dedicated failure state place. Therefore, the otherwise required $|F_{p_i}|$ arcs from T_{fail_i} to failure state places must not be present in the system model.

With the four-states process model chosen, the same means as for the three-states process model are required for the incoming arcs to p_i's failure transition T_{fail_i}. Additionally, $2 \cdot |F_{p_i}|$ outgoing arcs from p_i's failure transition T_{fail_i} to the process subnet places $p_j {}^{down}_{c:cur}$ and $p_j {}^{down}_{c:old}$ for each $p_j \in F_{p_i}$ must be incorporated into the system model as a process' state of being failed is represented by two places, depending on the process' replica status. The respective outgoing arc cardinalities are dependent on the current state of the process. If it is already failed, they evaluate to zero, regardless of its replica state. Otherwise, they depend on the process' state being either $p_j {}^{up}_{c:cur}$ or $p_j {}^{up}_{c:old}$. In the former case, the cardinality of the outgoing arc to the place $p_j {}^{down}_{c:cur}$ evaluates to p_j's process identity token count while in the latter case, this arc's cardinality evaluates to zero. Accordingly, the cardinality of the outgoing arc to the place $p_j {}^{down}_{c:old}$ evaluates to p_j's process identity token count in the latter case while it evaluates to zero in the former case.

Modeling directed dependent failures as described does not explicitly support *cascading failures*. For example, assume p_j is in p_i's failure dependency set and p_k is in p_j's failure dependency set. As modeled here, the failure of p_i results in its joint failure with p_j. If cascading failures were explicitly supported, the failure of p_i results in its joint failure with p_j and thereby also with p_k. However, as p_k fails jointly with p_j and thereby with p_i anyway, it may as well be directly included in p_i's failure dependency set.

Like the failure of processes, the recovery of processes may not be independent. For example, Chen and Wang [1996a,c] (cf. Section 4.2) have considered a single repairman resource that recovers failed processes in a FIFO order, a linear order, or a "best-effort" order such that the recovery of a process is potentially dependent on the preceding recovery of (some specific) other processes. The means described by Chen and Wang [1996a,c] are verbatim applicable to the system model and are therefore not paraphrased here.

Frequent Operations Assumption and Joint Process Failure or Recovery Events   As introduced in Section 4.2, assuming frequent operations means assuming that in between two failure or recovery events always at least one operation execution is triggered. This assumption is not valid if joint process failures or recoveries are possible since multiple processes may fail or recover simultaneously such that an operation cannot be triggered upon every single process failure or recovery. However, when assuming that in between two *(joint)* failure or recovery events always at least one operation execution is triggered, this frequent operations assumption is valid if joint process failures or recoveries are possible. Albeit not being able to instantly react to every single process failure or recovery of a joint process failure or recovery event, the dynamics is employed in the best-possible manner. No modifications to the system model presented so far are necessary to support this frequent operations assumption.

Effect of Dependent Failures on Timed Transitions   The clearing of process subnet places that represent a process' state of being non-failed – as a result of another process' failure because the process is included in the other process' failure dependency set – disables this process' timed failure transition. Eventually, the failure transition becomes enabled again upon the process' recovery. Then, the timed transition's memory policy determines whether the transition timer is continued or restarted. In case generally distributed firing time distributions are allowed, the memory policy may be set to a restarting policy, meaning that the remaining time to fire (that is, to fail) resembles the original lifetime of the recovered process, thereby presuming a repaired process is "as good" as a new process. If exponentially distributed firing times are assumed, the memory policy is irrelevant since the remaining time to fire is always exponentially distributed with the same mean due to the exponential distribution's property of being memoryless. In both cases, the physical aging of processes is neglected since the lifetime is always sampled from the same distribution function. Theoretically, this aspect can be accounted for by adapting the distribution function parameter(s) after the failure and prior to a new life cycle of a process by decreasing, for example, the mean. While the system model can be extended in this respect, tool support for changing distribution function characteristics at analysis run-time is lacking.

The next section illustrates how network topologies can be respected in the system model.

4.3.10 Network Topology Modeling

The system model due to Chen and Wang [1996b] as well as the system models based thereon explicitly model the network topology in terms of multiple channel subnets. For every channel interconnecting two processes, there are two places in a dedicated channel subnet indicating the channel's state of being functional or crash-failed. These two state places are connected via two timed transitions that model the channel's failure and recovery, respectively. The presence or absence of a network partition that hinders performing an operation is judged by a boolean expression on the channel states in terms of a guard that is an enabling condition to any attempt to perform operations. As of using the unstructured Dynamic Voting, the guard evaluates to true if an arbitrarily drawn majority of the set of processes is connected. Otherwise, it evaluates to false and the write operation – the only type of operation considered by Chen and Wang [1996b] – is not available due to network partitioning.

For example, in a ring network topology connecting five processes as considered by Chen and Wang [1996b] and shown in Figure 4.33 (a), the partition check guard evaluates to true if less than three arbitrary channels and less than four channels that form a sector of the ring have failed. As a second example, Chen and Wang [1996b] have considered a star network topology with a perfect central arbiter and five "satellite" processes as shown in Figure 4.33 (b). The according partition check guard evaluates to true if

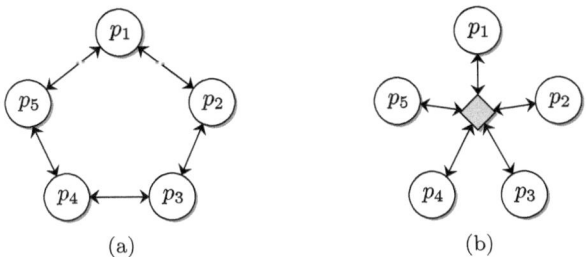

Figure 4.33: Example Ring (a) and Star (b) Network Topologies for Five Processes as considered by Chen and Wang [1996b]

less than three arbitrary channels have failed. If a channel interconnecting a process with the arbiter fails, then no communication of the partitioned process with the other processes is possible.

Channel Subnets   Such an explicit modeling of the network topology by channel subnets and stating enabling conditions to operation executions is applied to the system model as follows. A *channel subnet template* as illustrated in Figure 4.34 consists of a channel status place chn_i and two timed transitions $T_{chnrecover_i}$ and $T_{chnfail_i}$ that model the channel's recovery and failure, respectively. If the failure of a channel – in conjunction with already failed channels – results in a network partitioning such that a write operation cannot be performed, then the channel failure transition $T_{chnfail_i}$ outputs OPWRITE token to the newly introduced system model-global place *ispart*, given this place has zero token. If a read operation cannot be performed due to a partitioned network and the place *ispart* has OPWRITE token, then additionally OPREAD token are put thereon. If the place *ispart* has zero token and a read operation cannot be performed due to a partitioned network, then OPREAD+OPWRITE token are put thereon (since the existence of a partitioning that is fatal to the read operation is also fatal to the write operation but not vice versa). Otherwise, the arc cardinality evaluates to zero. A channel's recovery transition $T_{chnrecover_i}$ removes an according token count from the place *ispart* if this channel's recovery results in a rejoining of partitions such that operation(s) become available or the arc cardinality evaluates to zero. Hence, the network topology formed via channel subnets is reflected by the variable-cardinality arcs connecting the failure and recovery transitions to the place *ispart*.

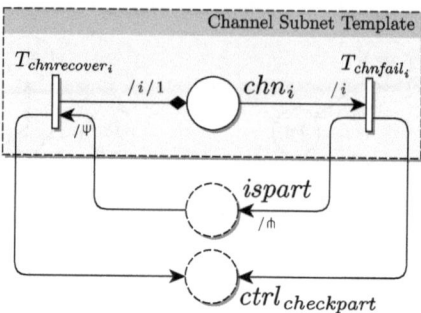

Figure 4.34: Channel Subnet Template

A channel subnet may not only model the communication means between two processes but may subsume and represent a set of channels whose failure results in a fatal partition to an operation. In this case, the channel's failure and recovery transition distribution functions must mimic the failure and recovery event distribution of the individual channels that are represented by this single channel subnet.

A channel's failure and recovery transitions put a token on the new system model-global place $ctrl_{checkpart}$, thereby activating the partition check subnet that is explained next.

Partition Check Subnet   When assuming frequent operations, the failure or recovery of a process triggers an operation execution. Since in between two process failure or recovery events no (further) operation executions are triggered, a meanwhile occurred channel failure that caused a network partitioning may affect the availability of operations as given by the token count of the place $opavail$: The previously available read (write) operation may become unavailable by the network partitioning. Conversely, a channel recovery resulting in a rejoining of partitions may render operations available that were previously unavailable. Hence, in order to reflect the actual availability of operations by the token count of the place $opavail$, the failure and recovery of channels must also trigger an operation execution. To some extent, this rationale also applies when not assuming frequent operations: Although usually many operations are triggered in between two process failure or recovery events, the operation driver firing frequency determines the actuality of operation availability as given by the token count of the place $opavail$. In between two operation executions, a channel failure that causes a network partitioning may render operations unavailable that were previously available (and vice versa for a channel recovery causing a rejoining of partitions).

Analogously to the argumentation in Section 4.3.8, the accounting of other quality measures besides operation availability is affected by the operation execution in response to channel failures and recoveries, albeit it is a special operation execution to determine the operations available (in terms of the token count on the place *opavail*). It may modify, for example, the epoch list marking or the replica status of processes. Avoiding the interference of this special operation execution with other quality measures requires to save and subsequently restore the state-constituting marking in the time domain. This is omitted here in favor of a more concise presentation.

Prior to executing an operation, the absence of a fatal partition to this operation must be examined. For this purpose, an operation execution is triggered upon a channel failure or recovery by the channel subnet's failure and recovery transitions depositing a token on the system model-global place $ctrl_{checkpart}$ whereby the *partition check subnet* as illustrated in Figure 4.35 is activated. Likewise, when assuming frequent operations, this subnet must be activated prior to the process list subnet upon a process failure or recovery. For this purpose, the process subnets' failure and recovery transitions must be adapted to place a token on $ctrl_{checkpart}$ instead of $ctrl_{op}$. When not assuming frequent operations, the process subnets' recovery transitions as well as the operation driver subnet(s) must be adapted to emit a token to the place $ctrl_{checkpart}$ instead of $ctrl_{op}$.

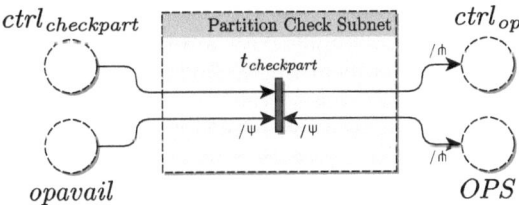

Figure 4.35: Partition Check Subnet

The partition check subnet illustrated in Figure 4.35 consists of the single transition $t_{checkpart}$. When fired, it (1) consumes the one token from the place $ctrl_{checkpart}$, (2) draws either none or an operation-specific number of token from the place *opavail*, and (3) outputs either one or none token to $ctrl_{op}$ with triggering the execution of an operation as determined by the token count emitted to or removed from the place OPS in the former case. If a partition that is fatal to the write (read) operation exists as indicated by the place $ispart$ having OPWRITE (OPREAD+OPWRITE) token, then OPWRITE (all) token are removed from the place $opavail$, provided that $opavail$ actually has this number of token. Otherwise, no token are drawn from the place $opavail$. The token count of the place OPS determines which operation(s) to execute. When assuming frequent operations and no fatal partition exists, the place OPS gets assigned OPREAD+OPWRITE token in order to concertedly perform a read operation and a write operation. If a partition exists that is fatal to the write operation only, then OPREAD token are deposited on the place OPS. In case a partition that is fatal to both operations exists, no token are placed on OPS. When not assuming frequent operations, the place OPS is populated with token by an operation driver subnet or a process' recovery and, depending on the existence of a fatal partition, token may have to be removed from the place OPS. The removal of token from the place OPS is as described above for the place $opavail$. If the place OPS has a non-zero token count, then according operation executions can be attempted and a token is emitted to the control place $ctrl_{op}$ to activate the process list subnet. Otherwise, no operation can be performed due to a fatal network partitioning and no token is put on $ctrl_{op}$.

The system model-global place OPS must be emptied after the operation execution as it is populated with token upon the next operation execution, either by an operation driver, a process' recovery, or by the transition $t_{checkpart}$, the latter when assuming frequent operations. Thus, the post-operation subnet must be adapted to always empty the place OPS and not only when not assuming frequent operations (cf. Section 4.3.5).

The above described semantics of removing token from the place $opavail$ upon the existence of a fatal partition to an operation may result in an operation execution influencing the availability of the other operation as determined by the token count of the place $opavail$. For example, consider two independent operation driver subnets with non-identical firing frequencies, one triggering read operations and the other one triggering write operations, and assume both operations are available. Eventually, a partition that is fatal to both operations has manifested. Then, the read operation driver triggers the execution of a read operation by which the place $opavail$ is emptied as no operation is available. Albeit no write operation execution is triggered, the write operation is marked as unavailable. This behavior is correct in the sense that leaving the write operation marked as available results in an overestimation of its availability since it is actually not available.

The Effect of Partitions on Operation Execution Whenever the partition check subnet deposits a token on the place $ctrl_{op}$, operations as determined by the token count of the place OPS can potentially be performed as there is no partitioning fatal to these operations. Hence, there may exist multiple partitions but the write (read) operation can be performed in (at least) one operation-enabled partition, given that a write (read) quorum can be formed therein. If both operations can be performed, then they must be performed in the same partition.

If a write operation has been performed and a process model having replica states is used, the replicas of processes not contained in the write quorum as well as the replicas of processes in other partitions must be outdated while the replicas of processes in the write quorum are updated. For example, consider a system using Majority Consensus Voting with four processes in a linear network topology such that a process p_i is connected to its neighbor process p_{i+1} by a channel $c_{i \leftrightarrow i+1}$ with $1 \leq i \leq 3$ as illustrated in Figure 4.36. Assume the channel $c_{1 \leftrightarrow 2}$ has failed such that process p_1 is partitioned from the other processes. A write operation can be performed with the processes p_2, p_3, p_4. The process p_1 cannot participate in the single write quorum and its replica status must be changed to outdated after having performed the write operation. If a read operation has been performed and a process model having replica states is used, the replicas of outdated processes in the read quorum are updated while the other processes' replicas retain their actuality status, regardless of their partition affiliation.

Hence, a read or write operation has to be performed with a quorum consisting only of those non-failed processes that are in the operation-enabled partition. Recall that a quorum is attempted to be formed out of the processes in the process list and only those processes that are in the process list may participate in the quorum. Thus, the process list must be filtered to contain only those processes that are in the operation-enabled partition prior to a quorum building. For this purpose, the cardinality functions of the process list subnet transition's outgoing arcs to process list places must

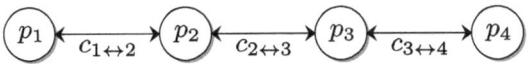

Figure 4.36: Example of a Linear Network Topology

consider a process' partition affiliation with the operation-enabled partition – which can be deduced from the combination of failed channels – in addition to the condition on epoch list places. After a successful operation execution, the post-operation subnet updates the replica status of processes in the operation-specific quorum(s) and marks the other processes' replicas as outdated if necessary.

Process list filtering according to partition affiliation is also required when using the two-states process model lacking replica states since the process list determines the processes with which a read or write quorum can be formed and thereby the ability to perform operations.

Read operation quorums do not need to mutually intersect. As a result, there is a special case in which no write operation-enabled partition exists but equally suited read operation-enabled partitions do. In this case, the arbitration in which partition to perform the read operation can be realized, for example, by choosing the partition having the highest sum of process identities. Depending on whether the read operation is available in the chosen partition or not, this is either a good choice or not. In the latter case, the read operation may be restarted by triggering the process list subnet such that the process list contains the processes of a read operation-enabled partition, given that such a partition exists. However, restarting an operation execution requires some modifications to the system model that are not described here.

Quorum system reconfiguration in terms of the epoch change operation relies on write quorums. Therefore, process list filtering is mandatory to determine its availability. In addition, the epoch change operation as implemented here (cf. Section 4.3.2) must be adapted to respect network partitioning. In particular, it may not consider all non-failed processes in the system but only all non-failed processes in the write operation-enabled partition. Analogously to the process list subnet, the epoch list subnet must filter processes according to their affiliation with the write operation-enabled partition in addition to their state of being failed or non-failed when populating the epoch list places.

Upon a process' recovery in a partition other than the single possibly existing write operation-enabled partition, the process' recovery transition may omit triggering an epoch change operation attempt as it cannot result in a quorum system reconfiguration by which this process is integrated into the quorum system. The same is true for a process' failure transition when assuming frequent operations. Alike, a channel recovery not resulting in the rejoining of a partition with the write operation-enabled partition cannot result in a quorum system reconfiguration. However, a channel recovery that does rejoin a partition with the single write operation-enabled partition must trigger an epoch change operation attempt to integrate the formerly partitioned processes into one quorum system. If the epoch change operation is not available, further processes must recover in the write operation-enabled partition or it must rejoin with further partitions.

Partition Conditions Unfortunately, even when assuming perfect processes, the decision of whether an operation execution is hindered by a partitioned network or not based on a threshold on the number of connected processes is only sufficient for some unstructured data replication schemes such as Majority Consensus Voting and the Read One Write All Protocol. For other data replication schemes – and in particular for structured ones – operation-specific knowledge about which individual processes are connected is required to judge on the ability to perform operations. For example, the ability to perform a read (write) operation using the optimized 3×3 Grid Protocol with nine processes depends on whether at least three processes forming a CC-Cover or (and) three processes forming a C-Cover are connected by non-failed channels. Like for Majority Consensus Voting and the Read One Write All Protocol, there is a threshold on the number of connected processes but unlike the condition for these data replication schemes, specific rather than arbitrary processes must be connected. Hence, the cardinality function of a channel subnet's failure transition arc to the place *ispart* deciding on whether a fatal partition exists or not must (1) consider the operation for which the channel's failure results in a fatal partition and it must (2) explicitly respect combinations of channel failures instead of just their number.

The combinations of failed channels marking a fatal network partitioning are specific to the subset of the set of processes constituting the current epoch. For example, consider a system using Dynamic Voting with four processes that are linearly interconnected by three channels as described above and illustrated in Figure 4.36. In stage four comprising all four processes, the failure of the channel $c_{2\leftrightarrow3}$ results in two partitions in neither of which the write operation is available as no three processes are connected. The read operation is available in both partitions. In stage three comprising the three processes p_1, p_2, and p_3 with process p_4 having failed, this channel's failure and the resulting partitioning does not render the write operation unavailable as the processes p_1 and p_2 form a write quorum (and a read quorum). Thus, depending on the processes forming the current epoch, the outgoing arc cardinality function of a channel subnet's failure transition arc to the place *ispart* must respect operation-specific conditions on channel states that mark a fatal network partitioning. Accordingly, the incoming arc cardinality function of a channel subnet's recovery transition arc from the place *ispart* must respect operation-specific conditions on channel states under which a fatal network partitioning no longer exists.

The next section describes how the system model is instrumented to evaluate quality measures such as operation availability.

4.4 Evaluating Quality Measures

A composed system model is instrumented with respect to a particular quality measure by a reward function assigning a positive reward to those markings in the time domain that positively contribute to the measure while assigning a reward of zero to the other markings in the time domain that negatively affect the measure. The marking-associated rewards translate to reward rates being attached to the states of the underlying stochastic process, which is a Markov reward model (cf. Section 4.1). Each state in the Markov reward model has associated a sojourn time and, for this reason, only rewards assigned to markings in the time domain (*tangible markings*) can be translated to reward rates. Markings in which immediate transitions are enabled (*vanishing markings*) are excluded from being assigned a reward as they have no sojourn times associated. Conceptually, tangible markings represent the states of the system among which it transitions while vanishing markings express a predicate against which the system states are tested. An example of such a predicate is read operation availability. The predicate outcome must be transported to the time domain, for example, by a dedicated outcome place's token count such that this place's tangible marking can be assigned a reward. Whenever the predicate-modeling subnet consisting of immediate transitions becomes activated by a timed transition firing, the outcome place is cleared and finally populated with an outcome-representing number of token such that it retains its marking in the time domain. Via calculating the steady state probability distribution of the system states (that is, the tangible markings) and evaluating the rewards assigned, a quantitative analysis with respect to a particular predicate is realized. For example, the (steady state) read operation availability is evaluated by a reward function that assigns a reward of 1 to those tangible markings in which the place *opavail* has at least OPREAD token whereas it assigns a reward of 0 to all other tangible markings in which the place *opavail* has fewer token. By the same means, other measures such as, for example, the write operation availability or the relative time spent in each stage of the dynamics can be evaluated as illustrated by an example evaluation given in the next chapter.

A measure of special interest is the relative time spent in each stage of the dynamics. The stage sojourn time distribution is evaluated by a reward function for each stage $1 \leq i \leq n$ of the dynamics that assigns a reward of 1 to those tangible markings in which $\sharp(stage) = i$ and a reward of 0 to all other tangible markings. This time distribution can be used to conclude overall quality measures of a (heterogeneous) dynamic data replication scheme from the respective quality measures of the static data replication schemes used in particular stages of the dynamics. For example, the message complexity – as a measure of operation costs in terms of the number of processes in a quorum and thus messages required to effectuate the quorum – of the overall dynamic data replication scheme calculates to the sum of its static data replication schemes' message complexities, each weighted by the relative time spent in that stage of the dynamics using this particular static data replication scheme. Unfortunately, this method is in general only applicable to structural – and in this sense static – quality measures (cf. Section 2.4) that consider quorum system characteristics in terms of a quorum system as being a tuple of two sets of subsets of the set of processes. Non-structural operational measures such as operation availability influence or actually determine the time distribution, for example, by the epoch change operation being available or not. The general relation of non-structural operational measures to the stage sojourn time distribution has not been investigated here and remains future work.

Closely related to the stage sojourn times is the operation availability provided in a particular stage of the dynamics. This measure is evaluated similar to the stage sojourn time distribution via an operation-specific reward function for each stage $1 \leq i \leq n$ of the dynamics: Those tangible markings in which $\sharp(stage) = i$ and the operation of interest is available – as indicated by the place *opavail* having (at least) an according number of token – are assigned a reward of 1 while a reward of 0 is assigned to all other tangible markings. From the relative operation availability, the operation availability provided in a particular stage of the dynamics can be deduced.

Being able to learn the relative (overall) and the per-stage operation availability as well as the sojourn time distribution may serve as a well-founded base for future work on characteristic quality measure functions for (hetero-geneous) dynamic data replication schemes as outlined in the next section on future work.

4.5 Future Work

This section presents some aspects that are left for future work.

State Space Composition A composed system model for the quality measure evaluation of a specific evaluation scenario consists of several sub-nets. Those subnets that are instances of the same subnet template are structurally equivalent in the sense that their reachability graph is isomor-phic, that is, identical except for labeling. For example, the reachability graphs of process subnets (of the same process subnet template) are struc-turally equivalent as they share a common graph structure but their labels differ to represent the individuality of the processes. The graphical repre-sentations of their underlying stochastic processes (in which state transition labels represent failure and recovery rates) also share a common graph struc-ture and are isomorphic. Thus, the multiple stochastic processes modeling the individual processes' status and behavior may be represented by a sin-gle one that is parameterizable with an individual identity and possibly individual failure and recovery rates.

Then, the reachability graphs must not be computationally constructed but instead can be composed of parameterizable reachability graphs while analyzing the system model. The composed reachability graph instances may even be a priori computed and stored such that they are already avail-able at analysis time. Unfortunately, the Stochastic Petri Net Package (SPNP) toolkit [Ciardo, Muppala et al., 1989] used here does not support the composition of state spaces in terms of reachability graph composition. Therefore, investigating the potential benefit of state space composition to analysis time is left for future work.

Characteristic Quality Measure Functions for Dynamic Schemes
In terms of the quorum system(s) specified, every (dynamic) data repli-cation scheme implements a particular trade-off between different quality measures. The unstructured static Majority Consensus Voting, for example, focuses on high operation availability and accepts a linear scalability in the number of processes and thus operation costs. The structured static Grid

Protocol's objective, on the contrary, is to provide high operation availability while allowing for a less than linear scalability in the number of processes. For such static data replication schemes, the effect of their quorum system construction rules on the resulting quality measures is well-understood. For example, the operation availability of static data replication schemes can be computed via calculating combinatorial formulas that can be found in the respective literature, for example, by Koch [1994].

Unfortunately, for dynamic data replication schemes – and in particular for heterogeneous ones – no such closed formulas do exist. The system model presented may serve as a base and validation framework to investigate regularities among, for example, operation availability and process availability of homogeneous (and heterogeneous) dynamic data replication schemes. A closely related research question is the impact of heterogeneity on the regularities found for homogeneous dynamic data replication schemes. Ultimately, the question of which data replication schemes – if existent at all – (almost) match given quality measure values may be addressed. Obviously, because of the trade-off between quality measures, a data replication scheme cannot be optimal in every respect and the given objectives may not be exactly met by any data replication scheme, if realizable at all even by the means of heterogeneous dynamic data replication schemes. Nonetheless, having an arsenal of characteristic quality measure functions – even if only for some prominent data replication schemes – greatly helps to quickly decide at run-time which data replication scheme to consider or to discard for a particular application scenario. Those data replication schemes for which characteristic quality measure functions have been developed are quickly evaluated by calculating the respective formulas as opposed to performing a full-fledged analysis, for example, with the system model presented in this chapter.

Optimizations in Network Topology Modeling   The approach to integrate a network topology into the system model presented in Section 4.3.10 explicitly distinguishes process and channel failures in accordance with the system model introduced in Section 2.1.1. The communication model allows the (external part of the) local state of a process to be observed from the outside, meaning by other processes or an external observer of the system. Hence, process failures cannot be identified with channel failures as a "failed" process can be observed making progress, for example, if the process is simply counting, by reading the (externally visible) counter variable value. However, processes may as well be modeled as automata only reacting on input to produce output such that a process cannot perform steps without being triggered by input.

For the purpose of the system model, processes may as well be considered as reactive automata only making progress upon being triggered by input. While in general not true, this assumption allows to model channel failures via process failures in the system model. What channel failure is modeled by which process failure is dependent on the concrete network topology. For example, consider the three processes p_1, p_2 and p_3 managed by Majority Consensus Voting and arranged in a linear network topology as illustrated in Figure 4.37 (a). The failure of channel c_1 must be modeled by the failure of process p_1. The failure of channel c_2 must be modeled by the failure of process p_3. If either channel failure is instead modeled by the failure of process p_2, then no operation can be performed although the processes p_1 or p_3 may not have failed and, in conjunction with process p_2, can perform operations. As a second example, consider the same three processes arranged in a triangular network topology as depicted in Figure 4.37 (b), also using Majority Consensus Voting. The sole failure of channel c_2 must not be respected by either one of the processes p_1 or p_3 failing since the three processes are still able to (indirectly) communicate with each other via the channels c_1 and c_3. Only if both channels c_2 and c_1 fail, then this channel failure incident must be reflected by process p_1 failing. However, if process p_2 has failed, then the failure of channel c_2 must indeed be respected. Otherwise, the processes p_1 and p_3 can communicate and can form a valid write quorum. The same reasoning applies to the failure of the channels c_2 or c_3.

Another aspect is that modeling channel failures by process failures requires both, channels and processes to have the same mean time to failure and mean time to repair. Otherwise, dedicated channel failure and recovery

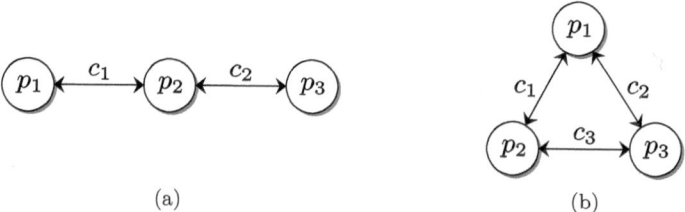

(a)   (b)

Figure 4.37: Three Processes in a Linear Network Topology with Two Channels (a) and a Triangular Network Topology with Three Channels (b)

transitions must be introduced into the system model, avoiding the up to $n \cdot (n-1)/2$ channel state places but not the up to $n \cdot (n-1)$ channel failure and recovery transitions when assuming that processes can directly communicate with each other. In case of processes and channels having different mean times to failure and mean times to repair, the failure of channels and processes can be distinguished because of the dedicated failure and recovery transitions. However, since a channel and a process failure (recovery) transition are enabled concurrently, a process or a (set of) channel(s) may fail (be repaired) prematurely. Otherwise, if one timed transition must model the failure (recovery) of a process and a (set of) channel(s), then it is indistinguishable whether the process or the (set of) channel(s) has failed (recovered). The problem of premature failure and recovery also applies to this case.

Investigating and exploiting the modeling of channel failures by process failures remains future work.

A further direction for future work is a compositional evaluation of the system model for (heterogeneous) dynamic data replication schemes and a given network topology by improving on the approach by Tsuchiya and Kikuno [1999] which, unfortunately, applies only to static data replication schemes and only to the write operation: For a given network topology, all minimal connected topology graphs that contain a write quorum are enumerated. The write operation availability is the probability that at least one of the graphs is operational, meaning that the process-interconnecting channels and the processes itself in this (sub)graph have not failed.

Essentially, a channel failure results in a modified network topology that can be considered as a new network topology representing a new evaluation scenario. The evaluation scenarios resulting from the different combinations of channel failures may be evaluated separately such that the overall quality measure of a (heterogeneous) dynamic data replication scheme is a composition of the individual evaluated measures.

4.6 Summary

Choosing a data replication scheme for a particular application scenario implies choosing a scheme-specific trade-off between quality measures. The chosen data replication scheme has to be carefully evaluated as it is crucial to the resulting overall quality-of-service and performance of the system. In this chapter, a comprehensive and versatile system model framework for the analytical evaluation of quorum-based data replication schemes has been presented. In contrast to previous approaches, it is not restricted to the evaluation of a specific subclass of unstructured data replication schemes, namely to the unstructured static Majority Consensus Voting and its homogeneous dynamic variants. Instead, via adopting tree-shaped voting structures to petri nets, the system model allows the evaluation of any unstructured or structured homogeneous and moreover the evaluation of any heterogeneous dynamic data replication scheme. It also supports static data replication schemes as a special case. A different data replication scheme is reflected in the system model simply by exchanging the quorum system specifications in terms of tree-shaped voting structure petri nets. Apart from the ability to evaluate quality measures with respect to the write operation as well as to the read operation, the system model allows the evaluation of other quality measures besides operation availability and its closely related measure reliability. This is illustrated in the next chapter by an evaluation example that considers the measures of read and write operation availability and the structural and average message complexity.

5 Example Evaluation

In this chapter, an example evaluation of three dynamic data replication schemes performed with the system model framework introduced in the previous chapter is presented. These three data replication schemes are (1) homogeneous Dynamic Voting, (2) the homogeneous Dynamic Grid Protocol, and (3) a combination of both in terms of a heterogeneous dynamic data replication scheme, called *Heterogeneous Protocol*.

Dynamic Voting, the homogeneous dynamic counterpart of the unstructured static Majority Consensus Voting, is highly resilient to process failures and provides high operation availabilities. However, its operation costs in terms of, for example, message complexity, scale only linearly in the number of processes. In contrast, the dynamic counterpart of the structured static Grid Protocol has lower operation costs because its quorum system construction rules exploit structural properties of the logical grid structure the processes are arranged in. The price, however, is lower operation availabilities compared to Dynamic Voting. As a blend of both, the Heterogeneous Protocol tackles these specific shortcomings and implements a new trade-off between operation availability and operation costs.

The exemplary quality measures of interest are the read and write operation availability, the structural message complexity, and the average message complexity (cf. Section 2.4). The latter is an example of a non-structural operational quality measure that can be evaluated by the system model. The three data replication schemes are evaluated under the frequent operations assumption as well as by using operation drivers (cf. Section 4.3.8).

This chapter is structured as follows. Next, the individual data replication scheme configurations are described. Then, the quality measures to be evaluated are discussed. Subsequently, the evaluation setting in terms of assumptions made considering the individual process availability, the network topology, and the operation intervals of the operation drivers is defined. Thereafter, the evaluation results of each data replication scheme are presented individually, followed by a comparative discussion of the results.

Data Replication Scheme Configuration

The three dynamic data replication schemes in this example evaluation each manage nine processes. The homogeneous Dynamic Voting as well as the homogeneous Dynamic Grid Protocol use their respective unstructured and structured static counterparts for all nine stages of the dynamics as illustrated in Figure 5.1 (a) and (b).

Number of Processes	Data Replication Scheme	Number of Processes	Data Replication Scheme
9	Majority Consensus Voting	9	Grid Protocol
8	Majority Consensus Voting	8	Grid Protocol
7	Majority Consensus Voting	7	Grid Protocol $_{rows}$
6	Majority Consensus Voting	6	Grid Protocol $_{cols}$
5	Majority Consensus Voting	5	Grid Protocol $_{rows}$
4	Majority Consensus Voting	4	Grid Protocol
3	Majority Consensus Voting	3	Grid Protocol
2	Majority Consensus Voting	2	Grid Protocol $_{cols}$
1	Majority Consensus Voting	1	Grid Protocol

(a)   (b)

Number of Processes	Data Replication Scheme
9	Grid Protocol
8	Grid Protocol
7	Majority Consensus Voting
6	Grid Protocol $_{cols}$
5	Majority Consensus Voting
4	Grid Protocol
3	Majority Consensus Voting
2	Majority Consensus Voting
1	Majority Consensus Voting

(c)

Figure 5.1: Data Replication Scheme Configuration of the Homogeneous Dynamic Voting (a), the Homogeneous Dynamic Grid Protocol (b), and the Heterogeneous Protocol (c), each with Nine Processes

Recall that the Grid Protocol arranges processes in a logical rectangular $k \times j$ grid where k is the number of columns and j is the number of rows in the grid. The Dynamic Grid Protocol's logical grid layouts for the individual stages of the dynamics are 1×1, 2×1, 2×2 with the lower right grid position unpopulated, 2×2, 2×3 with the lower left grid position unpopulated, 3×2,

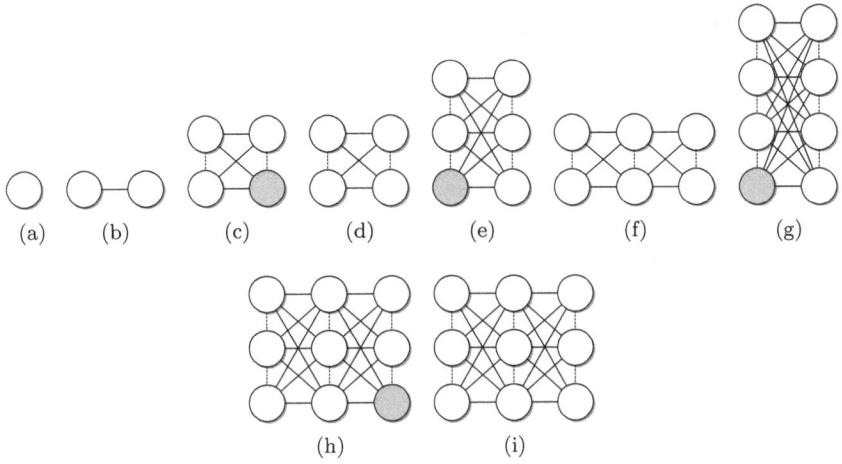

Figure 5.2: Logical Process Layouts used by the Homogeneous Dynamic Grid Protocol in Stages 1 to 9 of the Dynamics. Shaded Grid Positions are not populated by Processes.

2×4 with the lower left grid position unpopulated, 3×3 with the lower right grid position unpopulated, and 3×3 for the respective stages 1 to 9 of the dynamics as illustrated in Figure 5.2.

The Heterogeneous Protocol uses the structured Grid Protocol for the stages $4, 6, 8, 9$ and the unstructured Majority Consensus Voting for the other stages of the dynamics as illustrated in Figure 5.1 (c). In the four stages in which the Grid Protocol is used, the logical grid layouts as illustrated in Figure 5.3 are 2×2, 2×3, 3×3 with the lower right grid position

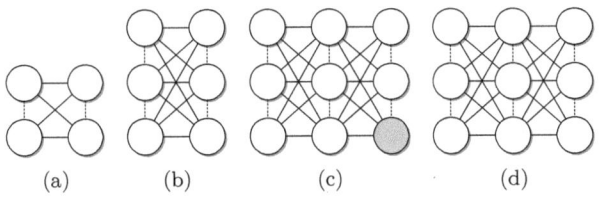

Figure 5.3: Grid Protocol Logical Process Layouts used by the Heterogeneous Protocol in Stages $4, 6, 8$, and 9 of the Dynamics. Shaded Grid Positions are not populated by Processes.

unpopulated, and 3×3. The reason to choose the Grid Protocol for the stages $4, 6, 8$ and 9 is twofold: First, in these stages, the logical grid structures are (mostly) symmetric allowing the Grid Protocol to unleash its potential of providing high operation availabilities at low costs in terms of the number of messages required to effectuate a quorum. Second, in low stages of the dynamics – in which the sojourn times cumulate for low process availabilities – an unstructured data replication scheme such as Majority Consensus Voting does not suffer from the restrained logical structure-induced quorum system construction rules, thereby offering a greater flexibility in quorum construction and consequently quorum- and operation availability.

Evaluated Quality Measures

The quality measures of interest in this example evaluation are read and write operation availability, structural message complexity, and average message complexity (cf. Section 2.4). The measure of average message complexity is a non-structural operational measure as it refers to the processes' (uniform) availability. Because it is a measure for static data replication schemes, it overestimates the actual average number of messages required for a dynamic data replication scheme. Specifically, it does not consider the system's evolution over time in terms of quorum system reconfigurations by which failed processes are removed from the quorum system (and recovered processes are reintegrated into the quorum system). Due to quorum system reconfiguration, the probability that a failed process is probed while forming a quorum is lower than the corresponding probability for a static data replication scheme having a static quorum system and no means of reconfiguration. The actual average message complexity of a dynamic data replication scheme depends on (1) the quorum probing strategy selecting quorums to perform operations with and on (2) when and which processes fail in an epoch prior to the next successful epoch change operation. This information can indeed be derived from the system model by tracking the process failures per epoch via a dedicated system model-global process failure accounting. Hence, the actual average message complexity of dynamic data replication schemes is an example of a non-structural operational measure that can be evaluated by the system model. However, in favor of a simpler system model, the average message complexity of a dynamic data replication scheme is calculated by the sum of its static data replication schemes' average message complexities, each weighted by the relative time spent in that stage of the dynamics using this particular static data replication scheme. Although it is not precise, this simpler average message complexity evaluation method is sufficient in the scope of this example evaluation.

For the evaluation of these measures, the two-states process model is sufficient as replica actuality or a particular process' participation in quorums need not to be considered.

Next, the average message complexity calculation for Majority Consensus Voting and the Grid Protocol is introduced in detail.

Average Message Complexity Calculation: Majority Consensus Voting   The average message complexity calculation for Majority Consensus Voting due to Saha, Rangarajan et al. [1996] is given by the formula

$$
\mathcal{M}_{\mathrm{MCV}}^{\varnothing}(n, a, m) = \begin{cases} 1 + (1 - a) \cdot \mathcal{M}_{\mathrm{MCV}}^{\varnothing}(n - 1, a, m) + \\ \quad a \cdot \mathcal{M}_{\mathrm{MCV}}^{\varnothing}(n - 1, a, m - 1) & \text{if } n \geq m \text{ and } m > 0, \\ 0 & \text{otherwise,} \end{cases}
$$

where n is the number of processes, m is the number of votes to collect among the n processes, and a is the uniform process availability.

The rationale for this formula is as follows. Unconditionally, one message needs to be sent to every process probed. Note that a message sent to a non-failed process is identified with this process granting its permission (vote) to the operation execution. Resource contention in terms of processes not granting their permission because of having granted it to a concurrent operation execution (for which they are locked) is not considered. With probability $1 - a$, the probed process has failed such that m votes must be collected from the $n - 1$ remaining processes. Otherwise, if the process has not failed, which is the case with probability a, then $m - 1$ votes must be collected from the $n - 1$ remaining processes. Eventually, either sufficiently many messages have been sent and thus the required votes have been collected ($m = 0 \wedge n \geq m$) or no quorum can be formed ($n < m \wedge m > 0$).

Note that to calculate the average message complexity, the case of $m = 0$ must not be explicitly considered. In contrast, when calculating operation availability, 1 must be returned in this case to account the probability mass of a successfully formed quorum.

The above formula is applicable to calculating the average message complexity for the read as well as for the write operation. For example, the average message complexity of Majority Consensus Voting with four processes is $\mathcal{M}^{\varnothing}_{\mathrm{MCV}}(4, a, 3)$ for the write operation and $\mathcal{M}^{\varnothing}_{\mathrm{MCV}}(4, a, 2)$ for the read operation.

Recall that Majority Consensus Voting defines no ordering in which to probe quorums (cf. Section 2.5.1). The above formula does not impose a probing order on quorums since, because of the uniform process availability, every quorum is equally suited for being probed (next).

Average Message Complexity Calculation: the Grid Protocol The average message complexity calculation for the Grid Protocol is dependent on the logical grid either being fully populated by processes or not. In the latter case, the order of probing the not equally populated columns has an impact on the average message complexity. For example, if the first probed column – which is without loss of generality assumed to be the leftmost column – is not fully populated, then the probability that all processes in this column have not failed (as required for a CC-Cover) is higher than the probability for columns that are fully populated by processes. Thus, the probability that a further column must be probed for a CC-Cover is higher if fully populated columns are probed first. On the other hand, for not fully populated columns, the probability that at least one process has not failed (as required for the C-Cover) is lower than the probability for fully populated columns. Hence, probing not fully populated columns first is favorable for a CC-Cover while probing fully populated columns first is favorable for a C-Cover.

In order to model not fully populated logical grid layouts, here, a particular grid layout is represented by a finite array of numbers with each array value reflecting the number of rows in a column (that is, the number of processes) and the array index representing the column number. Henceforth, the array index is referenced to by *col* and the numeric value in the col^{th} column is referenced to by *row*. The total number of columns is given by the array's length and is denoted col_{max}. For example, the logical grid layout for eight processes as illustrated in Figure 5.2 (h) is given by $grid_8 = [3, 3, 2]$ and col_{max} is 3.

The average message complexity calculation for the *read operation* in terms of a *C-Cover* is based on the formula by Saha, Rangarajan et al. [1996] but extended to also respect not fully populated grids. In the following formula, a is the uniform process availability, *col* is the current column to be probed (which defaults to zero as indicated by $col = 0$), row is the value of the grid layout array in the col^{th} position, and msgC – given below – is the average number of messages to be sent for this column.

$$
\mathcal{M}^{\varnothing}_{\text{GP}_{\text{ReadC}}}(a, col = 0) = \begin{cases} \text{msgC} + (1 - (1-a)^{row}) \cdot \\ \quad \mathcal{M}^{\varnothing}_{\text{GP}_{\text{ReadC}}}(a, col + 1) & \text{if } col < col_{\max} \\ 0 & \text{otherwise.} \end{cases}
$$

The rationale for this formula is as follows. With probability $1-(1-a)^{row}$, at least one process has not failed such that the next column is probed. The average number of messages required to either reveal that the column contains only failed processes (in which case no C-Cover can be formed) or to find a non-failed process is given by

$$
\text{msgC} = row \cdot (1-a)^{row} + \sum_{i=0}^{row-1} (i+1) \cdot (1-a)^i \cdot a
$$

$$
= \frac{1}{a} - \frac{(1-a)^{row}}{a}.
$$

If all processes have failed, which is the case with probability $(1-a)^{row}$, then row messages are needed. One message is needed if the first probed process has not failed, that is, $1 \cdot (1-a)^{i=0} \cdot a = 1 \cdot a$, which is the case with probability a. Two messages are needed if the first probed process has failed and the second probed process has not failed, that is, $2 \cdot (1-a)^{i=1} \cdot a = 2 \cdot (1-a) \cdot a$, which is the case with probability $(1-a) \cdot a$, and so forth.

The average message complexity calculation for the *write operation* which is inspired by the formula of Saha, Rangarajan et al. [1996] is given by

$$
\mathcal{M}^{\varnothing}_{\text{GP}_{\text{Write}}}(a, col = 0) = \begin{cases} \text{msgW} + (1 - a^{row} - (1-a)^{row}) \cdot \\ \quad \mathcal{M}^{\varnothing}_{\text{GP}_{\text{Write}}}(a, col + 1) + \\ \quad a^{row} \cdot \mathcal{M}^{\varnothing}_{\text{GP}_{\text{ReadC}}}(a, col + 1) & \text{if } col < col_{\max} \\ 0 & \text{otherwise,} \end{cases}
$$

with the variables defined as for the C-Cover read operation average message complexity calculation and msgW – given below – being the average number of messages to be sent for this column.

The rationale for this formula is as follows. With probability $1 - a^{row} - (1-a)^{row}$, not all but some processes have failed such that this column accounts for a C-Cover but not for a CC-Cover and the next column is probed for forming a CC-Cover. If no process in the current column has failed, which is the case with probability a^{row}, then a CC-Cover is found and a (partial) C-Cover remains to be formed with the subsequent columns. In summary, the processes of a column are probed for representing a CC-Cover until it is learned that this column (1) contains only non-failed processes and a CC-Cover is found, it (2) contains only failed processes in which case no write quorum can be formed, or it (3) contains some failed processes and at least one non-failed process in which case a partial C-Cover is found.

The probing needs at least two messages and on average a number of messages given by

$$\text{msgW} = row \cdot a^{row} + row \cdot (1-a)^{row} +$$
$$\sum_{i=2}^{row} i \cdot a^{i-1} \cdot (1-a) + i \cdot (1-a)^{i-1} \cdot a$$
$$= 1 + \sum_{i=1}^{row-1} a^i + (1-a)^i$$
$$= \frac{1 - a^{row-1} - (1-a)^{row-1}}{a \cdot (1-a)} - 1.$$

If processes are either all non-failed or all failed, which is the case with probability a^{row} and $(1-a)^{row}$, respectively, then row messages are needed. If the first probed process is non-failed but the second probed process has failed, then two messages are required. This is the case with probability $a \cdot (1-a)$. Conversely, if the first probed process has failed but the second probed process has not failed, then also two messages are required. This is the case with the same probability $(1-a) \cdot a$. If the first two probed processes have not failed but the third probed process has failed, then three messages are required. This is the case with probability $a^2 \cdot (1-a)$, and so forth.

The average message complexity calculation for the *read operation* in terms of a *C-Cover or a CC-Cover* (which is not considered by Saha, Rangarajan et al. [1996]) is given by the formula

$$
\mathcal{M}^{\varnothing}_{\mathrm{GP_{Read}}}(a, col = 0) =
\begin{cases}
\text{msgW} + (1 - a^{row} - (1 - a)^{row}) \cdot \\
\quad \mathcal{M}^{\varnothing}_{\mathrm{GP_{Read}}}(a, col + 1) + (1 - a)^{row} \cdot \\
\quad \mathcal{M}^{\varnothing}_{\mathrm{GP_{ReadCC}}}(a, col + 1) & \text{if } col < col_{\max} \\
0 & \text{otherwise}
\end{cases}
$$

with the auxiliary formula

$$
\mathcal{M}^{\varnothing}_{\mathrm{GP_{ReadCC}}}(a, col = 0) =
\begin{cases}
\text{msgW} + (1 - a^{row}) \cdot \\
\quad \mathcal{M}^{\varnothing}_{\mathrm{GP_{ReadCC}}}(a, col + 1) & \text{if } col < col_{\max} \\
0 & \text{otherwise}
\end{cases}
$$

and the variables a, col, row, and msgW as defined above.

The rationale for this formula is as follows. With probability $1 - a^{row} - (1 - a)^{row}$, some processes in the current column but not all of them have failed such that this column accounts for a C-Cover (but not for a CC-Cover) and the next column is probed. With probability $(1 - a)^{row}$, all processes in this column have failed such that a C-Cover cannot be successfully formed but a CC-Cover may be available. This case is handled by $\mathcal{M}^{\varnothing}_{\mathrm{GP_{ReadCC}}}$. A CC-Cover cannot be formed with the current column if not all processes are available. This is the case with probability $1 - a^{row}$. Then, a further column must be probed for the CC-Cover. The average number of messages sent in a column of the grid resembles the average number of messages as required for the write operation to form a CC-Cover because forming a CC-Cover is prioritized over forming a C-Cover.

Allowing a CC-Cover to be used as read quorum illustrates the trade-off between operation availability and – in a broader sense – performance: Being able to form a read quorum with a C-Cover or a CC-Cover renders the read operation more available compared to it being restricted to C-Covers only. This comes, however, at the cost of a higher average message complexity.

Note that the order of probing processes induced by the above formulas is to probe columns from left to right and to probe rows from top to bottom. Because of the uniform process availability a, the order in which to probe processes within a column is not significant as is the order in which to probe columns if the grid is fully populated.

Next, the evaluation setting in terms of assumptions made considering the individual process availability, the network topology, and the operation intervals of the operation drivers is presented.

Evaluation Setting

The above formulas to calculate the average message complexity of Majority Consensus Voting and the Grid Protocol are only valid if processes have uniform process availabilities. Otherwise, the average message complexity depends on the order in which processes are probed. If processes having a high availability are probed first and prior to processes having a low availability, the average message complexity is lower compared to them being probed last. Furthermore, these formulas are not applicable to evaluation scenarios in which the communication network is subject to failures. Therefore, (1) uniform process availabilities and (2) a fully interconnected network topology with perfect channels are assumed in this example evaluation for the sake of simplicity.

The mean time to repair (MTTR) for processes is assumed to be 3.88 days [Long, Muir et al., 1995] which is a value comparable to the result of 3.5836 days obtained by Warns, Storm et al. [2008]. The mean time to failure (MTTF) of a process depends on its availability a and the MTTR as given by the formula $MTTF = (MTTR \cdot a)/(1 - a)$.

The first set of experiments was conducted assuming frequent operations while the second set uses operation drivers. The artificial workload induced on the system by operation drivers is a read and a write operation attempt performed regularly every 5 minutes and an epoch change operation attempt performed regularly every 30 minutes. This workload describes a scenario in which a monitoring service triggers epoch change operations instead of them being triggered by process failures or by failed processes detected during quorum building attempts (cf. Section 4.3.8).

The analysis has been performed with the Stochastic Petri Net Package (SPNP) toolkit [Ciardo, Muppala et al., 1989] on a single dedicated core of a Core2Duo processor running at 1.2 GHz as, unfortunately, the SPNP toolkit is not able to benefit from multiple cores. The analysis involves reachability graph construction and calculating the stationary probability distribution of the resulting stochastic reward nets. Note that the evaluation result values presented in the following are generally rounded to five decimal places except for specific argumentation purposes requiring a greater precision.

Next, the individual evaluation results of Dynamic Voting, the Dynamic Grid Protocol, and the Heterogeneous Protocol are presented.

5.1 Individual Data Replication Scheme Evaluation Results

In this section, the individual evaluation results of Dynamic Voting, the Dynamic Grid Protocol, and the Heterogeneous Protocol with respect to read and write operation availability, structural message complexity, and average message complexity are presented. In addition, the relative time spent in each stage of the dynamics in relation to the (uniform) process availability is given to support the discussion of the results. The quality measures have been evaluated under the frequent operations assumption as well as by using operation drivers. Finally, specifics of the system model in terms of evaluation time and the size of the underlying continuous-time Markov chains are presented.

5.1.1 Dynamic Voting

Operation Availability The read and write operation availabilities of Dynamic Voting related to the (uniform) process availability with assuming frequent operations and by employing operation drivers are depicted in Figure 5.4 (a) and (b), respectively. The Figures 5.4 (c) and (d) show the operation availabilities related to process availability in log-scale, that is, the number of nines behind the decimal point in operation availability. As expected, the read operation is more available than the write operation, simply because of the way the respective quorums are constructed: While a write quorum requires a proper majority of all processes, half the processes suffice for a read quorum in case the total number of processes is even. Otherwise, if the total number of processes is odd, the read quorum set is identical to the write quorum set.

Note that the operation availability when employing operation drivers is not substantially lower than with assuming frequent operations for both operations. In fact, it is identical beyond a process availability of 0.97 for the read operation and beyond a process availability of 0.98 for the write operation. For the read operation, the difference diminishes starting from a difference of 0.0163 for a process availability of 0.01 (non-linearly) approaching a difference of $6 \cdot 10^{-12}$ for a process availability of 0.97. The corresponding values for the write operation are $8194 \cdot 10^{-8}$ for a process availability of 0.01 and $1.2 \cdot 10^{-11}$ for a process availability of 0.98.

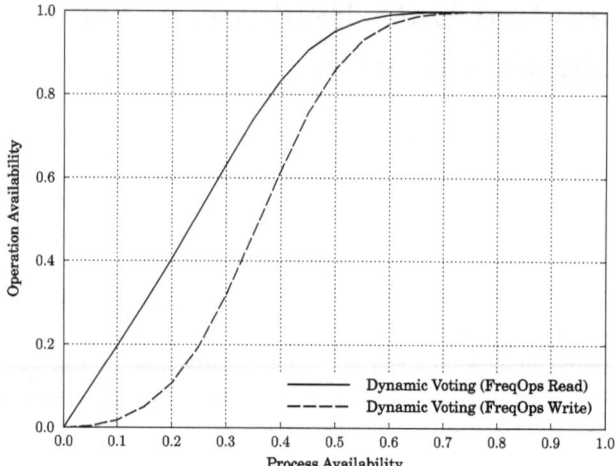

(a) Read Operation Availability (Solid Line) and Write Operation Availability (Dashed Line) over Process Availability Assuming Frequent Operations

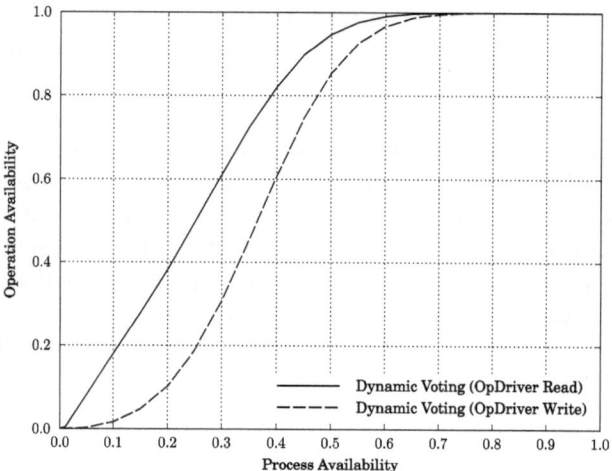

(b) Read Operation Availability (Solid Line) and Write Operation Availability (Dashed Line) over Process Availability using Operation Drivers

Figure 5.4: Dynamic Voting Operation Availability Results

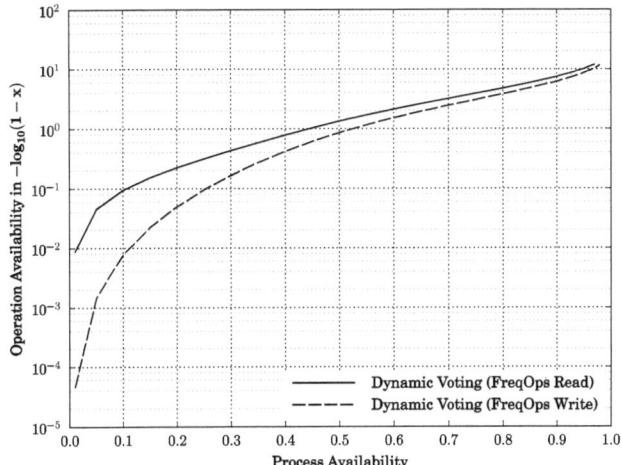

(c) Read Operation Availability (Solid Line) and Write Operation Availability (Dashed Line) in Log-scale over Process Availability Assuming Frequent Operations

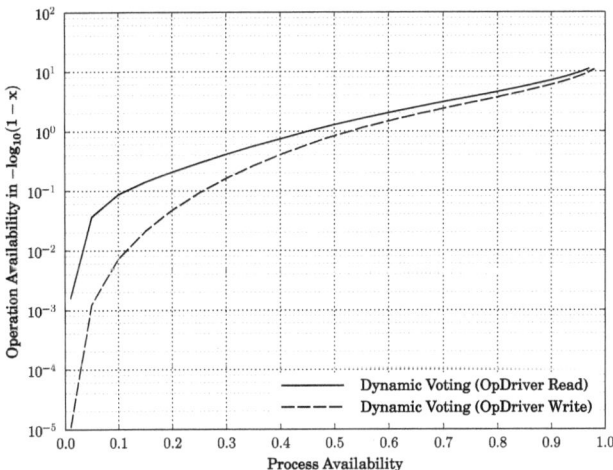

(d) Read Operation Availability (Solid Line) and Write Operation Availability (Dashed Line) in Log-scale over Process Availability using Operation Drivers

Figure 5.4 (cont.): Dynamic Voting Operation Availability Results

Message Complexity   The message complexity of Dynamic Voting with nine processes is related to the (uniform) process availability by Figure 5.5, again under the frequent operations assumption as well as with employing operation drivers. Note that in this figure – and henceforth – not all message complexity results are shown and that message complexity values differing by $1/10$th message are considered identical, both in favor of uncluttered graphs.

Message complexity figures are interpreted as follows: If the message complexity bar for a particular process availability is segmented, then the lower segment's bar height gives the message complexity value for an operation that is associated to the lower segment's bar color by the graph's legend. The absolute bar height, that is, the lower segment's bar height plus the upper segment's bar height, gives the message complexity value for an operation that is associated to the upper segment's bar color by the graph's legend. If a message complexity bar is not segmented, then its bar height accounts for both operations listed in the graph's legend. Note that the actual message complexity values of the two operations may differ by $1/10$th message but are depicted as identical due to the $1/10$th message filtering.

In Figure 5.5 (a) and (b), the structural message complexity, that is, the number of messages needed to effectuate a quorum as determined by the

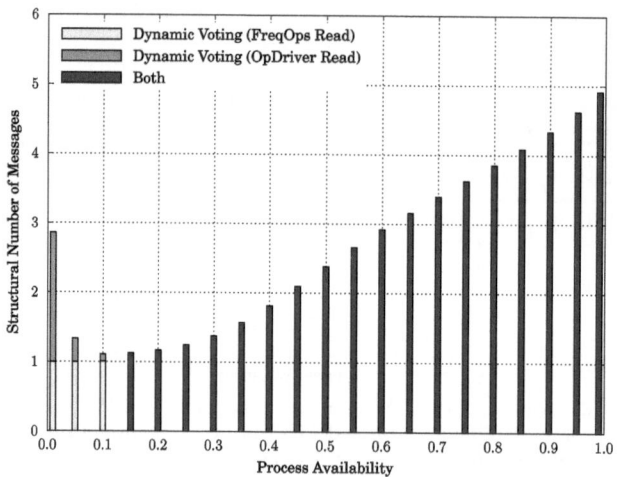

(a) Read Operation Structural Message Complexity Assuming Frequent Operations and using Operation Drivers

Figure 5.5: Dynamic Voting Message Complexity Results

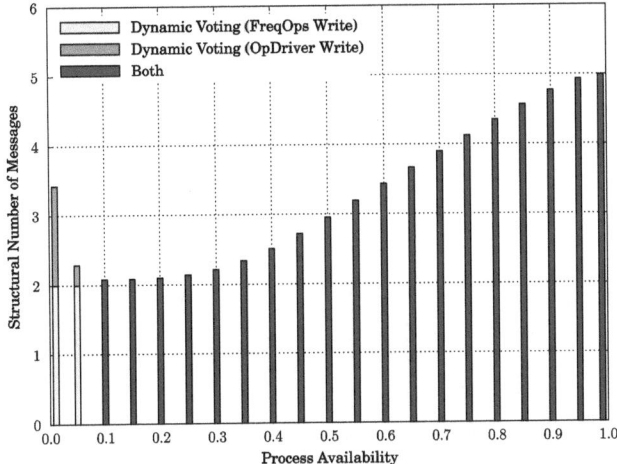

(b) Write Operation Structural Message Complexity Assuming Frequent Operations and using Operation Drivers

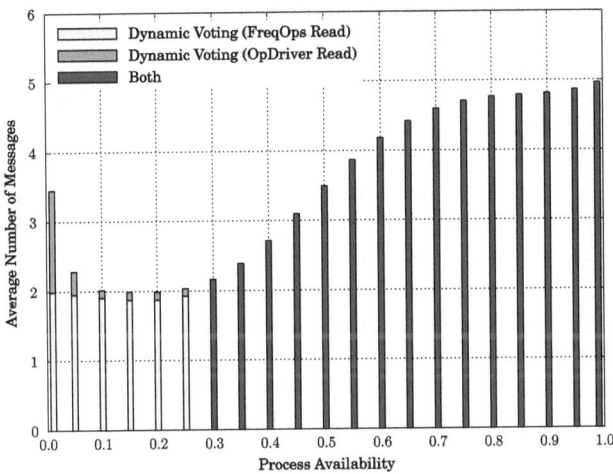

(c) Read Operation Average Message Complexity Assuming Frequent Operations and using Operation Drivers

Figure 5.5 (cont.): Dynamic Voting Message Complexity Results

quorum cardinalities, is related to process availability for the read operation and for the write operation, respectively. With the exception of process availabilities lower than 0.1 for the write operation and process availabilities

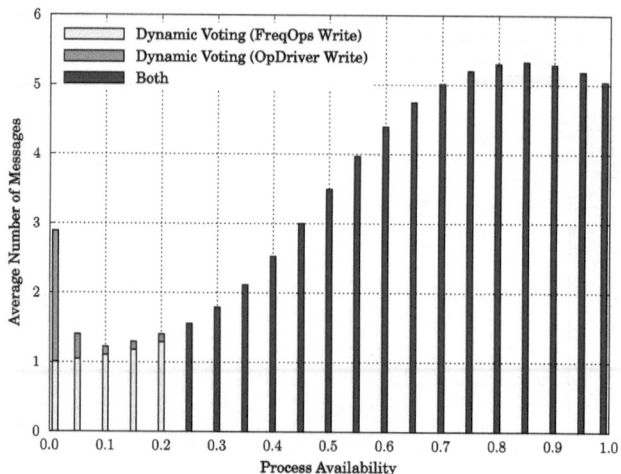

(d) Write Operation Average Message Complexity Assuming
Frequent Operations and using Operation Drivers

Figure 5.5 (cont.): Dynamic Voting Message Complexity Results

lower than or equal to 0.1 for the read operation, the structural message
complexity of the respective operation when assuming frequent operations
is identical to the structural message complexity when employing operation drivers. The same is true for the average message complexity but with
slightly higher process availabilities beyond which it is identical, as illustrated in Figure 5.5 (c) and (d).

The seemingly unfitting high message complexity values for low process
availabilities – and in particular for a process availability of 0.01 – when
employing operation drivers with respect to the structural as well as to the
average message complexity is explained by considering the sojourn times
in the different stages of the dynamics: For a process availability of 0.1, the
sojourn times in the respective stages from 1 to 9 are

Dynamics Stage	1	2	3	4	5
Relative Time	0.00000	0.88788	0.03123	0.07619	0.00138

Dynamics Stage	6	7	8	9
Relative Time	0.00163	0.00001	0.00157	0.00011

Dynamic Voting: Relative Time Spent in Stages for a
Process Availability of 0.1 and using Operation Drivers

The majority of time is spent in low stages, namely mostly in stage 2.
Surprisingly, for a process availability of 0.01, the time spent in specific

stages is more scattered:

Dynamics Stage	1	2	3	4	5
Relative Time	0.00000	0.17871	0.01197	0.17907	0.16627

Dynamics Stage	6	7	8	9	
Relative Time	0.13934	0.17047	0.07124	0.08294	

Dynamic Voting: Relative Time Spent in Stages for a
Process Availability of 0.01 and using Operation Drivers

Since more time is spent in higher stages of the dynamics – in which more messages are required to effectuate a quorum because of larger quorum cardinalities – the accumulated message complexity is, therefore, higher than the message complexity for a process availability of 0.1. A process availability as low as 0.01 handicaps the dynamics mechanism: It cannot scale down to a low stage as fast as it is able to if the process availability is at least high enough to successfully perform epoch change operations, therefore resulting in this time distribution. The epoch change operation availability for a process availability of 0.01 is 0.0000251650. The contribution of the individual stages to the overall epoch change operation availability is

Dynamics Stage	1	2	3	4	5
Rel. Availability	0.00000	0.00002	0.00000	0.00000	0.00000

Dynamics Stage	6	7	8	9	
Rel. Availability	0.00000	0.00000	0.00000	0.00000	

Dynamic Voting: Individual Stages' Contribution to the Epoch Change Operation
Availability for a Process Availability of 0.01 and using Operation Drivers

Note that this phenomenon does not occur when assuming frequent operations. In this case, an epoch change operation is attempted upon every process failure or recovery event such that – in contrast to using operation drivers – a process failure event is immediately acted upon, allowing for a fast down-scaling in stages and leaving no probability for joint or consecutive failure events which may render the epoch change operation unavailable when the redundancy in processes is exhausted. For example, for a process availability of 0.01, the stage sojourn times are

Dynamics Stage	1	2	3	4	5
Relative Time	0.00000	0.99999	0.00001	0.00000	0.00000

Dynamics Stage	6	7	8	9	
Relative Time	0.00000	0.00000	0.00000	0.00000	

Dynamic Voting: Relative Time Spent in Stages for a
Process Availability of 0.01 and Assuming Frequent Operations

The individual stages' contribution to the (overall) read operation availability of 0.01991 mostly stems from stage 2:

Dynamics Stage	1	2	3	4	5
Rel. Availability	0.00000	0.01990	0.00001	0.00000	0.00000

Dynamics Stage	6	7	8	9
Rel. Availability	0.00000	0.00000	0.00000	0.00000

Dynamic Voting: Individual Stages' Contribution to the Read Operation Availability for a Process Availability of 0.01 and Assuming Frequent Operations

Supporting the above argumentation of a fast scale-down in stages, from a per-stage read operation availability perspective, the stages 3–9 have a read operation availability of 1.0:

Dynamics Stage	1	2	3	4	5
Availability	0.00000	0.01990	1.00000	1.00000	1.00000

Dynamics Stage	6	7	8	9
Availability	1.00000	1.00000	1.00000	1.00000

Dynamic Voting: Read Operation Availability per Stage of the Dynamics for a Process Availability of 0.01 and Assuming Frequent Operations

Apart from this exception, in general, the higher the uniform process availability, the higher (lower) the percentage of time spent in high (low) stages of the dynamics. High stages have associated a higher message complexity because of larger quorum cardinalities. As depicted in Figure 5.5 (a) and 5.5 (b), the structural message complexity monotonically increases when assuming frequent operations. When employing operation drivers, the structural message complexity increases monotonically starting from a process availability of 0.1 for both operations.

As shown in Figure 5.5 (c) and 5.5 (d), the average write operation message complexity increases monotonically up to a process availability of 0.85 after which it decreases while the average read operation message complexity always increases monotonically starting from a process availability of 0.15, both with assuming frequent operations. In case of employing operation drivers, the average read operation message complexity monotonically increases starting from a process availability of 0.15. The average write operation message complexity monotonically increases starting with a process availability of 0.1 and up to a process availability of 0.85. Beyond this process availability, the average write operation message complexity decreases. In contrast to the structural message complexity, the average message complexity does not increase in an approximately linear manner for sufficiently high and increasing process availabilities. This observation is explained by the fact that the more available and reliable the processes become, the less messages are sent to failed processes, thereby avoiding the negative impact on the overall average message complexity.

Albeit not thoroughly visible in Figure 5.5 (a) and 5.5 (b) due to the $1/10$th message filter applied, the structural read operation message complexity is always lower than the structural write operation message complexity. This fact is due to read quorums having a smaller cardinality than write quorums for even-numbered stages of the dynamics, thereby resulting in a lower overall structural message complexity.

In contrast to the structural message complexity and regardless of assuming frequent operations or using operation drivers, the average read operation message complexity is higher than the average write operation message complexity for process availabilities lower than 0.5, albeit not visible in Figure 5.5 (c) and 5.5 (d) due to the $1/10$th message filter. This fact stems from the earlier abortion of write quorum probing in case a write quorum certainly cannot be formed, thereby resulting in – on average – fewer messages sent. For a process availability of 0.5, both operations have the same average message complexity. For process availabilities exceeding 0.5, the write operation has a higher average message complexity than the read operation.

Time Distribution   The time distribution, that is, the relative time spent in each stage of the dynamics related to the (uniform) process availability, is depicted in Figure 5.6. Similar to message complexity figures, not all results are shown in favor of uncluttered graphs. As expected and supporting the above discussion, in general, the higher (lower) the process availability, the more (less) time is spent in higher stages of the dynamics.

System Model Facts   Assuming frequent operations, the continuous-time Markov chains of Dynamic Voting with nine processes each have $14,326$ states, $128,934$ transitions, and took on average 47.88 seconds to be analyzed. Employing operation drivers, the continuous-time Markov chains of Dynamic Voting with nine processes have $1,542,144$ states, $15,990,332$ transitions, and took on average $2,293.82$ seconds (≈ 38 minutes) to be analyzed. This significant increase in the number of states, transitions, and analysis time stems from the computational complexity added by the (structurally simple) operation driver subnets in terms of additional and frequent timed transition firings.

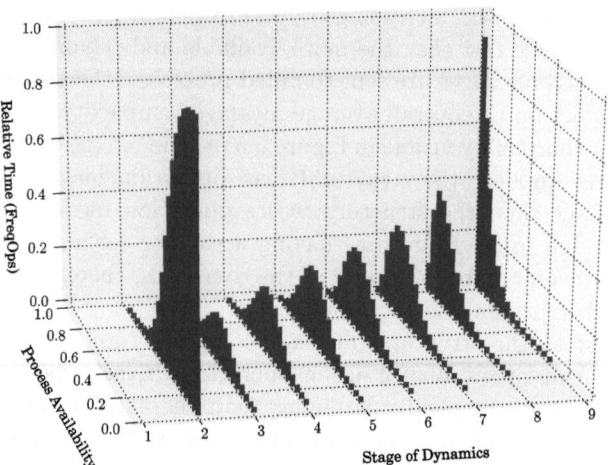

(a) Relative Time Spent in each Stage of the Dynamics over Process Availability Assuming Frequent Operations

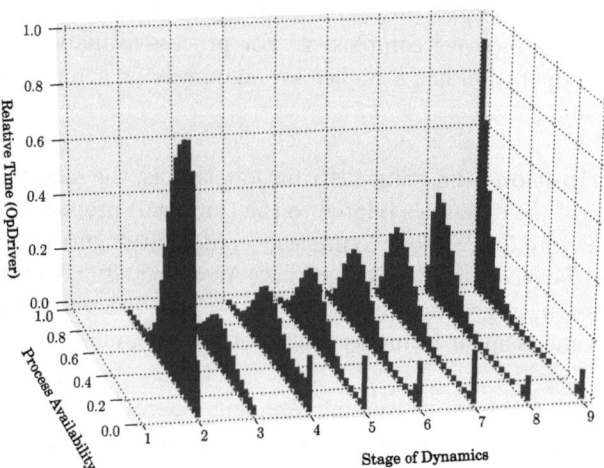

(b) Relative Time Spent in each Stage of the Dynamics over Process Availability using Operation Drivers

Figure 5.6: Dynamic Voting Time Distribution

5.1.2 The Dynamic Grid Protocol

Operation Availability The read and write operation availabilities of the Dynamic Grid Protocol related to the (uniform) process availability with assuming frequent operations and by employing operation drivers are depicted in Figure 5.7 (a) and (b), respectively. The Figures 5.7 (c) and (d) show the operation availabilities related to process availability in logscale. As it is the case for Dynamic Voting, the read operation is more available than the write operation. When assuming frequent operations, the write operation availability graph approaches the read operation availability graph with increasing process availabilities. They are identical for process availabilities higher than 0.99.

In case operation drivers are employed, the read operation is always more available than the write operation. The latter does not reach an availability of 1.0 even for a process availability as high as 0.999. This fact is attributed to the Dynamic Grid Protocol being a structured data replication scheme and, therefore, not being as resilient to process failures as the unstructured Dynamic Voting, in particular when employing operation drivers such that a process failure is not necessarily instantly reacted on. For example, for the Dynamic Grid Protocol and a process availability of 0.8, the relative

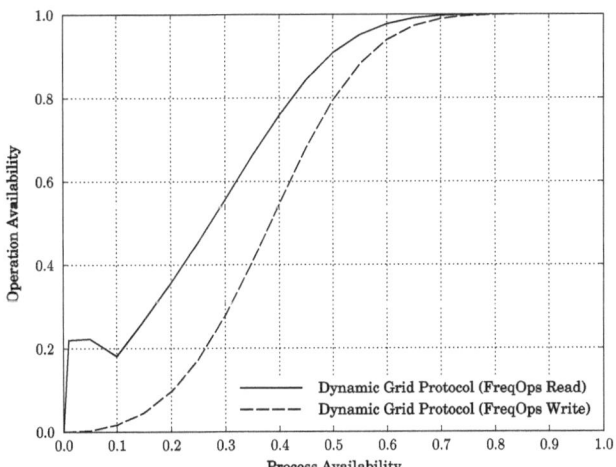

(a) Read Operation Availability (Solid Line) and Write Operation Availability (Dashed Line) over Process Availability Assuming Frequent Operations

Figure 5.7: Dynamic Grid Protocol Operation Availability Results

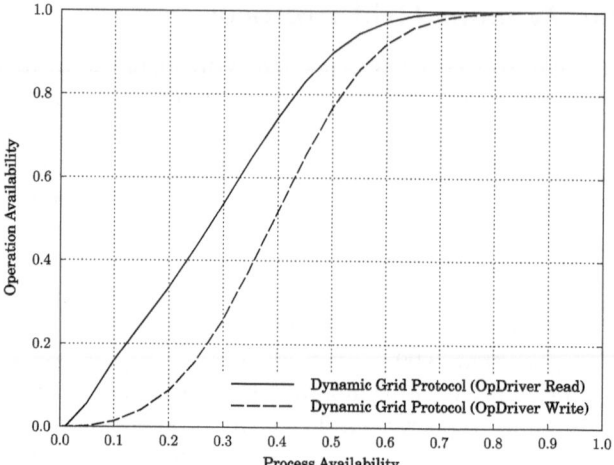

(b) Read Operation Availability (Solid Line) and Write Operation Availability (Dashed Line) over Process Availability using Operation Drivers

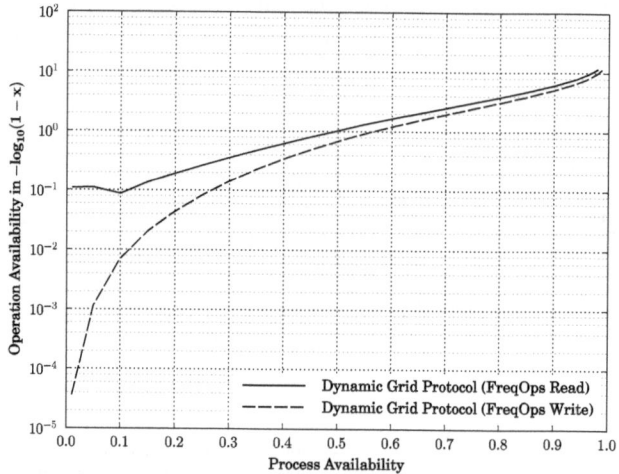

(c) Read Operation Availability (Solid Line) and Write Operation Availability (Dashed Line) in Log-scale over Process Availability Assuming Frequent Operations

Figure 5.7 (cont.): Dynamic Grid Protocol Operation Availability Results

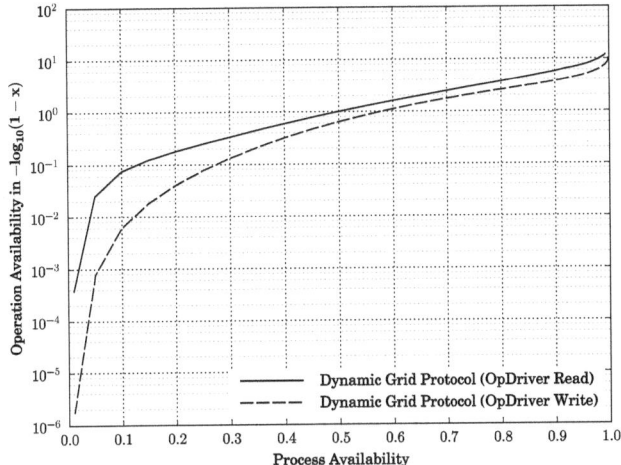

(d) Read Operation Availability (Solid Line) and Write Operation Availability (Dashed Line) in Log-scale over Process Availability using Operation Drivers

Figure 5.7 (cont.): Dynamic Grid Protocol Operation Availability Results

times spent in the individual stages of the dynamics are

Dynamics Stage	1	2	3	4	5
Relative Time	0.00000	0.00026	0.00316	0.01610	0.06527

Dynamics Stage	6	7	8	9
Relative Time	0.17568	0.30323	0.30208	0.13422

Dynamic Grid Protocol: Relative Time Spent in Stages for a
Process Availability of 0.8 and using Operation Drivers

For Dynamic Voting and also for a process availability of 0.8, the relative times spent in the individual stages of the dynamics are

Dynamics Stage	1	2	3	4	5
Relative Time	0.00000	0.00041	0.00272	0.01652	0.06603

Dynamics Stage	6	7	8	9
Relative Time	0.17614	0.30197	0.30198	0.13422

Dynamic Voting: Relative Time Spent in Stages for a
Process Availability of 0.8 and using Operation Drivers

The epoch change operation availability is 0.99725 for the Dynamic Grid Protocol with the individual stages from 1 to 9 contributing

Dynamics Stage	1	2	3	4	5
Rel. Availability	0.00000	0.00016	0.00252	0.01607	0.06509

Dynamics Stage	6	7	8	9
Rel. Availability	0.17549	0.30174	0.30196	0.13422

Dynamic Grid Protocol: Individual Stages' Contribution to the Epoch Change Operation Availability for a Process Availability of 0.8 and using Operation Drivers

The epoch change operation availability per stage is

Dynamics Stage	1	2	3	4	5
Availability	0.00000	0.64000	0.79825	0.99766	0.99724

Dynamics Stage	6	7	8	9
Availability	0.99895	0.99507	0.99963	0.99997

Dynamic Grid Protocol: Epoch Change Operation Availability per Stage of the Dynamics for a Process Availability of 0.8 and using Operation Drivers

In comparison, for Dynamic Voting, the epoch change operation availability is 0.99980, the individual stages' contribution is

Dynamics Stage	1	2	3	4	5
Rel. Availability	0.00000	0.00027	0.00272	0.01648	0.06603

Dynamics Stage	6	7	8	9
Rel. Availability	0.17613	0.30197	0.30198	0.13422

Dynamic Voting: Individual Stages' Contribution to the Epoch Change Operation Availability for a Process Availability of 0.8 and using Operation Drivers

and the per-stage epoch change operation availability is

Dynamics Stage	1	2	3	4	5
Availability	0.00000	0.64000	0.99892	0.99766	0.99999

Dynamics Stage	6	7	8	9
Availability	0.99998	1.00000	1.00000	1.00000

Dynamic Voting: Epoch Change Operation Availability per Stage of the Dynamics for a Process Availability of 0.8 and using Operation Drivers

From these values – and supported by the availability graphs in Figure 5.7 – the superiority of Dynamic Voting to the Dynamic Grid Protocol with respect to operation availability becomes apparent. It also explains the increasing discrepancy of the write operation availability when employing operation drivers and the write operation availability with assuming frequent operations for process availabilities higher than ≈ 0.6.

The remarkably high read operation availability for process availabilities lower than 0.1 when assuming frequent operations is explained by the fact

that for such low process availabilities, time is mainly spent in stage 2 and
to a – in comparison – negligible amount in stage 3:

Dynamics Stage	1	2	3	4	5
Relative Time	0.00000	0.97818	0.02182	0.00000	0.00000

Dynamics Stage	6	7	8	9
Relative Time	0.00000	0.00000	0.00000	0.00000

Dynamic Grid Protocol: Relative Time Spent in Stages for a
Process Availability of 0.01 and Assuming Frequent Operations

This time distribution suggests a fast scale-down in stages that is attributed
to the frequent operations assumption as already discussed for Dynamic
Voting. The relative per-stage contribution to the overall read operation
availability of 0.22020 is

Dynamics Stage	1	2	3	4	5
Rel. Availability	0.00000	0.21774	0.00246	0.00000	0.00000

Dynamics Stage	6	7	8	9
Rel. Availability	0.00000	0.00000	0.00000	0.00000

Dynamic Grid Protocol: Individual Stages' Contribution to the Read Operation
Availability for a Process Availability of 0.01 and Assuming Frequent Operations

and the per-stage read operation availability is

Dynamics Stage	1	2	3	4	5
Availability	0.00000	0.22260	0.11259	0.00000	1.00000

Dynamics Stage	6	7	8	9
Availability	0.00000	1.00000	0.00000	1.00000

Dynamic Grid Protocol: Read Operation Availability per Stage of the Dynamics for a
Process Availability of 0.01 and Assuming Frequent Operations

In stage 2, both processes are required to perform a write operation while
either also two or all three processes are required in stage 3. For performing
a read operation, only one process is required in stage 2 and either also
one or at most two processes are required in stage 3. Note that stage 2
marks the minimal stage of the dynamics since the failure of one of the two
processes in this stage renders an epoch change operation unavailable as
it requires a successfully formed write quorum. The read operation is still
available with the remaining process. For these reasons, the probability of
the read operation being available, which is 0.22020, is clearly higher than
the probability of the write operation being available, which is 0.00008,
supporting the discussion in Section 4.3.8.

In analogy to the discussion on the seemingly unfitting high message complexity values for low process availabilities when employing operation drivers and using Dynamic Voting, the sojourn times of the Dynamic Grid Protocol are also scattered throughout the stages of the dynamics due to the dynamics being handicapped and not being employed in an optimal manner. For example, for a process availability of 0.01, the relative times spent in the respective stages from 1 to 9 are

Dynamics Stage	1	2	3	4	5
Relative Time	0.00000	0.02606	0.00489	0.04069	0.05727

Dynamics Stage	6	7	8	9	
Relative Time	0.07333	0.05883	0.03117	0.70775	

Dynamic Grid Protocol: Relative Time Spent in Stages for a
Process Availability of 0.01 and using Operation Drivers

while the relative times for a process availability of 0.1 are

Dynamics Stage	1	2	3	4	5
Relative Time	0.00000	0.68614	0.15964	0.07338	0.01855

Dynamics Stage	6	7	8	9	
Relative Time	0.00493	0.03876	0.00181	0.01679	

Dynamic Grid Protocol: Relative Time Spent in Stages for a
Process Availability of 0.1 and using Operation Drivers

Due to the low process availability and because of the delayed reaction to process failure events, the read operation availability when employing operation drivers is not as high as with assuming frequent operations.

Message Complexity The Figures 5.9 (a) and (b) relate the structural message complexity to process availability for the read operation and the write operation, respectively. The average message complexity, also for both operations, is related to process availability by the Figures 5.9 (c) and (d). In contrast to Dynamic Voting, in which all quorums of an operation-specific quorum set have the same cardinality, the operation-specific quorums complying to the Grid Protocol may have different cardinalities. For example, consider a 3×2 logical grid layout as illustrated in Figure 5.8 (a) in which the processes are logically arranged in three columns and two rows. While write quorums have a uniform cardinality of 4, read quorums either have a cardinality of 2 or a cardinality of 3, depending on whether they represent a CC-Cover or a C-Cover. In case of a 3×3 logical grid layout as shown in Figure 5.8 (b), read quorums have a cardinality of 3 while write

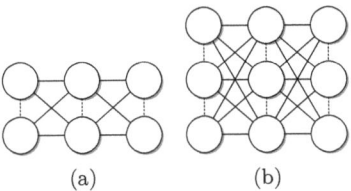

(a)   (b)

Figure 5.8: 3 × 2 (a) and 3 × 3 (b) Grid Protocol Logical Process Layouts

quorums have a cardinality of 5. For a fair comparison among the three protocols, the average instead of the minimal quorum cardinality is accounted
for the structural message complexity value if a quorum set has quorums of
different cardinalities to choose from.

As illustrated in Figure 5.9 (a) and 5.9 (b), the structural message complexity when assuming frequent operations is identical to the structural message complexity with employing operation drivers for process availabilities
beyond 0.1 for the read operation and beyond process availabilities of 0.3 for
the write operation. The same is true for the average message complexity
illustrated in Figure 5.9 (c) and 5.9 (d) but with the process availabilities
being 0.4 and 0.35, respectively.

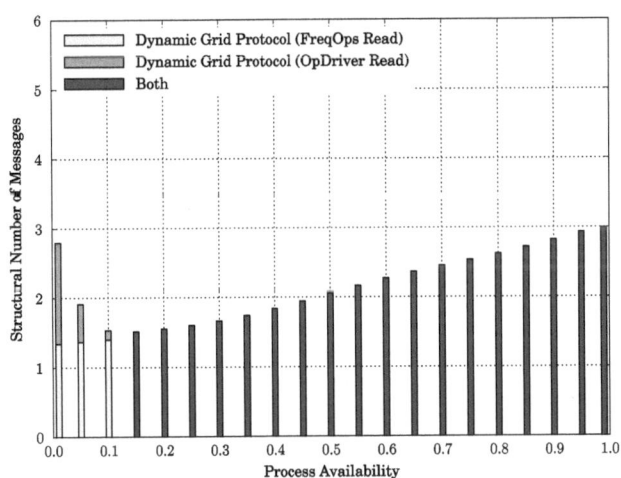

(a) Read Operation Structural Message Complexity Assuming Frequent Operations and using Operation Drivers

Figure 5.9: Dynamic Grid Protocol Message Complexity Results

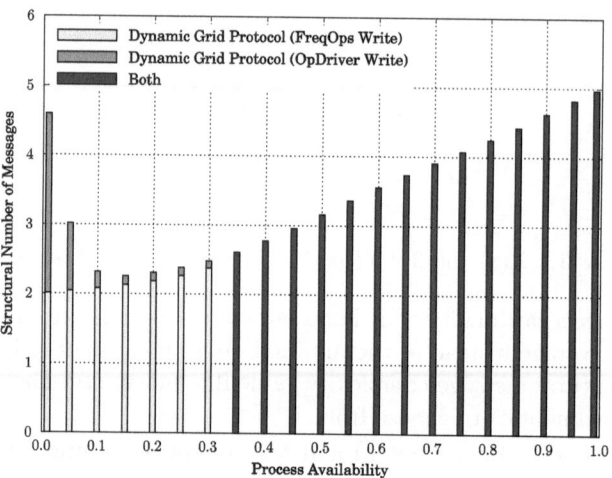

(b) Write Operation Structural Message Complexity Assuming Frequent Operations and using Operation Drivers

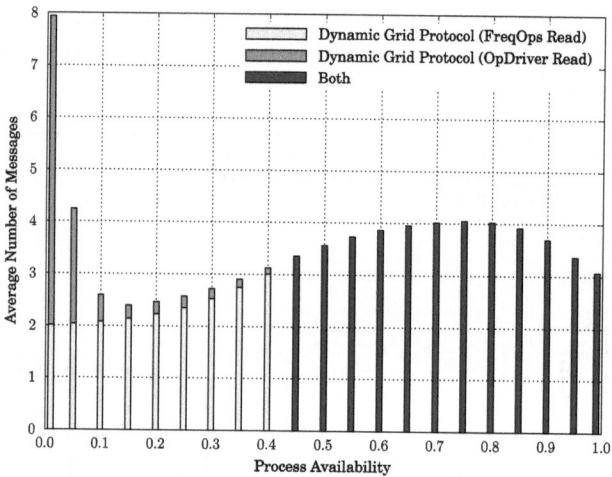

(c) Read Operation Average Message Complexity Assuming Frequent Operations and using Operation Drivers

Figure 5.9 (cont.): Dynamic Grid Protocol Message Complexity Results

The average read operation message complexity for a process availability of 0.01 is extremely high when using operation drivers (notice the different scale). It is – like for Dynamic Voting – explained by considering the sojourn

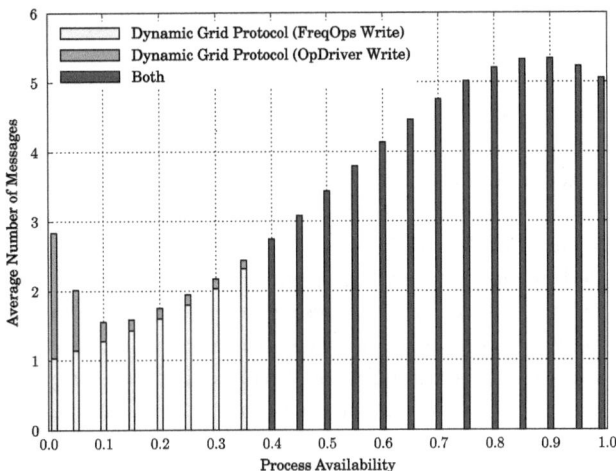

(d) Write Operation Average Message Complexity Assuming Frequent Operations and using Operation Drivers

Figure 5.9 (cont.): Dynamic Grid Protocol Message Complexity Results

times in the respective stages of the dynamics

Dynamics Stage	1	2	3	4	5
Relative Time	0.00000	0.02606	0.00489	0.04069	0.05727

Dynamics Stage	6	7	8	9
Relative Time	0.07333	0.05883	0.03117	0.70775

Dynamic Grid Protocol: Relative Time Spent in Stages for a
Process Availability of 0.01 and using Operation Drivers

revealing that 70.775 percent of time is spent in stage 9. In this stage, the nine processes are logically arranged in a 3×3 grid. In order to form a read quorum, three processes are to be probed in the best case and nine processes must be probed in the worst case. Hence, for a process availability as low as 0.01, rather more (namely 8.9406) than less processes are to be probed on average in stage 9, thereby resulting in such a high average read operation message complexity. In analogy to this argumentation, the high structural read and write operation message complexity as well as the high average write operation message complexity for low process availabilities are explained.

As depicted in Figure 5.9 (a) and 5.9 (b) and for the same reasons as for Dynamic Voting, the structural message complexity is monotonically increasing for both operations when assuming frequent operations. In case of employing operation drivers, the structural message complexity increases monotonically starting from a process availability of 0.15 for both operations. The average message complexity, on the other hand, does not monotonically increase. Apart from process availabilities lower than 0.1, the average read (write) operation message complexity reaches its peak value of 4.05 (5.34) at a process availability of 0.75 (0.9) and then decreases (nonlinearly) to a value of 3.01 (5.01).

As visualized in the structural message complexity Figures 5.9 (a) and 5.9 (b), the structural read operation message complexity is always lower than the structural write operation message complexity, regardless of whether frequent operations are assumed or operation drivers are employed. For the average message complexity shown in Figure 5.9 (c) and 5.9 (d), the read operation value is lower than the write operation value for process availabilities higher than or equal to 0.55 and vice versa, regardless of whether frequent operations are assumed or operation drivers are employed. Notice that the two average message complexity figures have a different scale.

The Dynamic Grid Protocol's maximal structural read operation message complexity of three messages is reached and excelled when using Dynamic Voting with a process availability higher than 0.617 (cf. Figure 5.5 (a)). The Dynamic Grid Protocol has a lower structural read operation message complexity than Dynamic Voting for a process availability higher than or equal to 0.45 when assuming frequent operations. When employing operation drivers, it has a lower structural read operation message complexity for a process availability higher than 0.4. For the write operation structural message complexity (cf. Figure 5.5 (b)), the values are 0.7 and 0.45, respectively.

Concerning the average message complexity, the Dynamic Grid Protocol is superior to Dynamic Voting with respect to the read (write) operation for a process availability higher than 0.5 (0.45) when assuming frequent operations as well as in case of employing operation drivers (cf. Figures 5.5 (c) and (d)).

While not true for the read operation, the structural and the average write operation message complexity of both protocols are substantially comparable for sufficiently high process availabilities (cf. Figures 5.5 (b) and (d)).

Time Distribution   The relative time spent in each stage of the dynamics related to process availability for the Dynamic Grid Protocol is depicted in Figure 5.10. As it is the case for Dynamic Voting and as expected, in

general, the higher the process availability, the more time is spent in higher
stages of the dynamics, and vice versa.

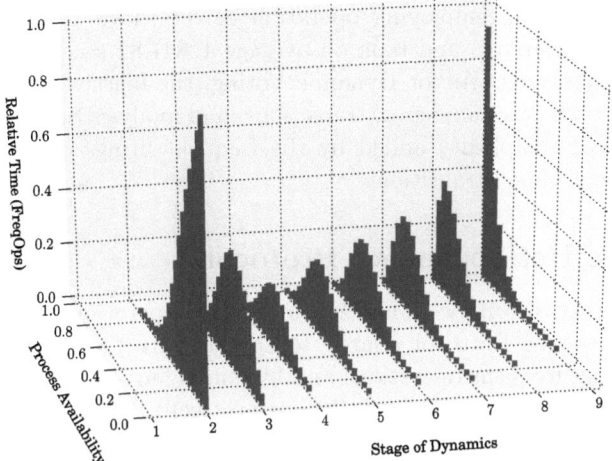

(a) Relative Time Spent in each Stage of the Dynamics over
Process Availability Assuming Frequent Operations

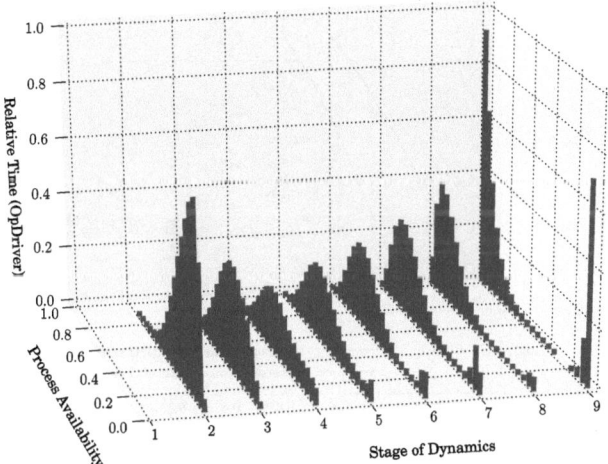

(b) Relative Time Spent in each Stage of the Dynamics over
Process Availability using Operation Drivers

Figure 5.10: Dynamic Grid Protocol Time Distribution

System Model Facts The continuous-time Markov chains of the Dynamic Grid Protocol with nine processes and assuming frequent operations have $40,821$ states, $367,389$ transitions, and took on average 97.13 seconds to be analyzed. The continuous-time Markov chains of the Dynamic Grid Protocol when employing operation drivers have $1,539,072$ states, $15,874,272$ transitions, and took on average $1,847.82$ seconds (≈ 30 minutes) to be analyzed. As for Dynamic Voting, the massive increase in the number of states, the number of transitions, and analysis time is due to the computational complexity added by the frequent firings of the operation driver subnets' timed transitions.

5.1.3 The Heterogeneous Protocol

Operation Availability The read and write operation availabilities of the Heterogeneous Protocol related to the (uniform) process availability with assuming frequent operations and by employing operation drivers are depicted in Figure 5.11 (a) and (b), respectively. The Figures 5.11 (c) and (d) show the operation availabilities related to process availability in log-scale.

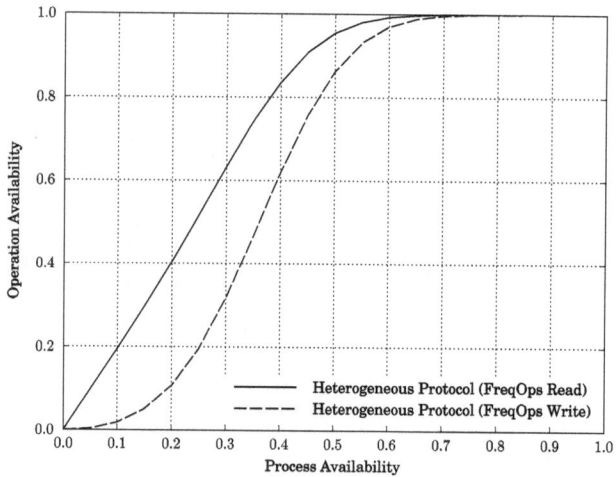

(a) Read Operation Availability (Solid Line) and Write Operation Availability (Dashed Line) over Process Availability Assuming Frequent Operations

Figure 5.11: Heterogeneous Protocol Operation Availability Results

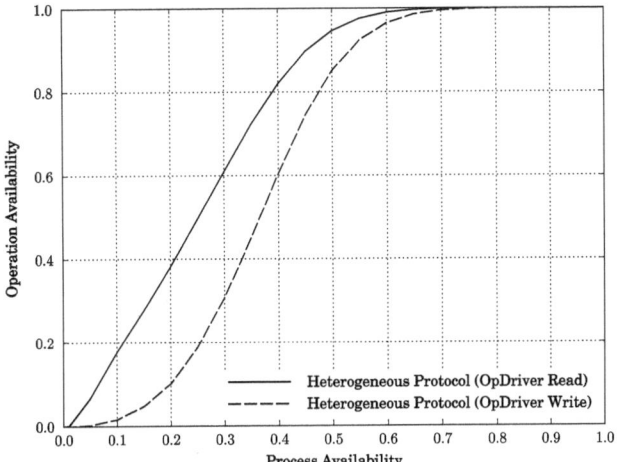

(b) Read Operation Availability (Solid Line) and Write Operation Availability (Dashed Line) over Process Availability using Operation Drivers

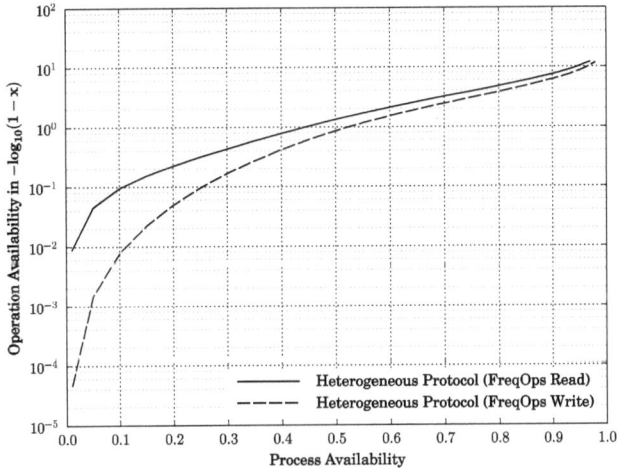

(c) Read Operation Availability (Solid Line) and Write Operation Availability (Dashed Line) in Log-scale over Process Availability Assuming Frequent Operations

Figure 5.11 (cont.): Heterogeneous Protocol Operation Availability Results

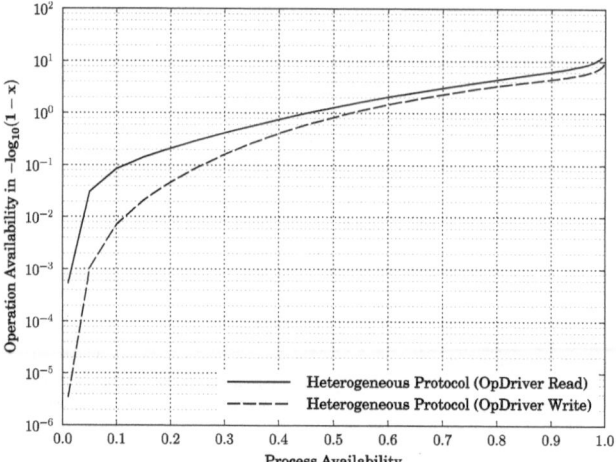

(d) Read Operation Availability (Solid Line) and Write Operation Availability (Dashed Line) in Log-scale over Process Availability using Operation Drivers

Figure 5.11 (cont.): Heterogeneous Protocol Operation Availability Results

Message Complexity   The Figures 5.12 (a) and (b) relate the structural message complexity to process availability for the read and the write operation, respectively. The average message complexity is related to process availability by the Figures 5.12 (c) and (d) for the read and the write operation, respectively.

Regardless of whether frequent operations are assumed or operation drivers are employed, the structural read operation message complexity is identical beyond a process availability of 0.15. With respect to the write operation, this is the case for a process availability exceeding 0.1. The same is true for the average message complexity with the respective process availabilities being 0.3 and 0.25.

Being a hybrid protocol composed of Majority Consensus Voting and the Grid Protocol, the high message complexity values for low process availabilities – and in particular for a process availability of 0.01 – are attributed to the stages using the Grid Protocol. The relative times spent in the stages of the dynamics for this process availability are

Dynamics Stage	1	2	3	4	5
Relative Time	0.00000	0.05619	0.00365	0.06056	0.03413

Dynamics Stage	6	7	8	9	
Relative Time	0.06809	0.09220	0.02890	0.65627	

Heterogeneous Protocol: Relative Time Spent in Stages for a
Process Availability of 0.01 and using Operation Drivers

revealing that 65.627 percent of time is spent in stage 9 in which the Grid
Protocol is used. Hence, the same argumentation as for the high message
complexity values of the Dynamic Grid Protocol applies to the Heterogeneous Protocol.

In contrast to the Dynamic Grid Protocol and Dynamic Voting, the structural read operation message complexity is not monotonically increasing
(for sufficiently high process availabilities). It reaches its peak value of 3.22
messages for a process availability of 0.8, regardless of whether frequent
operations are assumed or operation drivers are used. Neglecting the Grid
Protocol-induced high message complexity values for process availabilities
up to 0.1 for a fair comparison, the overall minimal structural read operation message complexity is 1.13 messages for a process availability of 0.15 if

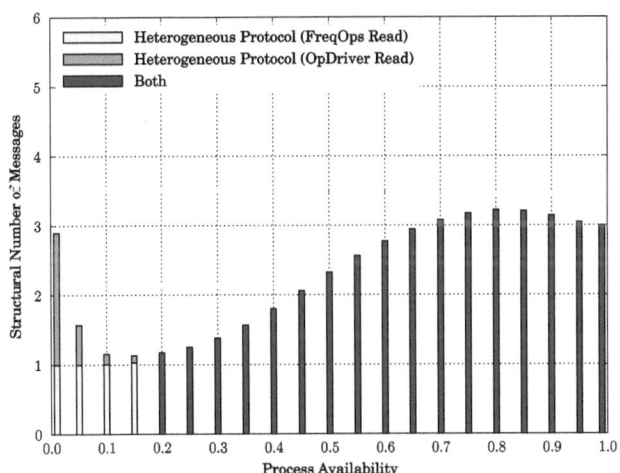

(a) Read Operation Structural Message Complexity Assuming Frequent Operations and using Operation Drivers

Figure 5.12: Heterogeneous Protocol Message Complexity Results

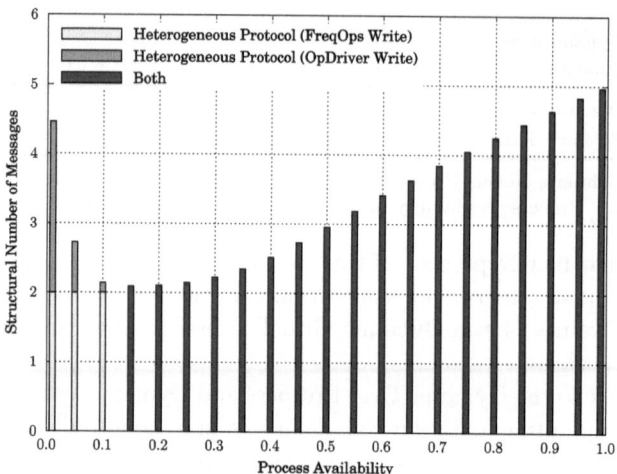

(b) Write Operation Structural Message Complexity Assuming Frequent Operations and using Operation Drivers

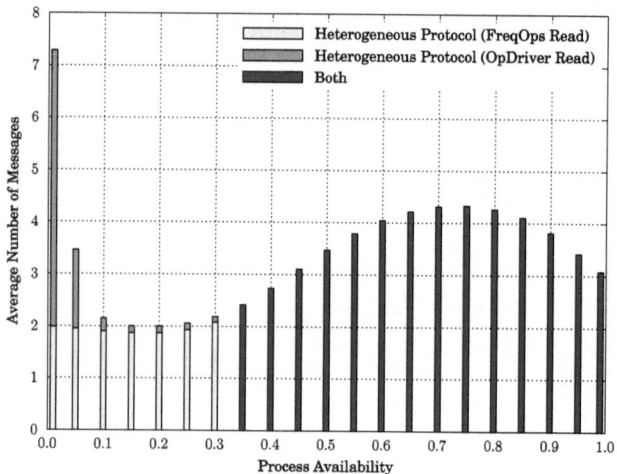

(c) Read Operation Average Message Complexity Assuming Frequent Operations and using Operation Drivers

Figure 5.12 (cont.): Heterogeneous Protocol Message Complexity Results

operation drivers are used. When assuming frequent operations, the overall minimal structural read operation message complexity is 1.01 messages for a process availability of 0.1. The structural write operation message

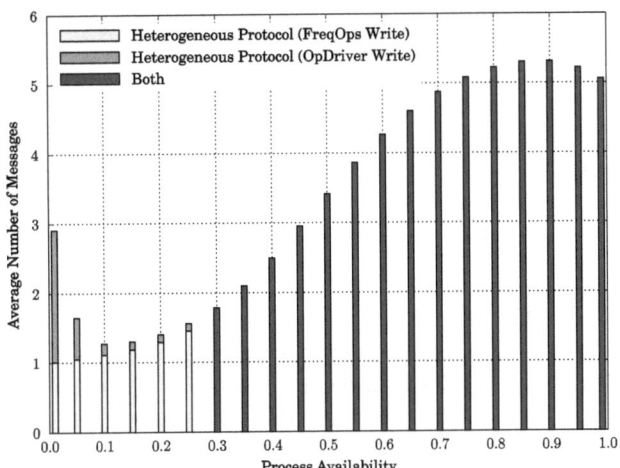

(d) Write Operation Average Message Complexity Assuming
Frequent Operations and using Operation Drivers

Figure 5.12 (cont.): Heterogeneous Protocol Message Complexity Results

complexity is – like for the Dynamic Grid Protocol and Dynamic Voting –
monotonically increasing, in case of using operation drivers starting from a
process availability of 0.15.

Concerning the average operation message complexity under the frequent
operations assumption, it reaches its peak value of 4.33 (5.33) messages for
a process availability of 0.75 (0.9) for the read (write) operation. Employing operation drivers, the average read operation message complexity peak
value of 4.33 messages is reached for a process availability of 0.75 when
not considering process availabilities lower than 0.1. The average write operation message complexity peak value of 5.32 messages is reached with a
process availability of 0.9.

As for Dynamic Voting and the Dynamic Grid Protocol, the structural
read operation message complexity in Figure 5.12 (a) is always lower than
the structural write operation message complexity in Figure 5.12 (b), irre-
spectively of using operation drivers or assuming frequent operations. As
shown in Figure 5.12 (c) and 5.12 (d), the average read operation message
complexity is lower than the average write operation message complexity
for process availabilities higher than 0.5, regardless of whether operation
drivers are employed or frequent operations are assumed. For process availabilities lower than or equal to 0.5, the read operation has a higher average

message complexity than the write operation. Note the different scale of the average message complexity figures.

Time Distribution The relative time spent in each stage of the dynamics related to process availability for the Heterogeneous Protocol is depicted in Figure 5.13. As expected, in general, the higher (lower) the process availability, the more (less) time is spent in higher stages of the dynamics.

System Model Facts The continuous-time Markov chains of the Heterogeneous Protocol with nine processes and assuming frequent operations have $14,326$ states, $128,934$ transitions, and took on average 59.71 seconds to be analyzed. The continuous-time Markov chains of the Heterogeneous Protocol when using operation drivers have $1,542,144$ states, $15,982,925$ transitions, and took on average $2,871.71$ seconds (≈ 47 minutes) to be analyzed. Here again, the increase in the number of states, the number of transitions, and analysis time stems from the computational complexity added by the frequent timed transition firings of the operation driver subnets.

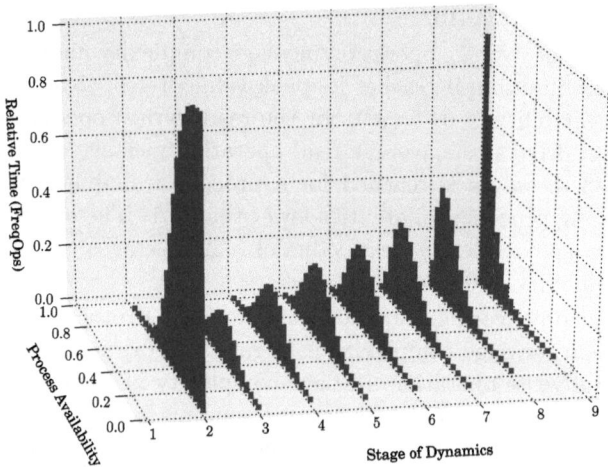

(a) Relative Time Spent in each Stage of the Dynamics over Process Availability Assuming Frequent Operations

Figure 5.13: Heterogeneous Protocol Time Distribution

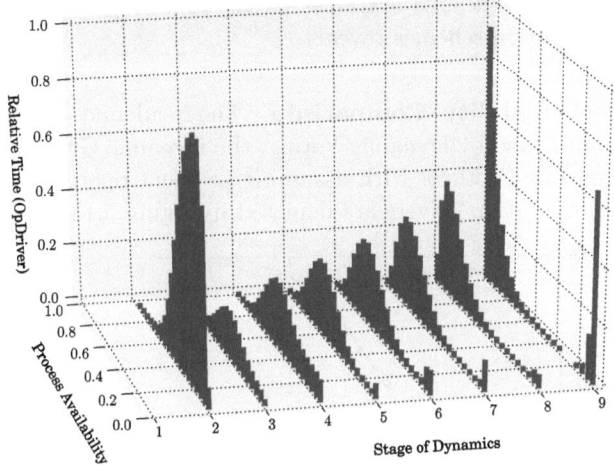

(b) Relative Time Spent in each Stage of the Dynamics over Process Availability using Operation Drivers

Figure 5.13 (cont.): Heterogeneous Protocol Time Distribution

After having presented the individual evaluation results, the data replication schemes are compared to each other in the next section.

5.2 Comparison of the Three Data Replication Schemes

The driving idea underlying heterogeneous dynamic data replication schemes is to harmoniously orchestrate several different static data replication schemes as one whole, thereby mitigating the individual deficiencies of their homogeneous dynamic counterparts with respect to a specific quality measure trade-off and allowing for a new and more balanced one. In this example evaluation, the Heterogeneous Protocol is composed of the structured static Grid Protocol and the unstructured static Majority Consensus Voting for the purpose of (1) providing operation availabilities like Dynamic Voting while (2) exhibiting a message complexity similar to the Dynamic Grid Protocol. Clearly, operation availability and message complexity are contradicting measures: Majority Consensus Voting prioritizes operation availability over message complexity while the Grid Protocol sacrifices some operation availability in favor of message complexity. The Heterogeneous

Protocol balances these two extremes as the following comparison of the three data replication schemes reveals.

Operation Availability Comparison The read and write operation availabilities provided by Dynamic Voting, the Dynamic Grid Protocol, and the Heterogeneous Protocol with assuming frequent operations as well as by employing operation drivers are depicted in Figure 5.14.

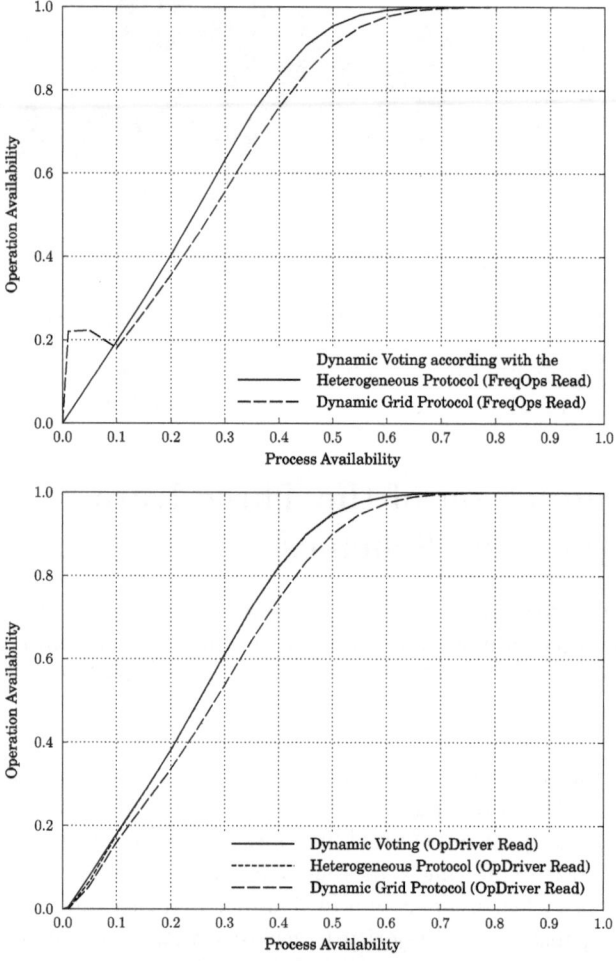

Figure 5.14: Operation Availability Results Comparison

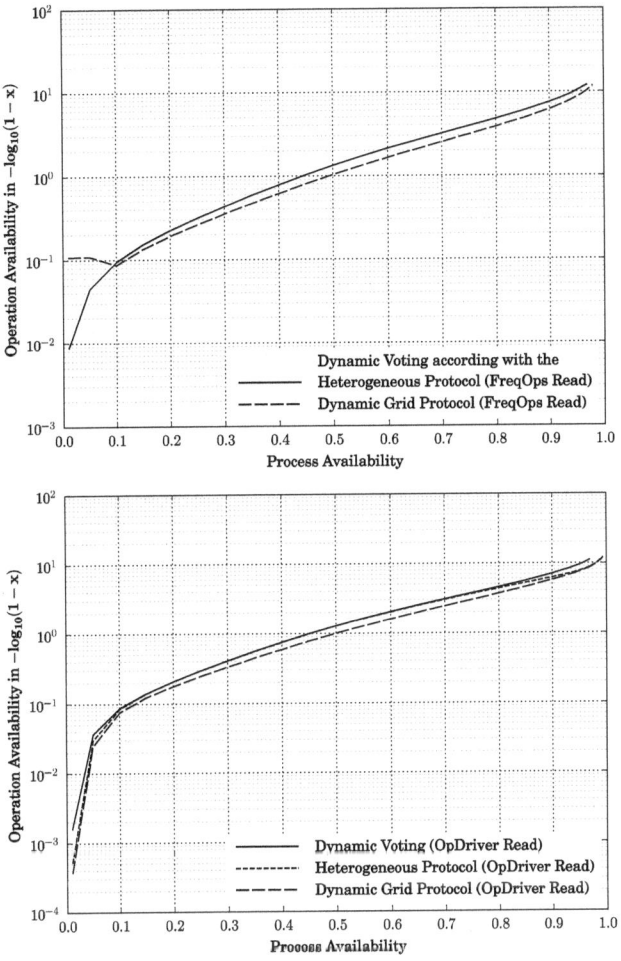

Figure 5.14 (cont.): Operation Availability Results Comparison

In case of assuming frequent operations, the Heterogeneous Protocol provides the exact same operation availability as the highly resilient Dynamic
Voting for both, for the read operation as well as for the write operation.
This is attributed to the fact that the Heterogeneous Protocol can tolerate
a process failure wherever Dynamic Voting can, due to the Heterogeneous
Protocol using Majority Consensus Voting particularly in low stages of the
dynamics (in which the Grid Protocol is not as resilient to process failures

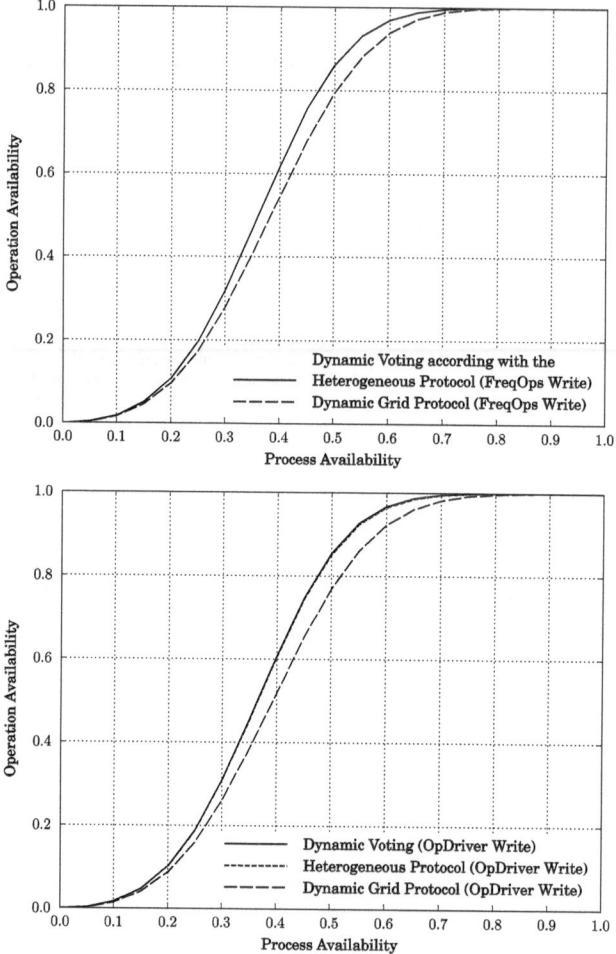

Figure 5.14 (cont.): Operation Availability Results Comparison

as Majority Consensus Voting). Not considering process availabilities lower than 0.1, the Dynamic Grid Protocol is only able to offer the same read operation availability as the Heterogeneous Protocol for a process availability as high as 0.98. The write operation availability of the Dynamic Grid Protocol matches the write operation availability of the Heterogeneous Protocol starting from a process availability of 0.991.

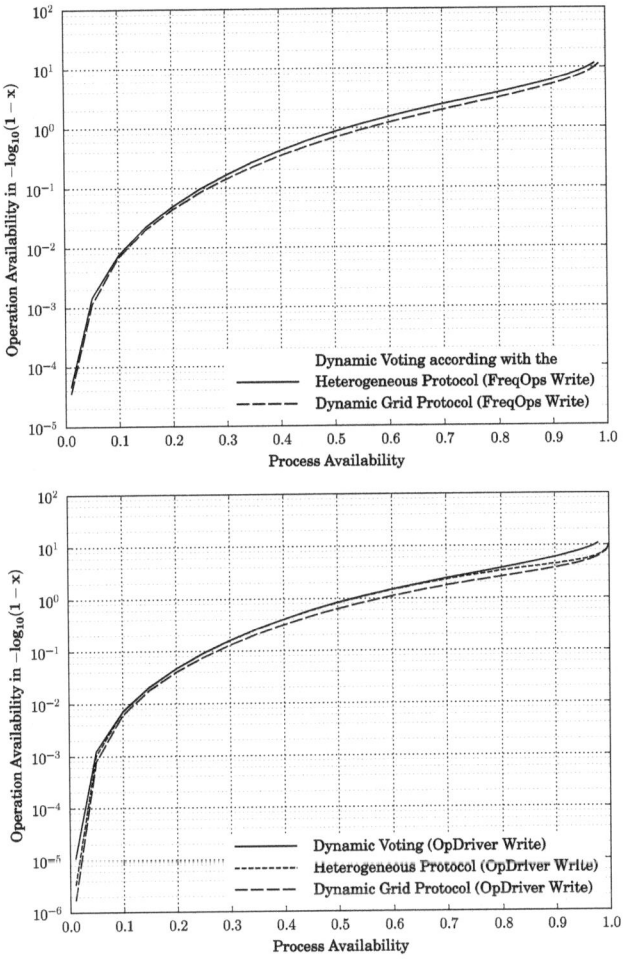

Figure 5.14 (cont.): Operation Availability Results Comparison

With the employment of operation drivers, the Heterogeneous Protocol offers slightly lower operation availabilities than Dynamic Voting, which is best perceivable in the log-scale availability graphs. For the read operation, it reaches the operation availability of Dynamic Voting with a process availability of 0.98 for process availabilities exceeding 0.994. For the write operation, it approaches but does not reach the write operation availability of Dynamic Voting, even for a process availability of and beyond 0.999. As discussed previously, this fact is attributed to Dynamic Voting employing the unstructured static Majority Consensus Voting for all stages of the dynamics while the Heterogeneous Protocol employs Majority Consensus Voting only for specific stages of the dynamics. However, the differences are not substantial as can be recognized from Figure 5.14. On average, the difference is 0.00075659546 for the read operation and 0.00059773805 for the write operation, diminishing with increasing process availabilities. The higher average difference for the read operation is explained by considering the read operation availability for a process availability of 0.1. For this process availability, the Heterogeneous Protocol offers a read operation availability of 0.067756 while Dynamic Voting provides a read operation availability of 0.080652. Cleared of this anomaly, the average read operation availability difference becomes 0.00041940259.

The Dynamic Grid Protocol shows an average operation availability difference to Dynamic Voting of 0.015891933 for the read operation and of 0.016251907 for the write operation, both of which are by two orders of magnitude higher than the differences from the Heterogeneous Protocol to Dynamic Voting. As it is the case for the Heterogeneous Protocol, the Dynamic Grid Protocol offers the same operation availability as Dynamic Voting for process availabilities exceeding 0.994 for the read operation while not reaching the write operation availability of Dynamic Voting. Compared to the Heterogeneous Protocol, the Dynamic Grid Protocol offers the same operation availability beyond a process availability of 0.99 for the read operation while approximating but not reaching the write operation availability offered by the Heterogeneous Protocol.

Message Complexity Comparison: Dynamic Voting and the Heterogeneous Protocol The read and write operation message complexity of Dynamic Voting and the Heterogeneous Protocol with assuming frequent operations as well as by employing operation drivers is shown in Figure 5.15. Apart from the high message complexity values for process availabilities lower than 0.1, the Heterogeneous Protocol has a lower structural and average read operation message complexity than Dynamic Voting, regardless of whether frequent operations are assumed or operation drivers are employed. Due to the $^1/_{10}$th message filter applied, the difference in read operation message complexity is not recognizable from the figure for process availabilities of about 0.5 but becomes more and more apparent with increasing process availabilities.

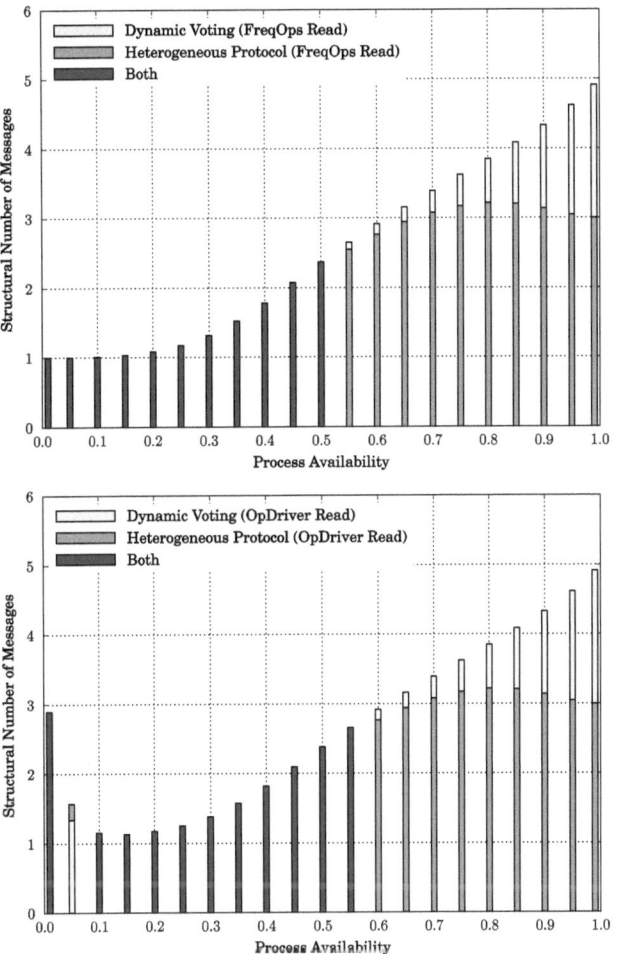

Figure 5.15: Message Complexity Results Comparison of Dynamic Voting and
the Heterogeneous Protocol

Alike, the Heterogeneous Protocol has a lower structural write operation
message complexity than Dynamic Voting, independent of whether frequent
operations are assumed or operation drivers are employed. However, the
difference is only marginal such that it is not thoroughly perceivable in
the figure. Concerning the average write operation message complexity
and assuming frequent operations, the two data replication schemes are

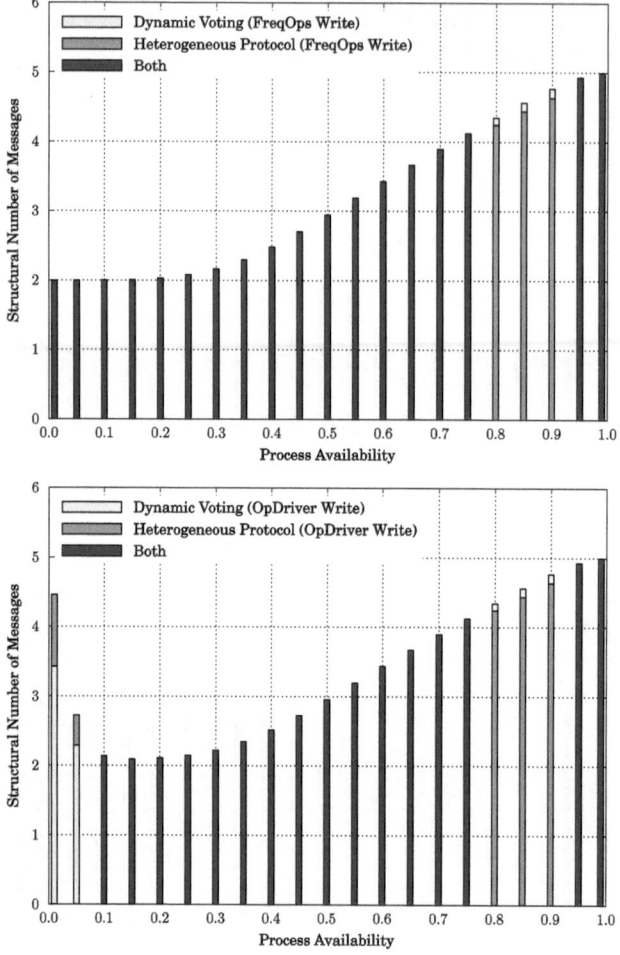

Figure 5.15 (cont.): Message Complexity Results Comparison of Dynamic Voting and the Heterogeneous Protocol

similar: Dynamic Voting requires on average 0.01895 fewer messages than the Heterogeneous Protocol for process availabilities exceeding 0.9 while the Heterogeneous Protocol – also on average – requires 0.05056 fewer messages for process availabilities lower than 0.9. The according average differences when employing operation drivers are 0.01842 and 0.06, also with respect to the process availability of 0.9 that represents the switching boundary.

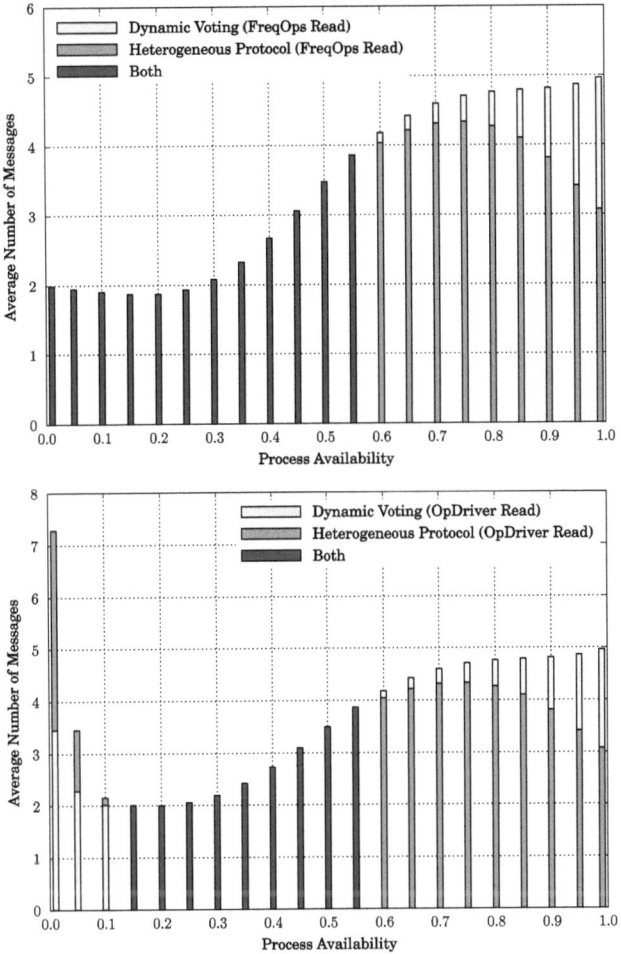

Figure 5.15 (cont.): Message Complexity Results Comparison of Dynamic Voting and the Heterogeneous Protocol

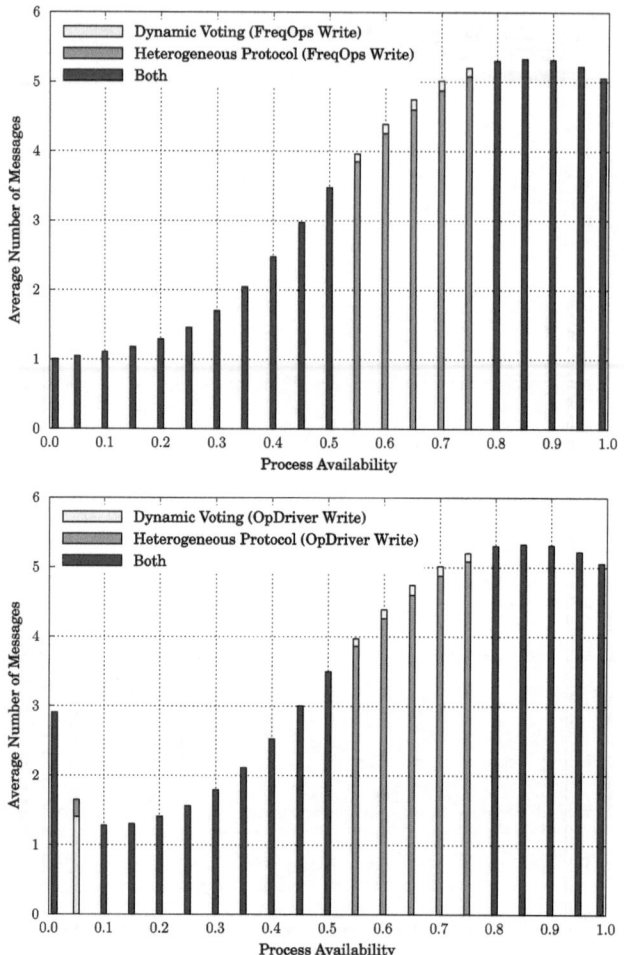

Figure 5.15 (cont.): Message Complexity Results Comparison of Dynamic Voting and the Heterogeneous Protocol

**Message Complexity Comparison: the Dynamic Grid Protocol
and the Heterogeneous Protocol** The read and write operation message complexity of the Dynamic Grid Protocol and the Heterogeneous Protocol with assuming frequent operations as well as by employing operation
drivers is shown in Figure 5.16. Under the frequent operations assumption, the structural read operation message complexity of the Dynamic Grid

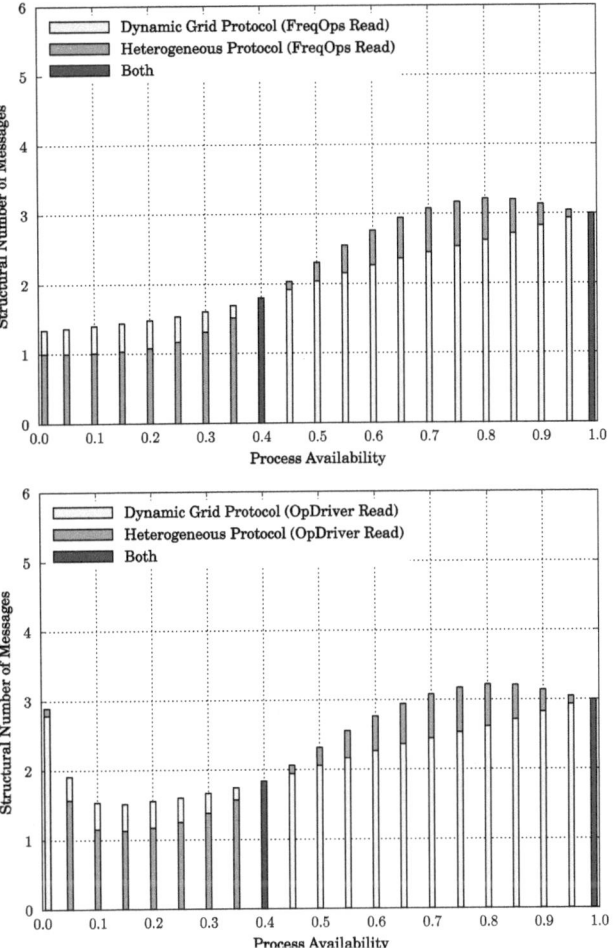

Figure 5.16: Message Complexity Results Comparison of the Dynamic Grid
Protocol and the Heterogeneous Protocol

Protocol is higher than that of the Heterogeneous Protocol for process availabilities lower than or equal to 0.4 while it is lower for process availabilities
higher than 0.4. The average differences are 0.31111 and 0.19482, respectively. The same is true when using operation drivers with the average
differences being 0.29125 and 0.20179, respectively. After all, the differences in the values are identical for a process availability exceeding 0.3,

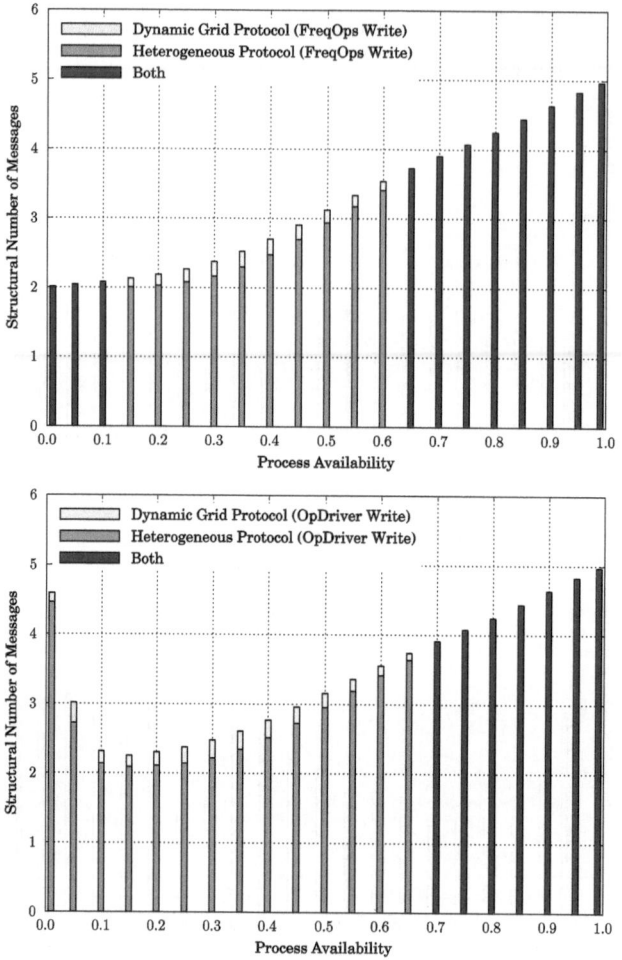

Figure 5.16 (cont.): Message Complexity Results Comparison of the Dynamic Grid Protocol and the Heterogeneous Protocol

independent of whether operation drivers are used or frequent operations are assumed. However, the structural read operation message complexity when employing operation drivers has slightly higher absolute values for lower process availabilities. This is also the case for the structural write operation message complexity and a process availability higher than or equal to 0.6. For a process availability lower than or equal to 0.75, the Dynamic

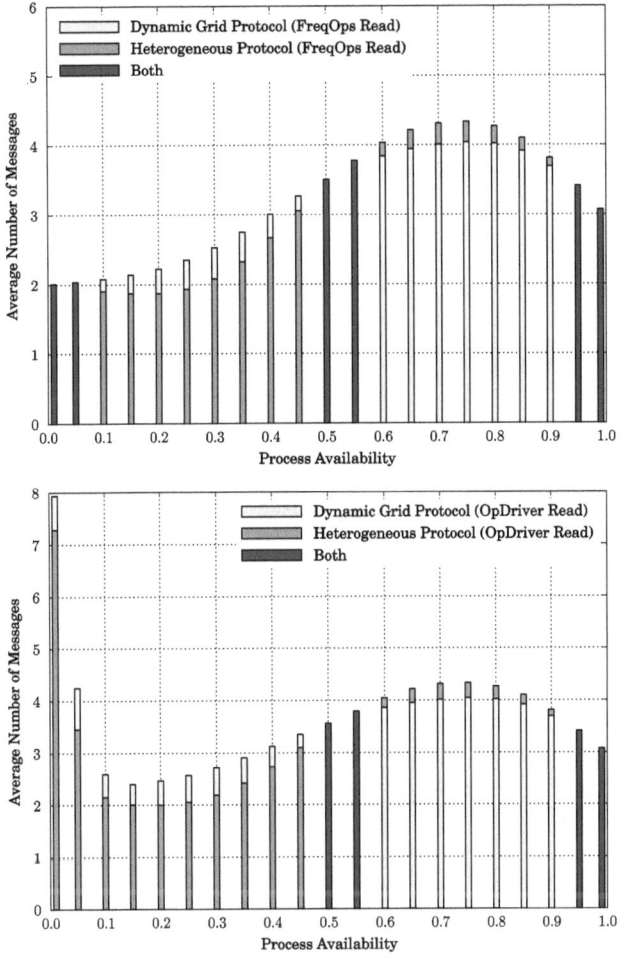

Figure 5.16 (cont.): Message Complexity Results Comparison of the Dynamic
Grid Protocol and the Heterogeneous Protocol

Grid Protocol has a higher structural write operation message complexity
than the Heterogeneous Protocol, and vice versa for process availabilities
beyond. The according average differences are 0.1325 and 0.00524 when
assuming frequent operations and 0.18125 and 0.00524 when employing operation drivers. In summary, the Heterogeneous Protocol has a structural
write operation message complexity that is almost identical to that of the

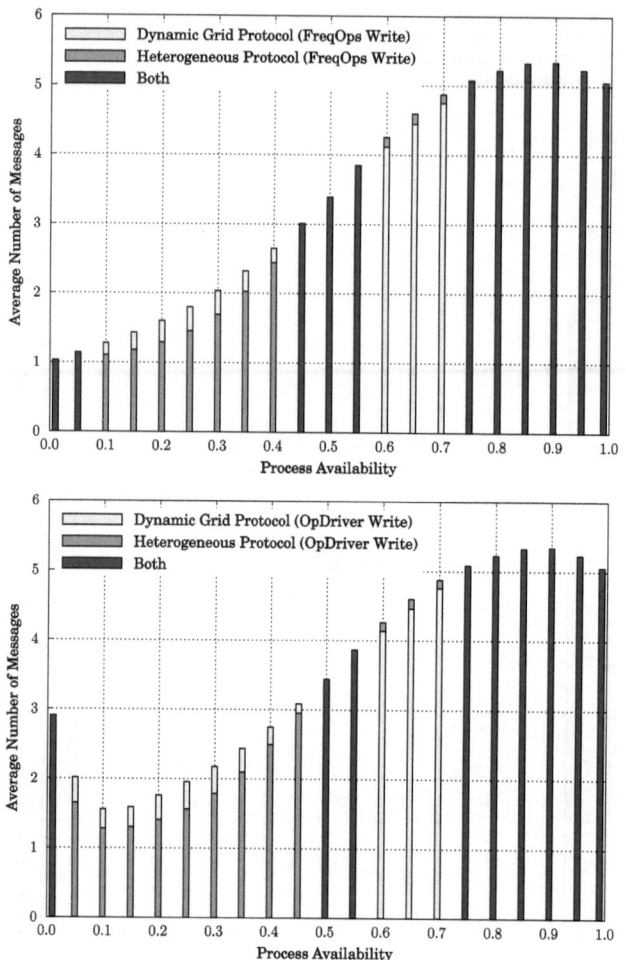

Figure 5.16 (cont.): Message Complexity Results Comparison of the Dynamic Grid Protocol and the Heterogeneous Protocol

Dynamic Grid Protocol. The structural read operation message complexity of the Heterogeneous Protocol compared to the Dynamic Grid Protocol is slightly inferior for high process availabilities and vice versa for low process availabilities.

The average write operation message complexity of the Dynamic Grid Protocol is rather similar to that of the Heterogeneous Protocol, regardless of whether operation drivers are employed or frequent operations are assumed. In general, for low to medium process availabilities, the values when using operation drivers are slightly higher compared to the case of assuming frequent operations. Irrespective of assuming frequent operations or employing operation drivers, the Dynamic Grid Protocol exhibits the same average write operation message complexity starting from a process availability of 0.75. Concerning the Heterogeneous Protocol, using operation drivers causes a minimal higher average write operation message complexity than under the frequent operations assumption throughout the process availability range. If assuming frequent operations, the average difference of the two data replication schemes is 0.213 for a process availability lower than or equal to 0.45, 0.08857 for a process availability in between 0.45 and 0.85, and 0.007 beyond a process availability of 0.85. In case of employing operation drivers, the respective average differences are 0.281, 0.09167, and 0.007. As for the average write operation message complexity, the average read operation message complexity of the Heterogeneous Protocol compared to the Dynamic Grid Protocol is quite similar. Notice the different scale caused by the extremely high average read operation message complexity value for a process availability of 0.01. Regardless of whether frequent operations are assumed or operation drivers are employed, the Grid Protocol has the same average read operation message complexity starting from a process availability of 0.8. With respect to the Heterogeneous Protocol, the according process availability is 0.75. Assuming frequent operations, the average difference of the two data replication schemes for a process availability lower than or equal to 0.5 is 0.25545 and it is 0.08269 for process availabilities beyond. In case of employing operation drivers, the average differences are 0.45454 and 0.08038, respectively.

Operation Mean Time to Failure Finally, in Figure 5.17, the operation mean time to failure of Dynamic Voting, the Dynamic Grid Protocol, and the Heterogeneous Protocol is compared for the read and the write operation when assuming frequent operations as well as by employing operation drivers. Recall that the mean time to repair (MTTR) is assumed to be 3.88 days [Long, Muir et al., 1995]. The mean time to failure (MTTF) of an operation depends on its availability a and the MTTR as given by the formula MTTF $= (\text{MTTR} \cdot a)/(1-a)$. Note that the operation availabilities given below are rounded to five decimal places and that the mean time to failure values are rounded to two decimal places while the calculation has been done with a precision of twelve decimal places.

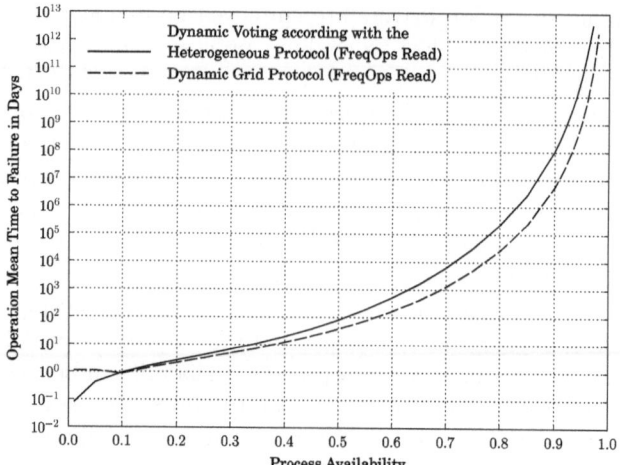

(a) Read Operation Mean Time to Failure Assuming Frequent Operations

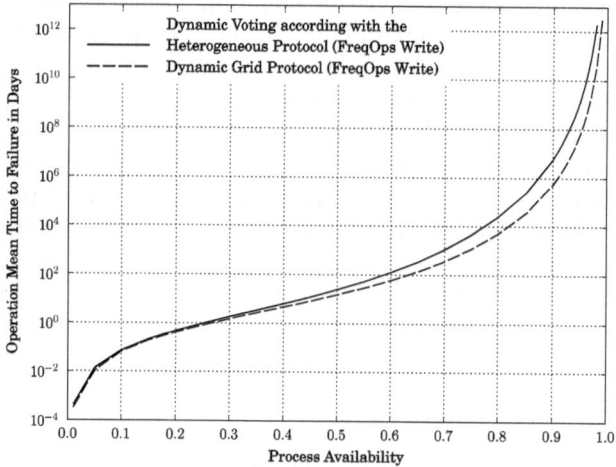

(b) Write Operation Mean Time to Failure Assuming Frequent Operations

Figure 5.17: Mean Time to Failure Results Comparison

When assuming frequent operations, the Heterogeneous Protocol has the same mean time to failure as Dynamic Voting for the read as well as for the write operation. For example, for a uniform process availability of 0.8,

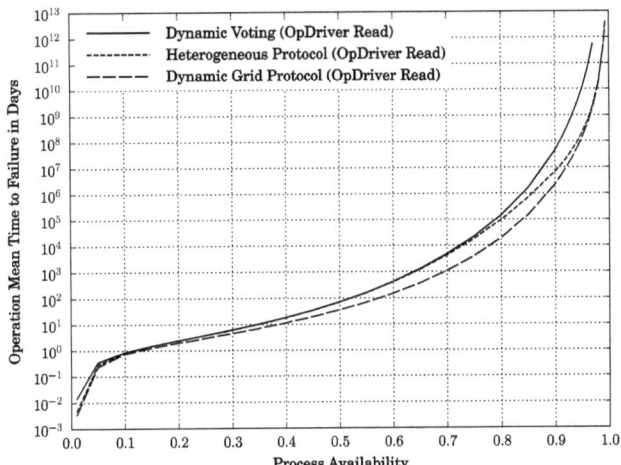

(c) Read Operation Mean Time to Failure using Operation Drivers

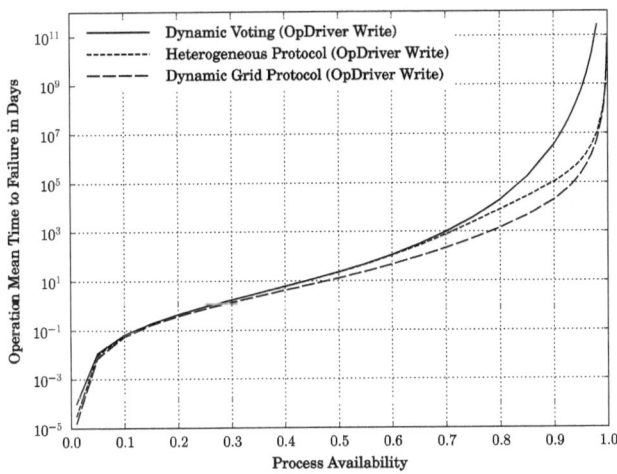

(d) Write Operation Mean Time to Failure using Operation Drivers

Figure 5.17 (cont.): Mean Time to Failure Results Comparison

the write operation availability is 0.99985, calculating to a mean time to failure of 25,036.27 days or 68.59 years. The read operation availability is 0.99998, calculating to a mean time to failure of 225,357.51 days or 617.41

years. The Dynamic Grid Protocol has a shorter operation mean time to failure for process availabilities higher than 0.1 for the read operation and an overall shorter write operation mean time to failure compared to Dynamic Voting, respectively, the Heterogeneous Protocol: Also for a uniform process availability of 0.8, its write operation availability is 0.99924, resulting in a mean time to failure of 5,081.86 days or 13.92 years. The read operation availability is 0.99986, calculating to a mean time to failure of 26,288.14 days or 72.02 years.

When employing operation drivers, the Heterogeneous Protocol has an overall shorter operation mean time to failure compared to Dynamic Voting but with the differences being small up to a process availability of 0.55. Beyond this process availability, the difference gradually increases with increasing process availabilities. The read operation mean time to failure of the Heterogeneous Protocol and the Dynamic Grid Protocol is identical starting from a process availability of 0.991. For the write operation mean time to failure, it is identical for a process availability starting from 0.995. However, the Heterogeneous Protocol improves on the Dynamic Grid Protocol's operation mean time to failure for process availabilities up to 0.991 and 0.995 for the read operation and the write operation, respectively. Again for a process availability of 0.8, the write operation of Dynamic Voting has an availability of 0.99980 and a mean time to failure of 19,866.41 days or 54.43 years. Its read operation availability is 0.99997, resulting in a mean time to failure of 145,424.09 days or 398.42 years. The write operation availability of the Dynamic Grid Protocol is 0.99725, calculating to a mean time to failure of 1,409.35 days or 3.86 years. Its read operation has an availability of 0.99980, resulting in a mean time to failure of 19,397.38 days or 53.14 years. The write operation of the Heterogeneous Protocol has an availability of 0.99950, resulting in a mean time to failure of 7,884.66 days or 21.60 years. Its read operation has an availability of 0.99996, resulting in a mean time to failure of 96,915.38 days or 265.52 years.

The high mean time to failure values in the order of years are explained by the very high operation availabilities in conjunction with a long mean time to repair of 3.88 days [Long, Muir et al., 1995]. In order to be able to provide such high operation availabilities, the long mean time to repair must be compensated by a very long mean time to failure. Otherwise, the high operation availabilities cannot be reached. For lower mean time to repair values, the mean time to failure values also become lower since high operation availabilities do not require such very long mean times to failure.

Recall that when employing operation drivers, the frequency of attempting epoch change operations was artificially set to 30 minutes. The read, write, and epoch change operation availabilities provided by a dynamic data replication scheme are integrally dependent on the individual process availabilities that determine in which stages of the dynamics the sojourn times cumulate as well as on the process failure patterns leading to those stages. Hence, for specific uniform process availabilities, the epoch change operation frequency of 30 minutes may not be optimal neither for Dynamic Voting, nor the Dynamic Grid Protocol, nor the Heterogeneous Protocol. In particular for the latter, a reconfiguration frequency that is adapted depending on the current stage of the dynamics using Majority Consensus Voting or the Grid Protocol allows to fine-adjust the Heterogeneous Protocol to specific process availabilities. Finding the optimal epoch change operation frequency per (uniform) process availability is beyond the scope and purpose of this example evaluation. Nevertheless, it can be found by employing the system model analogously to the manner described by Chen, Wang et al. [2004a]; Wang, Chen et al. [2000] for the original system model due to Chen and Wang [1996b] (cf. Section 4.2).

5.3 Summary

As shown by the comparison of the three dynamic data replication schemes in the previous section and under the evaluation setting as described in this chapter's introduction, the Heterogeneous Protocol offers – in case of assuming frequent operations – the very same operation availabilities as the highly resilient Dynamic Voting while having a message complexity in the order of the communication-efficient Dynamic Grid Protocol. With employing operation drivers, the operation availabilities provided by the Heterogeneous Protocol are to a small extent lower than those of Dynamic Voting while still being an improvement over the operation availabilities offered by the Dynamic Grid Protocol, at the cost of a slight increase in message complexity. Thus, if willing to trade a little message complexity for increased operation availability, the Heterogeneous Protocol may qualify as a drop-in replacement for the Dynamic Grid Protocol in application scenarios in which both, high operation availability as well as a low message complexity is required.

This simple evaluation example has exemplary illustrated the potential of heterogeneous dynamic data replication schemes in allowing to choose a more balanced trade-off between quality measures than possible using traditional homogeneous dynamic data replication schemes.

6 Conclusion

Quorum-based data replication is a well-established concept to improve operation availability on critical data objects in distributed systems whose components are (naturally) imperfect and subject to failures. Therefore, it is an important base concept to construct dependable distributed systems. In recent years, distributed systems have evolved from traditional statically deployed and fixed-sized systems to dynamic distributed systems. Their topology – in terms of the number of processes and their interconnecting communication infrastructure – cannot be immutably predetermined at design-time but instead is flexible and fluctuating with processes joining and deliberately departing from the system at run-time. The advent of such dynamic distributed systems demands for new means to cope with the emerging challenges posed by the dynamics. These challenges are a system's ability to dynamically adapt to changing topologies – and possibly also to changing application requirements – and this adaptation to be performed in a best-possible manner with respect to the quality measure trade-off the system is specified for and supposed to implement. The former demands for a multitude of quorum systems complying to various different static data replication schemes to be available to the system in order to be prepared for any topology (and application requirement) possibly arising at run-time. The latter requires an adequately fast evaluation means to guide the selection of a particularly appropriate data replication scheme among those ones available to the system. This thesis has contributed to both of these aspects by a uniform data replication scheme specification formalism that has been presented in Chapter 3 and by a system model framework for the analytical evaluation of data replication schemes that has been presented in Chapter 4.

Static and Dynamic Data Replication Schemes   Static data replication schemes have an upper bound on operation availability because of a symmetry constraint among the read and write operation availability graphs [Theel and Pagnia, 1998]. They cannot react to process failures beyond a scheme-specific threshold of processes. In contrast, the dynamics mechanism of dynamic data replication schemes allows to reconfigure the quorum system at run-time: A process whose failure has been detected is excluded from the quorum system until its eventual recovery upon which it is reintegrated into the quorum system. By this dynamics, dynamic data replication schemes can maintain operation availability in cases static data replication schemes have to cease operation. Although there are some cases in which the opposite holds true [Jajodia and Mutchler, 1990], dynamic data replication schemes usually provide increased operation availabilities.

Unbounded Homogeneous Dynamic Data Replication Schemes
Such a dynamics in reaction to process failures and recoveries is per design limited to vary the number of processes in an a priori defined and static upper-bounded range of processes for which all potentially required quorum systems are predetermined and known to the system, either implicitly or explicitly. It is not possible to integrate new processes into the system at run-time – and thereby surpassing the upper bound – due to the system lacking knowledge of appropriate quorum systems considering the new processes. For some dynamic data replication schemes such as for Dynamic Voting, there are add-on protocols that allow the integration of new processes at run-time [Jajodia and Mutchler, 1990]. But, these protocols are scheme-specific and thus are not applicable in general. This fact hinders the application of traditional dynamic data replication schemes to more dynamic environments demanding for enhanced flexibility in the number of processes manageable at run-time that exceeds the capability of failure-driven dynamics. Such environments cannot be adequately addressed by traditional bounded dynamic data replication schemes.

Exactly this flexibility is provided by voting structure shapes that have been introduced in Chapter 3. Essentially, a voting structure shape captures the specific inherent quorum system construction rules of a particular static data replication scheme in a semantics-enriched graph structure. From this graph structure, implicit quorum system representations complying to the particular static data replication scheme but for arbitrary numbers of processes can be derived by a universal instantiation algorithm. The resulting implicit quorum system representation for a particular number of processes – in terms of a tree-shaped voting structure as introduced in Chapter 3 – is interpreted by a universal algorithm that yields operation-specific quorums to perform operations with. Employing voting structure shapes, a quorum system reconfiguration that is due to the failure or recovery of a process or a process joining or deliberately departing from the system is handled uniformly by (1) instantiating a voting structure shape for the new number of processes and then (2) consistently switching to this new quorum system, thereby realizing homogeneous dynamic data replication schemes that are not restricted by an upper bound on the number of processes.

Heterogeneous Dynamic Data Replication Schemes A second dimension of flexibility – beyond being able to manage arbitrary numbers of processes at run-time – has been introduced in Chapter 3 by the uniform data replication scheme specification formalism that enables dynamic data replication schemes to become heterogeneous. Instead of homogeneously using the same data replication scheme-inherent quorum system construction rules for all numbers of processes, a heterogeneous dynamic data replication scheme is free to use different ones for different numbers of processes. Like there is no single data replication scheme superior for every application scenario, there is also none superior for every number of processes: Unstructured data replication schemes face scalability problems with increasing numbers of processes while structured data replication schemes can only unleash their full potential if the underlying logical structure the processes are arranged in is sufficiently populated by processes. Heterogeneity allows to counter these scheme-specific deficiencies by utilizing the respective best-option static data replication scheme per number of processes, thereby allowing a more individual and fine-grained trade-off between quality measures for a concrete application scenario than possible with traditional homogeneous dynamic data replication schemes. This flexibility in the selection of appropriate data replication schemes as well as in the number of processes manageable at run-time greatly expands the design- and application space of quorum-based data replication schemes.

Exploring the Data Replication Scheme Design Space Having the means to potentially use particularly well-suited data replication schemes apparently provokes the question of which concrete (heterogeneous) data replication scheme to employ for a given application scenario. Providing an answer to this question requires to explore the – due to heterogeneity greatly increased – data replication scheme design space in search for good candidates and these candidates to be evaluated with respect to the particular quality measure trade-off matching the application scenario requirements. In light of constantly evolving dynamic systems, this question cannot be answered definitely at design-time but also has to be (repeatedly) addressed at run-time, namely whenever the system's topology or the application scenario requirements change. For this reason, evaluation methods based on simulation are inappropriate because of their massive time complexity or, if run in a reasonably upper-bounded period of time, their approximate nature of results. Contrarily, methods based on stochastic analysis are fast and accurate but require a sensible and careful crafting of the system model for it to provide meaningful results and to remain tractable at all. This requirement is attributed to the necessarily higher degree of abstraction of an analytical model compared to a simulation model since an analytical model which is as detailed as a simulation model is often not tractable due to exponential time and space requirements.

Analytical Evaluation of Heterogeneous Dynamic Schemes While static data replication schemes can be modeled by and are easily analyzed via calculating combinatorial formulas (given some simplifying assumptions such as perfect channels), modeling and analyzing dynamic data replication schemes is a much more sophisticated task due to the additional complexity introduced by the dynamics. There have been some approaches to the analytical evaluation of dynamic data replication schemes [Chen and Wang, 1996a,b,c; Chen, Wang et al., 2004a; Dugan and Ciardo, 1989; Jajodia and Mutchler, 1990; Pâris, 1986a; Wang, Chen et al., 2000]. Exceeding these approaches, the analytical evaluation framework that has been presented in Chapter 4 is (1) not restricted to a very specific subclass of unstructured homogeneous dynamic data replication schemes in terms of homogeneous dynamic variants of Majority Consensus Voting, it is (2) not specifically tailored towards a particular data replication scheme and thereby inapplicable to the evaluation of other schemes, and it is (3) not limited to write operation availability and its closely related measures as the only quality measures of interest.

The ability to evaluate unstructured as well as structured homogeneous and moreover heterogeneous dynamic data replication schemes – with static ones as a simple special case – is provided by employing the petri net counterparts of tree-shaped voting structures as quorum system representations in the system model. By varying the tree-shaped voting structure petri nets in the system model, different data replication schemes are easily reflected without the need for further modifications to the general system model. Exploiting this fact, the uniform data replication scheme specification formalism employing voting structure shapes alongside with the automatized transformation of the resulting tree-shaped voting structures into their petri net counterparts enables the data replication scheme options for a given application scenario to be evaluated in an automated manner, simply by providing the different data replication scheme specifications found while exploring the data replication scheme design space.

The framework allows to evaluate other quality measures besides operation availability and its related measure reliability for the write operation as well as for the read operation. An example is message complexity – a measure of operation costs in terms of the number of messages needed to effectuate a quorum – as has been evaluated in the example given in Chapter 5. Although operation availability is probably the most important quality measure, a data replication scheme always implements a trade-off between various quality measures and this trade-off needs to be evaluated in entirety for a fair and thorough comparison with other data replication schemes, in particular if the optimization goal is manyfold such that operation availability is not the only measure to optimize for.

Directions for Future Work Beyond data replication schemes using strict intersecting quorum systems, the evaluation framework is – in principle – also suited for the evaluation of probabilistic quorum systems [Iakab, Storm et al., 2010; Malkhi, Reiter et al., 2001] or byzantine quorum systems [Malkhi and Reiter, 1998]. A tree-shaped voting structure is essentially just a different notation for a tuple of sequences of sets and is therefore not inherently limited to strict intersecting quorum systems. However, the modifications required to accommodate the system model to a different notion of consistency or a different functional failure model have not been addressed here and are left for future work.

Depending on the point of view, the design space to explore in search of a particular well-suited (heterogeneous dynamic) data replication scheme for a given application scenario is either fortunately or unfortunately very large: It is fortunate that the design space provides a wide range of data replication schemes to choose from and this is just as well unfortunate since this many data replication schemes have to be explored and evaluated. As exploration and evaluation may have to be (repeatedly) performed at runtime, namely whenever a successive quorum system has to be installed in the system, a means to accelerate the search and selection process is desirable for a fast adaptation. Heuristic methods that bisect and filter the encountered and worthwhile to be evaluated data replication schemes may serve as a "traveler's guide to the design space" and are certainly an option – if accepting the inherent inaccuracy of heuristic decisions.

Another option are characteristic functions as sketched in the future work section of Chapter 4. Essentially, characteristic functions for dynamic data replication schemes are the counterparts of the well-known quality measure functions for static data replication schemes such as the combinatorial formulas to calculate operation availability. Unfortunately, for dynamic data replication schemes – and in particular for heterogeneous ones – such functions are not known yet. The presented analytical evaluation framework may serve as a well-founded base and validation means for the research of such characteristic functions and the impact of heterogeneity on the quality measure trade-off implemented by homogeneous dynamic data replication schemes. Ultimately, the question of which data replication schemes – if existent at all – (almost) match a given specification of quality measures may be rapidly addressed and answered, simply by calculating characteristic functions.

Bibliography

Martín Abadi and Leslie Lamport. Conjoining specifications. *ACM Transactions on Programming Languages and Systems*, 17(3):507–535, May 1995.

Divyakant Agrawal and Amr El Abbadi. The tree quorum protocol: An efficient approach for managing replicated data. In *Proceedings of the 16th Very Large Data Bases Conference (VLDB'90)*, pages 243–254. Morgan Kaufmann, August 1990.

Divyakant Agrawal and Amr El Abbadi. The generalized tree quorum protocol: An efficient approach for managing replicated data. *ACM Transactions on Database Systems*, 17(4):689–717, December 1992.

Mustaque Ahamad, Mostafa H. Ammar, and Shun Yan Cheung. Multidimensional voting: A general method for implementing synchronization in distributed systems. In *Proceedings of the 10th International Conference on Distributed Computing Systems (ICDCS'90)*, pages 362–369. IEEE Computer Society Press, May 1990.

Mustaque Ahamad, Mostafa H. Ammar, and Shun Yang Cheung. Multidimensional voting. *ACM Transactions on Computer Systems*, 9(4):398–431, November 1991.

Mustaque Ahamad, James E. Burns, Phillip W. Hutto, and Gil Neiger. Causal memory. In *Proceedings of the 5th International Workshop on Distributed Algorithms (WDAG'91)*, volume 579 of *Lecture Notes in Computer Science*, pages 9 30. Springer, October 1991.

Mustaque Ahamad, Gil Neiger, James E. Burns, Prince Kohli, and Phillip W. Hutto. Causal memory: definitions, implementation, and programming. *Distributed Computing*, 9(1):37–49, March 1995.

Bowen Alpern and Fred B. Schneider. Defining liveness. *Information Processing Letters*, 21(4):181–185, October 1985.

Yair Amir and Avishai Wool. Evaluating quorum systems over the Internet. In *Proceedings of the 26th International Symposium on Fault-Tolerant Computing (FTCS'96)*, pages 26–37. IEEE Computer Society Press, June 1996.

Anish Arora and Mohamed Gouda. Closure and convergence: A foundation of fault-tolerant computing. *IEEE Transactions on Software Engineering*, 19(11):1015–1027, November 1993.

Anish Arora and Sandeep S. Kulkarni. Component based design of multitolerant systems. *IEEE Transactions on Software Engineering*, 24(1):63–78, January 1998a.

Anish Arora and Sandeep S. Kulkarni. Detectors and correctors: A theory of fault-tolerance components. In *Proceedings of the 18th IEEE International Conference on Distributed Computing Systems (ICDCS'98)*, pages 436–443. IEEE Computer Society Press, May 1998b.

Algirdas Avižienis, Jean-Claude Laprie, Brian Randell, and Carl Landwehr. Basic concepts and taxonomy of dependable and secure computing. *IEEE Transactions on Dependable and Secure Computing*, 1(1):11–33, January – March 2004.

Daniel Barbara and Héctor García-Molina. Mutual exclusion in partitioned distributed systems. *Distributed Computing*, 1(2):119–132, June 1986a.

Daniel Barbara and Héctor García-Molina. The vulnerability of vote assignments. *ACM Transactions on Computer Systems*, 4(3):187–213, August 1986b.

Rida A. Bazzi. Planar quorums. *Theoretical Computer Science*, 243(1–2):243–268, July 2000.

Michael Ben-Or. Another advantage of free choice: Completely asynchronous agreement protocols. In *Proceedings of the 2nd Annual ACM Symposium on Principles of Distributed Computing (PODC'83)*, pages 27–30. ACM Press, August 1983.

Philip A. Bernstein, Vassos Hadzilacos, and Nathan Goodman. *Concurrency Control and Recovery in Database Systems*. Addison Wesley, February 1987. ISBN-13 978-0201107159.

Tushar Deepak Chandra and Sam Toueg. Unreliable failure detectors for reliable distributed systems. *Journal of the ACM*, 225–267(2):43, March 1996.

Ing-Ray Chen and Ding-Chau Wang. Analysis of replicated data with repair dependency. *The Computer Journal*, 39(9):767–779, May 1996a.

Ing-Ray Chen and Ding-Chau Wang. Analyzing dynamic voting using petri nets. In *Proceedings of the 15th Symposium on Reliable Distributed Systems (SRDS'96)*, pages 44–53. IEEE Computer Society Press, October 1996b.

Ing-Ray Chen and Ding-Chau Wang. Repairman models for replicated data management: A case study. In *Proceedings of the 4th International Conference on Parallel and Distributed Information Systems (PDIS'96)*, pages 184–195. IEEE Computer Society Press, December 1996c.

Ing-Ray Chen, Ding-Chau Wang, and Chih-Ping Chu. Response time behavior of voting schemes for managing replicated data. In *Proceedings of the 23rd Annual Conference on Computer Software and Applications (COMPSAC'99)*, pages 139–144. IEEE Computer Society Press, October 1999.

Ing-Ray Chen, Ding-Chau Wang, and Chih-Ping Chu. Response time behavior of distributed voting algorithms for managing replicated data. *Information Processing Letters*, 75(6):247–253, November 2000.

Ing-Ray Chen, Ding-Chau Wang, and Chih-Ping Chu. Analyzing reconfigurable algorithms for managing replicated data. *Journal of Systems and Software*, 72(3):417–430, August 2004a.

Ing-Ray Chen, Ding-Chau Wang, and Chih-Ping Chu. Analyzing user-perceived dependability and performance characteristics of voting algorithms for managing replicated data. *Distributed and Parallel Databases*, 14(3):199–219, November 2004b.

Cho Cheng-Hong and Wang Jer-Tsang. Triangular grid protocol: An efficient scheme for replica control with uniform access quorums. *Theoretical Computer Science – Special Issue on Parallel Computing*, 196(1–2):259–288, April 1998.

Shun Yan Cheung, Mostafa H. Ammar, and Mustaque Ahamad. The grid protocol: A high performance scheme for maintaining replicated data. *IEEE Transactions on Knowledge and Data Engineering*, 4(6):582–592, December 1990.

Shun Yang Cheung, Mustaque Ahamad, and Mostafa H. Ammar. Optimizing vote and quorum assignments for reading and writing replicated data. *IEEE Transactions on Data and Knowledge Engineering*, 1(3):387–397, September 1989.

Ching-Tsun Chou, Israel Cidon, Inder S. Gopal, and Shmuel Zaks. Synchronizing asynchronous bounded delay networks. *IEEE Transactions on Communications*, 38(2):144–147, February 1990.

Gianfranco Ciardo. *Analysis of Large Stochastic Petri Net Models*. Ph.D. thesis, Duke University, Durham, North Carolina, NC, U.S.A., April 1989.

Gianfranco Ciardo, Alex Blakemore, Philip F. Chimento, Jogesh K. Muppala, and Kishor S. Trivedi. Automated generation and analysis of markov reward models using stochastic reward nets. *Institute for Mathematics and its Applications (IMA) Volumes in Mathematics and its Applications: Linear Algebra, Markov Chains, and Queuing Models*, 48:145–191, December 1993.

Gianfranco Ciardo, Jogesh K. Muppala, and Kishor S. Trivedi. SPNP: Stochastic petri net package. In *Proceedings of the 3rd International Workshop on Petri Nets and Performance Models (PNPM'89)*, pages 142–151. IEEE Computer Society Press, December 1989.

Gianfranco Ciardo, Jogesh K. Muppala, and Kishor S. Trivedi. Analyzing concurrent and fault-tolerant software using stochastic reward nets. *Journal on Parallel and Distributed Computing – Special Issue on Petri Net Modelling of Parallel Computers*, 15(3):255–269, July 1992.

Flaviu Cristian. A rigorous approach to fault-tolerant programming. *IEEE Transactions on Software Engineering*, 11(1):23–31, January 1985.

Flaviu Cristian. Understanding fault-tolerant distributed systems. *Communications of the ACM*, 34(2):56–78, February 1991.

Flaviu Cristian, Houtan Aghili, Ray Strong, and Danny Dolev. Atomic broadcast: From simple message diffusion to byzantine agreement. *Information and Computation*, 118(1):158–179, April 1995.

Flaviu Cristian and Christof Fetzer. The timed asynchronous distributed system model. In *Proceedings of the 28th Annual International Symposium on Fault-Tolerant Computing (FTCS-28)*, pages 140–149. IEEE Computer Society Press, June 1998.

Aldo Cumani. ESP - A package for the evaluation of stochastic petri nets with phase-type distributed transition times. In *Proceedings of the International Workshop on Timed Petri Nets*, pages 144–151. IEEE Computer Society Press, July 1985.

Carole Delporte-Gallet, Hugues Fauconnier, Rachid Guerraoui, and Petr Kouznetsov. Mutual exclusion in asynchronous systems with failure detectors. *Journal of Parallel and Distributed Computing*, 65(4):492–505, April 2005.

Krzysztof Diks, Evangelos Kranakis, Danny Krizanc, Bernard Mans, and Andrzej Pelc. Optimal coteries and voting schemes. *Information Processing Letters*, 51(1):1–6, July 1994.

Joanne Bechta Dugan, Andrea Bobbio, Gianfranco Ciardo, and Kishor S. Trivedi. The design of a unified package for the solution of stochastic petri net models. In *Proceedings of the International Workshop on Timed Petri Nets*, pages 6–13. IEEE Computer Society Press, July 1985.

Joanne Bechta Dugan and Gianfranco Ciardo. Stochastic petri net analysis of a replicated file system. *IEEE Transactions on Software Engineering*, 15(4):394–401, April 1989.

Joanne Bechta Dugan, Kishor S. Trivedi, Robert Geist, and Victor F. Nicola. Extended stochastic petri nets: Applications and analysis. In *Proceedings of the 10th International Symposium on Computer Performance Modelling, Measurement and Evaluation (Performance'84)*, pages 507–519. North-Holland Publishing Co. Amsterdam, December 1984.

Klaus Echtle. *Fehlertoleranzverfahren*. Studienreihe Informatik. Springer, April 1990. ISBN-10 3-540-52680-3.

Burkhard Englert and Alexander A. Shvartsman. Graceful quorum reconfiguration in a robust emulation of shared memory. In *Proceedings of the 20th International Conference on Distributed Computing Systems (ICDCS'00)*, pages 454–463. IEEE Computer Society Press, April 2000.

Christof Fetzer. Perfect failure detection in timed asynchronous systems. *IEEE Transactions on Computers*, 52(2):99–112, February 2003.

Christof Fetzer and Flaviu Cristian. On the possibility of consensus in asynchronous systems. In *Proceedings of the 1995 Pacific Rim International Symposium on Fault-Tolerant Systems (PRFTS'95)*. IEEE Computer Society Press, December 1995.

Michael J. Fischer, Nancy A. Lynch, and Michael S. Paterson. Impossibility of distributed consensus with one faulty process. *Journal of the ACM*, 32(2):374–382, April 1985.

Héctor García-Molina. Elections in a distributed computing system. *IEEE Transactions on Computers*, 31(1):48–59, January 1982.

Héctor García-Molina and Daniel Barbara. How to assign votes in a distributed system. *Journal of the ACM*, 32(4):841–860, October 1985.

David K. Gifford. Weighted voting for replicated data. In *Proceedings of the 7th Symposium on Operating Systems Principles (SOSP'79)*, pages 150–161. ACM Press, December 1979.

Cary G. Gray and David R. Cheriton. Leases: An efficient fault-tolerant mechanism for distributed file cache consistency. In *Proceedings of the 12th ACM Symposium on Operating Systems Principles (SOSP'89)*, pages 202–210. ACM Press, December 1989.

Felix C. Gärtner. Fundamentals of fault-tolerant distributed computing in asynchronous environments. *ACM Computing Surveys*, 31(1):1–26, March 1999.

Yehuda Hassin and David Peleg. Average probe complexity in quorum systems. *Journal on Computer Systems Science*, 72(4):592–616, June 2006.

Martin Hirt and Ueli Maurer. Complete characterization of adversaries tolerable in secure multi-party computation. In *Proceedings of the 16th ACM Symposium on Principles of Distributed Computing (PODC'97)*, pages 25–34. ACM Press, August 1997.

Ron Holzman, Yosi Marcus, and David Peleg. Load balancing in quorum systems. *Society for Industrial and Applied Mathematics (SIAM) Journal of Discrete Math*, 10(2):223–245, May 1997.

Kinga Kiss Iakab, Christian Storm, and Oliver Theel. Consistency-driven probabilistic quorum system construction for improving operation availability. In *Proceedings of the 11th International Conference on Distributed Computing and Networking (ICDCN'10)*, volume 5935/2010 of *Lecture Notes in Computer Science*, pages 446–458. Springer, January 2010.

Sushil Jajodia and David Mutchler. Integrating static and dynamic voting protocols to enhance file availability. In *Proceedings of the 4th International Conference on Data Engineering (ICDE'88)*, pages 144–153. IEEE Computer Society Press, February 1988.

Sushil Jajodia and David Mutchler. Dynamic voting algorithms for maintaining the consistency of a replicated database. *ACM Transactions on Database Systems*, 15(2):230–280, June 1990.

Pankaj Jalote. *Fault Tolerance in Distributed Systems*. Prentice Hall, April 1994. ISBN-10 0133013672.

Ricardo Jiménez-Peris, Marta Patiño-Martínez, Gustavo Alonso, and Bettina Kemme. How to select a replication protocol according to scalability, availability and communication overhead. In *Proceedings of the 20th IEEE Symposium on Reliable Distributed Systems (SRDS'01)*, pages 24–33. October 2001.

Ricardo Jiménez-Peris, Marta Patiño-Martínez, Gustavo Alonso, and Bettina Kemme. Are quorums an alternative for data replication? *ACM Transactions on Database Systems*, 28(3):257–294, September 2003.

Flavio Paiva Junqueira and Keith Marzullo. Coterie availability in sites. In *Proceedings of the 19th International Symposium on Distributed Computing (DISC'05)*, volume 3724/2005 of *Lecture Notes in Computer Science*, pages 3–17. Springer, September 2005a.

Flavio Paiva Junqueira and Keith Marzullo. The virtue of dependent failures in multi-site systems. In *Proceedings of the 1st IEEE Workshop on Hot Topics in System Dependability (HotDep'05)*. IEEE Computer Society Press, June 2005b.

Hans-Henning Koch. *Entwurf und Bewertung von Replikationsverfahren*. Ph.D. thesis, Department of Computer Science, University of Darmstadt, Germany, June 1994.

Sandeep S. Kulkarni and Ali Ebnenasir. The complexity of adding failsafe fault-tolerance. In *Proceedings of the 22nd International Conference on Distributed Computing Systems (ICDCS'02)*, pages 337–344. IEEE Computer Society Press, July 2002.

Akhil Kumar, Michael Rabinovich, and Rakesh K. Sinha. A performance study of general grid structures for replicated data. In *Proceedings of the 13th International Conference on Distributed Computer Systems (ICDCS'93)*, pages 178–185. IEEE Computer Society Press, May 1993.

Yu-Chen Kuo and Shing-Tsaan Huang. A geometric approach for constructing coteries and k-coteries. *IEEE Transactions on Parallel and Distributed Systems*, 8(4):402–411, April 1997.

Leslie Lamport. Proving the correctness of multiprocess programs. *IEEE Transactions on Software Engineering*, 3(2):125–143, March 1977.

Leslie Lamport. How to make a multiprocessor computer that correctly executes multiprocess programs. *IEEE Transactions on Computers*, 28(9):690–691, September 1979.

Leslie Lamport. On interprocess communication part I: Basic formalism. *Distributed Computing*, 1(2):77–85, June 1986.

Leslie Lamport and Nancy A. Lynch. Distributed computing: Models and methods. In *Handbook of Theoretical Computer Science: Formal Models and Semantics*, volume B, chapter 18, pages 1157–1199. MIT Press Cambridge, February 1991. ISBN-10 0-444-88074-7.

Leslie Lamport, Robert Shostak, and Marshall Pease. The byzantine generals problem. *ACM Transactions on Programming Languages and Systems*, 4(3):382–401, July 1982.

Butler W. Lampson. Atomic transactions. In *Distributed Systems – Architecture and Implementation*, volume 105 of *Lecture Notes in Computer Science*, pages 246–265. Springer, July 1981.

Butler W. Lampson and Howard E. Sturgis. Crash recovery in a distributed data storage system. Technical report, Xerox Palo Alto Research Center, June 1979. Unpublished technical report.

Yun Liu, Dongyan Chen, and Kishor S. Trivedi. Performance analysis of voting algorithms with non-zero network delay and site processing time. In *Proceedings of the 14th IEEE International Symposium on Software Reliability Engineering (ISSRE'03)*, pages 1–2. IEEE Computer Society Press, November 2003. Fast Abstract.

Darrell D. E. Long, Andrew Muir, and Richard A. Golding. A longitudinal survey of Internet host reliability. In *Proceedings of the 14th Symposium on Reliable Distributed Systems (SRDS'95)*, pages 2–9. IEEE Computer Society Press, September 1995.

Nancy A. Lynch. *Distributed Algorithms*. Morgan Kaufmann, March 1996. ISBN-13 978-1-55860-348-6.

Mamoru Maekawa. A $\sqrt{N}$ algorithm for mutual exclusion in decentralized systems. *ACM Transactions on Computer Systems*, 3(2):145–159, May 1985.

Dahlia Malkhi and Michael K. Reiter. Byzantine quorum systems. In *Proceedings of the 29th Annual ACM Symposium on the Theory of Computing (STOC'97)*, pages 569–578. ACM Press, May 1997.

Dahlia Malkhi and Michael K. Reiter. Byzantine quorum systems. *Distributed Computing*, 11(4):203–213, October 1998.

Dahlia Malkhi, Michael K. Reiter, Avishai Wool, and Rebecca N. Wright. Probabilistic quorum systems. *Information and Computation*, 170(2):184–206, November 2001.

Marco Ajmone Marsan, Giovanni Conte, and Gianfranco Balbo. A class of generalized stochastic petri nets for the performance evaluation of multiprocessor systems. *ACM Transactions on Computer Systems*, 2(2):93–122, May 1984.

Marco Ajmore Marsan, Gianfranco Balbo, Giuseppe Conte, Susanna Donatelli, and Giuliana Franceschinis. *Modelling With Generalized Stochastic Petri Nets*. Wiley Series in Parallel Computing. John Wiley & Sons, 1st edition, November 1995. ISBN-13 978-0471930594.

John F. Meyer, Ali Movaghar, and William H. Sanders. Stochastic activity networks: Structure, behavior, and application. In *Proceedings of the International Workshop on Timed Petri Nets*, pages 106–115. IEEE Computer Society Press, July 1985.

Jayadev Misra. Axioms for memory access in asynchronous hardware systems. *ACM Transactions on Programming Languages and Systems*, 8(1):142–153, January 1986.

Michael Karl Molloy. Performance analysis using stochastic petri nets. *IEEE Transactions on Computers*, C-31(9):913–917, September 1982.

Tadao Murata. Petri nets: Properties, analysis and applications. *Proceedings of the IEEE*, 77(4):541–580, April 1989.

Moni Naor and Udi Wieder. Scalable and dynamic quorum systems. *Distributed Computing*, 17(4):311–322, May 2005.

Moni Naor and Avishai Wool. The load, capacity, and availability of quorum systems. *Society for Industrial and Applied Mathematics (SIAM) Journal on Computing*, 27(2):423–447, April 1998.

Mitchell L. Neilsen. *Quorum Structures in Distributed Systems*. Ph.D. thesis, Kansas State University, Kansas, KS, U.S.A., May 1992.

Peter G. Neumann. Illustrative risks to the public in the use of computer systems and related technology. *ACM Special Interest Group on Software Engineering (SIGSOFT) Software Engineering Notes*, 19(1):16–29, January 1994.

Mirjana Obradovic and Piotr Berman. Voting as the optimal pessimistic scheme for managing replicated data. In *Proceedings of the 9th Symposium on Reliable Distributed Systems (SRDS'90)*, pages 126–135. IEEE Computer Society Press, October 1990.

Christos H. Papadimitriou and Martha Sideri. Optimal coteries. In *Proceedings of the 10th Annual ACM Symposium on Principles of Distributed Computing (PODC'91)*, pages 75–80. ACM Press, August 1991.

Jehan-François Pâris. Evaluating the impact of network partitions on replicated data availability. In *Proceedings of the 2nd IFIP Working Conference on Dependable Computing for Critical Applications*. IEEE Computer Society Press, February 1991.

Jehan-François Pâris. Voting with a variable number of copies. In *Proceedings of the 16th International Symposium on Fault-tolerant Computing (FTCS-16)*, pages 50–55. IEEE Computer Society Press, June 1986a.

Jehan-François Pâris. Voting with witnesses: A consistency scheme for replicated files. In *Proceedings of the 6th International Conference on Distributed Computing Systems (ICDCS'86)*, pages 606–621. IEEE Computer Society Press, May 1986b.

David Peleg and Avishai Wool. How to be an efficient snoop, or the probe complexity of quorum systems. *Society for Industrial and Applied Mathematics (SIAM) Journal on Discrete Mathematics*, 15(3):416–433, March 2002.

James Lyle Peterson. Petri nets. *ACM Computing Survey*, 9(3):223–252, September 1977.

James Lyle Peterson. *Petri Net Theory and the Modeling of Systems.* Prentice Hall, June 1981. ISBN-13 978-0136619833.

David Powell. Failure mode assumptions and assumption coverage. In *Proceedings of the 22nd International Symposium on Fault-Tolerant Computing (FTCS-22),* pages 386–395. IEEE Computer Society Press, July 1992.

Muhammad A. Qureshi and William H. Sanders. The effect of workload on the performance and availability of voting algorithms. In *Modeling, Analysis, and Simulation of Computer and Telecommunication Systems (MASCOTS),* pages 217–224. IEEE Computer Society Press, January 1995.

Michael Rabinovich and Edward Lazowska. The dynamic tree protocol: Avoiding "graceful degradation" in the tree protocol for distributed mutual exclusion. In *Proceedings of the 11th Annual International Conference on Computers and Communications (ICCC'92),* pages 101–107. IEEE Computer Society Press, April 1992a.

Michael Rabinovich and Edward Lazowska. Improving fault tolerance and supporting partial writes in structured coterie protocols. *ACM Special Interest Group on Management of Data (SIGMOD) Record,* 21(2):226–235, June 1992b.

Sampath Rangarajan, Pankaj Jalote, and Satish K. Tripathi. Capacity of voting systems. *IEEE Transactions on Software Engineering,* 19(7):698–706, July 1993.

Debanjan Saha, Sampath Rangarajan, and Satish K. Tripathi. An analysis of the average message overhead in replica control protocols. *IEEE Transactions on Parallel and Distributed Systems,* 7(10):1026–1034, October 1996.

Fred B. Schneider. What good are models and what models are good? In *Distributed Systems,* chapter 2, pages 17–26. ACM Press / Addison Wesley, 2nd edition, July 1993a. ISBN-10 0-201-62427-3.

Marco Schneider. Self-stabilization. *ACM Computing Surveys,* 25(1):45–67, March 1993b.

Dale Skeen. Non-blocking commit protocols. In *Proceedings of the ACM Special Interest Group on Management of Data (SIGMOD) Conference on Management of Data,* pages 133–142. ACM Press, April 1981.

Scott D. Stoller. Leader election in asynchronous distributed systems. *IEEE Transactions on Computers,* 40(3):283–284, March 2000.

Christian Storm. *Konzeption und Implementierung eines Rahmenwerkes für adaptiv-dynamische Replikationsstrategien.* Diploma thesis, Department of Computer Science, University of Oldenburg, Germany, January 2006.

Christian Storm and Oliver Theel. Highly adaptable dynamic quorum schemes for managing replicated data. In *Proceedings of the 1st International Conference on Availability, Reliability and Security (ARES'06)*, pages 245–253. IEEE Computer Society Press, April 2006.

Christian Storm and Timo Warns. Deriving highly available quorum systems from structural failure models. In *Proceedings of the 7th European Dependable Computing Conference (EDCC-7)*, pages 56–65. IEEE Computer Society Press, May 2008.

Richard N. Taylor. Complexity of analyzing the synchronization structure of concurrent programs. *Acta Informatica*, 19(1):57–84, April 1983.

Oliver Theel. *Ein vereinheitlichendes Konzept zur Konstruktion hochverfügbarer Dienste*. Ph.D. thesis, Department of Computer Science, University of Darmstadt, Germany, June 1993a.

Oliver Theel. General structured voting: A flexible framework for modelling cooperations. In *Proceedings of the 13th International Conference on Distributed Computing Systems (ICDCS'93)*, pages 227–236. IEEE Computer Society Press, May 1993b.

Oliver Theel. Meeting the application's needs: A design study of a highly customized replication scheme. In *Proceedings of the 1993 Pacific Rim International Symposium on Fault Tolerant Computing (PRDC'93)*, pages 111–117. IEEE Computer Society Press, December 1993c.

Oliver Theel and Henning Pagnia. Optimal replica control protocols exhibit symmetric operation availabilities. In *Proceedings of the 28th International Symposium on Fault-Tolerant Computing (FTCS-28)*, pages 252–261. IEEE Computer Society Press, June 1998.

Oliver Theel and Hans-Henning Pagnia-Koch. General design of grid-based data replication schemes using graphs and a few rules. In *Proceedings of the 15th International Conference on Distributed Computing Systems (ICDCS'95)*, pages 395–403. IEEE Computer Society Press, May 1995.

Oliver Theel and Thomas Strauß. Automatic generation of dynamic coterie-based replication schemes. In *Proceedings of the International Conference on Parallel and Distributed Processing Techniques and Applications (PDPTA'98)*, pages 1606–1613. CSREA Press, July 1998.

Robert H. Thomas. A majority consensus approach to concurrency control for multiple copy databases. *ACM Transactions on Database Systems*, 4(2):180–207, June 1979.

Kishor S. Trivedi. *Probability and Statistics with Reliability, Queuing and Computer Science Applications.* John Wiley & Sons, 2nd edition edition, 2002. ISBN-10 0-471-33341-7.

Tatsuhiro Tsuchiya and Tohru Kikuno. Availability evaluation of quorum-based mutual exclusion schemes in general topology. *The Computer Journal*, 42(7):613–622, 1999.

John von Neumann. Probabilistic logics and the synthesis of reliable organisms from unreliable components. *Automata Studies (Annals of Mathematics Studies)*, AM-34:43–99, April 1956.

Ding-Chau Wang, Ing-Ray Chen, and Chih-Ping Chu. Analyzing reconfigurable algorithms for managing replicated data with strict consistency requirements: A case study. In *Proceedings of the 24th Annual International Computer Software and Applications Conference (COMPSAC'00)*, pages 608–613. IEEE Computer Society Press, October 2000.

Timo Warns. *Structural Failure Models for Fault-Tolerant Distributed Computing.* Ph.D. thesis, Department of Computer Science, University of Oldenburg, Germany, September 2009.

Timo Warns, Christian Storm, and Wilhelm Hasselbring. Availability of globally distributed nodes: An empirical evaluation. In *Proceedings of the 27th International Symposium on Reliable Distributed Systems (SRDS'08)*, pages 279–284. IEEE Computer Society Press, October 2008.

Timo Warns, Christian Storm, and Oliver Theel. How to be a more efficient snoop: Refined probe complexity of quorum sets. In *Proceedings of the 2nd International Workshop on Reliability, Availability, and Security (WRAS'09)*, pages 354–359. IEEE Computer Society Press, December 2009.

Avishai Wool and David Peleg. The availability of quorum systems. *Information and Communication*, 123(2):210–223, December 1995.

Chienwen Wu and Geneva G. Belford. The triangular lattice protocol: A highly fault tolerant and highly efficient protocol for replicated data. In *Proceedings of the 11th Symposium on Reliable Distributed Systems (SRDS'92)*. IEEE Computer Society Press, October 1992.

Haifeng Yu and Amin Vahdat. Consistent and automatic replica regeneration. *ACM Transactions on Storage*, 1(1):3–37, February 2005.